Empires of Slavery

Max Planck Studies in Global Legal History of the Iberian Worlds

Editor

Thomas Duve

The book volumes in the *Max Planck Studies in Global Legal History of the Iberian Worlds* publish research on legal history of areas which have been in contact with the Iberian empires during the early Modern and Modern period, in Europe, the Americas, Asia and Africa. Its focus is global in the sense that it is not limited to the imperial spaces as such but rather looks at the globalization of normativities within the space related to these imperial formations. It is global also in another sense: The volumes in the series pay special attention to the coexistence of a variety of normativities and their cultural translations in different places and moments, decentring classical research perspectives and opening up for different modes of normativity.

The monographs, edited volumes and text editions in the series are peer reviewed, and published in print and online.

Brill's Open Access books are discoverable through DOAB and distributed free of charge in Brill's E-Book Collections, and through OAPEN and JSTOR.

VOLUME 7

The titles published in this series are listed at *brill.com/mpiw*

Empires of Slavery

Rights and Power in the Early Modern Iberian World

By

Daniel Allemann

BRILL | NIJHOFF

LEIDEN | BOSTON

ISSN 2590-3292
ISBN 978-90-04-76058-5
ISBN 978-90-04-76059-2 (PDF)
DOI 10.1163/9789004760592

Library of Congress Control Number: 2026938077

Brill and Koninklijke Brill BV are part of De Gruyter Brill.
www.degruyterbrill.com

Questions about General Product Safety Regulation: productsafety@degruyterbrill.com

Cover illustration: Detail of *Aula de Teología* by Martín de Cervera (oil on wood, 1613). Originally painted on the doors of the University of Salamanca's archive, it is now located in the manuscript room of the university's historical library.

Für Alban, Esthi & Sara

Contents

PART 3
Slavery and Labor Coercion in the Americas

Acknowledgments

This book grows out of my doctoral research. I am deeply grateful to Annabel Brett for her exceptional mentorship and unwavering support, far beyond my time in Cambridge. I am also indebted to Lauren Benton and Magnus Ryan, whose guidance was essential in bringing this research to publication. The History Department in Lucerne provided the perfect environment in which to complete the manuscript. I am particularly thankful to Valentin Groebner and Marie Schenk for their intellectual companionship.

Over the past years, I have benefited from the insights and discussions with many others: Anna Becker, Christiane Birr, Luisa Stella Coutinho, Francisco Cuena Boy, Eloise Davies, Max Deardorff, Mariana Dias Paes, José Luis Egío, Rômulo da Silva Ehalt, Mark Goldie, Anton Jäger, Charlotte Johann, Fernando Liendo Tagle, Shiru Lim, Emma Mackinnon, Giuseppe Marcocci, Alicia Mavor, Barret Reiter, Carla Roth, Jacopo Sartori, Mark Somos, Sarah-Maria Schober, Stefan Schweighöfer, Benjamin Slingo, Eveline Szarka, Birgit Tremml-Werner, Tim Twining, Andreas Wagner, and Romina Zamora. I also thank audiences in Aarhus, Cambridge, Frankfurt, Huelva, Oxford, Palermo, Paris, London, Tübingen, and Stockholm, where some of the arguments in this book were first presented.

Financial support from the Cambridge International Trust and the Jubiläumsstiftung der Basellandschaftlichen Kantonalbank was essential, as were three productive months spent at the Max Planck Institute for Legal History and Legal Theory in Frankfurt. The Institute has remained a cherished venue for scholarly exchange ever since, and I am grateful that this book is published in the *Max Planck Studies in Global Legal History of the Iberian Worlds*. I would like to thank Thomas Duve, Nicole Pasakarnis, and the anonymous referees for their suggestions and encouragement. I am also grateful to Gita Rajan for her careful reading of the manuscript.

All translations from early modern sources and modern scholarship are my own, unless otherwise indicated. That said, I have found modern translations of early modern texts to be a valuable resource, and I thank Matthias Kaufmann for sharing a draft of the German translation of Molina's *De iustitia et iure*, prepared in collaboration with Alexander Loose and Danaë Simmermacher, and now available in print.

Parts of Chapter 4 were first published as "Sklaverei, Heirat und 'Menschenrechte' in der iberischen Welt des 16. und 17. Jahrhunderts", in *Historische Zeitschrift* 317:2 (2023), 311–341.

Daniel Allemann
Luzern, November 2025

Introduction

On 5 July 1685, Charles II (1661–1700) sent an urgent letter to the Council of the Indies, the highest governing board of the Spanish empire in the Americas. The king was troubled by two central questions: What "benefit" did enslaved Black Africans bring to the New World and what "harm" would result from their absence? More fundamentally, the Habsburg monarch sought moral clarity about "whether it is licit to buy and trade them as slaves" and, as a corollary, if there were any "authors who have written about this issue".[1] The Council of the Indies, writing back immediately, promised to investigate the matter thoroughly.[2] Seven weeks later, the king's advisors put forward a powerful vindication of both the necessity and justice of Atlantic slavery. From the beginning of "the discovery and subjugation of the Indies", they argued, the imperial project had relied on enslaved African labor.[3] Now, with much of the Indigenous population decimated, they warned, "there would be no food to sustain human life" and "America would be exposed to total ruin" without Black slaves.[4] Yet the councilors were keen to insist that Atlantic slavery was not merely necessary, but also just. They claimed that "many authors" had already written extensively on the subject.[5] In their conclusion, imperial needs and authoritative approval made the possession and trade in enslaved Africans "a long-established and common custom of the kingdoms of Castile, America, and Portugal, without objection from His Holiness, the Papal States, but rather with the tolerance of all".[6]

1 Charles II of Spain, "Decreto de Carlos II a Vicente Gonzaga", ed. Pena González, 339: "El Consejo de Indias me informará luego de qué conveniencia son los negros en la América y qué daños seguirían de no haberlos [...] a fin de reconocer si es lícito comprarlos por esclavos y hacer asiento de ellos, si hay autores que hayan escrito sobre este particular, quiénes son".

2 Council of the Indies (Consejo de Indias), "Oficio del Consejo de Indias a Carlos II, Madrid, 6 agosto 1685", ed. Pena González, 339–341.

3 Council of the Indies (Consejo de Indias), "Oficio del Consejo de Indias a Carlos II, Madrid, 21 agosto 1685", ed. Pena González, 351: "se ha tenido siempre por tan necesaria la introducción de esclavos negros en las Indias, que aun en el principio de su descubrimiento y reducción".

4 Council of the Indies (Consejo de Indias), "Oficio del Consejo de Indias a Carlos II, Madrid, 21 agosto 1685", ed. Pena González, 350–351: "si estos faltasen totalmente, faltaría el alimento para mantener la vida humana [...] el común del reino, las haciendas, que principalmente consisten en el caudal de los esclavos negros, se perdería exponiéndose la América a una total ruina".

5 Council of the Indies (Consejo de Indias), "Oficio del Consejo de Indias a Carlos II, Madrid, 21 agosto 1685", ed. Pena González, 352–353.

6 Council of the Indies (Consejo de Indias), "Oficio del Consejo de Indias a Carlos II, Madrid, 21

 | DOI:10.1163/9789004760592_002

Some of the key themes and central figures in this book emerge from the exchange between King Charles II and his colonial administrators and advisors. The correspondence reveals that the ideology underpinning early Atlantic slavery was deeply rooted in the interface between individual rights and political power. Slaving was not just a commercial transaction between buyers and sellers but intimately intertwined with Spanish and Portuguese imperial ambitions in the wider world. It dominated the political discourse of the highest circles of power, including that of the monarch himself, for one reason: without enslavement, there could be no empire.

The opening vignette also illustrates that slavery was perceived as a problem of justice and morality. No one at the time seriously questioned the legality of slavery as such. Yet widespread reports of violent practices of captivity and human trafficking contrasted sharply with the Christian ideal of charity. Iberian slaving, in the Atlantic and beyond, put the Catholic moral order at risk. How could Iberians engage in such a trade without endangering their salvation? Were slaveholders safe in conscience when owning "human commodities" that had been captured and enslaved for profit? And what course of action did the Iberian monarchs have to take to avoid eternal damnation? Those who grappled with these pressing questions were the "many authors" mentioned by the Council of the Indies—an influential group of university theologians, canon lawyers, colonial jurists, and missionaries. They are the central figures of this book.

The Iberian imperial theorists, as I will call them, were the principal moral authorities of the Spanish and Portuguese empires in the 16th and 17th centuries. They formulated concrete solutions to the most pressing social, religious and political challenges of their era. What united these authors—whether writing scholarly treatises in Latin, manuals for merchants and confessors, or political tracts in the vernacular—was a preoccupation with the limits of moral human agency: they probed how far one could go while remaining safe in conscience. Their texts were read both by royal councilors and by confessors overseas, who confronted the violent reality of empire and enslavement on the ground. These thinkers provided the ideological tools considered necessary for safeguarding the souls of both the rulers and the ruled. In an age marked by

agosto 1685", ed. Pena González, 354: "Y así parece que no se puede dudar de la precisión de estos esclavos para mantenerse los reinos de las Indias […] por las razones que quedan representadas, autoridades referidas, costumbre inveterada y común en los reinos de Castilla, América y Portugal, sin repugnancia de Su Santidad, estado eclesiástico, antes bien con tolerancia de todos".

colonial expansion and global slavery, they redefined the boundaries of what was legally and morally permissible.

Empires of Slavery places the Iberian imperial theorists at the heart of early modern legal and political action. It builds on the insights of social historians who have transformed our understanding of law by shifting attention away from abstract norms and rules that traditional legal historians themselves have often cast as the counterpart of social reality.[7] Scholars like Lauren Benton have shown how actors across the early modern world used and produced legal arguments in moments of conflict and contestation. Viewing law as a product of jurisdictional politics not only foregrounds the agency of Indigenous peoples and unlettered settlers overseas. It also invites us to reconsider the role of European thinkers within a broader landscape of early modern legal and political thought and practice.[8]

By tracing the extensive debates among Iberian thinkers on enslavement, this book offers a new narrative about the relationship between individual rights and political power in the early modern period. Centered on the household, slavery blurred the line between private right and public authority, both conceptually and in practice. Recent scholarship in the history of political thought emphasizes the active role of women and wives in family governance, showing that early modern domestic and political spheres were conceptually entangled.[9] What is more, historians of empire have discovered that communities of households served as key nodes of authority in early European imperial expansion, where often the boundary between private raiding and princely warfare was ambiguous.[10] While building on these lines of inquiry, the present study also goes beyond them. It shifts our attention to the politics of slavery, showing how masters simultaneously owned enslaved persons as property and governed them as members of the household community. This nexus of rule

7 A recent example for such a traditional legal history is José Antonio Piqueras' study of slave laws in medieval Castile and early modern Spanish America. The author himself notes that his work "is not a history of slavery, but a history of the norms that regulated it" (Piqueras, *Derecho antiguo y esclavitud moderna*, 288: "el presente estudio no es una historia de la esclavitud sino de las normas que la regulaban").

8 The work of Lauren Benton and her co-authors provides a valuable entry point into the extensive literature on jurisdictional politics and legal pluralism. See e.g., Benton and Ross, "Empires and Legal Pluralism"; Benton and Clulow, "Interpolity Law and Jurisdictional Policits"; and, most recently, Benton, *They Called It Peace*.

9 See Becker, *Gendering the Renaissance Commonwealth*; and Haar, *Natural and Political Conceptions of Community*.

10 See Benton, *They Called It Peace*, ch. 3. For a related argument about the bottom-up formation of political authority in the Spanish empire in the Americas, see also Díaz Ceballos, *Poder compartido*.

and ownership granted slaveholders ample latitude to punish slaves. Coercive power was formally the prerogative of princes, but domination of slaves within households relocated aspects of public authority into the domestic sphere. By examining the master-slave relationship, Iberian theologians and jurists negotiated the question of where the "state" truly began.

Empires of Slavery also adds a new dimension to the study of early Atlantic slavery by examining the legal and theological frameworks that structured the possibilities of courtroom action by enslaved people. Legal historians like Michelle McKinley have emphasized how enslaved people in colonial Latin America could mobilize the law to assert their interests.[11] This perspective has been essential in recovering the voices and strategies of the enslaved. However, a closer look at the writings of Spanish and Portuguese theorists reveals that the precarious status of slaves as both persons and property ultimately conferred far greater legal agency upon slaveholders. If early modern Iberians recognized enslaved people as human beings created in the image of God who were not reducible to mere objects of possession, slaves were also subject to ownership and trade. This ambiguity did not sit well with the theological worldview of the time, but contemporaries made a virtue of this problem. They maintained the personhood of slaves, while commodifying these very humans in the arena of commercial exchange whenever it best served their interests. Capitalizing on the precarity of enslaved people, the Iberian imperial theorists formulated legal loopholes and expanded the bounds of moral agency to reinforce the rights of those who owned and traded "human commodities".

By approaching the writings of these intellectuals through the lens of slavery, the book likewise opens up new vistas on the language of Catholic natural law. In forward-looking genealogies of liberalism and the secular state, this strand of Iberian thinkers is portrayed as distinctly pre-modern because they had not yet separated politics from supernatural ends.[12] Yet, Spanish and Portuguese theorists are also celebrated for their religiously neutral understanding of natural rights as independent from the Christian faith or divine grace.[13] This study puts forward an alternative view. It argues that rights and religion remained deeply intertwined well into the period that we now call early modern, without casting the Iberian imperial theorists as outsiders in a future-focused narrative

11 See McKinley, *Fractional Freedoms*. On the legal agency of enslaved Indigenous people in 16th-century Castile, see Van Deusen, *Global Indios*.

12 For a recent iteration of this argument, see Mortimer, *Reformation, Resistance, and Reason of State*, 269–272.

13 See e.g., Pagden, *Burdens of Empire*, 65.

of secular modernity.[14] These thinkers affirmed that even "unbelievers" possessed natural rights, and that the legality of slavery was framed by universal juridical principles. Yet they also layered distinctly Christian privileges on top of this foundation. Charity, as they understood it, forbade the enslavement of fellow believers, while sanctioning the slavery of so-called "infidels". In this way, Iberian imperial thinkers promoted specifically Christian rights at the expense of non-Christian others.[15]

The centuries-long debates about empire and enslavement in the medieval Mediterranean shaped how early modern thinkers viewed European slaving in the Atlantic, Pacific, and Indian Ocean worlds. Scholars have shown that the idea of the Holy War against "Saracens" cast a long ideological shadow, animating both the "Reconquest" of the Iberian Peninsula and the subsequent "conquest" of the New World.[16] The polemical dehumanization of Muslim enemies during the Crusades—what Geraldine Heng has described as "race-as-religion"[17]—also left its mark on Spanish and Portuguese visions of enslavement. The Iberian imperial theorists never fully reduced slaves to the status of non-humans, and their constructions of human difference were by-products of broader reflections on the relationship between rights and power. However, the book asserts that early Atlantic slavery was shaped far less by attitudes toward skin color or non-European otherness than by Iberians' deep-seated belief in the hegemonic truth of the Christian faith. This reading aligns with the work of Chloe Ireton, who has shown that a select few enslaved Black Africans won their freedom in Iberian courts by arguing that they were illegally enslaved because they had always been Christians—thus invoking the logic of the Iberian imperial theorists to challenge their own enslavement.[18]

Finally, the study also contributes to broader debates on the nature of empires in world history, offering new insights into how early modern thinkers conceived of an imperial body politic. When Native slavery was formally abolished in Spanish America, a system of labor coercion continued, with old

14 This argument builds on insights developed in Muldoon, *Popes, Lawyers, and Infidels*, ch. 7. The role of religion remains significant in modern legal and political discourse, as argued in Moyn, *Christian Human Rights*.

15 Elsewhere, I have highlighted the nexus of natural rights and Christian rights with respect to justifications of the Spanish conquest. See Allemann, "Empire and the Right to Preach the Gospel".

16 See Huber, *Beute und Conquista*; and Mikhail, *God's Shadow*, ch. 6.

17 Heng, *The Invention of Race*, 149 and ch. 3.

18 See Ireton, "Black Africans' Freedom Litigation Suits"; and Ireton, *Slavery and Freedom in Black Thought*, ch. 5.

practices persisting in a new guise. Thousands of Indigenous individuals perished in the Andean mines, while settlers were exempt from such deadly tasks. Although the Catholic monarch sought to put an end to this regime, jurists and missionaries writing from colonial Peru insisted that the inclusion of "*indios*" in the body politic justified their obligation to perform labor for the common good. The book demonstrates that Iberian theorists envisioned a sharply stratified society of Spaniards and Andeans: a "composite commonwealth" of unequal elements that were pieced together in one political whole.

For many decades, historians approached slavery as a coherent and continuous institution across human history. Following the example of Orlando Patterson, they sought to "understand the universal features of the internal structure of slavery".[19] Patterson had posited that "the slave had no socially recognized existence outside of his master" and was therefore "a social nonperson", a condition he tracked from antiquity through the Age of Revolutions.[20] In addition to the emphasis on *longue durée* continuities, two historical sites of slavery received special attention: ancient Rome and the antebellum US South. Moses Finley cast them as the quintessential "slave societies", as opposed to all others, which were seen merely as "societies with slaves".[21] These studies from the 1980s have had a profound impact on the historiography of slavery in general and on the study of Atlantic slavery in particular. Roman slavery, and especially the slave economy on US-American plantations, continue to serve as the ultimate reference points for histories of slavery.[22]

Historians of Africa were among the first to challenge this view of slavery.[23] Joseph Miller, for instance, criticized the tendency of conventional narratives to take "the antebellum United States [as] the single source of the politicized epistemology of studies of slavery as an institution".[24] Rather than viewing "slavery as an outcome", he called on historians to study "slaving as a strategy".[25] Other

19 Patterson, *Slavery and Social Death*, x.
20 Patterson, *Slavery and Social Death*, 5.
21 Finley, *Ancient Slavery and Modern Ideology*.
22 For a recent example, see Rugemer, *Slave Law and the Politics of Resistance*, 1.
23 See especially Kopytoff and Miers, "Introduction", 3–7.
24 Miller, *The Problem of Slavery as History*, x. For a similar argument, see Epstein, *Speaking of Slavery*. For a recent critique of the US-dominated historiography of slavery, see also Herzog, "Enslaved as Outsiders, Enslaved as Property".
25 Miller, *The Problem of Slavery as History*, 4.

scholars have similarly argued that slavery must be more properly understood in the plural, as a history of *slaveries*.[26] This perspective aligns closely with the approach taken in this book. By tracing how Iberian intellectuals grappled with the problem of slavery in the 16th and 17th centuries, this study seeks to recover the conceptual vocabulary employed by past thinkers themselves. Historians of political thought have long emphasized that ideas are neither free-floating nor perennial—and cannot be abstracted from the social and cultural milieu from which they emerged.[27] Spanish and Portuguese visions of enslavement were no exceptions: they were part and parcel of an intimate interplay between concrete historical practices and the ideologies that drove and legitimated those practices.

Iberian theorists are famous for pondering the question of whether Indigenous communities in the Americas qualified as Aristotle's "slaves by nature"—people incapable of self-governance and independent political existence, so that the Spaniards had a just cause to subjugate and rule them. Francisco de Vitoria (1486–1546) and Domingo de Soto (1495–1560), both holders of the most important chair of Theology in Salamanca, questioned the validity of this retrospective justification of the Spanish conquest.[28] Yet the two founding figures of the so-called School of Salamanca also dealt with another, less studied, form of slavery.[29] What they referred to as *servitus civilis* had little to do with the natural aptitudes of individuals or the rule of entire communities. Civil slavery was a political and juridical category that entailed the loss of one's God-given freedom. It was a relationship between master and slave—what we would call "slavery proper". In the eyes of these Iberian thinkers, natural liberty could be legitimately deprived insofar as it preserved human life: slavery saved those who sold their freedom in the face of starvation, and in "just wars" the right to kill the enemy could be translated into a right of servitude. Whereas natural slavery was primarily debated in the context of the Americas, civil slavery

26 Zeuske, *Sklaverei*, 14–19; and Piqueras, *Derecho antiguo y esclavitud moderna*, 9–10. For an excellent panorama, see the contributions in Pargas and Schiel (eds.), *The Palgrave Handbook of Global Slavery*.

27 See Quentin Skinner's classic "Meaning and Understanding in the History of Ideas"; and Brett, "What is Intellectual History Now?". The importance of this is also emphasized in Miller, *The Problem of Slavery as History*, 1 and 11.

28 The classic study is Pagden, *The Fall of Natural Man*. See also Matsumori, *The School of Salamanca in the Affair of the Indies*. Unless stated otherwise, biographical information on the Iberian thinkers is drawn from the following two excellent resources: Schmutz, *Scholasticon*; and Barrientos García, *Repertorio de moral económica*.

29 On the School of Salamanca, see Belda Plans, *La escuela de Salamanca*; and Pena González, *La Escuela de Salamanca*.

spanned continents and contexts: from revolts in southern Spain and piracy in the Mediterranean to mercantile ventures along the African coasts and wars in Japan.[30]

Global issues like slavery preoccupied Spanish and Portuguese thinkers across the early modern Iberian world. Where earlier scholarship tended to overlook the shared intellectual enterprise of these theorists and focused exclusively on Spanish theologians such as Vitoria and Soto, historians have begun to place the "School of Salamanca" within a broader context. Some of the most influential works of theology and law were penned in the Portuguese lecture halls of Coimbra and Évora, in the Jesuit College in Rome, and in newly established universities overseas. The intellectual and political cultures of Spain and Portugal were deeply intertwined throughout the 16th and 17th centuries, both before and after the formal union of the Iberian crowns (1580–1640).[31] The continued scholarly division of Spain and Portugal, and their respective empires, has less to do with the lived reality of the early modern period than it does with the legacy of nationalist historiographies.[32] As Serge Gruzinski puts it, 21st-century scholars face the task of reconstructing and reconstituting these Iberian entanglements—"a bit like an electrician who comes to repair what time and historians have torn apart."[33]

In modern scholarship, the early modern Iberian thinkers examined in this book are often portrayed as antiquarians confined within a post-medieval bubble. They are frequently labeled as representatives of "scholasticism" due to their deep engagement with the works of Thomas Aquinas, both as readers and commentators.[34] But to cast these thinkers as "scholastics"—including such cognates as "late scholastics" or "colonial scholastics"—is to perpetuate a

30 The most important studies of Iberian thinkers' accounts of civil slavery have come from historians of the early modern Portuguese empire, focusing on Portuguese debates about the trade in enslaved Black Africans and the slavery of Indigenous Brazilians. I will discuss them in more detail below in Chapters 1 and 3. See Zeron, *Ligne de foi*; and Marcocci, *A consciência de um império*, chs. 11 and 12.

31 See Marcocci, "Iberian Theories of Empire", 671–683; Cardim and Monteiro, "Introduction", 4. See also Bouza, Cardim and Feros (eds.), *The Iberian World*; and Cardim, *Portugal y la monarquía hispánica*, 43–77.

32 For a critique of colonial and imperial history as organized according to 19th-century nation-state categories, see Gruzinski, *Les quatre parties du monde*, 33. Gruzinski's prime example for such an imperial history in the shadow of the nation state is Brading, *The First America*.

33 Gruzinski, *Les quatres parties du monde*, 35: "il s'agit de dégager ou de rétablir les connexions […] un peu à la manière d'un électricien qui viendrait réparer ce que le temps et les historiens ont disjoint."

34 For a recent example, see Koskenniemi, *To the Uttermost Parts of the Earth*, ch. 2.

polemical term from the past.[35] Although academics had been mocked as conceited "schoolmen" (*scholastici*) as early as the 12th century, the label "scholasticism" emerges as a coherent category only later and is properly an 18th-century invention. Only then did it become the epitome of an entire era, mobilized both to disparage the so-called Dark Ages, contrasting it with the self-styled novelty of the Enlightenment, and to romanticize the medieval past.[36] The term is also misleading because Iberian thinkers were not engaged in detached and abstract intellectual debates. Quite the contrary, even those who held chairs at universities were deeply involved in imperial affairs: they trained the future colonial elites and served as confessors to the Iberian monarchs. To that extent, their writings were far from irrelevant and could indeed have far-reaching political implications, as seen in the Council of the Indies' letter to the Spanish monarch on the justice of Atlantic slavery.

How, then, should we refer to these thinkers? In recent years, Portuguese scholars have coined the phrase "Iberian School of Peace" so as to expand a canon previously centered on Spanish writings.[37] Others have sought to retain the label "School of Salamanca", while emphasizing the global knowledge production of thinkers who recognized Vitoria as their founding father.[38] But neither of these designations is wholly convincing: the former is steeped in colonial apology and the latter obscures the fact that Iberian thinking was not exclusively tied to universities. The theologians, jurists, colonial administrators, and missionaries discussed in this book are more accurately described as Iberian imperial theorists, a term I adopt throughout. This designation highlights their crucial role as public intellectuals and influential political advisors whose work addressed the paradoxes of an expanding imperial world in the name of the common good and the Catholic faith.

---

35 See e.g., Schwartz, *The Political Morality of the Late Scholastics*; and Hofmeister Pich and Culleton, "Introduction".

36 See Rexroth, *Fröhliche Scholastik*, 40.

37 Calafate and Mandado Gutiérrez, *Escola Ibérica da Paz*; Calafate and Ventura, "The Iberian School of Peace"; Moreira and Azevedo Alves, *De Salamanca a Coímbra y Évora*. The "Iberian School of Peace" framework takes its cue from the so-called "Hispanic Corpus of Peace" (*Corpus Hispanorum de Pace*), a project that was launched in Franco-era Spain in order to celebrate the "great thinkers" of Spain's so-called Golden Age of empire and global domination. Originally led by the historian Luciano Pereña in the 1960s, the project continued after the regime change and was financed by the Spanish National Research Council. It rendered numerous critical, bilingual Latin-Spanish editions of early modern Iberian imperial writings into the 1980s and was renewed for a second series in the 21st century. The insistence on "peace" as an apologetic label for imperial ventures was never abandoned and still characterizes many of the contributions.

38 Duve, "The School of Salamanca".

A significant portion of the texts examined in this book are Latin treatises penned by university theologians. These include Francisco de Vitoria's lectures on Thomas Aquinas's *Summa theologiae* and the early modern genres that developed out of this tradition of commentary, notably the literature "On justice and right" (*De iustitia et iure*).[39] Tomes bearing this title were written by Domingo de Soto, and by Spanish Jesuits like Luis de Molina (1535–1600) and Juan de Lugo (1583–1660).[40] Yet this study also brings to light lesser-known writings by Portuguese professors such as Estevão Fagundez (1577–1645), non-denominational university theologians like Miguel de Palacio (c. 1515–1593), or American-based academics like Diego de Avendaño (1594–1688).[41] In all these writings, Iberian imperial theorists wove their statements on current political issues into meditations on questions Thomas Aquinas had formulated three centuries earlier. However, as they saw it, this endeavor was neither backward-looking nor antiquarian, as these theologians did not aim to historicize their own intellectual tradition. Spanish and Portuguese theologians treated Aquinas as they did the corpus of Roman law, the Bible, or late medieval canon law: as part of a living repertoire to address the problems of the present, offering new interpretations that suited their political aims.[42]

The university theologians were in dialogue with a range of other contemporary intellectuals, some of whom were also academics. Among them were prominent canon lawyers such as Martín de Azpilcueta (1492–1586)—professor in Salamanca and Coimbra and author of an influential handbook for confessors in the vernacular—and his Salamancan student and successor Diego de Covarruvias y Leyva (1512–1577).[43] Others composed guides for merchants on the morality of economic affairs. And still others wrote about the

---

39 Vitoria, *Comentarios a la Secunda secundae*, ed. Beltrán de Heredia. This commentary was compiled on the basis of surviving manuscript notes of Vitoria's pupils, who had written down their professor's dictated lectures.

40 Soto, *De iustitia et iure*; Molina, *De iustitia et iure*; Lugo, *De iustitia et iure*.

41 Fagundez, *De iustitia et contractibus*; Palacio, *Praxis theologica*; Avendaño, *Thesaurus indicus*.

42 On the use of Roman law as a repertoire for early modern imperial claim-making, see Benton and Straumann, "Acquiring Empire by Law". If we adopt this perspective, it makes little sense to criticize early modern Iberians for failing to properly understand Roman legal doctrines, as Francisco Cuena Boy does in his otherwise insightful study *De servitute*, 111–205. On this issue, see also Chapter 2, footnote 76.

43 Covarruvias, *Opera omnia*; Azpilcueta, *Manual de confessores*. The latter is a significantly revised Spanish edition, based on the first and second editions of the *Manual* that were printed in Portuguese (1549 and 1552). In 1573, a Latin edition was published in Rome. On the intricate book history of the *Manual*, see Bragagnolo, "Managing Legal Knowledge in Early Modern Times".

politics of imperial rule in the Americas, as the Salamanca-educated jurist Juan de Solórzano y Pereira (1575–1655) did in his *Política indiana* (1648).[44]

Some scholars have argued that intellectuals who wrote in the vernacular and did not pursue an academic career were concerned with more practical issues and addressed audiences beyond the university.[45] Yet it is misleading to draw a rigid distinction between "theoretical" and "pragmatic" texts.[46] All these Iberian thinkers read each other's work, across genres, and they cited and argued with each other. Tomás de Mercado (1530–1579), for instance, began his manual for merchants with a dense discussion of natural law that only made sense to readers trained in theology.[47] Conversely, Luis de Molina explicitly stated in his *De iustitia et iure* that the purpose of his examination of the justice of Atlantic slavery was "such that I may counsel confessors and other God-fearing people who inquire into this matter".[48] Indeed, even the academic treatises of Iberian theorists were ultimately handbooks. Like the vernacular manuals for merchants and confessors, these texts formed clusters around specific topics to examine concrete cases of conscience. These thick tomes were not intended to be read sequentially from cover to cover. Instead, readers could use the detailed tables of contents and indexes to jump right to the heart of the matter. In a fraught world of slavery and empire, the writings of the Iberian imperial theorists offered practical guidance on how to act morally and legally in almost any given situation.

Mapping the Book

To address these issues, the book is structured in three parts. The first examines how Spanish and Portuguese thinkers both confronted and bolstered the rise of global slavery. While Iberian theorists famously raised doubts about the

44 Solórzano y Pereira, *Política indiana*, ed. Ochoa Brun.

45 Duve, "Pragmatic Normative Literature", 17–25. See also Duve, "The School of Salamanca", 14.

46 For a related point on the close intellectual links between Jesuit missionaries in Brazil and the lecture halls of Coimbra and Évora, see Zeron, *Ligne de foi*, 36.

47 Mercado, *Suma*, ed. Sánchez-Albornoz, lib. I, *passim*.

48 Molina, *DIEI*, vol. 1, tr. II, disp. 35, introduction, col. 179: "non quod rem tantam solus definire audeam, neque quod tantum mihi tribuam, ut in ea meis dictis ac iudicio velim stetur: sed tum, ut pro mea tenuitate confessariis timoratisque aliis, qui de hac re interrogant, consulam". An English translation of Molina's treatise of slavery is now available but appeared too late to be consulted. See Molina, *On Slavery and the Slave Trade*, trans. Schwartz and Tellkamp.

scope and applicability of the idea that anyone could be a slave by nature, they upheld slavery, asserting that humans could lose their God-given freedom through legal slavery: a set of juridical mechanisms regulated the loss of natural liberty in "just wars" and equally allowed for the sale of oneself or one's children in extreme necessity. Legal slavery was framed by the *ius gentium* or "law of nations". While often celebrated as the origin of international law, this universal juridical framework also governed the morality of commerce between individuals. By situating slavery within this broader "moral economy", the book reconstructs how Iberian imperial theorists understood enslavement as a pivotal problem of conscience—as both a moral and juridical problem requiring reflection and justification.

Chapter One lays the groundwork for the analysis that follows by introducing the Iberian thinkers, their works, and their reception in modern scholarship. Chapter Two turns to the engagement of Spanish and Portuguese intellectuals with the mushrooming Mediterranean piracy and wars. It also examines how slavery became a pressing moral concern on the Iberian Peninsula through domestic rebellions. Challenging the view that Catholic natural rights were independent of divine grace and inherently "secular", this chapter shows instead that Iberian theologians and jurists crafted specifically Christian rights against those of Ottomans and "infidels" in Castile.[49]

Chapter Three focuses on the Portuguese slave trade, examining the spectacular growth of enslavement across Africa and Asia and the complex moral dilemma of Iberian merchants engaged in the commerce with "human commodities". Confronted with first-hand accounts of global Iberian slaving, Portuguese and Spanish thinkers acknowledged the plain injustice of human trafficking in the Atlantic and beyond. And yet, they expanded the boundaries of moral agency for all those who captured, traded, and owned slaves "in good faith".

The book's second part illuminates the place of slavery within the household. Although enslaved persons belonged to their owners, they could never be reduced to mere objects of possession. For Iberian theorists, slavery was equally about the power dynamics between the head of household and his domestic subjects. Rather than envisioning "an empire of private rights", Iberian thinkers emphasized the tensions and overlaps between ownership and authority, exploiting the ambiguities that resulted from the interplay between individual rights and domestic rule.[50] By reconstructing the legal and political imagina-

---

49 See e.g., Pagden, *Burdens of Empire*, 65.

50 The argument that Iberian thinkers theorized an "empire of private rights" is from Koskenniemi, *To the Uttermost Parts of the World*, 181. For an earlier version of this argument see Koskenniemi, "Empire and International Law", 32.

tion of slaves and their position in society, this section also brings previously overlooked conceptual perspectives in dialogue with social histories of enslavement in colonial Latin America.

Chapter Four explores the intricate nexus of slavery and marriage.[51] While early modern Spanish and Portuguese thinkers regarded slaves as both property and unfree subjects of their master—a status that seemed to preclude political agency—the institution of marriage complicated this picture, as enslaved individuals could simultaneously become heads of household and rule their own domestic community. The chapter demonstrates that this resulted in a tense situation where the agency of slaves conflicted with the agency of slaveholders.

Chapter Five examines the scope of masters' power over the bodies of their slaves. Iberian theorists universally agreed that slaveholders had no rightful authority to kill their slaves, but debates raged over whether slaveholders could brand their "human properties" or lock them up in private prisons. Equally contentious was the question under what circumstances enslaved people could claim the protection of civil and ecclesiastical authorities. In tackling these issues, Spanish and Portuguese thinkers redrew the line between private rights and public authority.

The book's final part focuses on Iberian voices from the New World. Theologians, missionaries, and imperial administrators were deeply concerned about an emerging system of labor coercion that perpetuated Indigenous slavery under new forms.[52] They also highlighted the troubling consequences of earlier apologies of the transatlantic trade in enslaved Africans. Slavery and forced labor formed the backbone of the Iberian imperial venture overseas, but at the same time threatened to undermine its material foundation: the exploitation resulting from Andean mining wiped out the human foundation on which the New World economy rested.

Chapter Six shows how Iberian theorists collectively engaged in vindicating forced Native labor in colonial Peru. It traces the jurisdictional politics involved in assigning different rights and duties to subjects of the same king. While scholars of colonial Latin America suggest that Spanish colonizers confronted this issue by distinguishing a "republic of *indios*" from a "republic of Spaniards",[53] this chapter challenges that view and argues otherwise: colonial

51 An article based on material from this chapter was published as Allemann, "Sklaverei, Heirat und 'Menschenrechte'".

52 Nancy van Deusen calls it a system of "thinly disguised slavery". See van Deusen, *Global Indios*, 7.

53 See e.g., Puente Luna, *Andean Cosmopolitans*, 15 and 159–160. Adrian Masters has shown that this two-republic-model is an invention of 20th-century historiography. See Masters, "The Two, the One, the Many, the None".

intellectuals assigned Andeans a place within the political community, by framing Indigenous labor coercion as a necessary contribution for the preservation of a sharply stratified "composite commonwealth".

The final chapter homes in on Epifanio de Moirans (1644–1689) and his polemic against the Iberian "moral economy" of the slave trade.[54] The French missionary stirred the highest political circles and became the impetus behind the Spanish monarch's alarmed letter to the Council of the Indies, which opens this book. Recent studies portray Moirans as a proto-abolitionist because he advocated the freedom of Black Africans.[55] This chapter shows instead that he crafted a new world-historical vision of salvation that reimagined Black Africans as Christians who were exempt from slavery by virtue of their faith. Moirans's critique of the Iberian imperial theorists ultimately deepened the nexus of enslavement and religion.

54 Moirans, *Servi liberi*, ed. Pena González et al.

55 See e.g., Weller, "Humanitarianism before Humanitarianism?", 167.

PART 1

Slavery in the Iberian World

CHAPTER 1

The Iberian Imperial Theorists in History

Charles II was certainly not the first Spanish monarch to be drawn to the writings of Iberian imperial theorists. Already in the sixteenth century, Francisco de Vitoria's critical examination of the justice of the Spanish conquest in his solemn lecture "On the American Indians" (*De indis*, 1539) drew the ire of the emperor himself. Charles V (1500–1558), addressing his complaint to the prior of the monastery of San Esteban in Salamanca, where Vitoria resided, wrote: "certain religious masters of your house have debated and treated in their sermons and lectures the right we have over the Indies, the islands and firm lands in the oceanic sea".[1] On matters of empire and slavery, the writings of early modern Spanish and Portuguese thinkers were politically explosive.

Before embarking on the task of reconstructing this strand of imperial theorists, I would like to outline how the book's approach relates to historical accounts provided by other scholars. The best-known figures among the Iberian theorists are Francisco de Vitoria and his fellow Dominicans at the University of Salamanca. While earlier scholarship focused primarily on their accounts of natural slavery, more recent histories tracing the ideological origins of European imperialism feature the Salamancan thinkers more broadly.[2] Central to these approaches is an appreciation of the language of natural law that the early modern theologians and jurists inherited from Aquinas. In their understanding, natural law was imprinted in the minds of human beings to such an extent that it was reason itself. It provided the basis for human beings

1 Emperor Charles V's letter from 10 November 1539 is edited in Getino, *El maestro fray Francisco de Vitoria*, 150: "Venerable padre prior del monasterio de santisteban de la cibdat de salamanca yo he sydo ynformado que algunos maestros religiosos de esa casa han puesto en platica y tratado en sus sermones y en repeticiones del derecho que nos tenemos a las yndias yslas e tierra firme del mar oceano". Vitoria's *De indis* was a so-called *relectio*, a solmen lecture in which Vitoria pondered current affairs that were related to themes of his ordinary lecture course on Aquinas's *Summa*. All fifteen special lectures held between 1527 and 1543 are available in a complete critical edition based on the surviving manuscripts of scribes: Vitoria, *Relecciones jurídicas y teológicas*, ed. and trans. Fernández-Largo et al. An English translation of the *De indis* is available in Vitoria, *Political Writings*, ed. and trans. Pagden and Lawrance.

2 See e.g., Benton, *They Called It Peace*; Tellkamp, "Introduction"; Pagden, *Burdens of Empire*, ch. 1; Benton and Straumann, "Acquiring Empire by Law"; Lupher, *Romans in a New World*, ch. 2; and Tuck, *The Rights of War and Peace*, ch. 2.

to act morally and set the terms for individual freedom.[3] But it also served as the conceptual framework through which Iberian theorists—both the Dominicans at Salamanca and later Jesuit thinkers—sought to understand the political and juridical world around them.[4] Based on this observation, Annabel Brett has provided a powerful re-evaluation of the significance of the Catholic natural law discourse for the emergence of the modern, man-made state with respect to both nature and the interpolitical arena transcending the commonwealth.[5]

A body of law closely related to, yet distinct from the law of nature was the *ius gentium* or "law of nations", a concept rooted in Roman law. Traditional scholarship on the *ius gentium* celebrated figures like Vitoria as progressive founders of international law.[6] More recent scholarship, however, has shown that the early modern *ius gentium* was embedded in a narrative of biblical history quite at odds with the principles of modern international law.[7] For Iberian theologians and jurists, its principal function was to reconstitute the natural

3 See Brett, *Liberty, Right and Nature*, ch. 4; Deckers, *Gerechtigkeit und Recht*, ch. 3; and Tuck, *Natural Rights Theories*, ch. 2.

4 The relationship between earlier Dominican and later Jesuit theologians and jurists has been the subject of debate among historians of political thought. In his *Natural Rights Theories*, Richard Tuck emphasized a sharp contrast between them (54). But in *The Rights of War and Peace*, Tuck revised his earlier stance and instead underlined the continuities between Iberian Dominicans and Jesuits (68). More recent scholarship has pushed in this direction, while also showing that there were nevertheless important differences between individual Dominican and Jesuit thinkers. See especially Brett, *Changes of State, passim*; and Decock, *Theologians and Contract Law*, 65–66. The present study takes its cue from these latter studies. Importantly, this also means that, in contrast to Harro Höpfl's treatment of Jesuit political thought, the focus in the present work is not on the general "Jesuit" label but on the thought of specific intellectuals, and on the respective continuities and discontinuities between them and earlier Dominicans. See Höpfl, *Jesuit Political Thought*.

5 See Brett, "Scholastic Political Thought and the Modern Concept of the State"; and above all Brett, *Changes of State*. The story that Brett tells tacitly resists the idea of placing the Iberian theorists in a binary framework between "absolutism" and "constitutionalism", as suggested in Burns, "Scholasticism"; and Skinner, "A Genealogy of the Modern State". More importantly, Brett also challenges the notion of a clear-cut Catholic/Protestant divide in the early modern natural law discourse that is advocated in Tuck's *Rights of War and Peace*. Brett's potision is also echoed in more recent scholarship. See e.g., Malcolm, *Useful Enemies*, ch. 11; and Grant, "Francisco de Vitoria and Alberico Gentili on the Juridical Status of Native American Polities".

6 See e.g., Brown Scott, *The Spanish Origins of International Law*. On the uses of Vitoria by Brown Scott and other interwar legal scholars, see Amorosa, *Rewriting the History of the Law of Nations*; and Rasilla del Moral, *In the Shadow of Vitoria*, ch. 3.

7 There is, however, a debate between scholars engaged in so-called "critical histories of international law" and historians of political thought on the validity of approaching Vitoria's thought, in particular, through the early 20th-century interpretation by James Brown Scott. For an excellent account of this debate; of the misconceptions that guide some of its participants; and of how many scholars who are writing global legal histories today in fact fruitfully

telos of humanity in the postlapsarian state.[8] In their account, in Eden, earthly possessions had been held collectively by all human beings. But after the Fall, the *ius gentium* was introduced to regulate the establishment of private property, distinct commonwealths, wars and—most importantly, for the purposes of this study—slavery. The complex relationships between the pristine and the fallen world, and between natural law and the *ius gentium*, have been studied extensively. Above all, scholars have focused on the political implications of the interplay between the notion of *dominium*—which signified both human liberty (under natural law) and mastery or ownership of external things (under the *ius gentium*)—and the concept of right.[9]

The *ius gentium* was also central to the Iberian theorists' engagement with the questions of conscience arising from economic dynamics in the wider Iberian world. It shaped their understanding of human contracts in such a way that interpersonal exchange was conceived primarily as an exchange of *rights* over things, governed by the principles of commutative justice. The Iberian impulse to interrogate the morality of trade has since become a point of interest for an entire scholarly tradition that views the early modern thinkers as forerunners of modern economic theory. As Marjorie Grice-Hutchinson observed in her 1978 monograph on *Early Economic Thought in Spain*: "[t]he Spanish Doctors made a useful contribution to the progress of value-theory".[10] Four years earlier, notably, Friedrich von Hayek had likewise underlined the significance of "the Spanish Schoolmen", describing them in his Nobel Prize Lecture as "remarkable anticipators of modern economics".[11] Even today, this view remains far from obsolete. As the theologian Diego Alonso-Lasheras has recently argued, "studies of the last 40 years have helped to establish the importance of the scholastics in economic thought and particularly their influence on Adam Smith and modern economics".[12]

---

draw on perspectives from the history of political thought as well as social history, see Benton, "Beyond Anachronism".

8 Kirstin Bunge offers a helpful metaphor in speaking of the *ius gentium* as having a *Scharnierfunktion*, a hinge function, between natural and civil law. See Bunge, *Gleichheit und Gleichmass*, 268.

9 See e.g., Brett, *Liberty, Right and Nature*, ch. 4; Brett, *Changes of State*, chs. 2–4; Seelmann, "Selbstherrschaft, Herrschaft über die Dinge und individuelle Rechte in der spanischen Spätscholatik"; Scattola, "Die weiche Ordnung"; and Tellkamp, "Rights and *Dominium*".

10 Grice-Hutchinson, *Early Economic Thought in Spain*, 98. The so-called "Austrian" tradition of the history of economic thought contributed extensively to the establishment of this approach. See especially Schumpeter, *History of Economic Analysis*, ch. 2; and von Weber, *Wirtschaftsethik am Vorabend des Liberalismus*.

11 Hayek, "Lecture to the Memory of Alfred Nobel".

12 Alonso-Lasheras, *Luis de Molina's* De Iustitia et Iure, 5. For a similar argument, see Mac-

Most scholars arguing along these lines note that it would be mistaken to treat the early modern theologians as "pure economists", conceding they were equally motivated by their duty to guide people's conscience.[13] And yet, early modern adherents of Aquinas are still considered worthy of study because they anticipated the emergence of modern economic theory.[14] Such readings, however, are anachronistic and misrepresent the core of early modern Iberian thinking. Spanish and Portuguese theologians understood economics as a sphere of concrete human agency that "was not seen as a reality *abstracted and apart from* the actions of individuals".[15] To understand early modern writings on justice, rights, and contracts, it is critical, therefore, to acknowledge that these texts were deeply concerned with the *salus animarum*, or the salvation of souls.[16] As Wim Decock has shown, the ultimate framework through which theologians and canon lawyers measured individual agency in an economic world was the *forum conscientiae*, or the forum of conscience. When they theorized notions such as the "just price", they did so in fundamentally moral terms.[17]

This emphasis on conscience also shaped how the Iberian imperial theorists envisioned politics. Historians have emphasized the importance of the Spanish and Portuguese "voices of conscience" in offering political guidance to the Iberian kings, both in domestic affairs and in imperial contexts.[18] Martti Koskenniemi, by contrast, shifts the focus back to the horizontal plane of inter-individual exchange. "The real Spanish contribution" of Vitoria and his colleagues, as Koskenniemi puts it, was their creation of an "empire of private rights"—a language of private property rights that served to legitimate European domination over the non-Western world.[19] In this reading, Vitoria and

---

Gregor, *Luis de Molina*, 210–216 and 225; and Azevedo Alves and Moreira, *The Salamanca School*, 73 and 85.

13 See e.g., Barrientos García, "El pensamiento económico en la perspectiva filosófico-teológica", 119–120.

14 Other recent, forceful accounts in this regard include Popescu, *Studies in the History of Latin American Economic Thought*, ch. 4; Gómez Camacho, *Economía y filosofía moral*; Chafuen, *Faith and Liberty*.

15 Idoya Zorroza, "Some Reflections on the Ethical Rationality in the Economic Theory of the School of Salamanca", 90, original emphasis.

16 Duve, "Kanonisches Recht und die Ausbildung allgemeiner Vertragslehren in der Spanischen Spätscholastik".

17 Decock, *Theologians and Contract Law*. For a helpful overview of early modern contexts of conscience more broadly, see Braun and Vallance, "Introduction". On the notion of economic justice in early modern Europe, see Trivellato, "The Moral Economies of Early Modern Europe".

18 See Marcocci, *A consciência de um império*; and Reinhardt, *Voices of Conscience*.

19 Koskenniemi, "Empire and International Law", 32.

those writing in his vein are worthy of study, not because they advocated Spanish jurisdiction overseas, nor because they anticipated modern economic theory, but because they laid the conceptual foundations of what we now call capitalism.[20] Yet a further, third, perspective challenges this exclusive focus on interpersonal exchange, highlighting instead the interplay between the horizontal plane of individual rights and the vertical plane of political authority. As Annabel Brett has shown, property was itself implicated in the language of the common good.[21]

However, with a few notable exceptions—above all the work of Carlos Alberto Zeron and Giuseppe Marcocci on Portuguese slavery in West Africa and Brazil—a sustained study of Iberian visions of enslavement remains strikingly absent from recent scholarship.[22] This book seeks to address this lacuna. It demonstrates that slavery was the quintessential prism through which Spanish and Portuguese imperial theorists reflected on the relationships between rights and power, rulers and subjects, and commerce and politics.

1 The Iberian Imperial Theorists in the History of Slavery

The Iberian imperial theorists drew a sharp distinction between *servitus naturalis* and *servitus civilis*. In their view, only the latter governed the loss of human freedom and the process of enslavement, as the following chapters will show. The meaning of natural slavery, by contrast, is far more difficult to pin down. According to Anthony Pagden's influential argument, Vitoria not only rejected natural slavery as the legitimate legal basis for Castilian domination over the newly "discovered" peoples in the Americas, but ultimately also abandoned this

20 Koskenniemi, "Empire and International Law", 28.

21 Brett, "Luis de Molina on Law and Power". See also Benton, *They Called It Peace*, 96–97. Meanwhile, Martti Koskenniemi has come to adopt a more balanced view of Iberian thinking that also addresses war and political power. See Koskenniemi, *To the Uttermost Parts of the World*, ch. 2. For a contrasting view that insists on a clear-cut separation of property rights from the language of vertical power in the later Jesuit Iberian theorists, see Tellkamp, "Francisco de Vitoria and Luis de Molina on the Origin of Political Power".

22 Zeron, *Ligne de foi*; Marcocci, *A consciência de um império*, chs. 11 and 12. Also worth mentioning are Francisco Cuena Boy's studies on the influence of Roman legal doctrines in early modern Iberian arguments about slavery, now collected in Cuena Boy, *De servitute*. Piqueras's recent *Derecho antiguo y esclavitud moderna* focuses solely on legal norms and rules, and as noted above, he confines his analysis of Castilian and Mediterranean slave laws to the medieval period, while treating the early modern period exclusively through the lens of Spanish American contexts.

category altogether. Vitoria, Pagden argues, "effectively destroyed the credibility of the theory of natural slavery as a means to explain the deviant behaviour of the Indian".[23] Vitoria was indeed cautious to decouple the notion of natural servitude from the legal discourse associated with civil slavery. As Brian Tierney has shown, however, Vitoria nevertheless did not fully relinquish the idea. The decisive point, as he argues, was that "Vitoria was envisaging a status for those who were servants by nature radically different from the chattel slavery of ancient Greece and Rome".[24]

But what, precisely, was that status? In the *De indis*, a lecture Vitoria delivered before Salamanca's most illustrious intellectuals in 1539, he argued that Indigenous people in the New World were perhaps "so close to being mad, that *they are unsuited to setting up or administering a commonwealth both legitimate and ordered in human and civil terms*", and indeed, "unsuited even to governing their own households".[25] If the "barbarians" truly lacked the capacity for political self-rule, Vitoria suggested, "[i]t might therefore be argued that for their own benefit the princes of Spain might take over their administration, and set up urban officers and governors on their behalf, or even give them new masters, so long as this could be proved to be in their interest".[26] In the end, Vitoria remained ambiguous, stating he did "not dare either to affirm or condemn" this line of reasoning.[27] Equally important, he made clear that natural slavery, understood in this way, was not a legal status and had nothing to do with owning another person as private property.[28] And yet, he left open the possibility that framing Indigenous people as "natural slaves" might justify the Spanish presence in the New World under the guise of political protection and guardianship.[29]

---

23 Pagden, *The Fall of Natural Man*, 104.

24 Tierney, *The Idea of Natural Rights*, 270. Tierney first articulated his critique of Pagden's reading of Vitoria in his earlier and less familiar essay "Aristotle and the American Indians", 311–315.

25 Vitoria, *De indis*, in *Political Writings*, trans. Pagden and Lawrance, q. 3, a. 8, 290, original emphasis.

26 Vitoria, *De indis*, in *Political Writings*, trans. Pagden and Lawrance, q. 3, a. 8, 290.

27 Vitoria, *De indis*, in *Political Writings*, trans. Pagden and Lawrance, q. 3, a. 8, 290–291.

28 See Vitoria, *De indis*, in *Political Writings*, trans. Pagden and Lawrance, q. 1, a. 6, 251.

29 According to Carlos Alberto Zeron, Vitoria thus regarded natural slavery as an "attenuated" form of political domination to be distinguished from a "truly legitimate title" of conquest (see Zeron, *Ligne de foi*, 397). On the relationship between empire and arguments of protection more broadly, see the contributions in Benton, Clulow, and Attwood (eds.), *Protection and Empire*; and in Haug, Weber, and Windler (eds.), *Protegierte und Protektoren*.

Other contemporary Iberian thinkers like Domingo de Soto—also a Salamancan—were less ambiguous and contested this sort of reasoning.[30] Theologians and jurists writing from the New World, however, prominently revived the notion of natural slavery, with all its inherent ambiguities. For some, it served as a justification of the conquest, in that it sanctioned the imposition of Iberian authority over peoples like the "Caribs", who were perceived as having failed to form proper commonwealths.[31] But first and foremost, I will argue, the concept resurfaced in a new debate that was no longer about the legitimacy of conquest but about Spain's model of imperial rule overseas. Jurists like Juan de Matienzo (1520–1579), university theologians like José de Acosta (1539–1600), and missionaries like Juan de Silva deployed the idea of natural slavery to justify forced labor imposed on Spain's Indigenous vassals in the Americas.[32]

In the writings produced in Iberia the notion of natural slavery ultimately functioned as a foil for introducing another kind of slavery: *servitus civilis*. As a juridical rather than a natural category, civil slavery was a specific type of property right established by the *ius gentium*. The question of how one could fall into servitude thus centered on what the Iberian theorists called "legitimate titles", a set of legal arguments for slavery. The principal titles included enslavement in "just wars", selling oneself or one's children out of necessity, and enslavement imposed as a punishment by public authority.

Scholars have made several valuable observations regarding Iberian accounts of slavery. We now know, for instance, that the canon lawyer Diego de Covarruvias played a foundational role in shaping the Iberian theorists' understanding of "just war" slavery;[33] that the theologians Domingo de Soto and Luis de Molina disagreed over whether voluntary slavery was permissible in the absence of necessity;[34] and that Molina maintained that slaves, despite their status as "human properties", could nonetheless own property rights themselves.[35] These points will be revisited in more detail in the chapters that follow.

Among the Iberian imperial theorists, Luis de Molina, who offered the most comprehensive discussion of slavery, warrants a more detailed introduction.

---

30 Soto, *DIEI*, lib. IV, q. 2, a. 2, 290: "Et per hac satisfieri illis debet, qui sciscitantur utrum iure naturalis dominii possimus Christiani infideles armis infestare, qui pro suorum morum ruditate, naturales videntur esse servi. Nullum enim inde ius contra eos acquirimus vi illos subiugandi".

31 See e.g., Acosta, *De procuranda*, ed. Pereña, vol. 1, lib. II, cap. 5, no. 1, 282–284. I have discussed this in more detail in Allemann, "After Vitoria".

32 This will be the subject of Chapter 6 of this book.

33 See the insightful discussion in Scattola, "Sklaverei, Krieg und Recht".

34 Zeron, *Ligne de foi*, 275; and Brett, *Changes of State*, 94–95.

35 Kaufmann, "Slavery between Law, Morality, and Economy", 218–221.

Born in Cuenca in 1535, he began studying law at Salamanca at the age of sixteen but dropped out just a year later to join the Society of Jesus.[36] This marked a decisive moment in Molina's life that would shape the trajectory of his future academic career. Although the Jesuits had slowly begun to establish a presence in European universities in the 1540s, they had yet to gain this status at the leading Spanish institutions. In Portugal, however, King João III (r. 1521–1557) entrusted the Society of Jesus with a college of its own at the University of Coimbra in 1542, which soon emerged as a leading hub for Jesuit education.[37] Little wonder, then, that Molina was sent to Coimbra, where he studied philosophy, subsequently embarking on a second degree in theology, and eventually obtaining his doctorate in that subject in 1562. Accordingly, Molina has been characterized as "a Spaniard of Portuguese formation".[38] He remained in Portugal after completing his studies, holding a double professorship in theology and philosophy at Coimbra before accepting a prestigious chair in theology at the University of Évora in 1568. Molina held this position for over a decade until his increasingly declining health forced him to resign from teaching in 1583. He died in Madrid seventeen years later.

Molina is best remembered for his controversial intervention in a theological debate on divine foreknowledge. In his *Concordia* of 1588, he attempted to reconcile the Augustinian notion of grace with human liberty by coining the notion of "middle knowledge" (*scientia media*).[39] Equally successful was his treatise on justice and right, *De iustitia et iure*, that went through more than ten editions across Europe in the early 17th century.[40] This treatise is largely based on Molina's lecture courses on Aquinas delivered at the University of Évora in the 1570s and 80s. The multivolume work became available in its entirety only after Molina's death and was published between 1593 and 1609.[41]

36 The next couple of paragraphs draw on biographical information on Molina provided by Barrientos García, *Repertorio de moral económica*, 293–295; and MacGregor, *Luis de Molina*, chs. 1–2. Further valuable information on Molina's life is available in Aichele and Kaufmann, "Introduction", xiv–xvi; and in Stegmüller, *Geschichte des Molinismus*, 1–9.

37 Höpfl, *Jesuit Policital Thought*, 10–11.

38 Moreira and Azevedo Alves, *De Salamanca a Coimbra y Évora*, 31: "Luis e Molina—un español de formación portuguesa".

39 See Molina, *Concordia liberi arbitrii*. A concise summary of the controversy is provided in Aichele and Kaufmann, "Introduction", xxiii–xxvi. For more extensive discussions, see Freddoso, "Introduction"; Ruhstorfer, "Sola Gratia"; and Cruz Cruz, "Predestination as Transcendent Theology".

40 Aichele and Kaufmann, "Introduction", xxix.

41 For details about the publication history of the *De iustitia et iure*, see Pena González, *La Escuela de Salamanca*, 156; and Barrientos García, *Repertorio de moral económica*, 295–296.

And it is this work on justice and right that is most important for understanding his political and legal thought.

A range of recent studies, emanating mostly from outside the Anglophone academia, has centered on Molina's extensive account of slavery in the *De iustitia et iure*.[42] However, several issues remain unresolved in existing scholarship. The few accounts attempting to contextualize his understanding of enslavement draw rigid contrasts between him and earlier Iberian Dominicans. In so doing, they gloss over some of the crucial legal underpinnings of slavery, above all the complex interplay between the various senses of *dominium* central to Molina's and other Iberian thinkers' understanding of slavery—human freedom of action, rights over external things, and power over others.[43]

What is more, the vast majority of studies offer little more than an exposition of Molina's treatise on slavery, merely recounting his arguments and celebrating the singularity of his comprehensive appraisal of the Portuguese slave trade.[44] Yet to fully assess the political and legal dimensions of Molina's work, it is crucial to not only put him in dialogue with his contemporaries but also combine the reconstruction of his thought with a critical analysis. Otherwise, the historian's voice risks becoming indistinguishable from the language of early modern texts—and reproducing, rather than examining, their arguments. Precisely this problem lies at the heart of Jesús María García Añoveros's study of early modern Iberian attitudes toward slavery: "We interpret the sources as they were interpreted at the moments and in the periods that they were used", he notes bluntly, "excluding any possible modern interpretations of these texts".[45] Buying into the early modern rhetoric is presented as a historical approach, when in fact it constitutes a political move, one that blocks off a critical examination of the role Molina and other Iberian theorists played in the ideological justification of slavery and empire.

42 The best studies of Molina's treatise of slavery are Kaufmann, "Slavery between Law, Morality, and Economy"; Zeron, *Ligne de foi*, 271–294; and Hespanha, "Luís de Molina e a escravização dos negros".

43 See e.g., Haar and Simmermacher, "The Foundation of the Human Being Regarded as a Legal Entity in the 'School of Salamanca'"; and Tellkamp, "Über den Zusammenhang von Freiheit und Sklaverei bei Vitoria und Soto".

44 See e.g., Coxito, "Luis de Molina e a escravatura"; and Brieskorn, "Die Sklaverei in der Beurteilung des Luis de Molina S.J.".

45 García Añoveros, *El pensamiento y los argumentos sobre la esclavitud*, 14: "A las fuentes les damos la interpretación que se les dio en los momentos y en la época que fueron usadas, excluyendo posibles interpretaciones modernas de esos textos".

The third and final historiographical problem centers on Luis de Molina's place in the history of antislavery thought.[46] In 1974, Frank Costello was among the first to argue that "Molina opposed the slave trade and was a highly articulate critic of it".[47] Half a century later, while Molina's acceptance of the validity of slavery has been largely recognized, the view advocated by Costello remains an important impetus in recent studies. The basic line of argument is that "deep inside", as it were, Molina was a fierce critic of slavery and sought to get rid of this institution, though he never actually managed to do so.[48] Even serious scholars like Matthias Kaufmann, who maintain that such a view is problematic, insist that Molina was "on the road to abolitionism" and point to his "indirect role" in that development.[49] It is therefore unsurprising that Molina is also cast as a critical voice in general histories of slavery and abolition, including by scholars like Manisha Sinha.[50] But a close reading of Molina's text, especially when considered alongside the arguments of his predecessors, reveals that he actually expanded the moral and legal latitude for trading and owning enslaved people.[51] As I will argue, Molina should not be counted among the early critics of slavery.

This brief overview of the historiography connecting Molina and slavery reveals both misunderstandings and unresolved questions. This situation is emblematic of the broader condition of scholarship on slavery in Iberian imperial thought. It is vital to stress, however, that numerous Spanish and Portuguese thinkers, writing both before and after Molina, have been almost entirely forgotten. Intellectuals such as Miguel de Palacio, Estevão Fagundez, and Diego de Avendaño all wrote extensively on the subject—and with politi-

46 For a similar historiographical critique, see Zeron, *Ligne de foi*, 18–19 and 31.

47 Frank Costello, *The Political Philosophy of Luis de Molina*, 191.

48 Most forcefully in Schirrmacher, *Die Politik der Sklaverei*, 194: "Molina [...] der den Handel mit subsaharischen *negro*-Sklaven scharf kritisierte". And in Coxito, "Luis de Molina e a escravatura", 136: "É certo no entanto que para Molina o ideal seria criarem-se condições para que o tráfico de escravos pudesse ser proscrito, em nome da liberdade e da dignidade da pessoa humana". See also the equally problematic portrayals of Molina as a defender of the liberty of sub-Saharan Africans in Joner, "Impressions of Luis de Molina about the Trade of African Slaves", 49; García Añoveros, "Luis de Molina y la esclavitud de los negros africanos en el siglo XVI", 328–329; Craveiro da Silva, "Luis de Molina", 554–546; and Brieskorn, "Die Sklaverei in der Beurteilung des Luis de Molina S.J.", 95.

49 Kaufmann, "Slavery between Law, Morality, and Economy", 222 and 225. The same is argued in MacGregor, *Luis de Molina*, 223 and 225.

50 See Sinha, *The Slave's Cause*, 10–11. See also Pétré-Grenouilleau, *Les traites négrières*, 72.

51 On this point, I disagree with Marcocci, who argues that Molina ultimately condemned the Portuguese trade in enslaved Africans. See Marcocci, *A consciência de um império*, 426.

cal weight, as we saw in the letter from the Council of the Indies to the Spanish monarch. Yet their names remain largely absent from the stories we tell about their era.

One explanation for this neglect is that many Iberian imperial theorists wrote in Latin without ever being translated into modern European languages (let alone a non-European one). Another lies in the handbook style of their texts. The Iberian thinkers structured their writings into different thematic clusters, frequently repeating the fundamentals of justice and right at various points in these volumes. The resulting redundancies may seem tedious. But they are a real treasure trove for historians: they allow us to bring into dialogue various thematic strands so as to identify tensions and ambiguities within these writings. For in fact, the Iberian thinkers not only cited their contemporaries and other authorities extensively, they also constantly cross-referenced passages in their own works, revealing a self-imposed commitment to argue coherently. And it is precisely where inconsistencies occur in the thinking of the Iberian imperial theorists that we find some of their most intriguing arguments—and instances where they compromised their own conceptual architecture in the face of present political needs.

2 Slavery, Empire, and Global Intellectual History

As will be clear by now, the history of rights and slavery in the Iberian world is in many ways a global history. In his 2016 book on the subject, Sebastian Conrad provides both a general introduction to an increasingly popular field and his own interpretation of it.[52] He acknowledges the revisionist impulse of global history, especially its attack on "container-based paradigms, chief among them national history".[53] At the same time, he rightly cautions that global history is not simply a synonym for histories that study the entire planet. For him, it is a distinct analytical lens through which to view the past, "like gender history or economic history".[54] Conrad, in other words, understands global history as a perspective that sharpens the historian's analysis of certain processes, networks, people, ideas, or events.[55] "As important as the quest for alternative spatial units may be", he argues, "the real challenge consists in shifting between, and articulating, different scales of analysis rather than sticking to fixed terri-

52 Sebastian Conrad, *What is Global History?*.
53 Conrad, *What is Global History?*, 4.
54 Conrad, *What is Global History?*, 12.
55 Conrad, *What is Global History?*, 116 and 135–136.

tories".[56] For Conrad, focusing on a continuous dialogue between micro- and macro-historical views allows us to transcend "such dichotomies of structure and agency, of necessity and the contingent".[57] His contribution is valuable for intellectual history in that it invites a focus on individual agents—whether theologians, jurists, or missionaries—so long as they are situated in the broader intellectual, social, and political world they inhabited.

But how exactly have intellectual historians engaged in the so-called global turn? It is noteworthy that the phrase "global intellectual history" has been invoked as the title of both an important essay collection and an emergent academic journal.[58] In the introductory contribution to the former, Samuel Moyn and Andrew Sartori discuss a set of avenues that intellectual historians might wish to explore.[59] Their "gallery of alternative models" explores the potential of global historical methods such as comparative approaches, or an attention to networks and processes of translation, for historians of ideas.[60] For David Armitage, one of the leading proponents of this field, the need for going global hinges on the fact that most human beings on the planet experienced their present as subjects of empires rather than states.[61] What is more, this spatial extension is linked up with an expanded temporal perspective in Armitage's view. His understanding of global intellectual history is tied to a call for reviving the *longue durée*, connecting disparate historical episodes and epochs through what he terms "serial contextualism".[62]

However, as Frederick Cooper warns in one of the essays in Moyn's and Sartori's collection, an overemphasis of the global carries significant risks. By focusing only on "unbounded connections but not the greater array of those [dimensions] that are border crossing but finite", Cooper warns that we risk

56 Conrad, *What is Global History?*, 118.

57 Conrad, *What is Global History?*, 160.

58 Moyn and Sartori (eds.), *Global Intellectual History*. The journal *Global Intellectual History* was launched in 2016, under the aegis of Richard Whatmore. Other recent studies bearing this title include Becker Lorca, *Mestizo International Law*; and Aydin, *The Idea of the Muslim World*, a part of which was published as Chapter 7 of the Moyn and Sartori volume mentioned at the start of this footnote.

59 Moyn and Sartori, "Approaches to Global Intellectual History".

60 Moyn and Sartori, "Approaches to Global Intellectual History", 4 and *passim*.

61 Moyn and Sartori, "Approaches to Global Intellectual History", 239.

62 On the notion of serial contextualism, see Armitage, "What's the Big Idea?". Armitage first applied this methodology in his recent global intellectual history of civil wars from ancient Rome to the 20th century: Armitage, *Civil Wars*. For an advocacy of the *longue durée* in the study of history more broadly speaking, see also Guldi and Armitage, *The History Manifesto*. For a critique of the latter, see Cohen and Mandler, "*The History Manifesto*: A Critique".

defining a field "in artificial terms".[63] Cooper's reservation is not only due to what may be lost in a process that privileges global breadth at the expense of local depth. More importantly, he argues that to redescribe imperial intellectual history as global intellectual history is problematic, as not all imperial discourses are properly global. In Cooper's view, retaining the notion of empire intentionally prevents an uncritical adoption of a universalizing and Eurocentric notion of globality.[64] Other intellectual historians, too, have expressed their concerns about championing the global.[65] When invoked uncritically, as Shruti Kapila maintains, this locution all too easily assumes the status of "a mere politically acceptable version of the 'expansion of Europe.'"[66] She further argues that this danger looms large in the work of those who endorse a "spatially literal view" that is "by definition always from above" and therefore "absorbs distinction and ignores disruption in favour of replicable and coherent patterns across contexts".[67]

If we return to Sebastian Conrad's fundamental insistence that global history should be understood as a perspective rather than simply a replacement of one container (the state) with another (the world), we might approach the matter from a different angle. Other scholars have also pushed in this direction. Rather than searching for "ideal-types of political-spatial configurations and their significance", Lauren Benton argues that it is more beneficial to focus instead on "repeating problems taken up by political writers and [to] analyze their approaches in attempts to address those problems".[68] Benton emphasizes the central role of the commonwealth or state in recent global histories of political thought because, in the early modern period and beyond, it "continued to sit beside or partially constitute other configurations of political community".[69] Indeed, the theologians and jurists examined in this book understood "empire" in ways not always clearly differentiated from other forms of political community. In reflecting on the problem of slavery, the Iberian theorists also considered the circulation of "human goods" in other spaces, such as the

63 Cooper, "How Global Do We Want Our Intellectual History to Be?", 286.
64 Cooper, "How Global Do We Want Our Intellectual History to Be?", 289. On this point, see also Moyn, "On the Nonglobalization of Ideas".
65 Tom Pye, for instance, has pointed to the danger of over-emphasizing global contexts at the expense of how space was construed intellectually, arguing that John Locke's imperial involvement is not the decisive context for understanding his theory of property. See Pye, "Property, Space and Sacred History in John Locke's *Two Treatises of Government*".
66 Kapila, "Global Intellectual History and the Indian Political", 260.
67 Kapila, "Armitage on Civil Wars", 320.
68 Benton, "Afterward".
69 Benton, "Afterward", 258.

domain of the pope or the sphere of Roman law—spaces that were not equivalent to commonwealths governed by princes. In this sense, the book takes its cue from Benton's assertion that it is particularly fruitful to study "the tension between spatial representations of political community and ideas about the spatial distribution of authority".[70]

And yet, the call for more global intellectual histories is also a call to engage with past political languages that did not originate in Europe. The task of navigating between "language-worlds" and reconstructing non-Western "systems of thought" on their own terms is daunting, as the late John Pocock remarked, given the breadth of linguistic and cultural knowledge it requires.[71] Nonetheless, he encouraged historians to undertake this challenge to win back what had, in his view, been lost in the shift from earlier Eurocentric histories of political thought to approaches solely concerned with economic relationships and power plays.[72] Pocock sought to carve out a space for global histories before the age of economic globalization as much as he wished to preserve a place for politics in an age defined by commercial society.[73]

The fact that language poses a challenge for global history has also been noted by other historians. As Jeremy Adelman provocatively put it in his widely read essay of 2017, "it is hard not to conclude that global history is another Anglospheric invention to integrate the Other into a cosmopolitan narrative on our terms, in our tongues".[74] Adelman struck a nerve with his critique of the cultural and symbolic dominance of history-writing in the English language. But his polemic is only partly applicable to students of the early modern world. That this book is written in English does not therefore mean that it overrides the language of any "Other" in the conventional sense. Quite the contrary, it recovers texts originally written in some of the most important global *linguae francae* of the 16th and 17th centuries. Not all those languages remain in active use anymore, quite unlike the tongues and cultures of the so-called "Global South" that Adelman has in mind. Latin, the language of more than half of the writings under scrutiny in this book, is effectively a dead language that makes translation unavoidable. Yet far from imposing English on the world at large, the process of reconstructing forgotten ways of talking about rights and power

70 Benton, "Afterward", 255. A masterful example of such a study is Brett's *Changes of State.*

71 Pocock, "On the Unglobality of Contexts", 9–12. See also Dunn, "Why We Need a Global History of Political Thought".

72 Pocock, "On the Unglobality of Contexts", 12.

73 This is a tacit critique of the work of István Hont and those writing in his vein, for whom the 18th century marked a sharp break from earlier visions of politics and anticipated the contours of the modern, global economic order. See Hont, *Jealousy of Trade.*

74 Adelman, "What is Global Histoy Now?".

serves to reveal the historical contingency of our own conceptual frameworks about these issues—and to unsettle the "language world" that we inhabit.

It is also critical to avoid drawing a rigid contrast between "Europe" and the so-called "non-Western" world.[75] In the "interpolity zones" where power and sovereignty were fragile or absent altogether, agents of European empires were in constant dialogue and negotiation with representatives of other polities.[76] Scholars have shown that "Native claims" had a profound impact on these colonial encounters.[77] Moreover, recent work by legal historians has demonstrated that political and legal theories that are traditionally considered "European" were significantly shaped by imperial realities. Famous tracts by thinkers like Alberico Gentili (1552–1608) and Hugo Grotius (1583–1645) not only responded to domestic issues but also to concrete circumstances on the fringes of early modern empires.[78] Indeed, socio-legal historians have made significant—even if not always acknowledged—contributions to the field of global intellectual history.[79] These studies underscore a crucial dimension of global histories more broadly: namely, the significance of paying attention to developments in the world "out there" that transformed discourses and realities "at home".

It is not least in this sense that the present study approaches early modern Iberian accounts of enslavement from a global intellectual historical perspective. Many of the issues that the Spanish and Portuguese thinkers grappled with were urgent, practical problems of the day that demanded authoritative resolution. Portuguese missionaries in Brazil, for instance, faced the thorny question of whether enslaved Africans could be re-married if their spouses had been left behind on the other side of the Atlantic—and none other than Luis de Molina shared his opinion on the matter with some of the highest representatives of the Society of Jesus.[80] What is more, in their discussions of the Portuguese slave trade in Africa and Asia, Iberian theorists drew extensively from travel narra-

75 On "Europe" as a historical category in medieval and early modern history, see Oschema, *Bilder von Europa im Mittelalter*; and Groebner, "Europas Grenzen?".

76 See Benton and Clulow, "Webs of Protection and Interpolity Zones in the Early Modern World".

77 See Belmessous, "Introduction". See also Premo and Yannakakis, "A Court of Sticks and Branches"; and Owensby and Ross, "Making Law Intelligible in Comparative Context".

78 See Benton, *A Search for Sovereignty*, ch. 3.

79 This point is highlighted in Benton, "Beyond Anachronism", 25 fn. 49: "Fitzmaurice misses the explicit aim of the works of many socio-legal historians (including me) to uncover the interrelation of juridical thought to legal practice. This is an unfortunate misrepresentation". Benton here refers to Fitzmaurice, "Context and the History of International Law".

80 We shall turn to this in more detail in Chapter 4.

tives and eyewitness accounts to assess what could be deemed just or unjust.[81] And as we shall see in the following chapter, Spanish and Portuguese subjects were themselves routinely taken captive by Muslims in the Mediterranean, and one vital question was whether those enslaved among the "Saracens" could, in good conscience, flee their captivity.

81 This will be the subject of Chapter 3.

CHAPTER 2

Mediterranean Geographies of Slavery

The practices of slaving in the medieval and early modern Mediterranean were sorely neglected by historians for a long time. Where medievalists traditionally focused on the Black Sea region and the late Byzantine empire, scholars of early modern slavery directed their attention to the rise of Atlantic slavery. The last two decades, however, have seen a veritable boom in studies on Mediterranean contexts of enslavement, which is part and parcel of the growing attention to the history of Europe's colonial entanglements.[1] The geographic and cultural diversity of enslaved persons in late-medieval cities like Barcelona, Genoa, Venice, or Palermo is impressive. There were Tartars, Circassians, and Abkhazians from the Black Sea region; enslaved Bosnians and Serbians—mostly children or adolescents—whom the Ottomans had taken captive in the Balkans; Muslims from the Iberian Peninsula and the Maghreb; and, increasingly, enslaved Canary Islanders and West Africans.[2]

One of the best-studied contexts of slavery is the trade in enslaved persons from the Black Sea region between the 13th and 15th centuries. This commerce rested on what Hannah Barker has described as "assumptions and practices that amounted to a common culture of slavery".[3] Christians enslaved Muslims and vice versa, but Latin Christians also captured Orthodox Christians as slaves, and Muslim Arabs subjected Muslim Turks to servitude.[4] Commercial relations flourished across religious boundaries. Genoese merchants in control of the Crimean city of Caffa, "an emporium for slaves", supplied the Mamluk Sultanate of Egypt and Syria with human commodities.[5] Yet Italian traders were not just intermediaries in the service of North Africans, for they also pursued their own interests as slavers in the Black Sea.[6] During the heyday of the Venetian empire in the first half of the 15th century, Venetian merchants transported numerous enslaved people into the Mediterranean from places as far away as Tana in

---

1 See the magnificent survey of the field by Hanß, "Sklaverei im vormodernen Mediterraneum". See also Schiel and Hanß, "Semantics, Practices and Transcultural Perspectives on Mediterranean Slavery".

2 Epstein, *Speaking of Slavery*, 81, 185, and 191; Armenteros Martínez, *La esclavitud en Barcelona*, 165–167; Schiel, "Sklavennahme in der Seerepublik Venedig", 589; Bono, *Schiavi*, 7–8 and ch. 2.

3 Barker, *That Most Precious Merchandise*, 3.

4 Barker, *That Most Precious Merchandise*, 209.

5 Epstein, *Speaking of Slavery*, 123.

6 See Schiel, "Slavery in the Western Mediterranean", 180; and Schiel, "Tatort Tana".

DOI:10.1163/9789004760592_004

the Sea of Azov to Trebizond, in what is now northeastern Turkey. It was only in the wake of the Fall of Constantinople (1453) and the subsequent Ottoman conquests of Trebizond and Crimea that the Italians were eventually pushed out of the Black Sea region.[7]

The aftermath was not, however, a straightforward turn from Eastern Europe to West Africa. The rise of Atlantic slavery from the mid-15th century coincided with increasing incursions into North African territories.[8] These raids extended practices familiar from the conflicts between Castile and al-Andalus on the Iberian Peninsula—the so-called *Reconquista*, or Reconquest.[9] But enslavement was not unidirectional. As Robert Davis has shown, Maghrebian enslavement of Christians alone "out-produced the trans-Atlantic trade during the sixteenth and into the seventeenth century".[10] The Mediterranean became a zone of intense activity of corsairs from various ethnic and religious backgrounds. Pirates of all persuasions raided ships and coasts, and "carried off thousands of slaves each year", as David Abulafia points out.[11] At the same time, the Ottoman empire was on the rise. Its fleet moved into the Western Mediterranean and most Maghrebian kingdoms, except for Morocco, came under indirect Ottoman control. The ensuing wars with Christian powers led to large numbers of captives on all sides.[12]

As a consequence, Iberian cities like Barcelona, Valencia, or Alicante became important Iberian centers for the trade in Mediterranean slaves in the 16th century.[13] Granada was another city with a substantial population of enslaved persons. As Aurelia Martín Casares has shown, two-thirds of the slaves from Mediterranean wars and piracy who ended up in Granada were female.[14] This astonishing fact is largely due to the gendered nature of warfare, as Martín Casares argues. While men were engaged in belligerent activities and often

7 Schiel, "Sklavennahme in der Seerepublik Venedig", 588–589.

8 Groebner, "The Carnal Knowledge of a Coloured Body", 223.

9 On the centrality of raiding to wars of (re)conquest, see Benton, "The Legal Logic of Wars of Conquest", 429–431; and Benton, *They Called It Peace*, ch. 2.

10 Davis, *Christian Slaves, Muslim Masters*, xxiv. The same point is also made in Zeuske, *Sklaverei*, 180.

11 Abulafia, *The Great Sea*, 413.

12 Malcolm, *Agents of Empire*, 209–210.

13 Phillips, *Slavery in Medieval and Early Modern Iberia*, 10–11 and 43–51. Noel Malcom argues that in the late 16th-century, there were 40,000–50,000 Muslim slaves in Spain (Malcom, *Agents of Empire*, 210). Alessandro Stella estimates that the total number of slaves brought to Iberia from the Mediterranean amounted to 300,000–400,000 from the mid-15th to the mid-18th centuries, roughly half the number of African slaves. See Stella, *Histoires d'esclaves dans la péninsule ibérique*, 79.

14 Martín Casares, *La esclavitud en la Granada*, 238.

died in battle, women and children were in turn the "principal booty of war".[15] Yet the best-remembered Maghrebian captive in Christian hands is a man, Leo Africanus (c. 1486–?), the former envoy of the Sultan of Fez, who was captured by pirates on the Mediterranean and eventually became a close diplomatic advisor to Pope Leo X. (in office from 1513–1521).[16]

The vast majority of Muslim captives in Christian hands, however, ended up serving perpetually as galley slaves. In Iberian and Italian ports alike, they equipped the triremes alongside those forced into that task as a form of public punishment. Ottomans and Maghrebians, by contrast, primarily captured Christians to sell them for a price.[17] This Mediterranean ransom economy generated close-knit webs of exchange across religious boundaries, with crucial players such as Christian orders like the Trinitarians and the Mercedarians, as well as the Roman Confraternity of the Gonfalone.[18] What is more, this practice not only cut across religious divides, but also applied to many ordinary people.[19] It was not just a privilege reserved for noblemen like Miguel de Cervantes (1547–1616), the author of *Don Quixote*, who spent five years in captivity in Algiers.[20] The mission to redeem captured compatriots was also a welcome opportunity for merchants to circumvent the prohibition of commerce with religious enemies.[21] But importantly, Iberians invested in privateering similarly made "huge profits" by selling captives they had raided on the shores of North Africa, even when these people were not ransomed back to their native cities but sold off as slaves.[22]

Many issues recent scholarship has brought to light, particularly on enslavement in the early modern Mediterranean, also preoccupied theologians and jurists at the time.[23] Yet while court cases, purchase contracts, or baptismal

15 Martín Casares, *La esclavitud en la Granada*, 241: "... convierte las mujeres y los hijos de los vencidos en uno de los principales botines de guerra".

16 See Zemon Davis, *Trickster Travels*. See also Leo Africanus' account of his diplomatic travels between Fez and Timbuktu, which is one of the earliest surviving acounts of sub-Saharan Africa: Africanus, "Della descrittione dell'Africa", ed. Ramusio.

17 Hanß, "Sklaverei im vormodernen Mediterraneum", 640; Martin Casares, *La esclavitud en la Granada*, 242. But despite the flourishing Mediterranean ransom economy, a significant proportion of Christians were captured and held as long-term slaves by the Ottomans in the sixteenth century. See Tarruell, "Prisoners of War, Captives or Slaves?".

18 Hanß, "Sklaverei im vormodernen Mediterraneum", 644–645; Epstein, *Speaking of Slavery*, 192–193.

19 Malcolm, *Agents of Empire*, 210–211.

20 See Garcés, *Cervantes in Algiers*; and Kaiser, "Sprechende Ware", 29.

21 Kaiser, "Sprechende Ware", 33.

22 Martín Casares, "Maghrebian Slaves in Spain", 98.

23 This includes Islamic legal scholars, as shown by Freamon, *Possessed by the Right Hand*.

records have been extensively studied by social and legal historians, the same cannot be said of the Iberian imperial theorists' accounts of slaving.[24] By turning to the works of Spanish and Portuguese intellectuals, this study revisits some of the central themes in recent scholarship, while also proposing new lines of inquiry that enrich our understanding of early modern slavery.

1 Theoretical Foundations: Natural Law, the *ius gentium*, and Civil Slavery

The natural law discourse owes its name to the central importance that early modern theologians and jurists accorded to the law of nature. The Iberian intellectuals inherited this framework from Aquinas, and agreed with the traditional Thomist understanding that, as Luis de Molina put it, natural law "is the intellect by which we separate and judge the things that are good by their own nature from the things that are bad by their own nature".[25] Some insisted that God not only imprinted the law of nature on the hearts or minds of humans but also on all natural things.[26] In the most pronounced articulation of this position, Domingo de Soto maintained that, as a consequence, all the beings on earth possessed natural rights to the extent that they followed their natural inclinations. This overlap between humans, animals, and nature at large reflected the original hierarchy and connectedness of laws in Aquinas. But all the Iberian theorists, including Soto, agreed that natural law in a narrower sense was a uniquely human affair.[27] It formed the God-given foundation of *dominium*: the capacity to act willingly, reasonably, and morally, which rendered humans free. Liberty, in this sense, distinguished the crown of creation from the rest of nature, which operated through instinct rather than moral choice.[28]

The notion of natural slavery as chattel slavery was problematic from a Thomist point of view because it contradicted the conviction that all human beings were naturally free by virtue of being made in the image of God. As Francisco de Vitoria stressed in the *De indis*, his lecture on the Indigenous peoples

---

24 See Martín Casares, "Maghrebian Slaves in Spain", 102, on the body of sources used in recent histories of Mediterranean slavery.

25 Molina, *DIEI*, tr. 1, disp. 3, no. 3, col. 9: "ipsa intellectus qua ea quae ex se et natura bona sunt, ab iis quae ex se mala sunt, secernimus ac diiudicamus".

26 Molina, *DIEI*, tr. 1, disp. 3, no. 3, col. 9: "ius naturale a Deo Optimo Maximo sit mentibus nostris inditum, naturisque ipsis rerum impressum".

27 On Soto's dual sense of natural law, see Brett, *Liberty, Right and Nature*, 142–146.

28 Brett, *Changes of State*, 37–39.

of the New World, "Aristotle does not suggest that natural slaves are by nature of someone else's right and did not have *dominium* over themselves and other things. This, in fact, is civil and legal slavery".[29] This distinction was echoed by all Iberian thinkers writing in Vitoria's vein.[30] Luis de Molina even went as far as to suggest that natural slavery "is inappropriately called slavery, since it does not bestow on others a right over such human beings".[31]

Legal enslavement was a consequence of the *ius gentium*, the body of law that governed the passage from Eden to the post-paradisal world. Domingo de Soto explained the necessity for this novel legal framework as follows:

> Let us restate this natural principle: Human life must be held out and preserved in peace and tranquility. Therefore, considering the other premise that after the corruption of nature it would not be possible to live in common and to cultivate the fields diligently, and neither to live in peace, the peoples [on earth] brought about the division of these possessions.[32]

In a world no longer in its pristine condition, the division of things was essential so that humans could pursue their natural end. This was also emphasized by Luis de Molina. To maintain peace and to impose justice in the wake of original sin, he explained, "it became necessary to introduce the *dominium* of jurisdic-

29 Vitoria, *De indis*, in *Relecciones jurídicas y teológicas*, ed. and trans. Fernández-Largo et al., vol. 2., q. 1, no. 23, 564: "Aristoteles non intellegit quod tales [i.e., natural slaves] sint a natura alieni iuris et non habebant dominium et sui et aliarum rerum. Haec enim est servitus civilis et legitima". The translation by Pagden and Lawrance is not exact: "Aristotle certainly did not mean to say that such men thereby belong by nature to others and have no rights of ownership over their own bodies and possessions (*dominium sui et rerum*). Such slavery is a civil and legal condition, to which no man can belong by nature" (Vitoria, *De indis*, in *Political Writings*, trans. Pagden and Lawrance, q. 1, concl., 251). The Latin edition from which I am quoting is based on the same manuscript of Vitoria's *De indis* that also provides the foundation for the translation by Pagden and Lawrance; the one preserved in the cathedral library of Palencia from c. 1540, which is most likely a direct copy of Vitoria's original script. See Allemann, "Re-Reading Vitoria", 339.

30 See e.g., Soto, *DIEI*, lib. IV, q. 2, a. 2, 288: "Duplicem enim servitutem scite Aristoteles dignovit 1. Politicorum. Alteram quidem naturalem alteram vero legalem".

31 Molina, *DIEI*, vol. 1, tr. II, disp. 32, no. 1, col. 158: "Quaedam est, quam vocat naturalem [....] Haec autem aptitudo improprie appellatur servitus, neque cuiquam alteri tribuit ius in huiusmodi homines".

32 Soto, *DIEI*, lib. I, q. 5, a. 4, 44: "Statuamus illud naturale principium: Vita humana in pace et tranquilitate sustentanda est et conservanda. Inde, subsumpta altera praemissa quod natura corrupta in communi vivens neque agros coleret diligenter, neque in pace viveret, gentes intulerunt dividendas esse possessiones".

tion with a certain coercive force".[33] And in the further course of sacred history, once human beings had multiplied and spread across the earth, "it became necessary that this *dominium* be divided and that rulers were set up to govern the various provinces, cities, and peoples".[34]

The new reality not only required divided political power, for the prospect of peace also hinged on the division of what had once been collective ownership of the movable and tangible things on earth.[35] In technical terms, this too was a division of *dominium*, a term that signified both mastery and property. If human beings were capable of owning and governing their own actions, the Iberian followers of Aquinas argued, they were likewise capable of possessing external things and ruling over other human beings.[36] In this sense, *dominium* denoted a set of interlocking phenomena: human freedom, private property, and political power.

The notion of *dominium* was closely related to right (*ius*). Molina defined the latter as "the faculty to do or possess anything, or to hold on to it, or to have it in any other way, so that if it is counteracted without a legitimate cause, the possessor suffers an *iniuria*, that is, his or her right is violated".[37] Like Vitoria and Soto before him, he understood subjective right as a "faculty" of the individual. Scholars have shown that there was some disagreement among the Iberian theologians as to whether *dominium* and right were the same or whether one was prior to the other.[38] For the purposes of this study, however, the more important point is that all the Iberian imperial theorists insisted on a close association between *dominium* and right, and sometimes used these concepts interchangeably.

---

33 Molina, *DIEI*, vol. 1, tr. II, disp. 20, no. 1, col. 99: "Etenim statim ac genus humanum ab innocentiae statu per peccatum corruit, necessarium fuit iurisdictionis dominium cum vi quadam coercente introduci".

34 Molina, *DIEI*, vol. 1, tr. II, disp. 20, no. 1, col. 99: "Multiplicatis praeterea hominibus, et per orbem dispertis, necesse etiam fuit eiusmodi dominium dividi, pluresque constitui rectores, qui varias provincias civitates ac populos moderarentur".

35 Molina, *DIEI*, vol. 1, tr. II, disp. 20, no. 5, col. 100: "necessarium est res quoad dominia esse divisas, ut ex communi rerum possessione gravissima oriretur". This point is also emphasized in Brett, "Molina on Law and Power", 169.

36 For an excellent history that traces the medieval heritage of early modern Iberian understandings of *dominium*, see Brett, *Liberty, Right and Nature*.

37 Molina, *DIEI*, vol. 1, tr. II, disp. 1, no. 1, col. 27–28: "Est facultas aliquid faciendi, sive obtinendi, aut in eo insistendi, vel aliquo se habendi, cui si, sine legitima causa, contraveniatur, iniuria sit eam habenti".

38 See Brett, *Changes of State*, 92–93; Brett, *Liberty, Right and Nature*, ch. 4; and Kaufmann, "Subjektive Rechte als Grenzen der Rechtssetzung bei Luis de Molina".

1.1 *The Idea of Civil Slavery*

Civil slavery was intimately connected to all of this. Enslaved persons were subject to the *dominium* of somebody else. Vitoria, as we saw above, stressed that slaves were not their own but *alieni iuris*; they belonged to the right of another.[39] One crucial consequence of this was that "the modes by which the *dominium* over a slave is transferred to other human beings are the same as those by which the *dominium* over other things is commonly transferred, namely by selling, exchange, donation, by a will, etc.", as Molina pointed out.[40]

Enslaved persons lacked the right to govern themselves and were deprived of their natural liberty. Slaves, in this sense, found themselves in an unnatural condition. Yet the Iberian theorists were keen to explain that enslavement did not contradict the law of nature for that reason. Domingo de Soto referred to Aquinas to underscore the difference between what was natural in Eden and what was natural after the Fall. As a consequence of original sin, punishment—including legal slavery—was introduced into the world, and this was "in accordance with corrupt nature".[41] The Augustinian Miguel Bartolomé Salón (1539–1621)—a now-forgotten professor at the University of Valencia, who wrote a treatise on justice and right like Soto before and Molina after him—similarly argued that "legal slavery is not by nature, but neither incompatible with nature; on the contrary, natural reason itself admonishes all humans that it is licit if it will be necessary to the preservation of life".[42]

Like other matters and entities regulated by the *ius gentium*, civil slavery was a consequence of the Fall. It thus belonged to a world in which human

39 See Vitoria, *De indis*, in *Relecciones jurídicas y teológicas*, ed. and trans. Fernández-Largo et al., vol. 2, q. 1, no. 23, 564.

40 Molina, *DIEI*, vol. 1, tr. II, disp. 33, no. 1, col. 160 [incorrectly labeled as 108]: "modis dominium illius transferri in alios, quibus dominia aliarum rerum transferri consueverunt, nempe venditione, permutatione, donatione, ultima voluntate, etc".

41 Soto, *DIEI*, lib. IV, q. 2, a. 2, 290: "servitutem non contra iri aut proprie derogari naturali iuri. [...] bifariam aliquid est a natura intentum: Uno modo secundum intentionem primam, quemadmodum generationem intendit, corruptibilis naturae conservatricem: Altero modo quantum ad secundam intentionem: quo pacto corruptionem intendit ut generet. [...] Attamen illa deficiente intentione, ex culpa subsequuta est poena, quae est conformis naturae curruptae. Atque inter poenarum genera unum est legalis servitus". See also Aquinas, *Scriptum super Sententiis*, ed. Alarcón and Busa, lib. 4, dist. 36, q. 1, a. 1, ad 2.

42 Salón, *Commentariorum in disputationem de iustitia*, q. 3, a. 1, concl. 4, 114: "servitutem legalem, de qua agimus non esse a natura, nec repugnare naturae, imo rationem ipsam naturalem omnes homines admonere eam licitam esse, quando fuerit necessaria ad vitae conservationem". The work was first published in 1591, and after 1608, it appeared under the title *Controversia de iustitia et iure atque de contractibus et commerciis humanis*. On matters of slavery, Salón closely followed Domingo de Soto's *De iustitia et iure*, and his Augustinianism was no cause for any substantial disagreements.

relations were no longer pristine, and in which it was possible to lose one's freedom. This was also underlined by Francisco Suárez, one of the most prominent Iberian thinkers. Suárez did not offer a comprehensive treatise of slavery, leaving only scattered remarks on this theme across his many writings.[43] But one of these is particularly illuminating. In his *Defensio fidei* of 1613, a polemic against the validity of James I of England's Oath of Allegiance of 1606, he put forward a powerful justification of enslavement. "Natural law", he argued,

> does not teach that every human should always be free, and (what is equally so) it does not absolutely prohibit that a human being may be enslaved, but only that this must not be done without his or her free consent, or without a just title and power.[44]

In the face of the Catholic insistence on God-given freedom, this was a remarkable thing to say. And yet, Suárez put forward a rhetorically forceful iteration here of a dictum shared by all the Iberian thinkers: even if the condition of the slave was not natural in itself, the process of enslavement could nevertheless be in accordance with the law of nature, provided it was properly regulated. Under certain conditions, both the voluntary act of self-submission and a set of legal mechanisms licensed the loss of human freedom.

1.2 *Enslavement in "Just Wars"*

The most fundamental of these so-called "titles" of slavery was a direct consequence of the *ius gentium*. It centered on the idea that in a "just war", it was permissible to enslave one's enemies. As Vitoria noted in his lecture "On the Law of War" (*De iure belli*, 1539), this dictum dated back to Roman law, "where it is stated that 'by the law of nations (*ius gentium*) all booty taken from the enemy

---

43 A helpful overview of Suárez's remarks on slavery is available in Seixas, "Trabalho livre e trabalho escravo na obra da Francisco Suárez". We shall turn to further important arguments of Suárez's at various points below.

44 Suárez, *Defensio fidei catholicae*, lib. III, cap. 2, no. 9, 220: "ius autem naturae non praecipit, omnem hominem semper manere liberum, seu (quod perinde est) non simpliciter prohibet, hominem in servitutem redigi, sed solum, ut id non fiat vel sine libero illius consensus, vel sine iusto titulo, et potestate." I owe this point to Benjamin Slingo, who drew attention to this passage in a paper presented at the University of Cambridge on 13 Feburary 2017. Suárez made a similar argument in his *De legibus*, vol. 3, lib. II, cap. 14, no. 18: "quamvis natura dederit libertatem et dominium eius, non tamen absolute prohibuisse ne auferri possit".

immediately becomes ours, to the extent that even free men may be taken into slavery by us.' "[45] The *ius gentium* not only regulated the division of jurisdiction and property but also sanctioned wars. This idea, rooted in the *Digest*, was a commonplace in early modern Iberian discussions of civil slavery.[46]

Domingo de Soto, along with later Jesuits like Luis de Molina or Juan de Lugo, emphasized the intimate nexus of enslavement and war by invoking an etymological account from Florentinus in the *Digest* and Justinian's *Institutes*: enslaved persons were called *servi* from the verb *servare*, because they had been saved by their enemies from a just death in war. What is more, these slaves were also called *mancipia* because they had been captured by hand, *manu capta*.[47] The idea of enslavement in "just wars" thus centered on a specific mode of protection: it was a commutation of the right to kill into the right of perpetual servitude.[48]

This testifies to the inherent complexity of how Iberian theorists understood the *ius gentium*. As shown above, this legal framework governed human relations in the postlapsarian state and was designed to mitigate the consequences of the Fall—chief among them, the need to preserve *peace*. And yet, at the very heart of the law of nations lies *war* as the foremost consequence of the division of things, which brought armed conflicts into being. The individual issues regulated by the *ius gentium* were no longer perfect in themselves; yet without it, as Molina emphasized, there would be "nothing that would remedy human nature sufficiently".[49] And it was precisely this line of reasoning that also licensed slavery in wars: even though enslavement was neither

45 Vitoria, *De iure belli*, in *Political Writings*, trans. Pagden and Lawrance, q. 3, a. 7, 322. Vitoria here quoted from Inst. 2.1.17.

46 D.1.1.5: "Ex hoc iure gentium introducta bella [...]".

47 See Soto, *DIEI*, lib. IV, q. 2, a. 2, 289: "Unde (ut lege citata et ff. De statu hominum, l. libertas docemur) servitutis nomen derivatum est. Videlicet quod imperatores bello captos vendere, neque occidere solent, sed servare. Et isti dicuntur mancipia: quia victores quos gladio transigere possent, manu capiunt, ut servent". See Molina, *DIEI*, vol. 1, tr. II, disp. 32, no. 2–3, col. 158: "Huiusmodi homines, ut *Institut. De iure personarum, § servi*, habeatur, servi dicti sunt a servando: quia videlicet Imperatores, quos bello capiebant, quosque fas illis erat interficere, servabant, commutata eorum morte in perpetuam servitutem. Dicti etiam sunt mancipia, quasi ab hostibus manu capta, ut ibidem subiungitur". See Lugo, *DIEI*, disp. 6, sect. 2, no. 10, 134, original emphasis: "a servando *servi* dicti sunt, sicut et dicuntur *Mancipia*, quia manu capiuntur". For the original passages in Roman law, see Inst. 1.3.3 and D.1.5.4.2–3.

48 As explicitly argued in Molina, *DIEI*, vol. 1, tr. II, disp. 33, no. 1, col. 160 [incorrectly labeled as 108]: "iure namque gentium mancipium sit capientum, morte in perpetuam servitutem commutata".

49 Molina, *DIEI*, vol. 1, tr. II, disp. 20, no. 5, col. 101: "nihil est quod naturae humanae sufficienter medeatur [...]".

natural nor good in itself, it was "introduced for the good of the slaves themselves, since perpetual servitude is a lesser evil for them than to be deprived of life".[50]

Although the *ius gentium* was universally valid, Iberian thinkers stressed that there was no such slavery among Christians. This position was already clear in Francisco de Vitoria's commentary on Aquinas's *Summa*. In his discussion of the Thomist hierarchy of laws, Vitoria pointed out that the *ius gentium* "can be partly abrogated" and that Christians had agreed not to enslave fellow believers captured in war.[51] Even more forcefully, Vitoria argued in his lecture "On the Law of War" that "it is not lawful to enslave fellow-Christians, at any rate during the course of the war".[52] This became a standard position endorsed by all the Iberian theologians and jurists.[53] The abolition of "just war" slavery among Christians had been introduced by human agreement, but it was considered permanently binding.[54]

But where did this idea originate? The most comprehensive answer was offered by the Salamanca-educated jurist Gregorio López (1490–1560).[55] López was appointed to the Council of the Indies at the height of his career (1543–1556), and he also wrote an influential gloss on the *Siete Partidas*. Originally commissioned by King Alfonso x. (r. 1252–1284) during the Spanish "Reconquest" of the Iberian Peninsula, the *Partidas* formed the foundation of Castilian civil legislation until the end of the colonial period.[56] But it was Gregorio López's extensive commentary from the 16th century that made the late medieval law code particularly useful for early modern readers.[57] His gloss, featured in every edition of the *Partidas* after it was first published in 1555, interpreted the law code through extensive references to Roman and canon law, as well as the opinions of jurisconsults and theologians. One of López's interventions concerned the validity of enslavement in "just wars". Like Vitoria, he insisted that "the laws regarding the captivity of persons captured in

50 Molina, *DIEI*, vol. 1, tr. II, disp. 32, no. 3, col. 158: "Quo sit, ut haec etiam servitus in bonum ipsorum servorum introducta sit, quatenus perpetua servitus minus malum illis est, quam privari vita".

51 Vitoria, *Comentarios a la Secunda secundae*, ed. Beltrán de Heredia, vol. 3, q. 57, a. 4, no. 5, 17: "potest abrogari ex parte ius gentium [...] sicut ius gentium est quod captivi in bello justo sint servi, sed [...] hoc non tenet inter christianos".

52 Vitoria, *De iure belli*, in *Political Writings*, trans. Pagden and Lawrance, q. 3, a. 3, 318–319.

53 See e.g., Soto, *DIEI*, lib. IV, q. 2, a. 2, 290; Molina, *DIEI*, tr. I, disp. 5, no. 4, col. 14.

54 On this point, see Iurlaro, *The Invention of Custom*, 5–6 and 62.

55 Biographical information on López is from Masferrer, "Las *Siete Partidas*".

56 On Alfonso x and the *Siete Partidas*, see O'Callaghan, "Alfonso x".

57 See Birr, "Tradition and Innovation in Knowledge Production".

war are not kept among Christians".[58] Instead, López explained, captives from another Christian commonwealth were detained in prisons.[59] He made this point with reference to the Renaissance Roman lawyer Bartolomeo da Saliceto (1330–1412), who had discussed the matter in his extensive commentary on Justinian's *Codex*.[60] The Christian abolition of "just war" slavery was a medieval idea that cast a long shadow.[61]

In many ways, the Iberian imperial theorists associated enslavement with Christian wars against "infidels" and with wars between non-Christian polities. The Jesuit Tomás Sánchez (1550–1610), "a luminary of the Spanish Golden Age most noted for his contributions to the moral theology and canon law of marriage", explained why.[62] The Christian custom of non-enslavement, he argued, was a consequence of "charity, which is common to all Christians through Christ".[63] This mindset was shared by all the Iberian thinkers. It colored their understanding of the Mediterranean wars between Castilians and Ottomans, as well as their accounts of Portuguese naval ventures in the Atlantic and Indian

58 *Las Siete Partidas*, l. 1, tit. 29, partida 2, gloss López: "Inter christianos non servantur iura captivitatis quoad personas captas in bello".

59 *Las Siete Partidas*, l. 1, tit. 29, partida 2, gloss López, verb. *alguna cosa*: "Tene menti istam l. nam de iure communi nulla l. cavet, quem effectum habeat ista captio personarum in bello, inter reges christianos, et conditor huius legis habuit respectum ad generalem consuetudinem, secundum quam christiani capti in talibus bellis, possunt detineri in carcere pro talea habenda, ut tradit Saly. c. in l. ab hostibus".

60 See Saliceto, *Ad V., VI., VII., VIII. et IX. libros Codicis commentarii*, commentary on C.8.50.2 (l. Ab hostibus, De postliminio et de redemptis ab hostibus), 330: "Nam christiano ad christianum guerram faciente servitus in captivis non inducitur. [...] Puto igitur quod solum in carcere pro talea habenda possit retineri".

61 In *De iustitia et iure*, published around the same time as López's edition of the *Partidas*, Domingo de Soto pointed to Bartolus of Sassoferrato (1313–1357), another important *trecento* lawyer, whose 16th-century editor of the *Opera omnia* also included a reference on the custom of non-enslavement among Christians. Yet Soto did not mention the alternative to detention in the way that López had, with reference to Saliceto (see Soto, *DIEI*, lib. IV, q. 2, a. 2, 290). As becomes clear from the editorial addition to Bartolus's text—to which Soto referred without quoting from it—Bartolus's editor in fact followed the rationale Saliceto had previously offered. See Bartolus of Sassoferrato, *In II. partem Digesti novi commentaria*, commentary on D.49.15.24 (l. Hostes, De captivis et postliminio reversis), no. 16, 638, verb. *Sed secundum mores*: "Salic in l. ab hostib. C. de postlim. ubi ait, in locum servitutis et captivitatis taleas subrogari".

62 The quote is from Domingo, "Tomás Sánchez", 225.

63 Sánchez, *Consilia*, lib. I, cap. 1, dub. 3, no. 6, 4: "nisi Christianus capiatur a Christiano, tunc enim quantumvis iustum sit bellum, non efficitur servus; sic enim generalis consuetudo obtinuit propter charitatem, quae in Christo omnibus Christianis communis est. Sic definit dicta *l. 1, tit. 29, part. 2* et ibi Gregorio Lopez *versic. Alguna*".

Ocean worlds. But before we turn to these contexts, we shall see that the issue of "just war" slavery was also at the heart of the greatest controversy over slavery on the early modern Iberian Peninsula.

2 War and Punishment in Castile

One of the most heated political issues in 16th-century Spain was the uprising of the formerly Muslim population of Granada.[64] The origins of this conflict date back to the Castilian subjugation of the last bastion of al-Andalus, the Nasrid Kingdom of Granada. But only much later did the so-called "Moorish New Christians"—as the forcibly converted Muslims were known in Castile's administrative language—experience a drastic change in their status within the Catholic monarchy.[65] In the wake of the Council of Trent (1545–1563) and the counter-Reformation, and with the ascension of Philip II to the throne in 1556, the Natives of Granada came under increasing political pressure. The crown had previously tolerated the cultural and religious practices of the converted Christians in exchange for special taxes. But under the new monarch, this kind of patronage and protection ended abruptly. Philip II's suppression of their privileges rested on the conviction that, as Stephanie Cavanaugh writes, "[c]onversion was a process greater than baptism", it was "a lengthy and contested project of subject making and an instrument of royal power".[66] Due to these circumstances, a group of leading Granadans called on their community to revolt against Castilian authorities in 1568. From their perspective, the act of rising up against the king and his troops was driven by "a political theology that sought to resist and transform the Christian sociocultural and political system that Moriscos deemed oppressive but that they also construed as divine punishment for deviating from the right path".[67] After two years of bloody warfare in the mountainous Alpujarra region, the king's troops succeeded in suppress-

64 This paragraph draws on the excellent historical context provided in Birr, "Rebellische Väter, versklavte Kinder", 282–299.

65 The Natives of Granada were referred to as *cristianos nuevos de moros* in Castilian administrative terminology. See Deardorff, "¿Quién es morisco?", § 1. The status of the formerly Muslim populations under Iberian control, both in Iberia and North African outposts (*presidios*), also preoccupied Maghrebian jurists in the 15th and 16th centuries. See Hendrickson, *Leaving Iberia*.

66 Cavanaugh, "Litigating for Liberty", 1284.

67 In so arguing, Mayte Green-Mercado pushes back against earlier understandings of the Morisco rebellion as motivated exclusively by economic and institutional needs. See Green-Mercado, *Visions of Deliverance*, 67.

ing the revolt. As a result, about two-thirds of the surviving Moriscos—as the Granadans came to be called after their revolt—were deported to other Spanish areas and more than 30,000 people were enslaved.[68]

In his *History of the Rebellion and Punishment of the Moriscos of the Kingdom of Granada* (1600), the chronicler Luis del Mármol Carvajal (1520–1600) explained that the question as to whether the revolting Moriscos were justly enslaved had been contested from the outset. "For although the general law permitted that enemies captured in war be enslaved", he wrote, "this was not to be understood as such among Christians; and because the Moriscos were Christians—or had, as they did, that name—it was not just that they be captured".[69] In Mármol Carvajal's eyes, the customary abstention from slavery in inner-Christian warfare ought to have protected the Moriscos from their ill-fated trajectory.

2.1 *Slavery in the Christian Commonwealth*

The very nature of the Morisco rebellion was, however, far from straightforward. Was the *Guerra de Granada* a war at all? An influential answer to this question came from the pen of Diego de Covarruvias y Leyva.[70] In 1527, the year after Vitoria had been appointed to the prime chair in theology at Salamanca, Covarruvias began his education in Roman and canon law at the same university. He studied under Martín de Azpilcueta and attended courses in theology with Vitoria and Soto. Before long, Covarruvias himself became a professor of canon law at Salamanca. And in one of his lectures in the late 1540s, he reflected on the question of what distinguished rebellions from wars.

Covarruvias was writing well before the uprising in the Alpujarras. He addressed the issue from a theoretical point of view, in a commentary on Boniface VIII's (in office from 1294–1303) *regula iuris* that no sin could be dismissed unless restitution was made, the so-called *regula "peccatum"*.[71] As Covarruvias

68 On the emergence of the category of Morisco, see Deardorff, "¿Quién es morisco?". On history of Morisco slavery, see Schirrmacher, *Die Politik der Sklaverei*, ch. 4.

69 Mármol Carvajal, *Historia del rebelión*, lib. V, cap. 32, fol. 124^{r}: "porque aunque por la ley general se permitía que los enemigos presos en guerra fuesen esclavos, no se debía entender ansí entre cristianos; y siéndolo los moriscos, o teniendo, como tenían, nombre dello, no era justo que fuesen captivos".

70 Biographical information on Covarruvias is from Helmholz, "Diego de Covarrubias y Leyva", 174–177; and Scattola, "Naturrecht und politische Theologie in der *Relectio regulae 'Peccatum'* von Diego de Covarrubias", 261.

71 The *Regulae iuris* were a collection of legal norms and principles issued by Boniface VIII, and listed at the end of the so-called *Liber sextus*, the sixth book that was added to the 13th-century *Liber Extra* to which we shall turn shortly.

put it in the published version of his lecture, those who classified a domestic conflict under the heading of war were mistaken. A rebellion was not, properly speaking, a war but rather "the execution of jurisdiction and punishment", Covarruvias maintained.[72] In so arguing, he followed the opinion of Pope Innocent III (in office from 1198–1216), whose authoritative opinion had entered the *Liber Extra* (completed in 1234) and thus become part and parcel of one of the most important works of late-medieval canon law.[73] The consequence of this redescription, according to Covarruvias, was that "those captured in a rebellion are not made the slaves of those who captured them".[74] It was impossible, he insisted, for a prince to enslave his own people. Malefactors of this kind had to be punished otherwise.

But not all the Iberian theorists agreed with this dictum. In his *De iustitia et iure*, Luis de Molina underscored that apart from the enslavement of the vanquished in warfare, another valid "title" of slavery was "if anybody, on account of a crime, is condemned to the punishment of slavery by someone who has the power to do so, if the crime is worthy of such punishment according to prudent judgment".[75] The reasoning Molina deployed here cast slavery as an intrapolitical affair. It brought enslavement into the commonwealth and was *servitus civilis* in quite a literal sense: slavery under the civil law of a particular polity.[76] Salamancans like Domingo de Soto had not mentioned the existence of such a title and tacitly aligned themselves with Covarruvias's view. The idea of slavery

---

72 Covarruvias, *In regula peccatum*, pars 2, § 9, no. 4, in *Opera omnia*, vol. 1, 541: "Innocentius communiter receptus in dict. cap. olim in 1. restit. spoliar. hanc esse justam belli causam opinatur, tametsi existimet potius esse executionem jurisdictionis punitionem rebellium in hoc casu, quam bellum, et ideo captos in eo non effici servos capientium: quod maxime est observandum".

73 The reference in the quote in the preceding footnote is X.2.13.12.

74 See the quote in the penultimate footnote.

75 Molina, *DIEI*, vol. 1, tr. II, disp. 33, no. 4, col. 160 [incorrectly labeled as 108]: "Secundus est, quando aliquis propter delictum, quod prudentis arbitrio tanta poena sit dignum, ab habente ad id potestatem, servitutis poena damnatur".

76 The Roman legal scholar Francisco Cuena Boy argues that Molina and his colleagues failed to differentiate Roman *ius gentium* slavery from other types of slavery governed by Roman civil law, effectively collapsing the latter into the former. According to Cuena Boy, this alleged conceptual impasse led early modern Iberian intellectuals to propose that Roman civil slavery was universally applicable, which in turn hindered them from criticizing Iberian slaving in the wider world. However, the Iberian theologians and jurists used Roman law as a flexible resource rather than a rigid template. They understood the *ius gentium* as a global legal framework—a prerequisite for all forms of slavery, even those confined to a given polity and thus governed by civil law. This was because the *ius gentium* introduced and framed slavery as a type of private property that had not existed before the Fall. See Cuena Boy, *De servitute*, 111–205.

as a punishment for crimes entered the Iberian natural law discourse only in the second half of the 16th century. As a form of enslavement principally identified with the laws of West African commonwealths, it loomed large in Iberian accounts of the Portuguese slave trade.[77] Luis de Molina, however, was keen to underscore that slavery by public authority was not just an extra-European issue:

> After in previous years those people in the kingdom of Granada, who descend from the Saracens, had apostatized—or, rather, revolted through the open manifestation of an apostasy that they had always had in their hearts—they were deservedly punished for their apostasy and rebellion by perpetual slavery, and the baptism they had previously received could by no means prevent their condemnation.[78]

In Molina's view, there was no doubt that the rebellion and apostasy of the Moriscos constituted crimes that warranted their enslavement. The Jesuit thus offered a retrospective vindication of what had, in fact, happened.

A more contentious issue, however, was whether the punishment of slavery could also be applied to the children of those who were actively involved in the upheaval. King Philip II commissioned a junta with the most prominent jurists of the Real Audiencia, Granada's administrative court, to resolve this issue. The outcome was a decree issued in 1572, in which the monarch stipulated that boys under the age of ten-and-a-half years and girls younger than nine-and-a-half years were exempt from slavery.[79] Philip II sought to preserve the liberty of the offspring of the Granadan rebels, even if he "required them to remain in the custody of their former masters in the capacity of servants until they reached the age of majority".[80] The primary rationale for this decision was to promote their integration into Catholic society, once they were separated from their "apostate"—and enslaved—parents. Yet the legal prohibition of driving minors into servitude was routinely ignored in practice. As

---

77 We shall return to this point in Chapter 2.

78 Molina, *DIEI*, vol. 1, tr. II, disp. 33, no. 6, col. 161: "Superioribus annis, cum in Granatensi Regno illi, qui a Saracenis originem trahebant, a fide apostando, seu potius internam, apostasiam, quam semper in corde habuerunt, aperte manifestando rebellassent, merito in apostasiae et rebellionis poena servitutis perpetuae, nihil baptismo, quod antea susceperant, impediente damnati sunt".

79 This was loosely based on the age limits for corporeal punishments laid down in the *Siete Partidas*. See Birr, "Rebellische Väter, versklavte Kinder", 314.

80 Cavanaugh, "Litigating for Liberty", 1283.

Aurelia Martín Casares argues, "this exemption was not respected by the Old Christians, who bought and sold Morisco children, above all girls, without any scruples".[81]

In the intellectual debate that followed in the wake of the *Guerra de Granada*, the question arose as to whether the king could have enslaved Morisco minors. It was a question about the limits of political power and the moral boundaries of princely rule.[82] In Molina's estimation, the apostasy and revolt of the Moriscos constituted such grave sins and crimes that both the parents as well as their innocent children could licitly be enslaved by public authority, because, as he wrote, "this punishment is expedient for the common good of the commonwealth and the deterrence of others".[83] He supported this claim with a reference to medieval canon law: "For the same reason", he explained, "children from marriages with clerics, who were ordained to sacred offices, are subjected to slavery".[84] In the face of the notable absence of any locus in Roman law by which the civil punishment of slavery could be legitimated, canon law appeared to be Molina's only means of establishing a legal analogy to underscore the validity of his claim.[85]

Yet Molina also offered an additional rationale for why it was licit to enslave the children of rebellious subjects, even though they were innocent. He did so by comparing the punishment of rebels to the dictum that "the offspring follows the womb", *partus sequitur ventrem*—the idea that the children of enslaved women inherited the servile condition from their mother. This principle, as Molina explained, was well-established and rooted in various commonplaces in Roman and canon law.[86] And while the cities on the Italian penin-

81 Martín Casares, *La esclavitud en la Granada*, 89: "las compraventas analizadas demuestran que esta salvedad no fue respetada por los cristianos viejos, que compraban y vendían niños moriscos, sobre todo niñas, sin reparos". On the limited but nevertheless real prospect of enslaved Morisco children to win their freedom in court, see Cavanaugh, "Litigating for Liberty".

82 As emphasized in Molina, *DIEI*, vol. 1, tr. II, disp. 33, no. 7, col. 161: "Dubium vero esse potest, an Rex in conscientia eam legem ferre tenetur".

83 Molina, *DIEI*, vol. 1, tr. II, disp. 33, no. 10, col. 162: "delictum [...], idque bono communi Reipublicae ad aliorum terrorem expediat".

84 Molina, *DIEI*, vol. 1, tr. II, disp. 33, no. 10, col. 162: "qua de causa filii suscepti ex matrimonio cum initiatis ordinibus sacris in commune bonum atque ad aliorum terrorem servituti subiiciuntur cap. *Cum multae*, 15, *qu.* 8". For the original passage in Gratian's *Decretum*, see C. 15, q. 8, c. 3.

85 It is noteworthy, however, that this canon law dictum had entered Castilian civil legislation through the *Siete Partidas*, a point that was made plain by Gregorio López. See *Las Siete Partidas*, l. 3, tit. 21, partida 4, gloss López, verb. *Siervos de la eglesia*.

86 Molina, *DIEI*, vol. 1, tr. II, disp. 33, no. 32, col. 166–167. Molina here referred to C.3.32.7, Inst. 1.3.4, Inst. 1.4, and X.4.10.

sula and their colonies in the eastern Mediterranean had turned away from it, as Sally Mckee has shown, in the Iberian empires it was preserved with reference to the *Siete Partidas*.[87] More importantly still, the idea that enslaved women gave birth to slaves had also been endorsed by Thomas Aquinas. In his commentary on Peter Lombard's *Sentences*—a text that will be at the heart of Chapter 4 of this book—Aquinas argued that slavery was a "bodily condition" bequeathed by the mother, from whom children inherited "the substance of the body". The father, by contrast, passed on only his dignity and honor to the child, the "formal complement" to the body.[88] The rationale of Roman and canon law, Aquinas concluded, was therefore consonant with reason.[89]

But what did all of this have to do with the offspring of the revolting Moriscos? Molina's point was to show that if mothers could pass on the punishment of slavery to their children at birth, then the same logic could justify enslaving children who had already been born because they were still their mothers' offspring.[90] It was, in other words, another analogy through which Molina sought to prove his point. What this actually entailed was later elucidated by Estevão Fagundez, one of the most important Portuguese imperial theorists of the 17th century. Having studied at Évora and Coimbra, Fagundez held a range of chairs at different Portuguese universities, with his longest appointment in Lisbon. In his *De iustitia et contractibus* of 1641, he closely followed Molina's line of argument, explaining that

---

87 *Las Siete Partidas*, l. 2, tit. 21, partida 4. On the Italian context, see McKee, "Inherited Status and Slavery in Late Medieval Italy and Venetian Crete". On the significance of this idea in the early modern Indian and Pacific Ocean worlds, see McManus, "*Partus Sequitur Ventrem* in Theory and Practice".

88 Aquinas, *Scriptum super Sententiis*, ed. Alarcón and Busa, lib. 4, dist. 36, q. 1, a. 4, corp.: "secundum leges civiles partus sequitur ventrem; et hoc rationabiliter; quia proles habet a patre complementum formale, sed a matre substantiam corporis. Servitus autem corporalis conditio est [...] sed in his quae pertinent ad dignitatem, quae est forma rei, sequitur patrem, sicut in honoribus et municipiis et hereditate et aliis".

89 Yet Aquinas also accepted that, outside the Christian-Roman world, where Roman and canon law did not apply, it was possible for commonwealths to legislate that children follow the condition of their father. That principle can be traced back to X.4.9.3 and was likewise endorsed by Iberian thinkers like Molina (see *DIEI*, vol. 1, tr. II, disp. 33, no. 32).

90 Molina, *DIEI*, vol. 1, tr. II, disp. 33, no. 11, col. 162: "si ob ventrem fas est filium mancipii innocentem redigere in servitutem tanquam fructum eius, qui ob suum, vel suorum antecessorum delictum iuste aliquando in servitutem redactus est, cur non etiam ob delictum eius, qui ut licere apostarent, in Reipublicae maximum detrimentum rebellavit erit vas [sic] redigere in servitutem filium eius, tanquam illius fructum?"

> […] this is so because to enslave the children of the Moriscos is not a punishment directed against the children themselves, but a punishment directed against the parents, who are punished in their limbs or parts […] that is, in their children. For they are children, as long as they remain under the power of their parents.[91]

2.2 *The Iberian Peninsula as a Space of War*

Molina had brought the civil punishment of slavery into the Christian commonwealth, but he was cautious not to push this argument too far. At no point did he, nor any of the Iberian theorists, suggest that slavery should be a public punishment for Christians—not even for the much abhorred "heretics" who followed Luther's sect, as Molina asserted.[92] In the end, therefore, he offered an alternative justification for enslaving the Moriscos:

> […] in reality, at the moment when they began to rebel they immediately elected a king and, together with their children who were with them, they formed a hostile commonwealth under their prince, and the Spaniards, therefore, had a just war against this whole commonwealth, and not against them as individual malefactors.[93]

By slipping into the discourse of "just war", Molina redescribed the Granada rebellion as an actual *Guerra de Granada*. From this perspective, the Moriscos were no longer internal criminals but external enemies: they were members of a hostile Muslim kingdom, against which the Spaniards had waged war under the full authority of the *ius belli*. Although the Moriscos had never left the southern part of the Iberian Peninsula and physically remained, in that sense, in the same place when they began to revolt, the political boundaries were fundamentally re-drawn by Molina. This vividly demonstrates that, in the early modern natural law discourse, the *civitas* or "state" was a metaphysical rather than a purely physical place.[94] In Molina's estimation, the Moriscos had formed

---

91 Fagundez, *De iustitia et contractibus*, lib. II, cap. 1, no. 8, 143: "Tum etiam, quia hoc non est punire ipsos filios innocentes, sed punire ipsos patres in membris suis, et praecipuis partibus suis, hoc est, in filiis; sunt enim liberi, dum sub patria potestate manent".

92 See Birr, "Rebellische Väter, versklavte Kinder", 308–309.

93 Molina, *DIEI*, vol. 1, tr. II, disp. 33, no. 9, col. 161: "revera eorum parentes, statim ac rebellarunt sibi elegerunt Regem, feceruntque cum liberis suis, quos secum habeant, Rempublicam unam iniquam sub illo Principe adversus quam totam, et non adversus singulos, qui nocentes erant, erat bellum iustum Hispanis".

94 See Brett, *Changes of State*, 1 et *passim*.

not only an enemy commonwealth but also one fundamentally opposed to the Christian faith. And it was for this reason that they could be enslaved without qualification.

Fernando Pérez (c. 1530–1595), another Spanish Jesuit and Molina's colleague at the University of Évora, disagreed.[95] Writing in the later 1580s, Pérez maintained that the Moriscos had been enslaved as "criminals" rather than as enemies in a "just war".[96] This is noteworthy because Pérez is sometimes cited as an important influence on Molina's understanding of slavery.[97] But the documentary evidence we have suggests the opposite. In two letters from 1582 and 1584, Molina complained about Pérez to the Jesuit Superior General himself, Claudio Acquaviva (1543–1615). By that time, Molina had completed the lectures that formed the basis of the first volume of his *De iustitia et iure*, and he accused Pérez of plagiarism.[98] Molina claimed that Pérez had plotted to appropriate his material on justice and contracts for use in the classroom, with the intention of eventually publishing it under his own name.[99] In the end,

95 Fernando Pérez (often referred to as Fernão Perez in Portuguese scholarship) was born around 1530 in Cordoba, where he was educated and joined the Society of Jesus. Appointed as one of the first professors at the newly established University of Évora in 1559, he became prime chair in theology (1567–1572) and rector (1572–1577). He then moved to the Jesuit College of Coimbra, where he remained professor of theology until his death in 1595. Biographical information on Pérez is from Guimarães Pinto, "Pérez, Fernando".

96 Pérez's account of slavery survives in two manuscripts: The first, dating from 1587, has an oral style that suggests that it consists of lecture notes taken by one of Pérez's students (Cod. 3860 in the National Library of Portugal). The second manuscript, dated 1588 in its title, largely follows the structure and content of the first but is more extensive (Cod. 2623 in the National Library of Portugal). See Ventura, "Sobre os textos da presente edição", 55–57.

97 See e.g., Zeron, *Ligne de foi*, 266; Guimarães Pinto, "Pérez, Fernando".

98 By 1580, Molina had completed the lectures for the first volume of the *De iustitia et iure* and by 1582, he had completed the lectures for the whole treatise (see Stegmüller, *Geschichte des Molinismus*, 6–7).

99 Molina's letters are edited in Stegmüller's *Geschichte des Molinismus*: In his letter from 29 August 1582, Molina wrote: "las materias de iustitia con otras que yo e leido está haziendo el Padre Fernan Perez. [...] Si a Vuestra Paternidad pareciere maior servicio de Dios, que lo que yo e hecho mejoren y impriman otros, yo soy contento dello" (559). In his letter from 21 April 1584, Molina wrote: "Lo que puedo dezir es, que muchos años a que experimento averseme dado aulas para leer, y el intento de muchos aver sido que yo hiziese lo que yva haziendo, y que se entregase despues a otros que paucis mutatis y concertado el stilo lo imprimiesen nomine alieno [...] Y el Padre Fernan Perez viendo que no yva adelante de la suma, siendo los contratos a juizio de muchos la mejor cosa o de las mejores que e hecho, sin nunca aver él leido aquellas materias, se a puesto a leellos estos años, y segun se an sonado con intento de imprimillos" (579–580).

Molina's fear did not materialize, as his own treatise made it to publication, while Pérez left only manuscripts. But the rivalry between the two remains remarkable. They never cited each other, and when it came to issues of slavery, they had significant disagreements—not just in this case, as we shall see.

Molina's insistence that the Moriscos' children could have been legitimately enslaved also marked a tacit disagreement with the Dominican Domingo Báñez (1528–1604), his fiercest rival in the controversy over free will. Less than a decade before the publication of Molina's treatise *On justice and right*, Báñez had argued that Morisco minors had justly been exempt from slavery. Like all the members of their community who had not actively opposed the king's authority, children rightly kept their liberty. For Báñez, this limitation was in accordance with the law of war. Yet in fact, he insisted that rebels were to be punished as individual malefactors, thereby insinuating that their enslavement was a matter of civil punishment rather than the outcome of a war against another commonwealth.[100]

In his somewhat convoluted account that blurred the boundary between war and punishment, Báñez failed to address how his argument about a limited right of enslavement in war related to the authoritative opinion of his fellow Dominican, Francisco de Vitoria. As the latter had stressed in his lecture *De iure belli*, in the "just wars" of Christians against Muslims, "it is not to be doubted that we may lawfully enslave the women and children of the Saracens".[101] Even though they were free of any guilt and could not be justifiably killed, as Vitoria stressed, "when the war is such that it is lawful to plunder all the enemy population indiscriminately and seize all their goods, it must also be lawful to enslave them all, guilty and innocent alike".[102]

Luis de Molina drew on precisely this reasoning. He argued that blameless children belonged to the enemy's body politic and could be punished like any other member of that polity.[103] And since the Moriscos had fallen from the faith, no barrier hindered the Spaniards from enslaving them indiscriminately, in the same way that Christians had always captured the children of Turks and

100 Báñez, *De fide, spe et charitate*, q. 40, a. 1, dub. 12, col. 1383: "Adulti, qui nihil contra Regem, aut contra fidem peccaverunt, non possunt in servitutem redigi. Nam poena quaedam est personalis, quod qui est iam sui iuris, sua libertate privetur. [...] Mihi videtur, quod iure belli infantes et innocentes, qui nihil mali cogitaverunt, non possunt redigi in servitutem". See the discussion in Birr, "Rebellische Väter, versklavte Kinder", 310–313.

101 Vitoria, *De iure belli*, in *Political Writings*, trans. Pagden and Lawrance, q. 3, a. 3, 318.

102 Vitoria, *De iure belli*, in *Political Writings*, trans. Pagden and Lawrance, q. 3, a. 3, 318.

103 Molina, *DIEI*, vol. 1, tr. II, disp. 33, no. 3, col. 160 [incorrectly labeled as 108]: "licet enim licite interfici non possunt, iure tamen belli et gentium, sunt mancipia capientium. Ratio est, quoniam illis, tanquam in propriis membris punitur iuste Respublica [...]".

Saracens in "just wars".[104] In that sense, the ideological justifications for the enslavement of the Moriscos were deeply intertwined with the ideology of the "holy war" of Christians against Muslims.

Yet the writings of Iberian theorists also reveal that the conflict over Granada was more complicated than a simple war. The question of whether the Moriscos were inside or outside the commonwealth, whether they were rebels or enemies, was a thorny issue—and not an entirely new one. Since the late 13th century, the relationship between Granada and Castile had been marked by truces and broken treaties. The Morisco uprising represents one episode in the long history of a tenuous alliance, in which violence was justified as peacemaking and directed against people positioned precariously between subjects and enemies.[105] This was precisely how Miguel Bartolomé Salón captured the complexity of the matter. Granadan membership in the Spanish body politic, he argued, had always been fraught and never final. When rebellion broke out, the state of war was immediately reinstated, allowing the Spaniards to justly enslave the Moriscos.[106]

In the mid-17th century, another Iberian theorist, the Spanish Jesuit Juan de Lugo, who was "strongly influenced by Luis de Molina" added his own perspective to the debate.[107] A trained philosopher and canon lawyer, Lugo became a professor of theology and held positions at Valladolid and Salamanca before being appointed to a chair at the prestigious Jesuit Roman College in the early 1620s. One of the fruits of two decades of teaching and research in Rome was the treatise *De iustitia et iure*, published one year before Lugo embarked on his second career as a cardinal in 1643.

104 Molina, *DIEI*, vol. 1, tr. II, disp. 33, no. 9, col. 161: "Ergo sicut Christianis iustum gerentibus bellum cum quacunque alia Turcarum aut Saracenorum Republica, fas est redigere in perpetuam servitutem infantes, quos ceperint […]".

105 On this point, see Benton, *They Called It Peace*, 13 and 39.

106 Salón, *Commentariorum in disputationem de iustitia*, q. 3, a. 1, concl. 4, 115: "illud regnum Granatense a Regibus Catholicis acquisitum fuit, permissi sint patres istorum in eo permanere sub hac conditione, ut si rebellarent, redigentur in servitutem omnes pertinentes ad illud regnum. Quia sub hac conditione fuerunt recepti, iuste facti sunt servi omnes isti Granatenses, tam adulti, quam parvuli eorum, sicut a principio potuerunt effici in illo bello iusto quo regnum illud obtentum fuit".

107 This quote and other biographical information on Lugo are from Jacob Schmutz's website *Scholasticon*.

In that work, he re-opened the question of whether the Morisco children could have been justly enslaved. He began by pointing to Molina's position that adults as well as minors could have been enslaved because they qualified as enemies of Spain and Christ alike.[108] Yet Lugo did not agree with the perspective of his Jesuit predecessor. The title of "just war" slavery, he argued,

> [...] does not seem to be legally valid, because these children were baptized, and it is precisely for this reason that they could not, by the law of war, become the slaves of Christians, even though they were members of a hostile commonwealth—by contrast, it would have been licit if they had been adults and enemies.[109]

Lugo argued that although Morisco minors belonged to an apostate, rebellious, and hostile commonwealth, they nonetheless retained a status distinct from that of their parents. Politically, they were enemies and formed a community with their parents, which justified enslavement. But Lugo maintained that the Morisco children still belonged to the very same spiritual community as the Spaniards and were a constitutive part of the global *respublica Christiana*.

He did not offer a straightforward explanation for how these children managed to preserve their faith in a community of Muslims. But Lugo was probably aware of what Domingo Báñez's proposal had put forth. In the latter's estimation, the potential for apostasy was tied to the age and use of reason, so that it was a priori impossible for minors to fall from the faith.[110] And Juan de Lugo here implied the very same point.

A better solution, he explained, was to approach the issue through the lens of civil punishment.[111] He agreed with Molina that the twofold offense of apostasy and rebellion was worthy of the punishment of slavery, and he likewise

---

108 Lugo, *DIEI*, disp. 6, sect. 2, no. 13, 134: "Unde probat Molina disp. 31 potuisse licite Hispanos redigere in servitutem non solum Mauros, seu Saracenos illos, qui cum baptizati essent, ut a fide apostaterent, rebellarunt contra Hispaniae regem, set etiam eorum parvulos [...] tum quia pars erant Reipublicae illius, quam Rebelles electo sibi Rege statim fecerunt".

109 Lugo, *DIEI*, disp. 6, sect. 2, no. 13, 134: "non videtur efficax, cum illi parvuli baptizati essent, atque adeo iure belli non poterant servi fieri Christianorum, licet essent pars reipublicae hostilis, imo licet fuissent adulti, et hostes". I have translated the second "licet" in the past perfect even if it is in the present tense in the original Latin. This is so, I think, because Lugo wanted to use the second "licet" as a pun on the first "licet", which is a homonym but means "even though".

110 Báñez, *De fide, spe et charitate*, q. 40, a. 1, dub. 12, col. 1381: "Pueri innocentes, qui sunt filii istorum apostatarum, retinent veram fidem, quam susceperunt in baptismate, et non potuerunt amittere illam ante usum rationis ergo saltem isti gaudent isto privilegio".

111 Lugo, *DIEI*, disp. 6, sect. 2, no. 13, 134: "Secunda vero ratio melior est".

conceded that this retribution could be "extended to the children".[112] However, Lugo pointed out a crucial caveat. In the face of the many fallen warriors in the bloody revolt, he argued, some of these children must have lost their parents. These orphans had to be placed under guardianship, but the issue was that tutors' actions had no legal effects on the children under their care. As such, there was no justification for forcing orphaned Moriscos into slavery.[113]

In the end, therefore, Lugo concluded that "the slavery of children before the age of puberty was wisely prohibited by the king, lest it perhaps befalls any innocent persons, on whom slavery could not be lawfully imposed".[114] Through a sophisticated re-reading of Molina, he offered a new perspective on the Morisco rebellion, ultimately supporting the official stance of Philip II.

2.3 *Slavery, Empire, and Protection*

The debate over the status of Morisco children reveals the underlying tension between bringing slavery into the Kingdom of Castile and the established principle of positioning slavery outside the web of human relations among Christians. In their accounts of slavery as a civil punishment, both Molina and Lugo emphasized that such punishment was possible solely because the Natives of Granada were considered both malefactors and apostates. In that way, slavery could be brought into Spain while still being framed as something external to and incompatible with Christianity. The significance of the Moriscos' apostasy to Iberian theologians and jurists was equally key to the "just war" perspective. Whether the Granadans and their children had fallen from the faith was a fundamental question that paved the way for bypassing the custom of non-enslavement among Christians. This case is first to illustrate just how central religious considerations were to the political thought of the Iberian imperial theorists and their language of natural law.

But the debate about the status of the Moriscos also highlights the significance of what Lauren Benton and Adam Clulow have termed "protection talk".[115] Following their incorporation into the Castilian monarchy, Emperor Charles V conceded extensive privileges to the Moriscos in exchange for trib-

112 Lugo, *DIEI*, disp. 6, sect. 2, no. 13, 134: "tum etiam quia apostasiae et rebellionis delictum dignum erat, ut puniretur servitute etiam ad filios extensa propter delicti atrocitatem".

113 Lugo, *DIEI*, disp. 6, sect. 2, no. 13, 134: "non probat de omnibus pueris: erant enim fortasse aliqui sine patribus, quo non poterant iuste poenam illam pati propter delictum suorum tutorum, vel curatorum, sub quorum cura erant".

114 Lugo, *DIEI*, disp. 6, sect. 2, no. 13, 134: "Quare sapienter illa impuberum servitus prohibita fuit a rege, ne innocentes forte aliqui eam incurrerent, quibus de iure imponi non posset".

115 Benton and Clulow, "Webs of Protection and Interpolity Zones in the Early Modern World", 49.

utary payments. These New Christians were initially able to retain their religious and cultural customs to a remarkable degree. Yet their position within the monarchy remained utterly fragile and ultimately unstable. As Miguel Bartolomé Salón observed, the political membership of the Moriscos had always been conditional. It could be revoked at the very moment they contravened the terms of their inclusion. In this sense, the relationship between Granada and Castile was emblematic of the "webs of protection" that shaped early modern empires more broadly.[116]

Iberian arguments in favor of enslaving the Moriscos eventually also traveled across the Atlantic into the New World. The New Laws of 1542 formally abolished Indigenous slavery in the Americas. In response to this sweeping policy shift, Iberian intellectuals forged arguments to legitimate a novel system of Indigenous labor coercion, as we shall see in Chapter Six. Yet, amid these changes, Spanish voices from the Americas maintained that slavery proper remained permissible in exceptional situations. The *Guerra de Granada* became a key precedent for missionaries and colonial administrators who sought to justify the enslavement of the rebellious Chichimeca in northern Mexico.[117] In colonial Peru, similar arguments for enslaving the Moriscos were deployed in reference to the Mapuche, a community in the Araucanía region of central Chile. Analogies between domestic and global phenomena shaped how early modern Iberians understood the imperial world they inhabited.[118]

The Mapuche's fierce resistance against Spanish colonization endured for centuries and became deeply entrenched in the Spanish cultural memory through Alonso de Ercilla y Zúñiga's (1533–1594) celebrated epic poem *La Araucana*.[119] The Salamanca-educated jurist Juan de Solórzano y Pereira, a judge in the colonial administration of Peru, also pointed to their political status in his widely-read *Política indiana* (1648).[120] The inhabitants of the Kingdom of

116 The phrase is from the title of Benton and Clulow, "Webs of Protection and Interpolity Zones in the Early Modern World".

117 On the debate over the enslavement of the Chichimeca, see Cook, *Forbidden Passages*, ch. 8.

118 See Brett, "Scholastic Political Thought and the Modern Concept of the State", 145; and Brett, *Changes of State*, ch. 1.

119 The poem was published in three successive parts between 1569 and 1589. The first complete edition I have been able to access was published in 1590 in Madrid. On Ercilla y Zúñiga, see Adorno, *Colonial Latin American Literature*, 63–68; and Brading, *The First America*, 55–56. On the long-standing conflict between the Mapuche and the Spaniards in the 16th and 17th centuries, see Jarra, *Guerra y sociedad en Chile*, ch. 8; and Korth, *Spanish Policy in Colonial Chile*, chs. 9–11.

120 Solórzano will be introduced in more detail in Chapter 6.

Chile, he explained, were so tenacious and belligerent in their resistance to Spanish authority that both Philip II and Philip IV had declared war against them in the early 17th century.[121] While the enslavement of Indigenous vassals was no longer permitted, Solórzano argued that this prohibition did not include Chileans. And as long as monarchs deemed it just to wage war against the Mapuche, he maintained, it was lawful to commute the right to kill enemies in warfare into the right to enslave them.[122]

The very same line of reasoning was also deployed by Diego de Avendaño, a Jesuit professor of theology in Lima.[123] In his *Thesaurus indicus* of 1688, he wrote: "Sometimes it is safe in conscience to reduce *indios* to perpetual slavery [...] because the *indios* can give us cause for a just war, and thus they can be killed, if this is admitted on account of our just defense: and thus they can be enslaved, by commuting death into slavery, which is the approved doctrine by common consent".[124] At the same time, however, Avendaño argued that Indigenous rebels were exempt from slavery.[125] How, then, did these seemingly contradictory claims fit together? His solution was to adopt the very same reasoning that Luis de Molina had previously invoked to justify the enslavement of the Moriscos: if it was evident that certain Indigenous peoples resisted Iberian authority and evangelization with full force, they could not be regarded as future subjects or Christians but only as "enemies of the faith, and must be counted alongside the Moors and Turks".[126] On these grounds, Avendaño concluded that there was justification for the enslavement of the Mapuche. He described them as a "cruel, treacherous, and refractory" people with whom the Spaniards had been at war "for many years".[127] In Avendaño's view, the formal

121 Solórzano, *Polícita indiana*, ed. Ochoa Brun, vol. 1, lib. II, cap. 1, no. 28–29.

122 Solórzano, *Polícita indiana*, ed. Ochoa Brun, vol. 1, lib. II, cap. 1, no. 32: "pareció justo derogar por la grande perfidia, y obstinacion de estos Indios Chilenos, y muchos daños, que nos han hecho. Y si por ellos se les pudo hacer guerra justa, y matarlos, tambien pudieron hacerse esclavos". See also the discussion in Cuena Boy, *De servitute*, 248–250.

123 Avendaño will be introduced in more detail in Chapter 6.

124 Avendaño, *Thesaurus indicus*, tit. I, cap. 11, § 2, no. 103, 23: "Aliquando Indi redigi in perpetuam servitutem tuta conscientia possunt [...] Quia Indis potest iustum bellum inferri, et ita etiam possunt occidi, si id ratio iustae defensionis admittat: ergo et servi fieri, servitute cum morte commutata, quae est communi consensu probata doctrina".

125 Avendaño, *Thesaurus indicus*, tit. I, cap. 11, § 2, no. 100, 23.

126 Avendaño, *Thesaurus indicus*, tit. I, cap. 11, § 2, no. 100, 23: "si videlicet ita resistentes non resipiscant, id concedit Pontifex, omnem in eo eventu scrupulum eximens, iam enim illi manifesti hostes Christi comprobantur, et cum Mauris et Turcis numerandi". For an explicit reference to Molina's account of Morisco slavery, see Avendaño, *Thesaurus indicus*, tit. I, cap. 11, § 2, no. 106, 24.

127 Avendaño, *Thesaurus indicus*, tit. I, cap. 11, § 1, no. 103, 23–24: "Tale autem bellum et esse potest, et iam multis retro annis experiemur in regno Chilensi, ubi durum satis a stirpe

prohibition of Indigenous slavery did not cover the kind of rebellion that the Mapuche had been staging. Their resistance was recurring, posed a continuous threat to the safety of the Spaniards, and offered no hope of reconciliation. For him, these were sufficient grounds to claim that their enslavement was legitimate.[128]

3 Fugitive Slaves in the Mediterranean

If the "Reconquest" wars against al-Andalus served as a crucial point of reference for Iberian theorists' understanding in their interpretation of the Morisco rebellion, the same holds true for their understanding of the wars between Christians and "Saracens" in the early modern period. As discussed in the introduction to this chapter, in the 16th and 17th centuries, the Mediterranean was a contested space marked by piracy and warfare, which led to the enslavement of numerous people on all sides. After all, the Mediterranean ransom economy was a lucrative business. But the Iberian imperial theorists were less interested in the economic dimensions of Mediterranean slavery. Their primary concern lay with the question of whether those enslaved in warfare could rightfully escape their bondage.

In histories of slavery, flight is routinely portrayed as the primary form of resistance available to enslaved persons.[129] However, Igor Kopytoff and Suzanne Miers have challenged this view as problematic. They have sought to demonstrate that "[i]n most African societies 'freedom' lay not in a withdrawal into a meaningless and dangerous autonomy but in attachment to a kin group, to a patron, to a power [...] Here, the antithesis of 'slavery' is not 'freedom' *qua* autonomy but rather 'belonging.'"[130] Indeed, we must be wary of retroactively imposing contemporary ideals of resistance onto other contexts, periods, and places.[131]

---

genus, infidum, refractarium, quod neque humana neque divina fides in rationabili contineat officio".

128 Avendaño, *Thesaurus indicus*, tit. I, cap. 11, § 1, no. 104, 24: "Dici potest a Regibus Catholicis hoc iudicatum illicitum, ut vidimus *num.* 100 verbis illis: *Porque estos no se pudieron hacer esclavos, aunque fuese por ocasion de rebelion.* Sed id non obstat. Concedimus enim non bellum quodlibet, aut rebellionem quamcumque ad servitutem sufficere, sicut superius explicatum: iteratam tamen, neque securitatem nostrorum, et eorum, qui Christianam sunt religionem amplexi, aut emendationis spe, titulum esse sufficientem affirmamus".

129 Forcefully in Phillips, "Slavery in the Atlantic Islands," 344.

130 Kopytoff and Miers, "Introduction", 17.

131 Kopytoff and Miers, "Introduction", 54.

And yet, the problem of runaway slaves was a major concern in early modern Iberia. It was especially acute along the southern coast, which lay closest to Africa. The journey from Almería to the now-Algerian city of Oran only took around a dozen hours. The chance to escape from Spanish hands was therefore very real for Maghrebians and Ottomans, as Aurelia Martín Casares has shown.[132] However, most enslaved people fled to other cities in the Iberian Peninsula, although it is difficult to estimate how many attempts were successful.[133] Most surviving records come from court cases, which inherently document failed escapes in which fugitives were apprehended and subsequently punished.[134] But the many individual cases that we do know of range from Barcelona to Setúbal, from Valencia to Granada, and from Mallorca to the Canary Islands—and they amply demonstrate that flight from servitude was a pressing problem in the eyes of contemporary authorities.[135] It is not surprising, then, that this issue also drew the attention of Iberian theologians and jurists. For them, the question of whether enslaved persons acted in good conscience when they fled brought into focus the limits of individual moral agency.

3.1 *Unjust Slaves among the Saracens*

From the perspective of the Iberian imperial theorists, a war could only be deemed just if it was waged for a just cause. As Francisco de Vitoria explained in his lecture on that topic, "*the sole and only just cause for waging war is when harm has been inflicted*", so that "there can be no vengeance where there has not first been a culpable offence".[136] Although determining when a cause was truly just, and thus when war could also be justified, was not a straightforward matter, Iberian intellectuals were unanimous that the conflict between Christians and Muslims was clear-cut.

Diego de Covarruvias, an important authority on interpolitical conflicts, addressed this issue in his commentary on the canon law rule *peccatum*. "The aggressions of the infidels", he asserted, "cannot be licit from any side, and neither their defenses, because they had occupied Christian provinces in a tyrannical, treacherous, and cruel way".[137] In principle, Covarruvias endorsed the "legal fiction" of the Roman law on captives and *postliminium*, which held

132 Martín Casares, "Maghrebian Slaves in Spain", 110.

133 Martín Casares, *La esclavitud en la Granada*, 398–402.

134 Phillips, *Slavery in Medieval and Early Modern Iberia*, 125.

135 Phillips, *Slavery in Medieval and Early Modern Iberia*, 124–126.

136 Vitoria, *De iure belli*, in *Political Writings*, trans. Pagden and Lawrance, q. 1, a. 3, 303, original emphasis.

137 Covarruvias, *In regula peccatum*, pars 2, §11, no. 6, in *Opera omnia*, vol. 1, 553: "Quorum quidem infidelium aggressiones, non possunt aliqua ex parte esse licita: nec itidem

that things or people captured by legitimate enemies became their rightful possession, implying that both sides in a war effectively enjoyed the full rights of war.[138] But he was keen to emphasize that this principle did not apply to wars of the "Turks and Saracens" against Christians, which he described as "most unjust" (*iniustissime*). For that reason, the laws of captivity, which extended only to proper enemies did not apply to them, and Christians captured by Muslims were not legally enslaved.[139] In so arguing, Covarruvias presented a *longue durée* perspective on interreligious contest from the so-called Reconquest of the Iberian Peninsula—the act of reclaiming illicitly "occupied" provinces—to the Mediterranean wars in his own time.[140] Across time and space, he suggested, the universal injustice of Muslim hostilities against the followers of Christ was self-evident.

Luis de Molina took a similar stance. Although he did not share the rationale behind the law of *postliminium*—an issue we will shortly explore—he insisted that all those who were held captive without a just cause "could flee wherever they want". There was no doubt that this principle applied to all the Christians who had been enslaved in the unjust wars of the "Turks and Moors".[141] Furthermore, he maintained that those unjustly enslaved also had the right to despoil their captors—and indeed anybody else who belonged to their commonwealth—during their flight. According to Molina, the Christians in hostile detention were not simply illegitimate human booty from a past raid, who would only be allowed to avenge themselves for the violation of their personal right. Rather, they were active participants in an ongoing "perpetual war" against the Saracens and hence authorized to act with the full force of the *ius*

---

defensiones: cum provincias Christiani nonminis tyrannice, et perfide, ac crudeliter occupaverint".

138 See the excellent discussion in Scattola, "Sklaverei, Krieg und Recht", 309. The reference was to D.49.15.5.2. On Covarruvias's use of the language of legal fiction, see the quote in the footenote below.

139 Covarruvias, *In regula peccatum*, pars 2, §11, no. 6, in *Opera omnia*, vol. 1, 553: "Quamobrem nisi aliud lege humana statutm in specie sit, opinor erga Christianos captos a Turcis, vel Sarracenis non esse servandas leges Romanorum, quae de captivis apud hostes loquuntur, nec esse necessarias fictiones legis Corneliae et postliminii [...] ego censeo iuste posse captivum Christianum indistincte fugere [...] cum tyrannice, et iniustissimo bello captus fuerit".

140 Covarruvias's allusion to the *Reconquista* is also underlined in Scattola, "Sklaverei, Krieg und Recht", 308.

141 Molina, *DIEI*, vol. 1, tr. II, disp. 37, no. 1, col. 197: "Dubium non est, eos homines, qui sine titulo iusto captivi detinentur, fugere posse [...] cum Turcarum et Maurorum bellum adversum nos ex eorum parte sit iniustum, dubium non est, nostros, qui apud illos captivi detinentur, licite posse fugere, quo velint".

belli, "with the presumed will of our prince".[142] By framing it that way, Molina demonstrated that his interpretation aligned with the authoritative opinion of Vitoria, who had underlined that "*soldiers may not plunder or burn without the authority of their prince or commander*".[143]

Estevão Fagundez closely followed Molina on this issue. The Portuguese Jesuit argued that, under the premise of a perpetual "just war", Christian slaves held by Muslims could even rightfully kill their "unjust masters".[144] Yet not all the Iberian thinkers agreed that fleeing Christian captives deserved the full rights accorded in the event of war. In Juan Azor's opinion, they were permitted to seize only what was needed for their return home. Despite their unlawful enslavement, Christians could not indiscriminately despoil Maghrebian and Ottoman enemies, as that would amount to theft "by private authority".[145] Azor insisted that only the prince could rightfully wage a war by virtue of his public power to defend the commonwealth, and his authority did not extend to fugitive slaves.[146]

3.2 *Just Slaves among the Christians*

The noteworthy interim conclusion is that the long-standing enmity between Christians and Saracens, dating back to crusades in Iberia and the Levant, had an immediate impact on the contemporary understanding of Mediterranean slavery. While theologians and jurists agreed that unjustly enslaved captives

142 Molina, *DIEI*, vol. 1, tr. II, disp. 37, no. 1, col. 197: "quia perpetuo nostris cum illis bellum est, accipere non solum ab eis, a quibus iniuria sunt affecti, competentem recompensationem damnorum et iniuriam [...] set etiam tam ab illis quam ab aliis iure belli atque ex praesumpta nostrorum principum voluntate accipere, quaecumque potuerint".

143 Vitoria, *De iure belli*, in *Political Writings*, trans. Pagden and Lawrance, q. 3, a. 7, 324, original emphasis.

144 Fagundez, *De iustitia et contractibus*, lib. II, cap. 5, no. 7, 155: "et per vim ad nostros possunt fugere, iniustos dominos occidendo, quia cum iniustie sint captivi, iniuste detinentur [...] quia Mauri, et Turcae, perpetuo nobis iniusti sunt hostes, perpetuumque nobis bellum ubique gerunt [...] ex tacito Principis consensu ab illis, in ratione hostium, et iure belli, quantumcumque potuerint accipere".

145 Azor, *Institutionum moralium*, vol. 2, lib. II, cap. 34, 141: "Nec enim arbitror Christiano servo fas esse, Turcis, et Saracenis, aut alii Christiani nominis hostibus quippiam furari, aut rapere, hoc est, privata auctoritate quidpiam auferre [...] nisi fortassis, quod est ad fugam necessarium". As the title of Azor's treatise reveals, he was deeply invested in Roman law, not just Justinian's *Institutes*, as we shall see more fully in Chapter 5 of this book. This point is also noted in Decock, "Spanish Neo-Scholasticism", 327.

146 Azor, *Institutionum moralium*, vol. 2, lib. II, cap. 34, 141: "fas non esse alicui privata auctoritate furari, vel rapere Turcis, vel Saracenis: secus vero publica auctoritate, videlicet iure belli quod quilibet Princeps Christianus habens auctoritatem incidendi bellum, ut suam Rempublicam defendat, potest illis inferre".

had the right to flee, a more complex question arose concerning those who had been taken in a "just war". Put differently: did the "Moors and Turks" also have a right to escape from Castilian and Portuguese servitude?

This question was prominently addressed by Domingo de Soto, who made a crucial distinction between prisoners of war and those who had sold themselves into slavery, a category that was intimately associated with the spaces of enslavement beyond the Mediterranean world, which will be discussed in greater detail in the following chapter. Soto insisted that voluntary slaves "cannot justly flee because they sold themselves freely and for a price". To escape, Soto insisted, would be tantamount to theft and a violation of contractual justice, "just as one cannot steal a horse from the person to whom one has sold it".[147] This principle found consensus among subsequent Iberian thinkers. Prisoners of war, by contrast, "did not voluntarily fall into this condition" and thus could not be coerced to endure the same "misery" as those who decided to subject themselves and all their possessions to the power of another human being.[148] As Soto made plain, there was a qualitative difference between these two kinds of enslavement that centered on the presence or absence of an act of will.

Diego de Covarruvias reached a similar conclusion, albeit from a different perspective. The canon lawyer drew from the law of *postliminium* we have encountered above. One particularly crucial consequence of this ample and nuanced legal principle was that "a Roman citizen captured by the enemy lost his citizenship but was restored to it (and *eo ipso* to his liberty) if he later returned, either to his native land or to a friendly city".[149] In Covarruvias's words, this meant that an enslaved person, even if they were "most justly a captive among the enemy, could licitly return to their people and escape by crossing the enemy's borders".[150]

---

147 Soto, *DIEI*, lib. IV, q. 2, a. 2, 289: "Illi enim qui se inopia pressi servituti manciparunt, quia libere se pretio vendidere, fugere iure nequeunt: sicut neque furari quem vendidisset equum".

148 Soto, *DIEI*, lib. IV, q. 2, a. 2, 290: "quoniam cum non sua sponte in illam conditionem inciderint, non est eorum miseria tanta afflictione coercenda [...] De illis autem qui seipsos vendiderint, aliquantulo est ratio apparentior, que quicquid sint, domini sint".

149 Brett, *Changes of State*, 181.

150 Covarruvias, *In regula peccatum*, pars 2, §11, no. 6, in *Opera omnia*, vol. 1, 553: "Imo et si captus esset apud hostes iustissimo bello, liceret ei ad suos redire, ac fugere hostium limites transgrediendo: ut ipse notavi lib. 1. Variar. resolut. c. 2. num. 10. et haec quidem de servis iure belli dicta sint, deque his qui ab hostibus capti servitutem serviunt iure gentium, procedente a ratione ipsa naturali". Covarruvias here referred to his more extensive treatment of this issue in his *Variarum resolutionum*, lib. 1, cap. 2, no. 10, in *Opera omnia*, vol. 2, 15.

When Luis de Molina addressed the matter toward the end of the 16th century, he rehearsed Soto's dictum that voluntary slaves were not entitled to escape.[151] He further emphasized that individuals reduced to servitude as a result of public punishment likewise lacked such a right because malefactors were obligated to serve the sentences inflicted on them.[152] Crucially, however, he took issue with the opinions advanced by Soto and, in particular, by Covarruvias. As Molina explained:

> Covarruvias confirms his sentence with the law *nihil interest* […] and also with law 23, title 14, *partida* 7 of the Laws of Castile, which expressly states: a Saracen who was justly captured by us and manages to flee to his own people gains his liberty. Indeed, even if at a later stage he voluntarily returns to do commerce with our people, he can no longer be coerced into his former condition of slavery.[153]

The passage highlighted here by Molina testifies to the immediate impact of the law of *postliminium* on the Iberian Peninsula. Firmly incorporated into the Castilian civil legislation, this legal doctrine effectively allowed all Muslim slaves in Iberia to escape the shackles of servitude.

Molina was dissatisfied with the fact that his intellectual predecessors had buttressed this logic. In his view, nobody enslaved under a just title had the right to escape, and this principle applied likewise to those captured in "just wars".[154] He insisted that this was not only a logical outcome but also a necessary one. If slaves were permitted to flee, Molina argued, they would attempt

151 Molina and those who were writing in his wake also added that this similarly extended to all those who had sold their children in extreme necessity, another title to which we shall turn in Chapter 3. See Molina, *DIEI*, vol. 1, tr. II, disp. 37 no. 2, col. 197–198; and e.g. Lugo, *DIEI*, disp. 6, sect. 3, no. 20, 136.

152 Molina, *DIEI*, vol. 1, tr. II, disp. 37, no. 3, col. 198: "qui ob delictum servitute communi sunt iuste mulctati, fugere de servitutem non possunt, sed per seipsos tenentur eam exequi poenam, eo ipso, quod per sententiam iuste est eis inflicta".

153 Molina, *DIEI*, vol. 1, tr. II, disp. 37, no. 4, col. 198: "Confirmat vero Covarruvias suam sententiam ex *lex nihil interest* […] etiam ex *lex 23. titulo* 14. *par.* 7. *legum Castella*, quae id expressius habet, dum statuit. Si Saracenus iuste a nostris captus fugiat, eo ipso, quod ad suos pervenit, consequi libertatem, adeo ut, si postea sua sponte regrediatur ad mercaturam inter nostros exercandum, cogi non possit ad pristinam servitutem". Molina here pointed to Covarruvias's discussion in *Variarum resolutionum*, as cited above. The legal references are to D.49.15.26 and *Las Siete Partidas*, l. 23, tit. 14, partida 7.

154 Molina, *DIEI*, vol. 1, tr. II, disp. 37, no. 10, col. 198–199: "Captus bello ita iusto […] lethaliter peccat, si fugiat dominum suum, teneturque seipsum restituere, esto ad suos perveniat. Probatur primo, quoniam possessor erat legitimus […]".

to do so "every day", thereby rendering them unreliable assets to their masters. The upshot, he warned, would be that nobody would spare the lives of their enemies, and "everyone would justly kill them in war".[155] In opposition to his predecessors, Molina argued that once *dominium* over a person had been legitimately transferred, "just war" slavery carried the same legal implications as any other form of servitude: it was equally permanent and equally binding. A similar stance was taken by the Portuguese Jesuit Perdo Simões, who held a post at the University of Évora in the 1570s and 1580s and addressed this issue in one of his manuscripts.[156]

3.3 *The Freedom to Flee and the Freedom to Chain*

This was a position most other Iberian theologians and jurists were unwilling to endorse. Fernando Pérez, for instance—Molina's *bête noir*—vigorously defended the rationale of the law of *postliminium*, insisting that "infidels" held in Iberian hands had a right to run away and were liberated if they managed to return to their own people.[157] The sharpest refutation of Molina's line of reasoning, however, came from Juan de Lugo. Those captured in wars, he argued, "do not seem more obliged to remain with their masters than those accused and detained for a crime are bound to stay in prison".[158] Echoing Covarruvias, he pointed to the Roman legal dictum that those captured in "just wars" who managed to escape to their people were as free as they had been before their captivity.[159] The right of masters over their slaves, Lugo insisted, was contin-

155 Molina, *DIEI*, vol. 1, tr. II, disp. 37, no. 10, col. 199: "Quotidie namque servi fugam arriperent ad suos [...] quare potius homines iuste interficerent hostes suos in bello, quam ad tale servitutis genus eos asportarent: quod in detrimentum ipsorummet servorum redundaret".

156 We know next to nothing about Simões's life and it is unclear whether he and Molina knew each others' texts, they certainly did not cite each other. Simões addressed the problem of slavery in a manuscript from 1585 that is preserved in the National Library of Portugal (cod. 6015), and which was recently edited. It was in this text that Simões argued that "just war" slaves could not licitly escape. See Simões, *Materia de restitutione*, ed. and trans. Maurício and Miranda, membrum 2, a. 5, 308.

157 Pérez, "De acquisitione dominii in homines", ed. and trans. Tarrío and Brito, dubitatio 7, 364; and Pérez, "Non nulla ante materiam de restitutione", ed. and trans. Tarrío et al., disp. 14, 456.

158 Lugo, *DIEI*, disp. 6, sect. 3, no. 22, 136: "non videntur ii magis obligari ad manendum apud dominum, quam reus ad manendum in carcere, quo ob delicta detinentur".

159 Lugo, *DIEI*, disp. 6, sect. 3, no. 22, 135: "prout habetur in § *item ea*, Inst. de rerum divisione, ubi expresse sermo est de servis captis a Romanis in bello iusto: *Liberi* (inquit) *homines capti in bello iusto in servitutem nostram reducantur: qui tamen, si evaserint, ad suosque reversi fuerint, pristinum statum recipiant*". Lugo here cited from Inst. 2.1.17. In this passage of Justinian's *Institutes*, a legal teaching book for students compiled in the 6th century,

gent upon the enslaved persons not exercising their right to flee.[160] An enslaved Ottoman who succeeded in escaping "from Spain to an African province with which the Turks have a union or confederation", he explained, "can be safe there in the same way that he would be safe in his native land".[161] In this sense, Lugo tacitly defended the rationale of the *Siete Partidas*, a legal doctrine that Molina had sought to undermine.

However, Lugo emphasized that all those fugitives who remained within their master's province and failed to move beyond enemy territory "do not regain their liberty".[162] According to the Portuguese theologian Fagundez, whose treatise appeared just a year before Lugo's, this meant that the privilege of flight could not be extended to enslaved individuals from the Iberian wars in West Africa. As Fagundez underscored, these slaves "lack the hope of fleeing to their people".[163] Both Lugo and Fagundez stressed that those who remained within the enemy's polity were vagabonds, who roamed around without a purpose. And this assertion constituted, at least implicitly, a reference to a forceful argument advanced by Domingo de Soto a century earlier in his influential *De iustitia et iure*. In his estimation, humans who wandered about aimlessly forfeited their very humanity, living the life of beasts rather than as *political* animals: "Aristotle says that just as we can hunt animals, so we can make war against those human beings who are natural slaves: we should give him a hearing just to this extent, that we can drive off or subject by force those who roam around straggling in the manner of wild beasts, keep-

---

the respective dictum from the law of captives and *postliminium*—D.49.15.5, which was originally from the 2nd-century lawyer Pomponius—was reiterated.

160 Lugo, *DIEI*, disp. 6, sect. 3, no. 25, 137: "Primo opponit Molina [...] Ius habet ad illos captivos deferendos, nemo tamen dicet, si ipsi tunc fugiant, antequam suae Provinciae fines egrediantur, furtum eos committere, quia totum domini ius erat sub conditione quod non fugerent".

161 Lugo, *DIEI*, disp. 6, sect. 3, no. 27, 138: "Sufficeret tamen Turcae, si ex Hispania confugiens rediret ad aliquam Africae provniciam, quaecum Turca unionem, et confoederationem haberet, ratione cuius posset ibi securus esse sicut in propria Patria".

162 Lugo, *DIEI*, disp. 6, sect. 3, no. 27, 138: "non liceat servo fugere ut maneat, et vagetur intra confinia eiusdem provinciae et in potestate eiusdem Principis: per hanc enim fugam non recuperat libertatem".

163 Fagundez, *De iustitia et contractibus*, lib. 11, cap. 4, no. 11, 153: "Procedit autem haec opinio de fuga ad suos, quia haec sola est iure, et consuetudine concessa ad recuperandam libertatem [...] fugas Aethiopum, qui in bello ex nostra parte iusto a nobis capti fuerunt, communiter esse iniustas, et vagabundas, quia ita carent spe evadendi ad suos". Fernando Pérez had made this argument as well, though neither Fagundez nor Lugo referred to him. See Pérez, "Non nulla ante materiam de restitutione", ed. and trans. Tarrío et al., disp. 14, 468.

ing none of the pacts of the nations, but trying to get their hands on other people's goods wherever they go".[164]

Yet even those who did have the right to flee, Lugo noted, rarely succeeded in doing so. Enslaved Maghrebians and Ottomans in Iberia, he argued, could rightfully be subjected to disciplinary measures under the threat of punishment. In this regard, Lugo maintained that slaveholders could justly "keep them in chains" or "cause them evil" to deter them from escaping for fear of retribution.[165] This point had likewise been underscored by several intellectual predecessors.[166] In this sense, Lugo concluded, Molina's argument that slaves would try to escape daily remained ultimately unfounded. For in fact, "they flee very rarely" on account of the master's extensive punitive powers.[167] Indeed, as we shall see more fully in Chapter 5 of this book, all the Spanish and Portuguese intellectuals were eager to emphasize the centrality of discipline and punishment to the master-slave relationship.

For now, we may conclude that the Iberian theorists' understanding of slave flight in the Mediterranean reveals an uneasy locus in the Catholic natural law discourse. In this context, the supposedly clear-cut separation of rights grounded in human nature, on the one hand, and non-legal implications of the faith, on the other, had been eroded. From the perspective of the Iberian theologians and jurists, Christians held in Muslim captivity did not possess the status of legal slaves and were therefore permitted to flee lawfully. This view was rooted in the deeply ingrained conviction that the wars by the "Saracens" were inherently unjust.

The wars waged by the Portuguese and Spaniards were not, however, confined to the Arab-Christian world. As shown above, Fagundez explicitly referred to the belligerent conflicts in sub-Saharan Africa. This extra-Mediter-

---

164 Soto, *DIEI*, lib. IV, q. 2, a. 2, qtd. and trans. in Brett, *Changes of State*, 26. On the same page, Brett emphasizes that it is therefore inaccurate to claim that natural slavery was categorically rejected as a just cause for war in the Catholic natural law discourse, as suggested in Tuck, *The Rights of War and Peace*, 70. Soto's argument was restated almost verbatim by Martín de Ledesma (1509–1574), who had studied with Vitoria in Salamanca and later became professor at the University of Coimbra. See Ledesma, *Secunda quartae*, Q. 18, a. 1, dub. 11, fol. 225^{v}.

165 Lugo, *DIEI*, disp. 6, sect. 3, no. 26, 137: "sicut enim potest dominus arctiori custodia, et vinculis tenere servum fugitivum, ne iterum fugiat: sic potest aliud aequivalens malum inferre, ut eius metu iterum non fugiat".

166 See e.g., See Azor, *Institutionum moralium*, vol. 2, lib. 11, cap. 34, 140; Rebelo, *Opus de obligationibus iustitiae*, pars 1, lib. 1, q. 12, no. 1; Sánchez, *Consilia*, lib. 1, cap. 1, dub. 7, no. 3, 8; and Fagundez, *De iustitia*, lib. 11, cap. 4, no. 10 and 13, 152–153.

167 Lugo, *DIEI*, displ 6, sect. 3, no. 26, 137: "neque enim quotidie fugiunt, sed rarissime, nec ideo noxia est dominis illa servitus propter expensas".

ranean dimension of warfare was also highlighted by Luis de Molina, who drew attention to the wars of "infidels" who were not Muslims, and who might, therefore, have justice on their side. It was in this context that Molina qualified his earlier categorical claim that slaves taken in a "just war" were a priori prohibited from escaping. His coreligionists, Molina argued, were always exempt from this rule, because "a Christian captive cannot dwell among infidels without notable spiritual harm".[168]

---

168 Molina, *DIEI*, vol. 1, tr. II, disp. 37, no. 12, col. 200: "Ad hac conclusione excipitur, quando fidelis aliquis iuste esset captivus apud infideles, indeque fugisset, neque sine notabili detrimento spirituali apud illos posset commorari".

CHAPTER 3

Trade and Trafficking in Sub-Saharan Africa and Beyond

In this chapter, the lens shifts from the Mediterranean into the Atlantic world and from enslavement in the Maghreb to the shores of West and southern Africa. The practice of slaving has a long history on the African continent, extending back at least to the year 500 AD.[1] Various kinds of inner-African slaveries existed, though our knowledge about them is limited. Some of these systems persisted into the early modern period. In 17th-century Morocco, for instance, nearly a quarter-million Black Africans were enslaved by Moroccans following the conquest of the Songhai Empire—today part of Senegal and Mali.[2] The kind of enslavement that historians have primarily studied, however, is commonly referred to as Atlantic slavery.

The prevailing historiographical view interprets the occupation and colonization of Madeira, the Canary Islands, Cape Verde, and São Tomé within the context of Portuguese and Spanish imperial expansion. In this story, the Iberian powers appear as agents of slaving, and the Atlantic as a space under European domination.[3] This perspective is not inherently problematic. After all, the Portuguese occupied the uninhabited island of Madeira in 1419 and turned it into a thriving, albeit short-lived, slave market in the second half of the 15th century. The Spaniards likewise colonized the Canary Islands, forcing large proportions of the Indigenous population into servitude around the turn of the 16th century.[4] Scholars have emphasized that these Atlantic islands "assumed the function of imperial laboratories" for subsequent Iberian ventures in the Americas.[5]

At the same time, historians have criticized the idea that West Africans were powerless subjects of European domination, exploitation, and enslavement. John Thornton, in particular, offered a powerful rebuttal to this perspective in his 1992 cultural history of the Atlantic world.[6] In the decades since, a substan-

1 Zeuske, *Sklaverei*, 191.
2 Zeuske, *Sklaverei*, 177.
3 See e.g., Abulafia, *The Discovery of Mankind*, ch. 8.
4 Phillips, "Slavery in the Atlantic Islands", 325–326.
5 Jorge, "The Iberian Empires", 275.
6 See Thornton, *Africa and Africans in the Making of the Atlantic World.*

tial body of scholarship has emerged that paints a more nuanced and complex picture of the cultural, social, and economic realities in the early modern Atlantic world. In his pre-history of the transatlantic slave trade, Toby Green was among the first to challenge an understanding of enslavement as practiced by European "states". He demonstrated that Atlantic slaving was shaped by the emergence of a dynamic, informal, and cross-cultural space.[7] Iberians had been lured to the shores of West Africa by rumors of gold but failed to conquer any territories. They also did not have any goods to offer the affluent local elites.[8] At least initially, all they could do was provide their service as intermediaries. This is how Portuguese merchants became involved in webs of commercial exchange between coastal African polities. As a reward, they were allowed to retain a share of enslaved persons they were transporting and put them to work on the Cape Verde and Sao Tomé archipelagos offshore.[9]

This dynamic fostered the emergence of a creole society that transcended national-imperial boundaries. So-called Luso-Africans or "Atlantic creoles" became key players in a thriving contraband trade.[10] They undermined the Castilian and Portuguese trade monopolies, which reserved privileges for a select group of noble merchants, and often intermarried with elite women from coastal kingdoms.[11] As translators and brokers of cultural and economic practices, Luso-Africans constituted an integral part of the slave ships that sailed from Africa to the New World and back.[12]

The significance of Atlantic creoles in the slave trade had already been highlighted by Luis de Molina in the 16th century. He noted that they were referred to as *tangomaos* in "Upper Guinea"—the region that is also known

7 Green, *The Rise of the Trans-Atlantic Slave Trade.*

8 Zeuske, *Sklaverei*, 82.

9 Zeuske, *Sklaverei*, 82. African economic agency is also highlighted in Toby Green's latest book, in which he argues that the demand of Atlantic elites shaped the trade between Iberians and Africans. His central claim is that it was not African powerlessness but an imbalance in the value of trading currencies—gold and silver as opposed to cowrie shells and cloth—that led to the long-term economic divergence between Western Europe and West Africa. See Green, *A Fistful of Shells*, 13–15 and *passim.*

10 Zeuske, *Sklavenhändler, Negreros, Atlantikkreolen*, 21 and *passim*. The importance of contraband trade and its association with creole slavery is also foregrounded in Green, *The Rise of the Trans-Atlantic Slave Trade*, ch. 7.

11 Zeuske, *Sklavenhändler, Negreros, Atlantikkreolen*, 179 and 188; Thornton, *A Cultural History of the Atlantic World*, 251–252 and 259; Mark and Silva Horta, "Being both Free and Unfree", 227–279.

12 Mark and Silva Horta, "Being both Free and Unfree", 227; Zeuske, *Sklavenhändler, Negreros, Atlantikkreolen*, 180.

as Senegambia, stretching from the Senegal river in the north to Sierra Leone in the South, with the Cape Verde islands offshore.[13] And in "Lower Guinea", the Luso-African slavers in the Kingdom of Kongo were known as *pombeiros*.[14] Molina viewed them as ruthless merchants who violently dragged enslaved Africans from the continent's interior to the coast. In a particularly graphic depiction of their cruelty, Molina recounted how *pombeiros* and *tangomaos* routinely used the arm cut off from one slave to beat others.[15]

By reconstructing how the Iberian imperial theorists grappled with the predicament of slaving in sub-Saharan Africa, I aim to show that their reflections went well beyond the cultural and commercial exchanges highlighted in recent scholarship.[16] Early modern intellectuals were keen to point out that enslavement in Africa was not reducible to trade, whether contraband or official, and was likewise a result of Portuguese wars against "infidel" commonwealths.[17] More significantly, the Iberian theorists also considered the extent to which commercial affairs were entangled with questions of political power. In what follows, then, I argue that Atlantic slavery must be understood not only in terms of individual moral agency but also as a matter of imperial politics and the conscience of Iberian kings.

---

13 Molina, *DIEI*, vol. 1, tr. II, disp. 34, no. 3, col. 169: "Commorantur praeterea inter Aethiopes illos Lusitani aliqui, qui inter eos mercaturam exercent quosque tangosmaos appellant". On "Upper Guinea" and "Lower Guinea", see Thornton, *A Cultural History of the Atlantic World*, 62–63. On Senegambia, see Green, *A Fistful of Shells*, 70.

14 Molina, *DIEI*, vol. 1, tr. II, disp. 34, no. 8, col. 170: "Ex hoc tamen regno [i.e., from Kongo] Lusitani, qui in eo habitant (quosque pomberos ibi appellant, ut Guinea superiori tangosmaos)". The *pombeiros* were also mentioned in Rebello, *Opus de obligationibus iustitiae*, pars 1, lib. I, q. 10, sect. 2, no. 8, 71; and in Fagundez, *De iustitia et contractibus*, lib. II, cap. 2, no. 5, 146. Serge Gruzinski describes the *tangomaos* as "aventuriers portugais implantés localement, largement africanisés et accoutumés à passer d'un monde à l'autre" (*Les quatre parties du monde*, 256). See also Zeron, "Pombeiros e tangomaus".

15 Molina, *DIEI*, vol. 1, tr. II, disp. 35, no. 18, col. 191: "eiusmodi mancipia tractantur, dum ab illis, quos tangosmaos aut pomberos appellant, ab interioribus locis ad navigia asportantur. Fertur enim praescindi interdum brachium unius mortuumque reliqui, eo vero tamquam flagello alios percuti atque agi, ut mortis timore iter faciant, aliasque saevitias in eo exerceri".

16 The lack of attention to the political dimension in recent scholarship is also emphasized in Herman Bennet's study of the ways in which early Atlantic diplomacy shaped European visions of political power. See Bennett, *African Kings and Black Slaves*, 9–12 and *passim*.

17 On the significance of "official" trade, see Thornton, "The Slave Trade and the African Diaspora", 138–141.

1 Slavery between Mission, War, and Commerce

The early stages of Portuguese slaving in West Africa in the mid-15th century were cast as a spiritual mission. A series of papal bulls, most notably Pope Calixtus III's *Inter caetera* of 1456, welcomed slavery as an instrument of evangelization.[18] The spread of Christianity was central to the justification of Portugal's imperial expansion well into the 16th century. While the legitimacy of papal concessions to conquest and slavery was hotly contested in Castile, no such public debate emerged concerning justice in the Portuguese empire—Portugal never had a Vitoria. It was only in the second half of the 16th century, when Salamanca students took up professorships in Portuguese universities, that Vitoria's ideas gained traction and the intellectual landscape slowly began to shift.[19]

The Iberian imperial theorists envisioned sub-Saharan Africa as a space marked by paganism.[20] Crucially, however, they insisted that "infidels", who were neither apostates nor enemies of Christ, were naturally free human beings. This was the central claim of Vitoria's lecture "On the American Indians" and applied equally to "unbelievers" across the globe. To argue otherwise would be to deny their humanity and *eo ipso* to question the magnificence of God's creation.[21] Concerning the enslavement of Black Africans, Luis de Molina acknowledged that one might be tempted to justify slavery for the sake of their spiritual salvation.[22] However, he went on to explain,

> [...] because bad things must not be done so that good things will come forth, and those who carry away slaves [from sub-Saharan Africa] do not strive for the slaves' spiritual good but for their own temporal good, it is not licit to approve of this commerce any more than justice and the love of one's neighbor permit it.[23]

---

18 See the discussion in Groebner, "The Carnal Knowing of a Coloured Body", 223.

19 See the excellent discussion in Marcocci, *A consciência de um império*, especially at 25–28, 310–314, and 329–331. We will return to this at the beginning of Section 2 of this chapter.

20 On the counterstrategies of enslaved Black Africans, who claimed that West Africa was a Christian space and, in some cases, succeeded in winning their freedom in so arguing before Castilian courts, see Ireton, "Black Africans' Freedom Litigation Suits".

21 As noted in Tierney, *The Idea of Natural Rights*, 270.

22 Molina, *DIEI*, vol. 1, tr. II, disp. 35, no. 19, col. 192.

23 Molina, *DIEI*, vol. 1, tr. II, disp. 35, no. 19, col. 192: "Quia tamen facienda non sunt mala, ut eveniant bona, iique, qui illos asportant, non spirituale eorum bonum, sed temporale suum quaerunt, non plus negotiationem hanc approbare fas est [...] quam iustitia et proximi caritas patiantur".

The "Aethiopeans", as Molina and his contemporaries referred to sub-Saharan Africans, were, like all other peoples, masters of their own affairs.[24] And for this reason, it was illicit to deprive them of their natural liberty without a just title.

Yet the Iberian theorists consistently emphasized that enslavement and evangelization were nevertheless compatible. This had already been underscored by Pope Gregory IX (in office from 1227–1241), the compiler of the famous *Liber Extra*. In a decretal of 1237, he addressed a particular situation in the crusader states, "where a Muslim slave's conversion to Christianity carried freedom", which prompted many to prevent conversions in order to keep their slaves.[25] To resolve this issue, the pope ruled that baptism did not confer freedom upon those who had previously been enslaved. In so arguing, he established a broader principle that enslavement and evangelization were compatible as long as slavery preceded conversion. As the Iberian intellectuals pointed out, even the Bible itself lent support to the idea that legal slavery did not stand in the way of spiritual freedom. This was clear from Saint Paul's Epistle to the Galatians, as Miguel Bartolomé Salón noted.[26] Francisco Suárez, too, highlighted that "there is nothing about bodily slavery which hinders the servitude of Christ".[27] While Christians customarily refrained from enslaving fellow believers, the Iberian theologians and jurists insisted that baptism did not alter the legal status of enslaved "infidels" in Christian hands.[28]

---

24 The notion of "Aethiopians" was inspired by biblical Ethiopia, but the Iberian theorists did not make this link explicit. Rather, they used that term to distinguish West and southern Africans from the Maghrebian "Saracens", whom they cast as enemies of the Christian faith. As Epstein notes, the locution "Ethiopians" was also widespread in early 15th-century Palermo, for instance, and was a common term in the Christian Mediterranean of the time. See Epstein, *Speaking of Slavery*, 188.

25 See Epstein, *Speaking of Slavery*, 175.

26 Salón, *Commentariorum in disputationem de iustitia*, q. 3, a. 1, concl. 4, 115: "servitutem legalem non prohibere libertatem spiritualem [...] De eadem libertate spirituali quae servitute legali non repugnat, loquitur Paulus ad Galatae 4". Salón here referred to Galat. 4:6–7.

27 Suárez, *De legibus*, vol. 1, lib. III, cap. 5, no. 12: "Huic autem servituti opponit [i.e., Paul] servitutem hominum; loquitur ergo de spirituali servitute, nam de corporali iam dixerat nihil obstare Christi servituti".

28 For a brief period in the late 1550s, enslaved persons throughout the Portuguese empire in Asia—including enslaved Black Africans—could be liberated upon conversion. In 1559, however, the crown reaffirmed the old principle that spiritual salvation did not entail temporal liberty. See Marcocci, "Blackness and Heathenism", 49.

1.1 *Rumor Has It …*

The central question, however, was how the inhabitants of the Atlantic world had initially come to be enslaved. The trade in sub-Saharan slaves was rife with vice and violence, as numerous contemporaries pointed out. One of the earliest and fiercest Iberian voices against the Portuguese ventures on the shores of West Africa was Fernando Oliveira (1507–c. 1580). A theologian by training, and a former Dominican, he made a name for himself as the author of a Portuguese grammar book and several treatises on the construction of ships.[29] It is his handbook *Arte da guerra do mar* (1555) or *The Art of War at Sea*, however, for which he is best remembered today. In this work, Oliveira synthesized his theoretical knowledge on matters of justice and morality into the language of soldiers, offering practical guidance on naval warfare in vernacular Portuguese. Above all, however, the text was a radical critique of Portuguese imperial ventures—and it landed Oliveira in prison.[30] In his discussion of the justice of war, Oliveira argued that the Portuguese had been waging "unjust wars" against "unbelievers" who were neither enemies nor apostates but peaceful people. And he insisted that in the absence of a just cause for war among the Portuguese, the practice of slavery fell short of legitimacy *tout court* because "we cannot capture nor buy those who were not captured in a just war".[31]

On the one hand, Oliveira's critique homed in on the injustice of enslavement in West Africa. He argued it was the presence of "buyers" that was responsible for the existence of "evil sellers". In Oliveira's view, "we give them occasion to deceive and steal one another […] We are the inventors of such evil trade that was never before practiced or heard of among humans".[32] On the other hand, Oliveira echoed the demands of the Portuguese Confraternity of Our Lady of the Rosary from the early 16th century. The brotherhood included Black Africans in a separate branch, and its Dominican leaders saw the emancipation of enslaved members as vital to their evangelization. Oliveira's critique can be seen as a response to this debate, Giuseppe Marcocci suggests, since he not only

29 Biographical information on Oliveira is from Metcalf, *Go-Betweens and the Colonization of Brazil*, 313–314 fn. 37.

30 See Marcocci, *A consciência de um império*, 318–320. The circumstances of Oliveira's imprisonment are not documented.

31 Oliveira, *Arte da guerra do mar*, cap. 4, 16^{v}: "nem temos justa causa pera ihe fazer guerra, i sem justa guerra não podemos cativar, nem comprar a cujos não sam".

32 Oliveira, *Arte da guerra do mar*, cap. 4, 15^{v}: "se não ouvesse compradores não haveria maos vendedores, nem os ladrões furtarião pera vender. Assi que nos ihe damos occasiam pera se enganarem huns a outros, i se roubarem […]. Nos somos os inventores de tam mao trato, nunca usado ne ouvido antre humanos".

denounced the illegality of the slave trade, but also advocated the liberation of enslaved Africans after a limited period.[33]

Rumors of Portuguese violations of rights had already been circulating before the publication of Oliveira's manual, and they also reached the lecture halls of Salamanca. Francisco de Vitoria did not address this problem in any of his preserved academic writings. But in a letter to his fellow Dominican Bernardino de Vique from c. 1546, Vitoria argued that warfare in sub-Saharan Africa was not simply a Portuguese affair. He noted that human beings "were enslaved in their own countries in war" and maintained that "the Portuguese are not obliged to discover the justice of wars between barbarians".[34] In Vitoria's estimation, "[i]t suffices that a man is a slave in fact or in law, and I shall buy him without a qualm".[35] This statement is particularly remarkable coming from a Thomist moral theologian.

But Vitoria went further, challenging the notion that the Portuguese themselves were capturing Africans unjustly.[36] In his view, there was insufficient evidence to condemn the deeds of merchants: "without further information, I see no reason why the gentlemen who purchased the slaves here in Spain should have any scruples".[37] The implication of Vitoria's narrative was that both Iberian traders operating at a distance and buyers of enslaved Africans at home in Spain acted in good conscience.[38] In this sense, Vitoria presented a straightforward defense of the slave trade.

---

33 See Marcocci, *A consciência de um império*, 406–410 and 418–419. Oliveira argued that enslaved people should be granted a "jubilee" (a reference to the Jubilee in the Hebrew bible) after serving the time mandated by law. See Oliveira, *Arte da guerra do mar*, cap. 4, 15ᵛ: "Ja que damos isto cor de piedade christam, dizendo que os trazemos a fazer christãos, nam seria mal usar co elles dessa Piedade i darlhes algum jubileu despoys de servirem certo tempo limitado per ley". However, in the new English translation of Oliveira's manual "jubilee" is incorrectly rendered as "holiday", which changes the entire meaning of Oliveira's argument. See Oliveira, *Arte da guerra do mar*, ed. Cardim, Pedro and Nuno Gonçalo Monteiro, trans. Igor Knezevic with the assistance of Rich Lizardo, 84: "Since we do this in the name of Christian piety, saying that we bring them over to make them Christians, it would not be amiss to show some of this mercy, and grant them a holiday after a certain period of time decreed by law".

34 Vitoria, "Letter to Fray Bernardino de Vique", in *Political Writings*, trans. Pagden and Lawrance, 335.

35 Vitoria, "Letter to Fray Bernardino de Vique", in *Political Writings*, trans. Pagden and Lawrance, 335.

36 Vitoria, "Letter to Fray Bernardino de Vique", in *Political Writings*, trans. Pagden and Lawrance, 334.

37 Vitoria, "Letter to Fray Bernardino de Vique", in *Political Writings*, trans. Pagden and Lawrance, 334.

38 This is also noted in Zeron, *Ligne de foi*, 236.

The same cannot be said of his Salamancan colleague and fellow Dominican Soto. The latter did not address the question of inner-African warfare. But Domingo de Soto did say something about the Castilian and Portuguese slavers:

> [...] if the rumor that has already spread everywhere is true [...] that these miserable people are seduced with tricks, and lured with whatever games, and cunningly attracted toward the port, and often compelled to do so [...] If this story is true, neither those who capture them, nor those who buy them from the captors, nor those who possess them can ever have a safe conscience until they set them free.[39]

Soto carefully phrased his argument in the conditional, but his emphasis was clear. It served as a stern warning not only to the traders on the shores of Africa but also to the buyers of slaves in Iberia. As Juan de la Peña (1513–1565), another Dominican theologian at Salamanca, later maintained, Soto suggested that the methods by which the Portuguese acquired their slaves in Africa amounted to "an unjust war".[40]

1.2 *Selling Oneself and One's Children*

Yet Vitoria and Soto's assessments of the slave trade did not end there. Both explored potential avenues open to the Portuguese to acquire "human commodities" in the African Atlantic. Vitoria mentioned "the case of those others who are condemned to death—doubtless an unjust death—and ransomed by Christians".[41] He explained that in his native Spain, saving someone by enslav-

39 Soto, *DIEI*, lib. IV, q. 2, a. 2, 289: "si, quae iam percrebuit, vera est fama [...] dolo calamitosam gentem seduci: inescarique nescio quibus iocalibus, et astu pellici versus portum, et nonnunque compelli [...] Quae si vera est historia, neque qui illos capiunt, neque qui captoribus coemunt, neque illi qui possident tutas habere unquam conscientias possunt, quosque illos manumittant".

40 Peña made this argument in his commentary on *quaestio* 10 of the *Secunda secundae* of Aquinas's *Summa*. See Peña, "An sit iustum bellum adversus insulanos (1560)", ed. in Pereña, *Misión de España en América*, 296: "regulariter mancipia quae venduntur a Lusitanis ex Ethiopia iniuste et per iniquitatem sunt servi, quia accipiuntur in bello iniusto. Videte de hac re Sotum (libro 4, de iustitia et iure, quaestione 2, art. 2)". For biographical and bibliographical information on Peña, who held the second most prestigious theology chair at Salamanca (the so-called Vespers chair), see Pereña, *Misión de España en América*, 235–243.

41 Vitoria, "Letter to Fray Bernardino de Vique", in *Political Writings*, trans. Pagden and Lawrance, 335.

ing them would be impossible.[42] "But in a country where one can be enslaved in numerous ways", Vitoria argued, "why should not a man voluntarily agree to become the slave of someone who is prepared to rescue him".[43] "In my view", he made clear, "he can be considered a slave for the duration of his life".[44]

Domingo de Soto also addressed this issue, expounding on the underlying rationale of voluntary slavery. "Even if men were created by God free", he argued, "nevertheless so innate in all animals is the desire and right of preserving life, that the wretched men can for its sake drive themselves into slavery".[45] Soto understood self-enslavement driven by necessity as a function of natural right, a principle universally valid for all humans everywhere. In a world characterized by divided *dominium*, where earthly possessions were no longer freely accessible, those facing starvation could legitimately alienate their freedom to secure their survival. The rationale for voluntary slavery, therefore, fundamentally resembled that for enslavement in "just wars": to protect one's life it was permissible to relinquish one's liberty.

Soto sidestepped Vitoria's critical qualification that the situation in Castile was different, a point that will be addressed further below. For now, however, it is important to highlight that Soto introduced yet another mechanism by which humans could be enslaved. Apart from the right to alienate one's own freedom, Soto argued that "parents forced by necessity could also sell their children by ancient law, in accordance with the same locus of Leviticus 25 and the chapter *On the fathers who have sold their children*, law 2 [...] although such laws are no longer in use among Christians".[46] With these references to the Bible and the Byzantine empire, Soto indicated that selling of youths had once been permissible in the distant past of sacred history and early Christendom, even though he failed to elaborate on the underlying rationale of this right.[47]

42 Vitoria, "Letter to Fray Bernardino de Vique", in *Political Writings*, trans. Pagden and Lawrance, 335.

43 Vitoria, "Letter to Fray Bernardino de Vique", in *Political Writings*, trans. Pagden and Lawrance, 335.

44 Vitoria, "Letter to Fray Bernardino de Vique", in *Political Writings*, trans. Pagden and Lawrance, 335.

45 Soto, *DIEI*, lib. IV, q. 2, a. 2, 289, qtd. and trans. in Brett, *Liberty, Right and Nature*, 152.

46 Soto, *DIEI*, lib. IV, q. 2, a. 2, 289: "Imo et parentes egestate compulsi, liberos suos antiquo iure vaenundare permittebantur: ut eodem loco Levi. 25 memoriae proditu mest. Et cap. De patribus qui filios suos distraxerunt [...] licet iam inter Christianos huiusmodi leges nun sunt in usu".

47 The Roman legal locus—C.4.43.2 (originally C.Th.5.10.1)—was introduced by the Christian emperor Constantine in 313 AD but revoked again around 374. See the discussion in Harris, "Child Exposure in the Roman Empire", 1 and 21. See also Epstein, *Speaking of Slavery*, 176–177 on the Bolognese jurist Azo's (c. 1150–1230) engagement with that law.

But his main point was to explain that "one says that this custom is still in place among Aethiopeans, where the Portuguese go with their ships to buy them. And if they sold them freely", he concluded, "there is no reason to term this commerce criminal".[48]

Soto, then, was far from optimistic about Iberian slavers acting morally. But he did not go so far as to frame the slave trade as an "unjust war" as Peña contended. Even though Soto had grave doubts about the practices of slaving in West Africa, he sidestepped the crucial question of whether Portuguese and Castilian slavers were acting on their own authority or as agents of the king in warfare.

1.3 *Contracts, Conscience, and the Slave Trade*

The authoritative but ambiguous account of Domingo de Soto shaped the writings of the Iberian imperial theorists based at Portuguese universities in the mid-16th century. Bartolomeu dos Mártires (1514–1590), for instance, closely adhered to Soto's view on African slavery in his lectures on the *Secunda secundae* at the Dominican convent of Batalha.[49] The same was true of Martín de Ledesma (1509–1574), a former student of Vitoria's, who joined the University of Coimbra after his studies and eventually held the prime chair of theology until his retirement (1557–1562).[50] In his *Secunda quartae* of 1560, Ledesma maintained that voluntary slavery and selling one's children under the pressure of necessity were just titles for slavery "among the Aethiopeans". And like Soto, he argued that if the rumors of unjust Portuguese raids on the shores of Africa proved true, slave traders and owners of enslaved Africans in Iberia would all be in a state of damnation.[51]

The most original accounts of Atlantic slavery after Soto, however, were penned by two thinkers in Castile: Tomás de Mercado and Miguel de Palacio.

48 Soto, *DIEI*, lib. IV, q. 2, a. 2, 289: "Aiunt tum apud Aethiopes eundem adhuc vigere morem: quo ad eorum mercatum Lusitani adnavigant. Quod si libere vaeneunt, non est cur mercatura illa crimini ullo denotet".

49 See Martyribus, *Theologica scripta*, ed. Almeida Rolo, Braga 1974, vol. 4, q. 66, a. 2, 690. Mártires had originally delivered his lectures in the 1540s, but revised his notes in the 1550s, following the publication of Domingo de Soto's *De iustitia et iure*. It is this later version of his lecture notes that has been preserved and published. See the discussion in Marcocci, *A consciência de um império*, 307–308 and 415.

50 For biographical information on Ledesma, see Idoya Zorroza, "Un discípulo salmantino en Coimbra: Martín de Ledesma".

51 See Ledesma, *Secunda quartae*, Q. 18, a. 1, dub. 11, fol. 225^r. Giuseppe Marcocci suggests that in following the argument of Domingo de Soto, Ledesma sought to contain the critique that Fernando Oliveira had put forward in his *Arte da guerra do mar* from 1555. See Marcocci, *A consciência de um império*, 417.

The two were writing in the 1570s and 1580s, when the perils of the slave trade increasingly preoccupied the intellectual, religious, and political elites in Portugal and Spain. To them, it was clear that Iberians sailed to the shores of West Africa as merchants rather than soldiers. Indeed, it was for this very reason that Mercado and Palacio addressed the issue of slavery in their tracts on the morality of contractual exchange.

Palacio was a former student of Vitoria's. In 1585, he founded his own theological college in Ciudad Rodrigo, located less than a day's hike from Salamanca. By that time, the Iberian crowns were already united, and the slave trade had become a pan-Iberian problem of conscience. It is not, therefore, surprising that Palacio addressed this matter in his *Praxis theologica de contractibus et restitutionibus*, a now-forgotten work published the same year.[52] Even before the 1580s, however, numerous enslaved Africans had been brought to Castile by Portuguese merchants, with Seville serving as the principal gateway. This was also where Tomás de Mercado had taught and lived after his studies with Vitoria and Soto at Salamanca.[53] Mercado worked as a confessor in this commercially thriving city and experienced the realities of slave trading with his own eyes. His symbiosis of conceptual rigor and the practice of confession culminated in the *Suma de tratos y contratos* (1571), a widely read handbook for confessors that owed much to the Iberian tradition of commentary on Aquinas.[54]

Although Mercado and Palacio cast Iberian slavers as buyers and sellers of "human commodities", they emphasized that the inter-individual dimension of trade was intimately connected to questions of vertical power. They argued that many enslaved Africans acquired by Portuguese and Spanish merchants had lost their freedom in wars between West African commonwealths. Moreover, Mercado also introduced a new element into the debate about Atlantic slavery among the Iberian theorists: the idea of enslavement as a civil punishment. "While our laws say: he who kills shall be killed", he explained, "theirs say: he shall be enslaved".[55] As we saw in the previous chapter, this form of enslavement was not quite impossible in Castile. But while Mercado associated the

---

52 The only historical study that takes Palacio's *Praxis theologica* into account is Annabel Brett's "The Good Man and the Good Citizen".

53 Mercado also spent some years in Mexico before his studies in Salamanca, but little is known for certain about his life. For a recent biographical account, see Lagares Clavo, "Seis incógnitas y algunas respuestas sobre la vida de Fray Tomás de Mercado".

54 As I have noted in the introduction to this book, Mercado began his treatise with an entire book on the law of nature. On Mercado's vision of the theologian as a confessor, see also Decock, "Collaborative Legal Pluralism".

55 Mercado, *Suma*, ed. Sánchez-Albornoz, lib. II, cap. 21, § 5: "Nuestras leyes dicen: Muera quien matare [...] Las suyas dicen: Quede hecho esclavo [...]".

civil punishment of slavery with sub-Saharan Africa, he did not suggest that the mere existence of this legal title licensed practices of slaving in African commonwealths. Quite the contrary, both he and Palacio argued that it was only rightful in theory. But in reality, it came with "a thousand deceptions and false testimonies", because "Aethiopean" kings routinely enslaved their subjects "with the mere pretext of crime".[56] The two theologians put forward a remarkably similar vision of the wars among African commonwealths, stressing the utter injustice of their belligerent affairs.[57] Mercado even went so far as to insist that the cause of unjust enslavement among the "Aethiopeans" was rooted in their character: "because they are barbarians, they do not act by reason but by passion, they neither examine nor consult the right they have".[58]

In Mercado's estimation, if princes failed to fulfill their duty of administering justice, there was yet another way for Iberian merchants to acquire slaves: if parents in dire necessity sold their children. This mechanism, while not directly involving the commonwealth, was embedded in a structure of vertical power too. "Fathers in extreme necessity", Mercado argued, "have the natural faculty to sell their children [...] if their life cannot be sustained or preserved in any other way".[59] What Soto had merely described as an ancient custom was portrayed by Mercado as a corollary of paternal power—as an authority vested in the head of household and thus tied to the teleology of the commonwealth, a theme more fully explored in the middle part of this book. And yet, Mercado underlined that purchasing enslaved children was no less problematic than buying any other person as a slave in West Africa. In his view, all Black Africans were enslaved without a just title.[60]

Despite his critical view of Black African societies, Mercado's ultimate target were the Iberian slavers themselves.[61] He did not accuse them of waging unjust wars. But Mercado argued that they committed numerous violations of

56 Mercado, *Suma*, ed. Sánchez-Albornoz, lib. II, cap. 21, § 9: "prendiéndolos con dos mil engaños y testimonios falsos [...]". And Palacio, *Praxis theologica*, lib. II, cap. 8, 156: "reges [...] praetextu delicti, eos [i.e., their subjects] adiudicant servituti".

57 Mercado, *Suma*, ed. Sánchez-Albornoz, lib. II, cap. 21, § 8; and Palacio, *Praxis theologica*, lib. II, cap. 8, 155.

58 Mercado, *Suma*, ed. Sánchez-Albornoz, lib. II, cap. 21, § 8: "Al primer título de guerra justa se mezcla ser muchas o casi todas injustas. Como son bárbaros, no se mueven por razón, sino por pasión, ni examinan ni ponen en consulta el derecho que tienen".

59 Mercado, *Suma*, ed. Sánchez-Albornoz, lib. II, cap. 21, § 6: "los padres en extrema necesidad tienen facultad natural de vender sus hijos [...] cuando no se puede de otra manera sustentar o pasar la vida de los padres".

60 Mercado, *Suma*, ed. Sánchez-Albornoz, lib. II, cap. 21, § 10.

61 This is also noted in Zeron, *Ligne de foi*, 244.

right, ignoring the impotent mandates of their monarch.[62] The injustice of the "Christian merchants" against the "Blacks", he maintained, was worse than "the cruelty of the Turks against Christian captives".[63] Mercado believed that at the end of the day, the actual "barbarians" were the Portuguese and Spanish slavers, whose involvement in this business he sharply condemned.

Miguel de Palacio reached remarkably similar conclusions, despite not knowing, or at least not citing, the work of Mercado. He likewise observed that the Iberian presence on the shores of sub-Saharan Africa fostered raids and robberies among the local population.[64] Yet, ultimately, he argued otherwise. Despite persistent rumors of injustice, Palacio maintained, it was not the task of merchants to examine the legitimacy of enslavement in foreign commonwealths. "If they buy from parents or magistrates", he argued, "it is sufficient if it is not evident that the parents or the magistrates or the deputies of the king are selling these slaves without due caution, which one could recognize from public outcries".[65] In the end, therefore, Palacio sought to pacify the conscience of Iberian slavers in a way that bears striking resemblance to Vitoria's earlier defense of the trade in enslaved Africans.

2 Luis De Molina on Atlantic Slavery

The detailed discussions of Mercado and Palacio reveal that it would be misleading to draw a rigid contrast between the Iberian imperial theorists based in Spain and those writing from Portugal, and to claim that only the latter discussed enslavement in concrete juridical terms.[66] Nonetheless, it is true that the most comprehensive discussion of Iberian slaving in sub-Saharan Africa was penned by a Spaniard in Portugal: the Jesuit Luis de Molina, to whom we now turn.

---

62 Mercado, *Suma*, ed. Sánchez-Albornoz, lib. II, cap. 21, § 20–21.

63 Mercado, *Suma*, ed. Sánchez-Albornoz, lib. II, cap. 21, § 13: "Después espantémonos de la crueldad que usan los turcos con los cristianos cautivos [...] cierto, muy peor tratan estos mercaderes cristianos a los negros [...]".

64 Palacio, *Praxis theologica*, lib. II, cap. 8, 155.

65 Palacio, *Praxis theologica*, lib. II, cap. 8, 156: "Caeterum haec exquirere, non tenentur mercatores, illo comigrantes, sed sat est, si a parentibus, aut a magistratibus emant, modo evidens non sit parentes, vel magistratus, aut regis procuratores, temere, vendere Aethiopes, id quod ex clamoribus publicis dignoscere [...]".

66 This point is argued in Zeron, *Ligne de foi*, 258 and 299–300. The idea that the Spaniards argued more abstractly and theologically, in contrast to the more concretely juridical Portuguese theorists, is also false when considering Salamancan theologians such as Vitoria and Soto, as the second part of this book shows.

2.1 *A History of Portuguese Slaving in Africa*

Molina's account of enslavement in *De iustitia et iure*, most remarkably, begins with a historical narrative absent from writings of other Iberian theorists before or after him. In Disputation 34 of the Second Tractate, he put forward a short history of the Portuguese ventures in the Atlantic. Molina took his cue from a body of works typically composed by officials and scribes aboard ships sailing along the shores of Africa, namely, the Portuguese travel narratives widely popular at the time.[67] These early eyewitness accounts rendered a relatively differentiated portrayal of the various geographical regions and peoples on the African coastlines.[68] This feature had already distinguished the chronicles of Gomes Eanes de Zurara (1440–1474), the "founding father" of Lusophone travel writing, who documented the early Portuguese endeavors in Africa.[69] Molina's historical perspective went beyond the monolithic portrayals of "Aethiopia" found in the accounts of his intellectual predecessors and outlined diverse relationships Portuguese traders and authorities had established and maintained with various commonwealths in sub-Saharan Africa. This had profound political and legal implications.[70]

Molina began his historical account with the Portuguese seizure of the Cape Verde archipelago in the mid-15th century. "The Portuguese found these islands unoccupied", he wrote, and therefore acquired control over them "because they were the first to occupy them".[71] He was keen to emphasize that the appropriation of Cape Verde was uncontentious because the archipelago had not previously belonged to anybody; it had been a so-called *res nullius*.[72] In so arguing, Molina offered a tacit counter-history to earlier conceptions of the

67 A number of historians have pointed to Molina's historical account as well but do not place it in the context of contemporary travel writing. See e.g., Kaufmann, "Slavery between Law, Morality, and Economy", 201–207. As Josiah Blackmore points out, a wealth of such travel accounts are still available today, but only very few of these early Portuguese histories have been subject to scholarly inquiry, especially in comparison to well-known contemporary Hispanic equivalents. See Blackmore, *Moorings*, xxii. For an overview of understudied printed sources, see Winius, "Bibliographical Essay: A Treasury of Printed Source Materials Pertaining to the 15th and 16th Centuries".

68 On this piont, see Rubiés, *Travel and Ethnology in the Renaissance*, 172; and Silva Horta, "Perspectivas para o estudo da evolução das representações dos Africanos", 420.

69 Blackmore, *Moorings*, xv. See e.g., Zurara, *Chronicle*.

70 The significance of early modern European chronicles for colonial and imperial legal discourses is also emphasized in Benton, *A Search for Sovereignty*, ch. 1.

71 Molina, *DIEI*, vol. 1, tr. II, disp. 34, no. 1, col. 167: "Has insulas Lusitani vacuas invenerunt, easque colere et habitare coeperunt. Quo sit, ut gentium iure Lusitanorum dominio, tanquam primo occupantium, legitime accesserint".

72 On the right of occupation, see also Vitoria, *De indis*, in *Political Writings*, trans. Pagden and Lawrance, q. 3, a. 1, 280. For an excellent of discussion of occupation and the idea of

Portuguese empire and its legal foundations. As noted above, the papal concessions of dominion over "infidel" lands and peoples had played a significant role in the Portuguese expansionist ideology up to that point. Even if conflicting claims to imperial overlordship between João III (r. 1521–1557) and Pope Clement VII (in office from 1523–1534) had spurred tensions between Lisbon and Rome, the rationale for empire remained much the same in the first half of the 16th century. This conflict ultimately led to the establishment of the *Mesa da Consciência*, the so-called Board of Conscience, a royal advisory body whose principal purpose was to pacify the king's conscience when his decisions appeared to infringe upon the pope's jurisdictional claims.[73] The court theologians who staffed this body advanced a temporal justification of Portugal's imperial project, accepting at the same time the idea that the right to conquer, enslave, and evangelize "infidels" in the wider world rested on papal bulls.[74]

From Molina's point of view, this was unthinkable. His project thus aimed to re-write the history of the Portuguese endeavors in the Atlantic, to render them compatible with his own understanding of inter-political relations. He firmly insisted that the Portuguese territorial acquisition had not entailed the subjugation of peoples and was, therefore, not comparable to near-contemporary ventures like the Spanish conquest of the New World: enslaved persons from Senegambia came into Portuguese possession "not by the law of any war" but "solely through purchase".[75] And yet, in choosing Cape Verde as the starting point of his narrative, Molina likewise foregrounded that the history of the Portuguese empire was a history of trade relations that went hand in hand with territorial occupation.

In 1473, Molina continued, the Portuguese seized another uninhabited archipelago further south they called São Tomé. This colony, similar to the Cape Verde islands, served as a strategic trading post from where the Portuguese established commercial relations with the neighboring coastal commonwealths.[76] But in the region that Molina called "Lower Guinea", there were two polities that held a special status in the Luso-Atlantic world. One was the "Kingdom of the Manikongos, which received the faith along with its king many years

res nullius, see Benton and Straumann, "Acquiring Empire by Law". For a critical view of early modern uses of the term *res nullius*, largely directed against Benton and Straumann's reading, see Fitzmaurice, *Sovereignty, Property and Empire*, 51–58.

73 Marcocci, "Conscience and Empire", 479–481. See also Marcocci, *A consciência de um império*, 134–144.

74 Marcocci, "Conscience and Empire", 483–487.

75 Molina, *DIEI*, vol. 1, tr. II, disp. 34, no. 3, col. 168: "mancipia haec Lusitanorum servituti subiiciuntur, non est ius aliquod belli, quod Lusitani cum illis gentibus habeant; sed sola emptio".

76 Molina, *DIEI*, vol. 1, tr. II, disp. 34, no. 7, col. 170.

ago".[77] The 1491 conversion of this African polity was remarkable and unique.[78] Not only did the Portuguese episcopate of Cape Verde claim spiritual jurisdiction over the kingdom. But more importantly, it meant that none of the Kongolese could be enslaved thereafter "because they are all Christians".[79] Whereas previously, the Manikongo had been permitted to enslave malefactors, he was now obliged to resort to other punitive measures.[80] This account powerfully demonstrates Molina's effort to push enslavement beyond the borders of the Christian commonwealth, despite his assertions about the slavery of the apostate Moriscos in Castile. But it also raises the question of what this meant for Portuguese practices of slaving in "Lower Guinea". The answer, Molina elucidated, was that the alliance with Kongo provided the Portuguese with a unique gateway into the "infidel" African heartland. From there, Kongolese and creole merchants obtained "a huge number of slaves" they brought to the coast and sold to Iberian merchants.[81]

In the province of "Ambundu", situated further south, the dynamic was markedly different. Once divided into many smaller provinces, akin to Italy and France, as Molina explained, each was ruled by "quasi kings, called *sobas*".[82] With the help of the Portuguese, one such *soba* managed to gain the upper hand, subjecting all others to his overlordship. Since his name was Angola Inene, the Portuguese now called this realm "the Kingdom of Angola".[83] It had all started peacefully, and the Angolan ruler had been a treasured trading partner of the Iberian merchants. But the situation changed, as Molina noted, resulting in a conflict between the Portuguese and Inene's great-grandson.[84]

---

77 Molina, *DIEI*, vol. 1, tr. II, disp. 34, no. 8, col. 170: "Primum est Manicongi regnum, quod a multis annis fidem cum suo rege suscepit [...]".

78 As Toby Green notes, it cannot therefore be explained in purely economic terms but was bound up with Kongolese cosmology. He argues that ruling *mwissikongo* elite saw the Portuguese as their albino ancestors. See Green, *A Fistful of Shells*, 206–207.

79 Molina, *DIEI*, vol. 1, tr. II, disp. 34, no. 8, col. 170: "cum omnes Christiani sint, nullum asportatur mancipium [...]".

80 Molina, *DIEI*, vol. 1, tr. II, disp. 34, no. 8, col. 170: "neque propter delicta servituti subiiciuntur, sed aliis poenas a suo rege puniuntur".

81 Molina, *DIEI*, vol. 1, tr. II, disp. 34, no. 8, col. 170: "aliis Aethyopes, interiora alia infidelium loca ac dominia [...] ingentem emunt mancipiorum copiam, quam vinctam, publice asportant, venduntque mercatoribus Lusitanis [...]".

82 Molina, *DIEI*, vol. 1, tr. II, disp. 34, no. 9, 170: "nomine Ambundi vocantur et provincia Ambundia divisaque est in multas alias provincias, eo pacto quo Italia et Gallai in provincias multas sunt divisae. Constat praeterea, multis quasi regibus, quos sobas vocant".

83 Molina, *DIEI*, vol. 1, tr. II, disp. 34, no. 9, col. 170.

84 Molina, *DIEI*, vol. 1, tr. II, disp. 34, no. 9, col. 170: "Cum rege hoc bellum [...] est hodie Lusitanis".

In a lengthy account, he narrated that the present king almost became yet another Christian ally in Lower Guinea. But then he seized vast quantities of Portuguese goods, killed numerous merchants aboard Iberian ships, and started a war against their commander.[85] The consequence was momentous: "On the grounds of the reported violations of justice and many more that this barbarous king has brought upon us", Molina maintained, "there is no doubt that this war is just and that our enemies, who are captured in this war, are legitimately enslaved".[86] With this, Molina introduced a novel perspective into the debate about enslavement in West and southern Africa among the Iberian imperial theorists: the idea of a just Portuguese war against an "Aethiopean" commonwealth.

Molina's accounts of Kongo and Angola reveal that slavery was deeply entangled with broader questions of evangelization and empire. But like his intellectual predecessors, he too confronted the by-then classic justifications for enslavement. "In both Guineas and any other place", Molina argued, "it is right to buy those who on the grounds of a sufficiently serious crime were enslaved by the public authority of the local government".[87] He likened the civil punishment of slavery in "infidel" African commonwealths to the punishment of galley slavery in the Christian polities of the Mediterranean.[88] The implication was that both these forms of retribution were legitimate alternatives to the death penalty.[89] But, according to Molina, even crimes that would warrant more lenient punishment "among us" could justly lead to enslavement in an African context.[90] What did this mean?

As Molina narrated in his "mini chronicle", in Upper Guinea even minor offenses, like the theft of a chicken, were punished with the death penalty or

85 Molina, *DIEI*, vol. 1, tr. II, disp. 34, no. 9, col. 171–172.

86 Molina, *DIEI*, vol. 1, tr. II, disp. 34, no. 10, col. 172: "Ob commemoratas iniurias, aliasque multas a barbaro illo Rege nostris illatas, non dubitatur bellum illud esse iustum, eosque ex hostibus, qui eo bello capiuntur, legitime in servituem redigi".

87 Molina, *DIEI*, vol. 1, tr. II, disp. 35, no. 4, col. 161: "In utraque Guinaea, et in quocunque alio loco, fas est emere eum, qui ob sufficiens ad id crimen publica authoritate pro loci regimine in servitutem est redactus".

88 See the quotation in the footnote below the next.

89 On the equivalence of capital punishment and galley slavery in early modern Iberia, see Pike, *Penal Servitude in Early Modern Spain*, 4.

90 Molina, *DIEI*, vol. 1, tr. II, disp. 35, no. 6, col. 181: "Crimen, quod inter nos prudentis arbitrio iuste puniretur poena deputationis alicuius ad perpetuo remigandum in triremibus, nec non crimen quod inter nos paulo leviori poena esset dignum, iudicari debet sufficiens, ut iuste aliqui damnetur servituti perpetuae".

perpetual slavery.[91] Similarly, under a law in the Kingdom of Angola, whoever tore out a feather from one of the king's peacocks would be dispossessed and then killed or enslaved, along with the relatives.[92] In Molina's estimation, the decisive point was that these punishments served to counteract the proliferation of wrongdoings that endangered the body politic.[93] Severe retributions for seemingly insignificant transgressions, he underscored, likewise existed in Iberia. In the Portuguese armed forces, the most minor wrongdoing led to the death penalty or perpetual galley slavery. This was just "because military discipline and the common good of the army require it", according to Molina, and the same was certainly true of such punishments that "are necessary for the common good of the commonwealth".[94]

This point was emphatically restated by Estevão Fagundez.[95] But neither he nor Molina paused to acknowledge that the military and the city were two rather different bodies. Even if both were subject to princely authority, only the latter constituted a political community. The attempt to explain a political practice in Africa in terms of a familiar example from Iberia was thus grounded in a markedly uneven comparison. This offers a first impression of how forcefully Molina, and Fagundez for that matter, sought to vindicate the slave trade against contemporary critics like Mercado. In the story that they were telling, Portuguese merchants were free of any qualms if they acquired slaves condemned by public authority.

2.2 *Revisiting Voluntary Enslavement*

The title of self-enslavement underwent a transformation in the hands of those writing in Domingo de Soto's wake. The latter, as recounted above, had been

91 Molina, *DIEI*, vol. 1, tr. II, disp. 34, no. 4, col. 169: "Levissimum vero furtum, etiam unius gallinae aut rei levioris, consueverunt punire poena capitis aut perpetuae servitutis".

92 Molina, *DIEI*, vol. 1, tr. II, disp. 34, no. 14, col. 174: "Solus Angolae rex pavones habet [...] Legem tulit, ut, si quis pennam aliquam ex illis extraherent, ipse et omnes propinqui eius bonis omnibus spoliati interficerentur aut servituti subicerentur".

93 Molina, *DIEI*, vol. 1, tr. II, disp. 35, no. 6, col. 182: "sic etiam cuando bonum commune Reipublicae indigeret, ut minima quaeque furta severe punirentur, licita esse ea poena [...]".

94 Molina, *DIEI*, vol. 1, tr. II, disp. 35, no. 6, col. 181–182: "Quemadmodum enim in exercitu non damnamus minima quaeque sub mortis poena prohibita capiti plecti aut servitute in triremibus, quoniam id exigit militaris disciplina et bonum commune exercitus, sic etiam, quando bonum commune reipublicae indigere, ut minima quaeque furta severe puniretur, licita esset ea poena". It is therefore inaccurate to claim that Molina described sub-Saharan African polities as wholly unjust and tyrannical, as argued in Hespanha, "Luís de Molina e a escravização dos negros", 959.

95 Fagundez, *De iustitia et contractibus*, lib. II, cap. 4, no. 4, 151.

reluctant to allow the alienation of human freedom, permitting it only in cases where life itself was at stake. For Soto, it was morally problematic to surrender the core of what distinguished humans from the rest of creation.[96] A different approach was put forward by Miguel de Palacio. He did not discuss voluntary slavery in his account of Aethiopia but argued, in the abstract, that it did not require a life-threatening situation. As long as someone's self-enslavement could be justified "by any rational cause, he does not sin; for instance, so that his daughter may enter a marriage".[97]

A more radical interpretation that entirely stripped the idea of voluntary enslavement of its moral dimension emerged in colonial Brazil. Unlike Spanish America, where Indigenous peoples were integrated into the colonial body politic and their enslavement was formally outlawed in 1542—an issue we will explore in more detail in Chapter 6—the imperial policy toward Indigenous peoples in Brazil was markedly different.[98] Even after the union of the Iberian crowns, Native slavery remained legal in Portuguese America, provided it resulted from a "just war" against rebellious peoples or if Indigenous individuals "voluntarily" relinquished their freedom.[99] Yet the meaning of voluntary slavery was deeply contested. In 1567, a debate among Jesuit missionaries in Bahia escalated into a veritable controversy. One of the protagonists, Quirício Caxa, argued that all human beings were naturally endowed with the right to dispose of their freedom at will. So long as civil legislation did not explicitly prohibit it, he insisted, individuals could sell their liberty like any other commodity. His opponent Manuel da Nóbrega, the founder of the Jesuit mission in Brazil, did not criticize the idea of Native slavery as such. But he denounced Caxa's line of argument, claiming that it ultimately served to cover up the pervasive violence and injustice of Indigenous slavery in Brazil.[100]

---

96 This point is also stressed in Brett, *Changes of State*, 94.

97 Palacio, *Praxis theologica*, lib. II, cap. 8, 156: "si [...] ob causam rationalem quispiam se faceret vendere, non peccaret, verbi causa ut filiam traderet nuptui".

98 For a concise overview, see Marcocci, *A consciência de um império*, ch. 11. For a fuller account, see Zeron, *Ligne de foi*.

99 There were several attempts to limit or even abolish Indigenous slavery in Brazil, but they were always short-lived due to massive resistance from Portuguese settlers and, at times, Jesuit missionaries. In 1570, a law limited Native slavery to "just war" and prohibited voluntary slavery, but the latter was legalized again in 1573. And in 1609, a law decreed that Indigenous Brazilians could no longer be enslaved at all, but this was abolished again in 1611. See the discussion in Zeron, *Ligne de foi*, 251–252 and 323–368.

100 On the debate between Caxa and Nóbrega, see Zeron, *Ligne de foi*, 105–155; and Eisenberg, "Cultural Encounters, Theoretical Adventures".

Caxa's understanding of voluntary slavery fundamentally departed from that of Soto and even Palacio. It remains uncertain whether the Iberian theorists in Europe ever laid eyes on his unpublished polemic, but José Eisenberg suggests that it was Caxa who inspired Luis de Molina's famous argument that every human being "is the owner (*dominus*) of his own liberty, and therefore, even standing solely under natural law, he can alienate it and enslave himself".[101] But Caxa did not, in fact, develop a novel argument of his own. Rather, he tacitly defended an earlier ruling of the Board of Conscience (*Mesa da consciência*), the Portuguese monarch's advisory body that held that it was legal for parents to sell their children in cases of necessity, and that all Indigenous Brazilians over the age of 20 could freely alienate their liberty.[102]

It is difficult to determine the extent to which the debate about voluntary slavery in Brazil shaped Molina's understanding of the issue. What is certain, however, is that the legitimacy of self-enslavement remained controversial among the Iberian imperial theorists. Juan de Lugo endorsed Molina's view in his own *De iustitia et iure*, written in the mid-17th century.[103] But not all the Iberian thinkers were ready to accept the idea that human freedom could be sold like chattel.[104] Some returned to Palacio's view that at least a reasonable cause, if not extreme necessity, was required.[105] Others argued differently. In

---

101 Molina, *DIEI*, vol. 1, tr. II, disp. 33, no. 3, col. 108, qtd. and trans. in Brett, *Changes of State*, 94. See Eisenberg, "Cultural Encounters, Theoretical Adventures", 392–393. However, none of the Iberian imperial theorists pointed to Caxa's polemic. I have not been able to consult Caxa's text myself, as the only surviving manuscript is preserved in the Municipal Library of Évora (MS "Livro sobre os indios do Brasil", cod. CXVI/1–33). I regret that I cannot therefore offer a comprehensive assessment about the extent to which Caxa's language and his line of argument shaped the subsequent discussion of thinkers in Europe.

102 See Marcocci, *A consciência de um império*, 448–450.

103 Lugo, *DIEI*, disp. 6, sect. 2, no. 14, 134–135. Molina's rival Fernando Pérez also touched upon this problem and left an ambiguous account. In one of his manuscripts, he insisted that voluntary slavery was permissible only when life itself was at stake, while in another he argued that human freedom could be sold like any other property. See Pérez, "De acquisitione dominii in homines", ed. and trans. Tarrío and Brito, dubitatio 3, 338: "Si quis pro vita conservanda se vendat, imo ipsa venditio in extrema aut gravissima necessitate, quando nemo aliter venit succurrere, bene potest fieri sine peccato". See also Pérez, "Non nulla ante materiam de restitutione", ed. and trans. Tarrío et al., disp. 12, 436: "Et qui ita se ipsum venditit, servus manebit, quia homo de sua libertate potest disponere sicut de aliis bonis".

104 See also Brett, *Changes of State*, 94.

105 See e.g., Rebello, *Opus de obligationibus iustitiae*, pars 1, lib. I, q. 9, no. 11, 68: "Semper tamen, et ubique illicitum est se ipsum vendere, si causa rationabilis non subsit". Another example would be the Palermitan theologian Antonino Diana (1585–1663), a Theatine who wrote a casuistic work on the resolution of moral doubts in 12 volumes, and who closely

Juan Azor's estimation, humans could alienate their liberty however cheaply, even if it was morally reprehensible. Yet in such cases—for instance, if somebody used his or her liberty as a stake for gambling—enslavement was only just if it did not result in a "grave detriment to the family".[106] Azor highlighted that voluntary slavery was not merely a contract between two individuals. It often involved other parties who depended on the person in question and even had certain rights over them, such as spouses.[107]

But there is also another dimension of voluntary slavery that we briefly encountered in Vitoria's remarks on the subject. In his letter to Bernardino de Vique, the Salamancan maestro pointed out that self-enslavement often occurred in the context of unjust punishments in the Atlantic world. Viewed from that perspective, purchasing a slave could be construed as a form of rescue from certain, though illicit, death among the "barbarians". This issue was also taken up by Martín de Azpilcueta, who was known among contemporaries as "the best jurist among the theologians and the best theologian among the jurists".[108] Formerly a colleague of Vitoria's at Salamanca, he became professor of canon law at the University of Coimbra in 1538. The years spent in Portugal left a deep imprint on Azpilcueta's *magnum opus*, his manual for confessors, where he noted that Portuguese settlers in Brazil routinely enslaved Indigenous people who would otherwise be sacrificed for cannibalism.[109] He acknowledged that this justification served as an excuse for Christian slavers, who were safe in their conscience in acquiring *soi-disant* voluntary slaves who had been "maliciously captured".[110] Azpilcueta thus deployed a more elaborate version of the very same argument Vitoria had sketched in his letter.

followed his Jesuit predecessors not just on matters of slavery. See Diana, *Resolutionum moralium*, tr. VII, resol. 7, 235. The only sustained discussion of Diana's work is available in Burgio, *Teologia barocca*; and in Burgio, "Antonino Diana e la rivolta del Portogallo".

106 Azor, *Institutionum moralium*, vol. 1, lib. II, cap. 31, 135: "qui seipsum lucri causa aleae ludo exposuerit: nam quamvis libertatem periculo obiiciat, lucrum nihilominus [...] sibi potest acquirere: hoc tamen locum habere puto solum, quando, hoc non est, cum gravi detrimento familiae". See also Diana, *Resolutionum moralium*, tr. VII, resol. 43, 257.

107 This problem will be explored in greater depth in the chapter that follows.

108 Biographical information on Azpilcueta is from Decock, "Martín de Azpilcueta", 116–119.

109 Azpilcueta, *Manual de confessores*, cap. 23, no. 95, 480: "los paganos, que compran los christianos en el Brasil, y en otras partes de otros paganos enemigos suyos, que los tienen presos, y los cevan para matar, y comerlos".

110 Azpilcueta, *Manual de confessores*, cap. 24, no. 9, 511: "Y por esta via se podrian salvar los Christianos, que en el Brasil, y otras partes, y venden los negros, que sus enemigos los quieren matar para los comer, aunque de suyo sean libres, y sean mal presos". I thank Christiane Birr for pointing me to this passage.

It was none other than Luis de Molina, the staunch defender of self-enslavement under natural law, who identified that as a problem. In his view, several scenarios rendered it impossible to acquire a person as a slave under these circumstances. For instance, if the potential buyer could forcibly liberate the captive without suffering any harm in so doing, or if the liberated captive was able to reimburse the person who bought them from the "cannibals".[111] Molina conceded, however, that "unbelievers" facing an unjust death could indeed be saved by enslavement: "The reason is that someone who has the strength to work and who is apt to serve is not considered poor absolutely so that we would need to provide any value whatsoever merely for free by the precept of almsgiving".[112] In this sense, Molina shared the conclusion that voluntary slavery was a way of winning infidels from "the region of Brazil and Aethiopia" for the Christian faith.[113]

The religious asymmetry that was at the heart of Molina's account of slaving was even more pronounced in his remarks on the idea that parents in necessity could justly alienate their children. Having restated the validity of this dictum, Molina said the following:

> I have spoken of the grave necessity of unbelievers: because slavery under the power of Christians results in their spiritual benefit, charity demands to buy their liberty, so that they become Christians by this occasion. But if they were Christians, the law of charity would postulate not only that they be left in liberty, but, oftentimes, that they be rescued merely for free.[114]

111 Molina, *DIEI*, vol. 1, tr. II, disp. 33, no. 30–31, col. 164. For a simiar view, see Azor, *Institutionum moralium*, vol. 2, lib. II, cap. 30, 134; and Diana, *Resolutionum moralium*, resol. 7, 236.

112 Molina, *DIEI*, vol. 1, tr. II, disp. 33, no. 31, col. 165: "Ratio est, quoniam non censetur simpliciter pauper, qui vires habet ad laborandum aptusve est ad serviendum, ut mere gratis eleemosyne praecepto teneamur illi exhibere valorem quemcumque, quo ad evadendam extremam aut gravem necessitatem indivuerit".

113 Molina, *DIEI*, vol. 1, tr. II, disp. 33, no. 31, col. 166: "servitus confert, ut, qui ita emitur, una cum vita corporis salutem animae consequatur, quod saepe in Brasilica regione et in Aethiopia eveniret".

114 Molina, *DIEI*, vol. 1, tr. II, disp. 35, no. 9, col. 183: "Locutus sum de gravi infidelium necessitate: quoniam cum servitus sub Christianorum potestate in bonum ipsorum spirituale cedat, charitas est libertatem eorum emere, ut ea occasione Christiani fiant. Quod si Christiani essent, lex charitatis postularet, non solum ut liberi relinquerentur, sed etiam ut mere gratis saepe eis subveniretur."

Molina's insistence on the significance of charity underscores just how problematic it is to portray the early modern language of natural law as religiously neutral.[115] While all humans on earth possessed natural rights by virtue of their humanity, Christians were deemed to enjoy additional privileges beyond these rights. Charity was at the heart of a specific mode of protection that saved coreligionists not only from death but also from losing their liberty. It was not so much the love of one's neighbor *tout court*, but a quasi-legal precept that obliged Christian toward other Christians, as Molina forcefully put it.[116] In contrast, for "infidels" charity meant welcoming them into the faith, even though the protection of their soul came at the expense of their temporal freedom.[117]

2.3 *Possession in Good Faith and the Limits of Morality*

In Molina's view, however, one particular title of slaving could be justified neither by appeal to Christian charity, nor by the "just war" against Angola, nor by pointing to the civil power of "Aethiopean" kings: the idea that captives of inner-African wars were, in general, licitly enslaved. Palacio, who had previously acknowledged this problem, argued that Iberian merchants remained invincibly ignorant in the absence of public outcry, meaning that they could not know the truth and were thus free of any moral culpability.[118] But according to Molina, the rumors of injustice were simply too widespread and well-known for such ignorance to be plausible for Portuguese and Castilian slavers. The implications were far-reaching. If Iberian traders engaged in slaving in Senegambia or southern Africa without a proper investigation into the circumstances of enslavement, Molina argued, they would sin mortally and could not take possession of their slaves in good faith.[119] This verdict did not go

115 To some extent, this was also echoed in the Protestant natural law discourse. See e.g., Grotius, *De iure belli*, lib. III, cap. 1, a. 4, no. 2: "Sed sicut antehac monuimus saepe, non semper ex omni parte licitum est quod juri stricte sumto congruit; saepe enim proximi caritas non permittet ut summo jure utamur". For an excellent discussion, see Tierney, *Liberty and Law*, 244–247.

116 Molina, *DIEI*, vol. 1, tr. II, disp. 35, no. 12, col. 186: "proximi charitate, praesertim quae in Christianis esse debet maxime ad fidei domesticos".

117 For a similar argument, see also Fagundez, *De iustitia et contractibus*, lib. II, cap. 4, no. 9, 152.

118 On the idea of invincible ignorance, see Toste, "Invincible Ignorance and the Americas", 284.

119 Molina, *DIEI*, vol. 1, tr. II, disp. 35, no. 16, col. 189: "ut emendo illa [i.e. the slaves], sine ulla inquisitione de titulo, quo servituti sint subiecta, et sine iusta causa depellendi praesumptionem, quae est, aut esse debet in contrarium, lethaliter peccet, neque incipiat bona fide possidere".

unnoticed. At least one contemporary Iberian denounced the "thousand lies" Molina allegedly spread about the injustice of slaving in "Guinea".[120]

Crucially, however, Molina insisted that it was impossible to fully ascertain what had actually transpired in the African heartland.[121] For this reason, he argued, whoever acquired enslaved people in good faith was free from moral culpability: even if, at some point, a slaveholder began to harbor doubts, there was no cause for concern—unless he had "persuaded himself that the slave is *not at all* his own thing: for in doubt the condition of the possessor is better".[122] In so arguing, Molina invoked a legal principle traditionally associated with debates about the acquisition of territory in warfare and transposed it into the context of private law.[123] This move not only eased the conscience of Iberian merchants.[124] This principle of *bona fide* possession also extended protection to all those who acquired enslaved Africans in Iberia and the Americas. Given their distance from the original site, Molina argued, such buyers were even less likely to uncover the true circumstance of what had transpired there.[125] In this sense, he maintained, "even if someone has convinced him or herself that slaves, who are carried away from the aforementioned places, were for the most part unjustly enslaved, he or she can licitly buy them".[126]

---

120 This account, recorded by Alonso de Sandoval in early 17th-century Cartagena de Indias, was given by a clergyman who had arrived from West Africa. See Sandoval, *Naturaleza*, lib. I, cap. 17, fols. 69^{v}–70^{r}.

121 Molina, *DIEI*, vol. 1, tr. II, disp. 35, no. 16, col. 189–190.

122 Molina, *DIEI*, vol. 1, tr. II, disp. 35, no. 20, col. 193, emphasis mine: "neque esto ipse merito incipiat dubitare an sua res sit, tenetur quicquam illius dare, quosque omnino sibi persuadeat rem nullo modo esse suam: eo quod in dubio melior sit conditio possidentis".

123 See Vitoria, *De iure belli*, in *Political Writings*, trans. Pagden and Lawrance, q. 2, a. 3: "once the case has been examined as long as is reasonable, if the doubt remains unresolved, the legitimate owner is not required to relinquish his territory, but may henceforth own it lawfully". The reference to Vitoria shows that it is not entirely correct to claim that the idea of the stronger position of the possessor only became central to the "scholastics" who were writing at the end of the 16th century, as argued in Schüssler, "Moral Self-Ownership and *ius possessionis* in Scholastics".

124 This is also noted in Perdices de Blas and Ramos Gorostiza, "The Debate over the Enslavement of Indians and Africans", 312; and in Cuena Boy, *De servitute*, 216 and 227–228.

125 Molina, *DIEI*, vol. 1, tr. II, disp. 36, no. 3, col. 196: "asportata vero in longinquam aliquam regionem, eo [i.e., an inquiry into the circumstances of enslavement] commodo privarentur: quod tamen raro admodum eveniet".

126 Molina, *DIEI*, vol. 1, tr. II, disp. 36, no. 3, col. 195: "Etiam postquam ex iis, quae duabus praecedentibus disputationibus dicta sunt, aut aliunde sibi persuaderet, mancipia quae ex praedictis locis asportantur, magna ex parte iniuste esse redacta in servitutem, posset licite ea emere".

Molina did not entirely dismiss the possibility of moral obligation and introduced an important qualification. Those who, on account of his treatment of the subject, began to doubt but nevertheless proceeded to purchase enslaved people were, he argued, "obliged to make restitution to their slaves, and the amount will depend on the extent of the doubt about the justice of their initial enslavement".[127] This position appears to resonate with Michelle McKinley's characterization of slavery as a condition of dependency between absolute liberty and full-blown domination, which she terms "fractional freedom".[128] Yet Molina's stance becomes clearer in the broader context of his discussion of doubtful possession and restitution. On the one hand, the obligation to make restitution applied only to those who already harbored doubts about the legitimacy of enslavement at the time of the purchase of the slave. Even then, that obligation remained partial and did not involve freeing an enslaved person.[129] On the other, Molina's caveat did not undermine his earlier stance that all those who had acquired slaves in good faith were not obliged to make any restitution at all—not even a partial one, and not even if they began to doubt at a later stage—unless they were convinced that the slaves in their possession were "not at all" their own.[130] Although Molina acknowledged a limited duty of restitution, his broader insistence on possession in good faith left ample room to shield slaveholders from moral and legal obligations. This intervention had a lasting impact on the Iberian theorists' understanding of the slave trade.[131]

---

127 Molina, *DIEI*, vol. 1, tr. II, disp. 36, no. 5, col. 196: "Quidubius, propter rationes nostras, aut propter quascunque alias [...] sane teneretur ad restitutionem mancipiis faciendam, maiorem vel minorem pro quantitate dubii, an iuste a principio fuerint in servitutem redacta".

128 McKinley, *Fractional Freedoms*, 11. For a similar point without reference to McKinley, see Schwartz and Tellkamp, "Introduction", 18.

129 On this point, see Molina, *DIEI*, vol. 1, tr. II, disp. 35, no. 20, col. 193: "qui eam accipit, etiamsi dubius an res aliena sit, eam accipiat, succedit in totum ius certum, aut dubium, quod is, qui illam tradidit, habebat; [...] Atque ex hoc fundamento dicimus, emptorem rei alicuius in dubio, an res tempore venditionis fuerit venditis, non teneri integre eam restituere, interim dum omnino non constat eam venditis non fuisse."

130 Molina, *DIEI*, vol. 1, tr. II, disp. 35, no. 20, col. 193: "quis bona fide coepit possidere, suum non esse, nullum ius est, ut in totum, vel in partem illa re spolietur, neque esto ipse merito incipiat dubitare an sua res sit, tenetur quicquam illius dare, quosque omnino sibi persuadeat rem nullo modo esse suam."

131 Some followed Molina's forceful stance that slaveholders could rest secure in conscience unless they were convinced that the person was "*nullo modo*" their own. See e.g., Azor, *Institutionum moralium*, vol. 3, lib. VIII, cap. 6, col. 638. Others argued that the doubt at least had to be "equal", which meant that the probability of unjust enslavement had to be equal or smaller than the probability of a just title. See e.g., Rebello, *Opus de obligationi-*

At the same time, however, Molina recognized that many Iberian slavers were largely indifferent to such moral and legal considerations. "They worry about nothing else in this trade than their own profit and advantage", he noted, and "indiscriminately accept all the slaves, as long as there will be an agreement on the price".[132] Did this render his elaborate account of *bona fide* possession meaningless?

2.4 *The King's Conscience*

The answer to that question brings us back to the political and imperial dimension of the inter-individual trade in "human commodities" from sub-Saharan Africa. By that, I do not mean the "empire of private rights" the traders themselves established, but rather how the horizontal dimension—so-called commercial imperialism—was itself implicated in the power structure of the commonwealth.[133] Several Iberian theorists writing from Portugal emphasized that the justice of the slave trade was ultimately the monarch's responsibility. One of them was the Jesuit Pedro Simões, briefly introduced in the previous chapter. "It is not up to the buyers to examine the just title of their slaves", Simões wrote in 1585, "this pertains to the king and the king's governors".[134] In his estimation, those who bought enslaved Black Africans "in the middle of the market" could not possibly inquire into the justice of the enslavement—and he further argued that "it is not a sufficient verdict when the slave affirms that he has been unjustly captured, since one must assume that the slave is lying on this occasion in order to obtain his freedom".[135] The upshot of this sweep-

---

bus iustitiae, pars 1, lib. I, q. 10, sect. 1, no. 3, 70; and Sánchez, *Consilia*, lib. I, cap. 1, dub. 4, no. 15, 6. Fernando Pérez had made this argument as well, but he also maintained—in the same text—that if slavery and liberty were equally probable, then the right to liberty was stronger and had to be favored both in the forum of conscience and in the judicial forum. See Pérez, "Non nulla ante materiam de restitutione", disp. 11, 430 and 440.

132 Molina, *DIEI*, vol. 1, tr. II, disp. 34, no. 6, col. 169: "illi [i.e., the Portuguese] nihil aliud curant in hac negotiatione, quam suum lucrum et commodum"; and Molina, *DIEI*, vol. 1, tr. II, disp. 34, no. 14, col. 175: "Lusitani mercatores [...] promiscue omnia accipiunt, modo in pretio conveniant".

133 The phrase in quotes is taken from Koskenniemi, "Empire and International Law", 32.

134 Simões, *Materia de restitutione*, ed. and trans. Maurício and Miranda, membrum 2, a. 1, 249: "ad ementes in hac materia non pertinet examiare de titulo iusto eorum servorum, id enim pertinet ad regem et ad regni moderatores". For a similar argument, see Pérez, "De acquisitione dominii in homines", ed. and trans. Tarrío and Brito, dubitatio 4, 344–346; and Pérez, "Non nulla ante materiam de restitutione", ed. and trans. Tarrío et al., disp. 12, 442.

135 Simões, *Materia de restitutione*, ed. and trans. Maurício and Miranda, membrum 2, a. 1, 249: "Nec video quam diligentiam possit facere qui huiusmodi servos in medio fori emit;

ing statement was clear: in Iberia, enslaved persons could always be purchased with a clear conscience.

In a sense, this understanding of Atlantic slavery resembles the Iberian imperial theorists' view of the duties of individuals in warfare. As Francisco de Vitoria explained in his lecture *De iure belli*, "lesser subjects who are not invited to be heard in the councils of the prince nor in public council are not required to examine the causes of war [...] because it would be impossible, and inexpedient, to put the arguments about difficult public business before every member of the common people".[136] A remarkably similar logic also applied to the trade in enslaved Africans.

Luis de Molina tapped into this line of reasoning too, but he added an important qualification. He noted that the moral issues involved in the slave trade were analogous to the controversies about the justice of Indigenous slavery in Spanish America and Morisco slavery in Andalusia. And in both cases, the Castilian kings had summoned juntas of theologians and jurists to debate these matters.[137] When it came to the problem of Iberian slaving in Africa, however, nothing of the sort had happened: "Why, I ask, does the king not order this to be examined, and if it is found that something is being done unjustly, put an end to it, and let whatever is just and licit be approved by public authority and mature judgment?"[138]

One might think that Molina was attacking the *Mesa da Consciência*, the king's theological advisory board. In keeping with its purpose of pacifying the conscience of Portuguese monarchs, it had refrained from taking a definitive stance on the problem of Atlantic enslavement.[139] However, the Board of Conscience had lost its power and importance with the union of the Iberian crowns

---

nec est sufficiens iuditium si servus affirmet se fuisse iniuste captum, praesumitur enim ipso mentiri propter libertatem consequendam".

136 Vitoria, *De iure belli*, in *Political Writings*, trans. Pagden and Lawrance, q. 2, a. 2, 308.

137 Molina, *DIEI*, vol. 1, tr. II, disp. 35, no. 1–2, col. 179–180.

138 Molina, *DIEI*, vol. 1, tr. II, disp. 35, no. 2, col. 180: "cur, inquam, rege id iubente non examinabitur resecabiturque, si quid compertum fuerit iniuste fieri, publicaque auctoritate ac maturo iudicio approbabitur, quicquid iuste et licite sit?"

139 See Marcocci, "Conscience and Empire", 485–486. Marcocci also suggests that Tomás de Mercado criticized the *Mesa* for sidestepping this issue, but this was not in fact the case. On the contrary, Mercado argued that the Portuguese king and his "council" had done what they could, in contrast to the Portuguese slavers in Africa. See Mercado, *Suma*, ed. Sánchez-Albornoz, lib. II, cap. 21, § 21: "En lo que toca al rey de Portugal, digo que me huelgo sea rectísimo y tenga crédito de ello, y creo que cuanto es en sí él y los de su consejo hacen y proveen lo que conviene. Mas mucho es lo que los reyes mandan y poco lo que los vasallos, en caso de interés, obedecen".

in 1580, and never regained its previous stature.[140] The subject of Molina's critique, therefore, was the Portuguese king himself, *dom Filipe o primeiro*, who was none other than Philip II of Spain, the ruler of the united Iberian empires.

Fernão Rebello later concurred with this critique.[141] A professor of philosophy when Molina was still at Évora, Rebello was later appointed to the prime chair of theology, like his former colleague.[142] The two Jesuits insisted that the stakes of the Portuguese trade in enslaved persons could not be offloaded onto traffickers operating in peripheral waters or slaveholders in Iberia. African slavery was a problem of the commonwealth. As such, Molina and Rebello maintained, it was the task of the king and his ministers, not that of individual subjects, to investigate the titles of the commercial goods imported and put on sale in Iberia.[143] At the end of the day, therefore, those who owned enslaved Africans were safe in conscience and could be regarded as "possessors in good faith".[144] The spiritual salvation of the king, however, was at grave risk.

3 Sites of Slaving in the Indian and Pacific Oceans

In the final pages of this chapter, I would like to highlight that some of the Iberian theorists were keenly aware that Portuguese sites of slaving were not confined to the Mediterranean and Atlantic worlds, but also extended to Asia.[145] Once again, it was Luis de Molina who made this issue explicit. By pointing to the Portuguese spaces of enslavement in the Indian and Pacific

140 Marcocci, "Conscience and Empire", 491 and 494.

141 Rebello, *Opus de obligationibus iustitiae*, pars 1, lib. 1, q. 10, sect. 2, no. 15, 72.

142 Stegmüller, "Zur Literaturgeschichte der Philosophie und Theologie an den Universitäten Evora und Coimbra", 405–406.

143 This is also noted in Simmermacher, *Eigentum als ein subjektives Recht bei Luis de Molina*, 195.

144 Molina, *DIEI*, vol. 1, tr. II, disp. 36, no. 1, col. 194–195: "cum ad subditos non spectet examinare, an merces, quae ad hoc regnum asportantur et in eo venduntur, legitime a subditis huius regni asportentur et vendantur, sed id ad principem et ad eius ministros pertineat [...] facillime omnes, qui hactenus mancipia [...] emerunt, bonae fidei possessores erunt talesque merito sunt censendi". See also Rebello, *Opus de obligationibus iustitiae*, pars 1, lib. 1, q. 10, sect. 1, no. 4, 70.

145 Scholarship on early modern slaveries in Asia has gained increasing attention in recent years. For an excellent overview, see the contributions in McManus and Ehalt (eds.), *Regimes of Bondage*.

Oceans, he took his cue from contemporary chronicles like João de Barros' *Decada primeira da Asia* (1552), in which the so-called "discovery" of Africa no longer served as the ultimate reference point but was framed as a pre-history of the Portuguese ventures in Asia.[146]

The connecting link between the Atlantic and the Asian slave trades was Mozambique. The vast majority of the enslaved persons loaded onto the Portuguese slave ships in East Africa were transported across the Atlantic.[147] However, historians have shown that slaves from Mozambique were also routinely sold in the Philippines, especially following the union of the Iberian crowns. Manila emerged as a major trading hub for "human commodities", sourced from a vast region stretching from East Africa and the Bay of Bengal to Japan. Between 1565 and the end of the 17th century, an estimate of 8,000 enslaved persons were brought to the Americas aboard the Manila galleon.[148]

Luis de Molina explained that the Portuguese had begun to establish a trading colony in Sofala in the early 16th century. But it was only in the 1560s that the situation changed drastically. The Portuguese reached the Karanga state of Mutapa in the interior of southern Africa with the ambition of turning it into "another Kongo".[149] The outcome of that mission was, however, quite the opposite. As Molina recounted, the missionary leader Gonçalo da Silveira (1521–1561) was murdered "unjustly and disgracefully against the Christian religion" because the Mutapan ruler had been corrupted by the counsel of "Mohammedans" in the area.[150] The notion that Muslim merchants had warned the *Mwene*, the king, of Portugal's imperial ambitions was widespread at the time. It is not entirely certain if this was indeed the cause of Silveira's death or if the story that Molina and others were telling was merely the product of "Portuguese Islamophobic fantasy".[151] The consequence, however, was clear. Rather than turning Mutapa into another allied Christian kingdom, it ushered in another Portuguese war on the African continent. Only this time,

---

146 Barros, *Decada primeira da Asia*. The links between European slaving in the Atlantic and Indian Oceans are also highlighted in recent scholarship. See e.g., Chakraborty, "Slavery in the Indian Ocean World", 340.

147 Zeuske, *Sklaverei*, 182–183.

148 Seijas, *Asian Slaves in Colonial Mexico*, 32, 52–55 and 241.

149 Strathern, "Catholic Missions and Local Rulers", 168.

150 Molina, *DIEI*, vol. 1, tr. II, disp. 34, no. 15, col. 175: "a rege Sebastiano missus est Franciscus Barreto [...] ut de rege Monomotapae, Sofalae finitimo, iustam sumeret vindictam, eo quod quorundam Mohumetanorum invidia ac suasu patrem nostrae societatis Gondisalvum a Silveira [...] iniuste et in Christianam religionem ignominiose interfecisset".

151 Strathern, "Catholic Missions and Local Rulers", 169.

it was steeped in the centuries-long vision of warfare against "Saracens", which made any inquiries into the justice of enslavement superfluous in the eyes of contemporaries.[152]

This global extension of "holy wars" had been at the heart of the Portuguese colonial pursuits in the Indian Ocean from the very outset. When Vasco da Gama (c. 1469–1524) and his fellow explorers first set foot in Kerala in 1498, they were convinced that the world beyond the Cape of Good Hope was another Mediterranean of sorts, one similarly conditioned by enduring conflicts between Muslims and Christians, who had previously been evangelized by the Corsicans and Italians.[153] By the time Molina was writing, it had become increasingly evident that this binary vision—Islam versus Christianity—failed to do justice to the complex webs of religious, political, and commercial relations in the so-called *Estado da Índia*.[154] And yet, the idea of Portuguese wars against Muslim kingdoms was central to the Iberian understanding of slaving in the Indian Ocean. This was pointed out explicitly by Estevão Fagundez, the most illustrious Portuguese imperial theorist of the 17th century. He underscored that the inhabitants on Java and Sumatra "professed the sect of Mohammad" and "killed preachers who announced the true Gospel to them".[155] Both Molina and Fagundez invoked familiar arguments about the "just war" against the "enemies of the faith" in novel contexts and placed them alongside other wars against "infidels" in the wider world.[156]

However, for the Iberian imperial theorists, not all individuals Portuguese slavers had acquired in Asia resulted from warfare, let alone their own bel-

152 Molina, *DIEI*, vol. 1, tr. II, disp. 34, no. 16, col. 176. This was later restated by Fagundez, *De iustitia et contractibus*, lib. II, cap. 3, no. 1, 148.

153 Subrahmanyam, *Empires Between Islam and Christianity*, 28. On the Corsican and Italian ventures in the Indian Ocean, see Subrahmanyam, *Empires Between Islam and Christianity*, ch. 3.

154 The canon lawyer Martín de Azpilcueta, for instance, qualified the idea that Christians were waging "just wars" against any and all "Saracens" and pointed out that there were also Muslim vassals in Portuguese Asia, who were exempt from war and slavery. See Azpilcueta, *Relectio cap. ita quorundam*, 40–43. See also the discussion in Marcocci, *A consciência de um império*, 304–305.

155 Fagundez, *De iustitia et contractibus*, lib. II, cap. 3, no. 4, 149: "De illis Samatrensibus [...] sectam Mahumetanam profitentur, saepe intestino odio in fidem Catholicam, evangelico praedicatores veram illis salutem annuntiantes occiderunt". On the same argument with regard to Java, see Fagundez, *De iustitia et contractibus*, lib. II, cap. 3, no. 9, 150.

156 In Fagundez's account, other sites of Portuguese "just wars" in the Indian Ocean included Calicut, Malacca, and Sri Lanka. See Fagundez, *De iustitia et contractibus*, lib. II, cap. 3, no. 3, 10, and 11, 149–150. The war against Calicut was also mentioned by Molina, *DIEI*, vol. 1, tr. II, disp. 34, no. 18, col. 176.

ligerent enterprises. A special case was Japan, where the Portuguese had been present since the 1540s.[157] As Rômulo da Silva Ehalt has shown, one of the foremost debates about enslavement in Japan centered on "the practice that most closely resembled voluntary slavery [...] *nenki hōkō* 年季奉公 or *temporary servitude*, in which a person subjected him or herself to serve another, voluntarily or not, for a set period of years".[158] Missionaries in Japan had routinely held such temporarily enslaved persons since the 1560s. But the first substantive inquiry into the legitimacy of this form of servitude only followed three decades later, in a dialogue between missionaries and Jesuit theologians in Goa.[159] What is remarkable about this episode is that the fathers of the Society of Jesus offered exactly the same justification of voluntary slavery that Luis de Molina later advanced in his *De iustitia et iure*: the Jesuits in Goa insisted that their fellow friars in Japan could justly acquire Indigenous individuals as "voluntary slaves" because every human being could alienate their freedom "*standing solely under natural law*".[160]

Molina made no reference to this debate, nor did he mention the title of self-enslavement in relation to Japan. Instead, he wrote that there were frequent wars among the "Japanese princes" whose legitimacy was highly doubtful, because "these infidels do not seem to have any regard for justice when starting wars".[161] Those who resisted such illicit aggression had justice on their side, Molina explained, and he also stressed that wars waged by Christianized kingdoms in Japan produced legitimate slaves. But he questioned whether the Portuguese merchants cared to inquire into the justice of Japanese slavery in the first place.[162]

Even more doubtful, Molina argued, was the title of all those humans who were subjected to slavery in Ming China. There was "perpetual peace" in that part of the world, the Chinese provinces were "most abundant" and thus

157 Sousa, *The Portuguese Slave Trade*, 15.

158 Ehalt, "Jesuit Arguments for Voluntary Slavery", 7.

159 Ehalt, "Jesuit Arguments for Voluntary Slavery", 7–8.

160 Ehalt, "Jesuit Arguments for Voluntary Slavery", 14, original emphasis and expansion of the contraction: "*estando in solo iura n*[atur]*ali como vno puede disponer de sus cossas, puede disponer de su libertad, et volenti non fit iniuria*". Ehalt cites from a text composed by Jesuit theologians in Goa c. 1569, which is preserved on microfilm at the University of Saint Thomas in Manila, entitled "Cassos resueltos en Goa por los Padres de la Compañia cerca del ministerio de Japon".

161 Molina, *DIEI*, vol. 1, tr. II, disp. 34, no. 20, col. 177: "inter Iapponenses principes intestina bella frequentissima sint, de eorum tamen bellorum iustitia merito dubitari potest, eo quod nulla ab infidelibus illis iustitiae ratio haberi videatur in bellis inferendis".

162 Molina, *DIEI*, vol. 1, tr. II, disp. 34, no. 20, col. 177.

spared from famines, and civil punishment in the form of slavery did not exist.[163] In Molina's estimation, there was "not a single just title" by which Portuguese merchants could licitly acquire enslaved persons from that region.[164] This assessment sharply contrasted with historical reality. Portuguese slavers had been trafficking in "human properties" from China since the mid-16th century, initially via Japan and later via the Portuguese colony in Macao, established in 1557.[165] Once the Iberian crowns were united, Portuguese traffickers began to sell off countless enslaved Chinese men and women in Manila, who were subsequently shipped to the Americas.[166]

It was Estevão Fagundez who pointed out that practices of slaving were thriving in China. In direct contrast to Molina, he posited that there was "no scruple" concerning the justice of these slaves.[167] To reinforce this point, Fagundez set out to quote "an entire paragraph" from Matteo Ricci's (1552–1516) journal from China.[168] The famous Italian missionary, who had arrived in Macao in 1582, remained in China for almost three decades.[169] His diaries, which were posthumously published by his fellow Jesuit Nicolas Trigault, served as a source from which Fagundez quoted: "Many of them", as Ricci had written about the Chinese,

> [...] sell themselves to wealthy patrons, so as to find a wife among his servants, and in so doing, subject their children to perpetual slavery. Others buy a wife when they can save money enough to do so, and when their family becomes too numerous to be supported, they sell their children

---

163 Molina, *DIEI*, vol. 1, tr. II, disp. 34, no. 20, col. 177: "Sinarum provincias perpetua pace frui [...] eas provincias abundantissimas esse neque umquam inter ipsos esse famem [...] iudices neminem suorum servitutis perpetuae damnare".

164 Molina, *DIEI*, vol. 1, tr. II, disp. 34, no. 20, col. 177: "nullus iustus titulus ex his, quos disputatione 33 commemoravimus, sese offerat, quo in servitutem redigi Sinae huiusmodi potuerint".

165 Before the establishment of the Macao trading colony in 1557, Portuguese merchants had routinely acquired Chinese slaves from local traders in Japan. In fact, it was not until the 1570s that the majority of enslaved humans acquired in Japan were actually of Japanese origin. See Sousa, *The Portuguese Slave Trade*, 48.

166 Sousa, *The Portuguese Slave Trade*, 183–184.

167 Fagundez, *De iustitia et contractibus*, lib. II, cap. 3, no. 7, 150: "De Sinensibus mancipiis nullus scrupulus esse potest".

168 Fagundez, *De iustitia et contractibus*, lib. II, cap. 3, no. 7, 150, original emphasis: "ut causam huius rei percipias, integrum paragraphum Nicolai Trigautii nostrae Societatis, *libri sui de expeditione ad Sinas primi cap. 9*".

169 On Ricci, see Laven, *Mission to China*.

> into slavery [...]. Sometimes this is done when there is really no necessity, and children are separated from their parents forever, becoming slaves to the purchaser, to be used for whatever purpose he pleases. The result of this practice is that the whole country is virtually filled with slaves. [...] Many of them are also taken out of the country as slaves by the Portuguese and the Spaniards.[170]

Ricci's account of enslavement in China was fundamentally incompatible with the moral and juridical foundations of slavery that Iberian theorists, and indeed Fagundez himself, advocated. But faced with the realities of slaving in the Ming empire and the equally real presence of Chinese slaves in the wider Iberian world, he was prepared to abandon his principles. In this remarkable passage, Fagundez not only argued against the opinion of his fellow Jesuit Molina. To drive home the point that all the owners of enslaved persons from China were safe in conscience, he was prepared to abandon the language of natural law.

This radical shift exemplifies how Portuguese slaving practices in Asia put considerable pressure on Iberian intellectuals. Yet China was an extreme example. Molina, Fagundez, and others agreed that the vast majority of people who came into Portuguese possession in the "East Indies" had been subjected to the same titles that regulated, and licensed, enslavement in the Atlantic and Mediterranean worlds.

3.1 *Asian Slaves or Indigenous Vassals?*

A completely different approach to the problem of Portuguese slaving in Asia was put forward by the Spanish imperial jurist Juan de Solórzano y Pereira. If the matter was viewed from a Castilian perspective, Solórzano maintained in his *Política indiana* of 1648, it was impossible to accept the legitimacy of *any* of the slaves the Portuguese had acquired in the Indian and Pacific Ocean worlds. Even if they were enslaved with a just title and, indeed, "even if the Portuguese say that they had taken and obtained them from among Moors", he argued, they could not be licitly acquired by subjects of the Crown of Castile.[171]

---

170 Fagundez, *De iustitia et contractibus*, lib. II, cap. 3, no. 8, 150, quoting verbatim from Trigault, *De christiana expeditione apud Sinas*, lib. I, cap. 9, 96. Here, I quote from Trigault, *China in the Sixteenth Century*, trans. Gallagher, lib. I, cap. 9, 86.

171 Solórzano, *Política indiana*, ed. Ochoa Brun, vol. 1, lib. II, cap. 1, no. 17, 136: "Eso mismo obligó á no permitir, que aún por titulo de compras, y ventas, que llaman rescates, se consintiese en las Indias de la Corona de Castilla a tener por esclavo los Indios, que los Portuguesses traían á vender a ellas, cogidos, y sacados para este efecto del Brasil, o de la

How was it possible for Solórzano to advance such an astonishing line of argument? In fact, he had previously justified the enslavement of captives taken in Portuguese "just wars" against Muslim polities in the Indian Ocean, referring to them as legitimate slaves by citing Portuguese legislation in his *De indiarum iure* (1629).[172] Yet in his vernacular *Política indiana*, Solórzano highlighted Castilian royal decrees from the 16th century that expressly forbade the enslavement of any "*indios*" from regions under Portuguese jurisdiction—even if they were "from among the Moors" in Asia.[173] In his estimation, the "good faith" that allowed for the possession of enslaved Black Africans "without scruple" did not apply to enslaved Asians.[174]

Although the Iberian Union had already been dissolved by the time the *Política indiana* was published, Solórzano insisted that the prohibition of Indigenous slaving in the Spanish empire, which had been formalized with the New Laws of 1542, also extended to all the peoples subject to the Portuguese "East Indies".[175] As he went on to explain,

> [...] even though father Molina and others make us understand that there, laws and provincial councils have introduced that one can enslave and sell those who are from certain kingdoms, against which the Portuguese are usually waging just wars, or they are mixed with [slaves from] Moors like Javans, Malayans, Bengals [...] or from the nations that customarily

India Oriental, o de otras tierras, y Provincias de la demarcacion de Portugal: aún quando decian, que los havian sacado, y ganado de entre Móros, y que seguian la secta Maometana, o estaban infectos de ella, sobre que se despacharon apretadas, y repetidas Cedulas del año 1550 y 1570".

172 Solórzano, *De indiarum iure*, ed. and trans. Baciero et al., lib. III, cap. 7, no. 115–116, 460–462: "aliquas esse Orientalis Indiae provincias, maurorum ut plurimum colluvione et infectione premixtas [...] quim quibus lusitani iustis et legitimis bellis quotidie decretant; et mancipia, quae in illis capiuntur, lusitanis legibus et Conciliarum Provincialium declarationibus capientibus cedere et ab eis vendi atque ab emptoribus ubique legitime possideri".

173 See the quotation in the footnote before the last.

174 Solórzano, *Política indiana*, ed. Ochoa Brun, vol. 1, lib. II, cap. 1, no. 26, 138: "A lo qual no contradice la práctica, que vemos tan asentada, é introducida de los esclavos Negros, que se traen de Guinéa, Cabo Verde, y otras Provincias, y rios, y pasan por tales sin escrupulo a España, y en las Indias. Porque en estos vamos con buena fé".

175 Solórzano, *Política indiana*, ed. Ochoa Brun, vol. 1, lib. II, cap. 1, no. 18, 136–137: "No se puede pasar en silencio el capitulo de las que llamaron Nuevas Leyes, del año 1542 que ciñendo todo esto con gran generalidad de palabras; dixo las que se siguen: *Item, ordenamos, y mandamos, que de aqui adelante por ninguna causa de guerra, ni otra alguna, aunque sea só titulo de rebelion, ni por rescate, ni de otra manera, no se pueda hacer esclavo Indio alguno*".

> sell themselves to one another, and where fathers even sell their children on account of famines and other urgent necessities; all of this seemed to contradict the laws and decrees of Castile that we have cited.[176]

In fact, Solórzano here not only disagreed with Molina, but also with his own earlier stance in the *De indiarum iure*.

As Tatiana Seijas has demonstrated, the trajectory of Solórzano's writings reflects a broader shift in imperial attitudes toward enslaved Asians, so-called *chinos*, in the Spanish empire. In the late 17th century, "a series of royal decrees condemned the enslavement of native peoples, broadly termed as Indians (*indios*) and ordered officials throughout the empire to liberate them, from the Spanish Philippines to Chile."[177] This mandate also included all Asian slaves who had been transported to colonial Mexico aboard the Manila galleon, even if they came from the regions outside the Spanish empire. In this way, "all chinos became Indians—as a group, they went from being slaves to being free indigenous vassals."[178] But as the final part of this book will show, what it meant to be a free "*indio*" in the Spanish empire remained entangled in thorny legal and political ambiguities.

---

176 Solórzano, *Política indiana*, ed. Ochoa Brun, vol. 1, lib. II, cap. 1, no. 25, 138: "aunque el Padre Luis de Molina, y otros dán á entender, que allí por leyes, y Concilios Provinciales está introducido, que se puedan hacer, y vender por esclavos los que son de algunos Reynos, con quien los Portugueses tienen de ordinario guerras Justas, ó están mezclados con Móros, como son los Javos, Malayos, Bengalas [...] y otros semejantes; ó de las Naciones, que acostumbran entre sí venderse unos á otros, y aún los padres a los hijos por causa de hambre, ú otras urgentes necesidades; tódo esto pareció contradecir á las Leyes, y Cédulas de Castilla, que se han referido".

177 Seijas, *Asian Slaves in Colonial Mexico*, 212.

178 Seijas, *Asian Slaves in Colonial Mexico*, 213. On the making of the category of "*indio*", see also Van Deusen, *Global Indios*.

PART 2

Slavery and the Household

Introduction to Part 2

In recent years, scholars have begun to emphasize the importance of the household in Renaissance and early modern political thought. The modern conceptual divide between public and private does not map onto how political life was understood by commentators of Aristotle. As Anna Becker has shown, in the Aristotelian tradition the sphere of the household and the sphere of the city were "mutually dependent, and conceptually interwoven".[1] One of the lenses through which Becker has chosen to investigate the central role of the household in the power structure of the commonwealth is marriage. As is well known, Aristotle himself had insisted that a husband could never be ruled by his wife and that the dynamic of ruling and being ruled, which characterized the government of the city, was absent in the domestic context. But the so-called "civic humanists" understood the rule of the household as a joint venture between husband and wife: "the way that citizens related to each other in the city", as Becker powerfully shows, "was like the husband-wife relationship in marriage".[2] Renaissance commentators of Aristotle like Donato Acciaiuoli (1428–1478) did not deny the natural superiority of men over women. But they were keen to stress the conjugal equality of the spouses. Viewed from this perspective, "[h]usband and wife appear as magistrates, jointly ruling the household".[3]

Scholarly attention to the early modern household and its relation to society is not an altogether new phenomenon. German-speaking historians, in particular, have long been interested in the so-called *Hausväterliteratur* or "patriarchal literature" that flourished in the Holy Roman Empire between the 16th and early 18th centuries.[4] Vernacular manuals on the management of domestic and agricultural affairs, written for noble owners of large estates, became famous through Otto Brunner's ideologically charged work of the mid-20th century.[5] Brunner, also known as co-editor of the *Geschichtliche Grundbegriffe*, was less concerned with using these texts as a window into the social and economic realities of early modern Germany. Rather, he projected his own discontent with modern society onto a mythical past. In Brunner's imagined long

1 Becker, "Gender in the History of Early Modern Political Thought", 853. See also Becker, *Gendering the Renaissance Commonwealth*.
2 Becker, "Gender in the History of Early Modern Political Thought", 859.
3 Becker, "Gender in the History of Early Modern Political Thought", 859–860.
4 See e.g. Hohberg, *Georgica Curiosa*.
5 See above all Brunner, "Das 'ganze Haus' und die alteuropäische Ökonomik".

Middle Ages, the patriarchal power of the paterfamilias served as a nostalgic counterpoint to the allegedly bygone social hierarchy and order of his own present.[6]

Despite its shortcomings, Brunner's work has nonetheless inspired more recent generations of historians to re-examine the household as a crucial site of social and political inquiry.[7] This has been especially true for scholarship on the relationship between domestic and political power in colonial Spanish America.[8] The most intriguing contribution stems from the Argentinian historian Romina Zamora, who has shown that in the early modern Spanish Indies, heads of household not only presided over a "populated house", a *casa poblada*, as Zamora puts it—which encompassed wives, children, enslaved persons, and Indigenous tributaries. They often also held offices in the city they inhabited.[9] This close interconnection of domestic and political power was reflected both in practice and theory. As the jurist Jerónimo Castillo de Bobadilla (c. 1546–1605) wrote in his manual for civil administrators, "the well-governed family is the true image of the commonwealth, and domestic authority is similar to supreme authority".[10]

In his study of the household community in early modern Jesuit thought, Christoph Haar likewise emphasizes the interdependence of household and commonwealth.[11] At the same time, Haar maintains that the domestic sphere was merely "a para-political space" for Iberian theologians of the 16th and 17th centuries. He concludes that "it is imperative to note that the household as such was not political".[12] According to Haar, theologians like Domingo de Soto or Tomás Sánchez inherited from Aquinas a dual account of matrimony: on the one hand, as a hierarchically ordered partnership between man and woman, centered on the male-dominated act of procreation, and on the other, as an equal union between husband and wife, grounded in marital friendship and

6 See the excellent discussion in Groebner, *Das Mittelalter hört nicht auf*, 119–122.

7 See e.g., Schmidt-Voges, "Das Haus in der Vormoderne"; and Duve, "Der blinde Fleck der 'Oeconomia'?". For a recent account of the presence of enslaved Black Africans in German households that builds on Brunner's analytical toolkit, see Dürr, "'German Home Towns' Reloaded".

8 On this point, see Tau Anzoátegui, "Provincial and Local Law of the Indies", 244–245.

9 Zamora, *Casa poblada y buen gobierno*, 24 and 90–91.

10 Bobadilla, *Política para corregidores*, lib. III, cap. 8, no. 18: "la familia bien regida es la verdadera imagen de la Republica, y la autoridad domestica semejate a la autoridad suprema". See the discussion in Zamora, *Casa poblada y buen gobierno*, 179–180. We shall turn to Bobadilla in more detail in Chapter 5.

11 Haar, *Natural and Political Conceptions of Community*, 180–181 and 247.

12 Haar, *Natural and Political Conceptions of Community*, 279.

joint management of the household. In Haar's estimation, it was precisely this uneasy tension between hierarchy and equality that ultimately set the household apart from the truly political sphere of human action.[13] Yet does Haar's strict dichotomy between a natural-hierarchical and a political-equal vision of marriage truly hold up in the writings of early modern Iberian theorists? And how might the idea of slave marriage complicate that conceptual divide?

---

13 Haar, "Tomás Sánchez and Late Scholastic Thought on Marriage and Political Virtue", 82. The argument is restated in Haar, *Natural and Political Conceptions of Community*, 208 and Chapter 4, *passim*.

CHAPTER 4

Marriage and Slavery

For over a millennium, the idea that enslaved persons could enter matrimony was inconceivable from the perspective of the Church. But the medieval canon law tradition fundamentally transformed the Catholic position on the validity of slave weddings. As David d'Avray explains, the "crucial milestone" was the 13th-century incorporation of a decree into the *Liber Extra*, which granted enslaved people a right of marriage, even against their master's will.[1] Contemporary theologians like Aquinas were quick to pick up this novel dictum, as we shall see. But above all, scholars have emphasized the "global implications" of this shift in the ecclesiastical account of servitude.[2] With the imperial expansion of the Iberian crowns, the idea of slave matrimony was exported across the Atlantic and profoundly shaped the colonial societies of the Americas. An increasingly pressing issue at councils and synods held in the New World, it led to the excommunication of many who had prevented their slaves from entering into marital union. It also figured prominently in the concerns of priests, who in their pastoral visitations sought to convey the Church's teachings to its subjects on the ground.[3]

Yet enslaved humans not only featured in societies on the imperial fringes. Marriages of and among slaves, as well as informal relationships between Iberian masters and their servile concubines, were already commonplace in Lisbon and Seville in the second half of the 15th century.[4] Enslaved men and women entered into matrimony not only with their owners, but also with free persons who were not their owners, and just as often they celebrated matrimony with other enslaved persons.[5] Legally speaking, the weddings of slaves were regulated under the *Siete Partidas*, which had incorporated the notion of a servile right to matrimony shortly after the completion of the *Liber Extra* in the 13th century.[6] While most historians resist what Michelle McKinley has termed

1 D'Avray, "Slavery, Marriage and the Holy See", 348. The key locus in the *Liber Extra* is X.4.9.1.

2 D'Avray, "Slavery, Marriage and the Holy See", 349.

3 McKinley, *Fractional Freedoms*, 74–76. On pastoral visitations, see Ramos, "Pastoral Visitations".

4 Velázquez Gutiérrez, *Mujeres de origen africano*, 101–105.

5 Bono, *Schiavi*, 152–153.

6 The *Liber Extra* was completed in 1234, and the *Siete Partidas* assumed the force of law as early as 1265.

a "biopolitic vision of law",[7] the relevance of legal discourse to the history and scholarship surrounding slaving is undisputed, as reflected in its ubiquitous presence in archival records.[8]

Domestic slavery was a decidedly urban phenomenon, and the sphere of the household extended not just to the family house and estate but also beyond its physical boundaries.[9] This meant that enslaved persons operated in networks beyond the reach of their owners.[10] But "Iberian litigiousness" was such a pervasive social practice that slaves on both sides of the Atlantic were also routinely exposed to legal discourse in the very homes of their masters.[11] Especially in the urban centers of the New World, enslaved persons "navigated juridical and institutional channels with ease"[12] and made "modest demands for liberty decorously veiled in a paternalistic discourse".[13] Colonial authorities actively encouraged marriages among the predominantly Black African slave population, principally "as a way to ensure the continuity of slave labor".[14]

In practice, the right of matrimony was far more limited for enslaved persons in Iberia. Despite legal provisions affirming that right, masters often opposed their slaves' marriages so that, in fact, "their consent was necessary".[15] Slaveholders, as Aurelia Martín Casares notes, adopted "an attitude of frank hostility against the laws that permitted the union of their slaves, so that marriages between enslaved persons were relatively exceptional".[16] It was only in the wake of the Council of Trent that ecclesiastical authorities also increased the support of slave marriages in the Old World.[17] The famous *Tametsi* decree, which was passed at Trent in 1563, determined that the foundation of Catholic marriage

7 McKinley, *Fractional Freedoms*, 7. The importance of law is most forcefully emphasized in Phillips, *Slavery in Medieval and Early Modern Iberia*, ch. 6 and *passim*.

8 On the regulation of slavery in the *Siete Partidas*, see Piqueras, *Derecho antiguo y esclavitud moderna*, 139–184.

9 On slavery in the rural context of Spanish America, see O'Toole, *Bound Lives*.

10 Many of the less affluent owners of enslaved persons, for instance, rented them out as daily wage laborers. See Martín Casares, *La esclavitud en la Granada*, 330–332; and McKinley, *Fractional Freeedoms*, 16.

11 McKinley, *Fractonal Freedoms*, 4.

12 Bennett, *Africans in Colonial Mexico*, 128. This point is also emphasized in Proctor, "*Damned Notions of Liberty*", 39 and 57–59.

13 McKinley, *Fractional Freedoms*, 5.

14 Martín Casares and Delaigue, "The Evangelization of Freed and Slave Black Africans", 230.

15 Bono, *Schiavi*, 153: "il matrimonio fra schiavi, per il quale occorreva il consenso del padrone o dei padroni rispettivi, tendezialmente contrarii".

16 Martín Casares, *La esclavitud en la Granada*, 360: "Los amos mostraban una actitud de franca hostilidad contra la legislazión de las uniones de sus esclavos/as y los casamientos entre personas esclavizadas eran relativamente excepcionales".

17 Phillips, *Slavery in Medieval and Early Modern Iberia*, 90–91.

was the will and consent of the spouses.[18] This marked emphasis on the free election of one's marital partner also put pressure on the Spanish vision of promoting strictly endogamous matrimony among slaves in the Americas.[19]

In what follows, however, I will argue that the nexus of slavery and marriage was not just a legal problem. Weddings of enslaved persons also carried far-reaching political, social, and economic implications. This becomes clear when we shift our focus from the court records studied by social historians to the writings of the intellectual and political authorities of the time. The Iberian imperial theorists conceptualized slaves as objects of possession that were subject to the logic of commodification. Yet enslaved persons were always also embedded in household communities. They were integrated into a patriarchal space in which the head of household exercised authority over his wife, children, and enslaved subjects alike. As Luis de Molina put it, "the three powers of the domestic sphere are united in the paterfamilias".[20] Conceptually speaking, slavery thus oscillated between a horizontal legal relationship and a vertical power structure, and the status of enslaved persons shifted between property and person.

The notion of slave matrimony added yet another dimension to these issues and further complicated the matter. For through marriage, enslaved persons became spouses, parents, and even heads of their own household—roles that clashed in fundamental ways with their simultaneous status as commodities and subordinates within the masters' domain. In this sense, the coupling of marriage and slavery seemed to destabilize the very categories that Iberian theologians and jurists were advocating, creating an aporia within their political theory. But this issue was not merely conceptual. It was also a practical problem, since the legal protection of the marriage bond posed a serious threat to the free disposal of "human commodities" so central to the Spanish and Portuguese colonial endeavors. How, then, did the Iberian imperial theorists confront these issues? What was their vision of the "politics of slave marriage"? And how did they situate the agency of enslaved persons vis-à-vis the authority of slaveholders?

---

18 Latasa, "'If they remained as mere words'", 13.

19 See Velázquez Gutiérrez, *Mujeres de origen africano*, 251–252, who notes that marriages between enslaved Africans and free Spaniards were not uncommon.

20 Molina, *DIEI*, vol. 1, tr. II, disp. 22, no. 7, col. 113: "Tres potestates explicatae in patrefamilias uniuntur".

1 Slaves, Children, and the Nature of Marriage

The Iberian imperial theorists' discussions of marriage and enslavement have been sorely absent from modern scholarship because they grew out of a tradition of commentaries on Peter Lombard's *Sentences* that has since fallen into obscurity.[21] Much of the early modern "renewal of theology" was advanced through commentaries on the *Summa theologiae*, which was the primary theological source to be taught and commented on.[22] But the text to be re-read on the theme of slave matrimony was Aquinas's commentary on Book Four of the *Sentences*.[23] This early and neglected text from Aquinas's student days was "the first and also the most extensive Thomist treatment on marriage".[24] And it is also a veritable treasure trove of Aquinas's otherwise scarce remarks on slavery.[25] Little wonder, then, that the early modern Iberian theologians and jurists would form their own views on the subject in conversation with Aquinas's foundational stance.[26]

1.1 *The Natural Right of Marriage and the Limits of Slavery*

Aquinas addressed the question of marriage and enslavement in his commentary on Distinction 36 of the Fourth Book of the *Sentences*. He began by stating that marriage, in its most basic definition, was a contract in which the two spouses obliged themselves "to render to each other what they were due".[27] The

21 Notable exceptions are Lanza and Toste, "The *Sentences* in Sixteenth-Century Iberian Scholasticism"; Brufau Prats, *La escuela de Salamanca*, 114–117; and Höffner, *Kolonialismus und Evangelium*, 327–341.

22 This phrase is borrowed from the title of Belda Plans's *La escuela de Salamanca y la renovación de la teología en el siglo XVI*.

23 Aquinas, *Scriptum super Sententiis*, ed. Alarcón and Busa, lib. 4, dist. 36, q. 1.

24 Haar, "Tomás Sánchez and Late Scholastic Thought on Marriage and Political Virtue", 86.

25 This is largely unknown even among historians of medieval enslavement. See e.g., Epstein, *Speaking of Slavery*, 145–146. Epstein solely points to Aquinas's brief reflections on slavery in the *Summa* and concludes that "Aquinas knew less about slavery and did not write much about it" (145).

26 Although Francisco de Vitoria also investigated questions relating to marriage and equally lectured on the Fourth Book of the *Sentences*, it is unlikely that he ever comprehensively addressed the nexus of slavery and marriage. He did not address the matter in his *Relectio de matrimonio*. The only other surviving work that reflects Vitoria's teaching on Book IV of the *Sentences* does not examine the issue either: Chavez, *Summa sacramentorum ecclesiae*. On the question of Vitoria's authorship of this work by his disciple Chavez, and how it relates to Vitoria's own manuscripts, see Lanza and Toste, "The *Sentences* in Sixteenth-Century Iberian Scholasticism", 442–451.

27 Aquinas, *Scriptum super Sententiis*, ed. Alarcón and Busa, lib. 4, dist. 36, q. 1, a. 1, corp.: "in matrimonii contractu obligatur unus conjugum alteri ad debitum reddendum".

problem was, however, that slaves were unfree and thus incapable (*impotens*) of freely performing their conjugal duties by their own will.[28] Slavery, it thus seems, constituted a severe impediment to marriage from the Thomist perspective. Yet Aquinas proceeded to explain that anyone could voluntarily accept a detriment in what they were owed. The marriage between a free and an enslaved person could thus be licit and binding, provided the stakes were clear.[29] The only condition under which such a union would be invalid, as the authoritative stance of the *Liber Extra* proclaimed, was if the free spouse entered into the contract unaware of the other's enslaved status, which canonists called *error conditionis*.[30]

Domingo de Soto, in his own commentary on the *Sentences*, confirmed the opinion of his intellectual predecessor. While the condition of enslavement might not necessarily hinder the marital purpose of procreation, the mutual obligation of the spouses, Soto emphasized, consisted in "performing certain duties toward each other in turns; to administer the household, to educate one's offspring, and to govern the family".[31] Slavery hindered this "thick" account of marriage. Enslaved persons, he insisted, were obligated to disclose their enslaved status to their future spouse and to clarify that they were not going to be able to perform those services at will.[32] In this sense, Soto made clear that the *error conditionis* did not lie in the condition of slavery as such. Rather, what was problematic was the concealment of that status and the resulting lack of informed consent.[33] As the Jesuit Tomás Sánchez would later add in his eminent multivolume treatise on the sacrament of marriage, such deceptive silence brought about "a most serious violation of the free spouse's right" and thus voided the contract of marriage.[34]

---

28 Aquinas, *Scriptum super Sententiis*, ed. Alarcón and Busa, lib. 4, dist. 36, q. 1, a. 1, corp.

29 Aquinas, *Scriptum super Sententiis*, ed. Alarcón and Busa, lib. 4, dist. 36, q. 1, a. 1, corp.

30 Aquinas, *Scriptum super Sententiis*, ed. Alarcón and Busa, lib. 4, dist. 36, q. 1, a. 1, s. c. 1: "quod decretalis, dicit de conjugio servorum, quod error conditionis impedit contrahendum matrimonium, et dirimit contractum". The reference was to X.4.9.2.

31 Soto, *In quartum*, vol. 2, dist. 35, q. unica, a. 2, 244: "Contractus coniugalis eam vim habet, ut alterutrum se coniuges obligent, tum debitum sibi invicem reddere, tum in eadem domo et proles educare, et gubernare familiam".

32 Soto, *In quartum*, vol. 2, dist. 35, q. unica, a. 2, 244: "si ergo aut vir aut foemina impotens est haec munera persolvere, ignorantia eiusmodi personae contractum vitiat, atque adeo matrimonium tollit". Soto, too, referred to X.4.9.2.

33 Soto, *In quartum*, vol. 2, dist. 35, q. unica, a. 2, 246: "Conditio enim servitutis non est per se impedimentum, ut cognatio, sed re lata ad consensum".

34 Sánchez, *DSMS*, vol. 2, lib. VII, disp. 19, no. 15, 136: "Quando liber contrahit cum serva, conditionis ignarus, sequitur ut non habeat verum consensum in illude matrimonium. [...] Cum enim gravissima iniuria irrogaretur coniugi decepto".

The theological discussion of this abstractly contractual vision of marriage mirrored pressing practical concerns. As Michelle McKinley's analysis of *error de persona* lawsuits in 17th-century Lima shows, marriages between free and enslaved persons were not infrequent.[35] Yet the question was how slaves could enter into a valid marriage contract at all, given that they were under the authority of their masters and lacked the legal liberty to act on their own will.

Aquinas had offered an influential solution to this conundrum. In his view, marriage was rooted in human beings' "natural appetite" for self-preservation: just as eating and sleeping helped preserve the individual, so too was marriage necessary for "the conservation of one's kind through procreation".[36] For this reason, enslaved people were autonomous with regard to acts of natural necessity, and they could transfer the power (*potestas*) over their bodies to their spouse.[37] Early modern Iberian theologians concurred with Aquinas and translated his stance into the language of right. Domingo de Soto insisted that matrimony was a function of the *ius se conservandi*, the natural right of self-preservation.[38] This right, as Soto had shown earlier in his *De iustitia et iure* (1556), was the fundamental right of all natural beings, insofar as "a thing's natural activity constituted its (natural) right".[39] Soto had thus preserved Aquinas's view of marriage as deriving from "natural appetite", that is, as a consequence of natural necessity. In that sense, the right of marriage stood in stark contrast to the notion of *ius* as an expression of human liberty and free will.[40]

Two important consequences followed from this. The first concerned the validity of Roman law. According to Justinian's *Codex*, marriages with enslaved women were strictly forbidden, for the offspring of such unions would inherit

35 McKinley, *Fractional Freedoms*, 109 and ch. 3, *passim*.

36 Aquinas, *Scriptum super Sententiis*, ed. Alarcón and Busa, lib. 4, dist. 36, q. 1, a. 2, corp.: "Sicut autem appetitus naturae est ad conservationem individui, ita est ad conservationem speciei per generationem. Unde sicut servus non subditur domino quin libere possit comedere et dormire, et alia huiusmodi facere quae ad necessitatem corporis pertinent, sine quibus natura conservari non potest".

37 Aquinas, *Scriptum super Sententiis*, ed. Alarcón and Busa, lib. 4, dist. 36, q. 1, a. 2, ad 1: "unde in his quae ad actus naturales pertinent, servus potest alteri, invito domino, sui corporis potestatem per matrimonium praebere".

38 Soto, *In quartum*, vol. 2, dist. 35, q. unica, a. 1, 243: "ita ius servitutis non potuit hominibus ius naturae adimere conservandi tum propria individua, tum et per matrimonia propria specie".

39 Brett, *Liberty, Right and Nature*, 153. For the original passage in Soto, see his *DIEI*, lib. III, q. 1, a. 3, corp.

40 On Soto's distinction between "natural" and "human" natural right, see Brett, *Liberty, Right and Nature*, 149–154.

the servile condition of their mother.[41] This was an issue Aquinas had sidestepped. But Soto argued that slavery, which was introduced by the *ius gentium*, and thus not natural in itself, could not override the most fundamental natural right of self-preservation. The sentence of canon law thus prevailed on this matter, for it was "consonant with natural and divine law".[42]

A further consequence was that the ownership of enslaved persons was limited. "A slave", Soto argued, "does not belong to the master in things concerning nature, but only in view of those services that are added to what is natural".[43] Since matrimony clearly belonged to the former, the slave was "exempt from the master's slavery" regarding the obligations incurred by the marriage contract.[44] In these remarkable passages, Soto highlighted the limits of masters' rights over their slaves, while emphasizing the rights that enslaved persons themselves retained.

Miguel de Palacio even went so far as to suggest that enslaved persons were "*sui iuris* regarding natural acts",[45] as they could perform those actions necessary for their self-preservation—eating, drinking, or sleeping—against their master's will. This was a powerful rhetorical move, given that slaves were precisely *not* of their own right, as Palacio himself conceded.[46] The Dominican Pedro de Ledesma, another Salamancan theologian writing at the end of the 16th century, restated this dictum and added that an enslaved human being "is by nature his or her own guardian regarding natural matters".[47] As a consequence, Ledesma argued, "in marriage, the slave can hand over a right and *dominium* to the other spouse with respect to natural matters, without preju-

41 C.5.5.3.

42 Soto, *In quartum*, vol. 2, dist. 35, q. unica, a. 1, 243: "quicquid civile ius propter suam Rempublicam statuat, non tamen potest iuri canonico, quod naturali et divino consonantius est officere". This point was later restated by Sánchez, *DSMS*, vol. 2, lib. VII, disp. 19, no. 13, 135.

43 Soto, *In quartum*, vol. 2, dist. 35, q. unica, a. 1, 243: "servus non est heri in iis, quae sunt naturalia, sed in aliis servitiis, quae naturalibus adijciuntur".

44 Soto, *In quartum*, vol. 2, dist. 35, q. unica, a. 1, 243: "potest tamen quantum ad munus illud generandi, quod sibi a natura conceditur, in quo a domini servitute exemptus est".

45 Palacio, *Disputationes theologicae*, vol. 2, dist. 30, disp. unica, 669: "Siquidem in actionibus naturalibus sunt sui iuris, omnes servi: quandoquidem, etiam repugnante domino dormire, et comedere, et bibere possunt, et videre, et audire, et caetera".

46 Palacio, *Disputationes theologicae*, vol. 2, dist. 36, disp. unica, 795. See also Soto, *In quartum*, vol. 2, dist. 35, q. unica, a. 1, 242.

47 Ledesma, *De magno matrimonii sacramento*, q. 52, a. 2, 343: "servus non subditur domino nisi in ordine ad civilia obsequia: in his autem quae pertinent ad officia naturae sunt sui iuris […] ab ipsa natura habet ius circa ipsa naturalia, et ad disponendum de seipso circa naturalia: cum sit custos per naturam sui ipsius circa naturalia".

dice to the power and *dominium* that the master has over the slave".[48] The idea that marriage consisted in a mutual exchange of ownership and mastery had already been invoked by Francisco de Vitoria.[49] But Ledesma revived Vitoria's dictum in a novel context and with a twist. Like Soto and Palacio, he sought to underline that the alienation of freedom in slavery and the mutual transfer of rights in marriage were neither all-encompassing nor necessarily overlapping. It was possible for one and the same person to be ruled and owned by both a master and a spouse.

The view that the right to marriage derived from "nature nature" rather than "human nature" was widely accepted among Iberian theorists into the 17th century, and was also affirmed by Tomás Sánchez, the principal Jesuit authority on marriage.[50] Sánchez maintained that it was therefore not lawful for masters to punish enslaved subjects for having entered into the bond of marriage.[51] They could, however, licitly revoke any benefits granted to the slave, for these had been conceded on a purely voluntary basis. "In the same way, the father cannot hinder his son's marriage through grave threats, but he can still threaten his son insofar as is permitted by his rights, such as with disinheritance, for instance".[52] In so arguing, Sánchez concluded his discussion of the natural marriage rights of enslaved persons by understanding the master's power over slaves in terms of the father's authority over children.

1.2 *Filial Obedience and the Limits of Natural Right*

This analogy between sons and slaves was not, in fact, Sánchez's innovation. In the context of his discussion of obedience in the *Summa*, Aquinas had made a remarkably similar statement more than three centuries earlier. In response to the question of whether subjects were obliged to obey their superiors in all things, Aquinas had posited that

48 Ledesma, *De magno matrimonii sacramento*, q. 52, a. 2, 344: "Et ita servus per matrimonium potest tradere facultatem et dominium alteri coniugi in ordine ad naturalia sine praeiudicio potestatis et dominii, quod habet dominus supra servus".

49 See Vitoria, *De matrimonio*, in *Relectiones theologicae XII*, vol. 1, no. 1, 435–436.

50 See Sánchez, *DSMS*, vol. 2, lib. VII, disp. 21, no. 3–5, 147–148. On the distinction between "human nature" and "nature nature", see Brett, *Changes of* State, 5–6.

51 This point had also been made by Ledesma, *De magno matrimonii sacramento*, q. 52, a. 2, 343.

52 Sánchez, *DSMS*, vol. 2, lib. VII, disp. 21, no. 5, 148: "Sicut nec pater potest matrimonii contractum filio impedire, mala minando, potest tamen quae iure permissa sibi sunt, minari: ut exhaeredationem casu, quo ius sibi permittit". This was later reiterated by the Portuguese Jesuit Fagundez, *In quinque praecepta decalogi*, vol. 1, lib. IV, cap. 14, no. 5, 575.

> [...] man is not bound to obey another man, but only God, in those things that pertain to the nature of the body, because all humans are equal by nature, such as in those things that pertain to the preservation of the body and the procreation of children. For this reason, slaves do not have to obey their masters, and neither do children have to obey their parents, regarding the celebration of marriage, the preservation of chastity, or other things of this sort.[53]

Children and enslaved persons, it thus seems, were both equally free to celebrate marriage by their own will, precisely because marriage was ultimately grounded in self-preservation.[54]

When Francisco de Vitoria revisited this issue in his commentary on the *Secunda secundae*, he noted that the question of whether children could licitly marry against paternal will was, in fact, a thorny matter. "It is astonishing", he wrote, "that Aquinas argued that children are not bound to obey their parents regarding the celebration of matrimony, the preservation of virginity, and things of the like".[55] The problem was that this dictum was incompatible with the idea that the daughter could be punished with disinheritance if she married against her father's will. Although Vitoria did not make this point explicitly, this had been laid down in the contemporary civil legislation of Castile.[56] The fact that the daughter could be punished, Vitoria insisted, meant that "therefore she sins, for she would not be punished if she did not sin".[57] How, then, could these two clashing perspectives be reconciled?

Vitoria reminded his readers that, apart from the passage under consideration in the *Summa*, Aquinas had also articulated a somewhat different position

---

53 Aquinas, *Summa*, ed. Alarcón and Busa, 2a2ae, q. 104, a. 5, corp.: "In quibus tamen etiam, secundum ea quae ad naturam corporis pertinent, homo homini obedire non tenetur, sed solum Deo, quia omnes homines natura sunt pares, puta in his quae pertinent ad corporis sustentationem et prolis generationem. Unde non tenentur nec servi dominis, nec filii parentibus obedire de matrimonio contrahendo vel virginitate servanda, aut aliquo alio huiusmodi".

54 On the implications of Aquinas's notion of obedience for the relationship between the individual and the *civitas*, and its reception in early modern Catholic natural law, see Brett, *Changes of State*, 144–149.

55 Vitoria, *Comentarios a la Secunda secundae*, ed. Beltrán de Heredia, vol. 5, q. 104, a. 5, no. 3, 213: "est mirabile, quia dicit [i. e., Aquinas] quod filii non tenentur parentibus obedire de matrimonio contrahendo vel virginitate servanda aut aliquo alio huiusmodi".

56 See the *Leyes de Toro*, l. 49. We shall return to this law in more detail below.

57 Vitoria, *Comentarios a la Secunda secundae*, ed. Beltrán de Heredia, vol. 5, q. 104, a. 5, no. 3, 213: "Sed in contrarium est de filia, quia ipsa punitur gravi poena, quia potest exheredari a parentibus: ergo peccat, quia non puniretur si non peccaret".

in his commentary on the *Sentences*. In this latter text, Aquinas argued that while fathers lacked any coercive force over their children's marriage choices, they still had some indirect power over them. A father, as Aquinas had put it, "can induce his son to marry by a rational cause" and his command was thus compelling insofar as "this cause obliges the child by necessity or honesty".[58] It therefore appeared, as Francisco de Vitoria commented, that in ignoring the father's "licit and morally right (*honestum*)" command, the child "sins mortally".[59]

Yet, at the same time, Vitoria emphasized that only *law* could oblige in conscience.[60] And, for that reason, it was possible to argue that disobeying the father's *will* was not a sinful act after all:

> [...] if the daughter approaches the bishop and tells him: 'Lord, I'd like to marry so-and-so, and my father does not let me', then the bishop will give her permission, saying, 'you may marry with God.' [...] Hence, since God made her free, and the same applies to the son, it seems that he wanted to give them this privilege for the sake of marriage, so that they could marry whomever they wished.[61]

In his final words on the issue, Vitoria considered filial liberty in marriage as a consequence of the specifically human freedom that God had granted to mankind alone. This is significant because it suggests that marriage could not be entirely reduced to the necessity that governed the natural world at large. But in integrating Aquinas's commentary on the *Sentences* into the discussion

58 Aquinas, *Scriptum super Sententiis*, ed. Alarcón and Busa, lib. 4, dist. 29, q. unica, a. 4, corp.: "sed potest eum inducere ex rationabili causa; et tunc sicut se habet filius ad causam illam, ita se habet ad praeceptum patris; ut si illa causa cogat de necessitate vel de honestate, et praeceptum similiter cogat, alias non".

59 Vitoria, *Comentarios a la Secunda secundae*, ed. Beltrán de Heredia, vol. 5., q. 104, a. 5, no. 3, 214: "Si tamen rationabiliter pater vellet quod filia non nubat, et hoc esset licitum et honestum, et ipsa non vellet facere, peccaret mortaliter, quia est in re gravi."

60 Vitoria, *Comentarios a la Secunda secundae*, ed. Beltrán de Heredia, vol. 5., q. 104, a. 5, no. 3, 214: "Secundo potest dici quod saltem non est peccatum mortale; nam leges dant actionem in foro conscientiae." On the broader political and philosophical implications of this argument, see Brett, "Later Scholastic Philosophy of Law", 352–359.

61 Vitoria, *Comentarios a la Secunda secundae*, ed. Beltrán de Heredia, vol. 5., q. 104, a. 5, no. 3, 214: "Quia si filia veniret ad episcopum et diceret ei: señor, yo me quiero casar con fulano, y no me deja mi padre, ipse episcopus daret ei licentiam et diceret: nubas cum Domino. Ergo signum est quod non est peccatum mortale, quia alias episcopus non daret ei licentiam nubendi. Unde quia Deus fecit illam liberam, et ita filium, videtur quod voluerit ratione matrimonii dare illis hoc privilegium, quod possint cuicumque voluerint nubere".

of filial obedience in the *Summa*, Vitoria also highlighted that the question of whether children could licitly marry against the will of their parents was highly ambiguous, and a lot less straightforward than a reading of the *Secunda secundae* alone might suggest. Vitoria did not propose a definitive solution to the conundrum raised by Aquinas's paradoxical accounts, and by the uneasy tension between the natural right of matrimony and the legal punishment of filial disobedience. Nor did he address the broader implications of this issue, or the fact that Castilian civil law regulated marriage in a markedly gendered way.

Domingo de Soto sought to provide a more comprehensive account, but he began by complicating the matter. The decisive argument that compelled Aquinas to reject the idea of forcing children to marriage, Soto explained, was that "matrimony is a certain kind of perpetual slavery, as it were, and the father cannot force his son to this, because of the son's free condition".[62] Yet the analogy between marriage and enslavement threatened to undermine the very conclusion it was supposed to support. After all, Soto himself had conceded that under the pressure of necessity, fathers could legitimately sell their children into slavery.[63] His first challenge, then, was to explain that forcing one's offspring into the quasi-servile condition of marriage differed from the parental alienation of children into *servitus civilis*.

Soto's solution homed in on the idea that marriage was more than just a bodily condition. While slavery "does not require love, and it is sufficient for the slave to serve with fear", he explained, "the marriage relation, by contrast, demands the mutual love of the spouses".[64] In Soto's view, the key difference between marriage and slavery was that the latter coerced the child solely in the body, and not the mind. This originally Senecan dictum had found its way into the early modern Iberian discourse through the writings of Aquinas. In drawing on Seneca's idea that a slave's "mind is independent, *sui juris*", Aquinas had argued that "in matters that pertain to the interior motion of the will, a man is not bound to obey man, but God alone; but a man is bound to obey man in those things that are enacted externally by means of the body".[65]

---

62 Soto, *In quartum*, vol. 1, dist. 29, q. 1, a. 4, 158: "probat Divus Thomas [...] matriomonio sit quaedam quasi servitus perpetua, nequit pater filium quippe qui liberae conditionis, est, cogere". For the original passage in Aquinas, see *Scriptum super Sententiis*, ed. Alarcón and Busa, lib. 4, dist. 29, q. unica, a. 4, corp.

63 See Soto, *In quartum*, vol. 1, dist. 29, q. 1, a. 4, 158. We have also encountered Soto's argument above in Chapter 3.

64 Soto, *In quartum*, vol. 1, dist. 29, q. 1, a. 4, 158: "Negatur consequentia, tum quia servitus non exigit amorem, sed satis est, ut servus timore serviat, cum tamen coniugale commercium suapte natura mutuum amorem coniugum exposcat".

65 Aquinas, *Summa*, ed. Alarcón and Busa, 2a2ae, q. 104, a. 5, corp., qtd. and trans. in Brett,

On the one hand, this reinforced the idea that marriage was not rooted merely in natural necessity, but was also bound up with the distinctly human ability to direct and express one's will through the use of reason. But, on the other, as Soto went on to explain, it demonstrated that only marriage was truly perpetual. Whereas an enslaved person could, in principle, be freed from servitude, marriage endured until death. And it was precisely for this reason, Soto concluded, that a father could lawfully sell his children into slavery, yet he could not compel them to marry.[66]

Like Vitoria before him, however, Soto also pointed to Aquinas's idea that a father's command, when issued under the pressure of necessity, and for a morally upright reason, obliged his children under the punishment of mortal sin.[67] Soto was aware that this latter assertion appeared to contradict his own emphatic insistence on the freedom of marriage. For if children were bound, under the punishment of mortal sin, to obey their parents, he conceded, "this just is coercion".[68] The task he set for himself, then, was to show that this was not in fact the case.

Soto approached the matter through the lens of Roman law, specifically the law *Si patre cogente* in the *Digest*. In his view, this law epitomized how licit paternal coercion was compatible with the notion that children married by their own volition.[69] Indeed, the Roman legal text declared that the son "marries a wife that he would not have married, had he been left to his own free will, but he still celebrates marriage because marriage cannot take place without the consent of the parties".[70] Soto had thus, in a sense, solved the issue, while sidestepping questions at the heart of the matter: How was it possible to assume that children would consent to such coercion? And what *was* the coercive force of paternal commands regarding the marriages of their children?

Changes of State, 144. For the original passage in Seneca, see *De beneficiis*, in *Moral Essays*, ed. and trans. Basore, vol. 3, lib. III, 20.

66 Soto, *In quartum*, vol. 1, dist. 29, q. 1, a. 4, 158.

67 Soto, *In quartum*, vol. 1, dist. 29, q. 1, a. 4, 158.

68 Soto, *In quartum*, vol. 1, dist. 29, q. 1, a. 4, 158: "Videtur secunda conclusio tertiae repugnare, quippe quae concedi teneri filium nonnunquam parere parenti sub poena peccati mortalis: hoc enim est cogi".

69 Soto, *In quartum*, vol. 1, dist. 29, q. 1, a. 4, 158: "Respondetur nullam esse repugnantiam. [...] Et sic intelligitur l. Si patre cogente".

70 D.23.2.22: "Si patre cogente ducit uxorem, quam non duceret, si sui arbitrii esset, contraxit tamen matrimonium, quod inter invitos non contrahitur".

1.3 *Filial Freedom of Marriage after Trent*

When Tomás Sánchez turned to the issue of filial obedience in his treatise *On Marriage*, he noted that the critical question was whether "the child commits a mortal offense if he or she marries against the parents' will without a just cause".[71] By the time Sánchez was writing, the law of the church had undergone several crucial changes. Most relevant for our purposes is that in the wake of the Council of Trent, clandestine marriages were legally prohibited.[72] This entailed, as Sánchez explained, that "children, under mortal guilt, are bound to ask for their parent's advice about marriage"[73] in order to make their intentions known. Although this measure was intended to increase paternal oversight over children's marital choices, after the Council of Trent the church prioritized spouses' free consent for weddings.[74] Much as ecclesiastical authorities protected the right of enslaved persons to marry against their masters' will, they also punished fathers who coerced their children into matrimony.[75] In keeping with the legal reality of the time, Sánchez argued that children were not therefore obliged to comply with their parents' wishes, and "they may licitly marry whomever they want".[76]

Sánchez anchored this point in Aquinas's view on obedience in the *Secunda secundae*, which asserted that "in matters pertaining to the preservation of their own body and the procreation of their offspring, children are not subject to their parents and do not therefore have to follow their advice and will".[77] But in fact, he did not fully abandon the Dominican idea that it was occasionally sinful to resist parental command. Sánchez explained that children were

71 Sánchez, *DSMS*, vol. 1, lib. IV, disp. 23, no. 9, 801: "Difficultas autem est, quando deficit haec causa iusta in filio, an lethaliter delinquat invitis parentibus iniens matrimonium?"

72 Sperling, "Marriage at the Time of the Council of Trent", 98.

73 Sánchez, *DSMS*, vol. 1, lib. IV, disp. 23, no. 10, 802: "teneri filios sub culpa lethali consilium parentum circa matrimonium petere, non tamen illud sequi".

74 Sperling, "Marriage at the Time of the Council of Trent", 77–78. In colonial Mexico, clandestine marriages were encouraged by the church, precisely to push back against the influence of parents (Sperling, "Marriage at the Time of the Council of Trent", 98).

75 Latasa, "'If they remained as mere words'", 25–26.

76 Sánchez, *DSMS*, vol. 1, lib. IV, disp. 23, no. 10, 802: "et ita licite posse ipsis invitis, prius tamen consultis, inire matrimonium, quod volunt". See also Sánchez, *DSMS*, vol. 1, lib. III, disp. 47, no. 13, 660: "Unde valde distat inter matrimonium absque consensu parentum initum, et clandestinum: illud enim non punibile est, sed permissum iure canonico, hoc autem eo prohibetur, gravibusque poenis afficitur".

77 Sánchez, *DSMS*, vol. 1, lib. IV, disp. 23, no. 10, 802: "Probatur posterior pars, ex doctrina D. Thomae 2.2, q. 104, a. 5, corpore, ubi ait, in his quae ad proprii corporis sustentationem, prolique generationem attinent, omnes homines esse pares, nec filios subiici parentibus: ergo non tenentur sequi consilium et voluntatem parentum".

bound to obey their parents' will if marriage was "a means to settle grave conflicts between their parents and relatives, with whom the marriage is to be celebrated".[78] And in so arguing, he was ultimately grappling with the same question that had already troubled Aquinas, Vitoria, and Soto: how could one simultaneously affirm both filial freedom and filial obligation?

Sánchez's solution was to suggest that what obliged the children was not the parental command in and of itself. Rather, it was "by the virtue of piety" that "the son is obliged to look after the father's necessity".[79] This insistence on piety went back to Pedro de Ledesma. In his *De magno matrimonii sacramento* (1592), the Dominican argued that "the father cannot, in itself and absolutely speaking, force his son to enter marriage by command" because he "is neither a prince nor a superior, and thus he cannot properly and rigorously place a command".[80] Ledesma tacitly reminded his readers that only law could oblige in conscience. In so doing, he not only repudiated the idea of filial obedience in marriage but radically diminished the scope of paternal authority. Sánchez appeared to avoid this problem by shifting his focus from a strictly legal duty towards a broader moral one. But in fact, the obligation that piety placed on the child acquired a quasi-legal force that equally obliged the child in conscience.[81]

The discussions by Sánchez and Ledesma thus confirm Christoph Haar's recent observation that the neglected virtue of *pietas* played a significant role in early modern Catholic natural law thinking.[82] But they also reveal that the division between the Dominican and Jesuit theologians on the question of fil-

78 Sánchez, *DSMS*, vol. 1, lib. IV, disp. 23, no. 4, 800: "tenetur filius sub lethali culpa, obedire parenti illud praecipienti. Ut si esset medium ad graves inimicitias componendas, quae essent inter parentes, et consanguineos eorum cum quibus est contrahendum matrimonium".

79 Sánchez, *DSMS*, vol. 1, lib. IV, disp. 23, no. 7, 800: "non tam ex praecepto paterno, quam ex pietatis virtute filium obligantis consulere paternae indigentiae, tenetur obedire. [...] Sic tenet Petrus de Ledesma, De matrimonio, q. 47, arg. 6, dub. 2, concl. 3". See also Sánchez, *DSMS*, vol. 1, lib. IV, disp. 23, no. 4, 800: "Quia ex virtute pietatis tenentur filii subvenire parentum necessitati, ergo quando parentes indigent tali matrimonio, tenebuntur filii obedire".

80 Ledesma, *De magno matrimonii sacramento*, q. 47, a. 6, 270: "Pater per se et absolute loquendo non potest compellere per praeceptum filium, ut contrahat matrimonium [...] nam pater non est princeps nec superior, ergo proprie et in rigore non potest ponere praeceptum".

81 On Sánchez, see the two passages quoted in the footnote before the last. Ledesma, although he clearly disentangled the two virtues, likewise emphasized the binding character of the "superior" virtue of piety. See Ledesma, *De magno matrimonii sacramento*, q. 47, a. 6, 271: "Nam pater non habet virtutem praeceptivam, nam in rigore obedientia, non est erga parentes, sed peccat contra virtutem pietatis quae est superior quam obedientia".

82 Haar, *Natural and Political Conceptions of Community*, 265–276.

ial obedience in matrimony was not clear cut.[83] By drawing on the theory of Pedro de Ledesma, Sánchez translated Aquinas's insistence on the *honestum* into the language of piety. In this sense, Sánchez did not resolve the fundamental tension between the filial freedom of marriage and the moral obligation to follow parental will when it was deemed the morally right course of action—he merely repositioned it.[84]

∴

The final issue Sánchez revisited concerned the validity of contemporary Castilian legislation. A daughter who married against her father's will could justly be disinherited, according to the *Leyes de Toro* (1505), a piece of early 16th-century legislation that was later integrated into king Philip II's civil law code of 1566.[85] This law, as noted above, had put considerable pressure on early modern Iberians' understanding of filial obedience. Vitoria had not offered a comprehensive answer to the question of how it was compatible with the idea of a natural right of matrimony. The first sophisticated solution was offered by Domingo de Soto, who argued that this was a question of the prince's power to regulate marriage—not the father's. While noting that "kings cannot alter that which concerns the substance of marriage", the ruler could nevertheless "define what counts as worthy of punishment, as soon as a marriage offends the common good".[86] This seemed to contradict the dictum that children were free on the question of marriage, a point that Soto insisted was not the case: "For although by this liberty the marriages contracted without paternal consent are valid, this does not mean that the spouses are therefore always exempt from committing a crime that the prince can punish".[87] Viewed from this perspective, as Tomás Sánchez later explained, the lawgiver's intervention was based

83 This calls into question whether the virtue of obedience had particular salience in Jesuit political thought, as Harro Höpfl argues in his *Jesuit Political Thought*, 26–34.

84 This was also noted by the Jesuit Estevão Fagundez, *In quinque praecepta decalogi*, vol. 1, lib. IV, cap. 14, no. 7, 575: "quamvis pater nequeat filii matrimonium impedire minis et terroribus gravibus, potest tamen quando tale matrimonium ipsum non decet, prudenti modo illi obsistere iure suo utens, ut optime docet Sanchez".

85 See the *Leyes de Toro*, l. 49; and the *Nueva Recopilación*, which was published as *Recopilacion de las Leyes destos Reynos*, lib. 5, tit. 1, l. 1. On the relationship between the *Leyes de Toro* and the *Nueva Recopilación*, see Martín Casares, "Domestic Service in Spain", 195.

86 Soto, *In quartum*, vol. 1, dist. 29, q. 1, a. 4, 159: "Non quod principes ea possint, quae sunt de matrimonii substantia demutare, sed tamen quae valeant contrahentes mulctare, ubi in bonum publicum contrahendo delinquerint".

87 Soto, *In quartum*, vol. 1, dist. 29, q. 1, a. 4, 159: "Quod si arguas. Ius canonicum liberam potestatem tribuit filiis matrimonia contrahendi. [...] Nam etsi ob eandem libertatem

on the idea that matrimony was not simply a sacrament of the church, but likewise "a natural and political contract", and it was for this latter reason that marriages, which endangered the peace of the *civitas*, could justly be punished by civil power.[88]

Sánchez himself, however, disagreed with Soto's account of the politics of marriage. "Secular law", he argued, "cannot bring about such punishments, for the administration of marriage pertains to canon law alone".[89] But Sánchez did not seek to undermine the validity of Castilian legislation. Rather, he maintained that the dictum in the *Leyes de Toro* made a crucial point that his Dominican predecessors had sidestepped: "it concerns clandestine matrimony, which is not the same as contracting marriage without the father's consent".[90]

Not only did this close the circle of Sánchez's framing of the whole discussion. Ultimately, it meant that the civil law under consideration solely "imitates and sustains" the sentence of canon law, as Sánchez put it.[91] In so arguing, he tacitly defended the rationale of the *Tametsi* decree passed in Trent in 1563. While spouses were free to choose their husband or wife without parental consent, marriages were only valid if celebrated before a pastor and at least two witnesses.[92] This also meant that the distinctively gendered regulation of marriage in Spanish civil law had lost its purchase in Sánchez's hands. For him, it was merely an iteration of the more fundamental, and non-gendered, sentence of canon law.

---

matrimonia inconsultis parentibus sint valida, non tamen semper contrahentes excipiuntur a delicto, quod princeps punire potest".

88 Sánchez, *DSMS*, vol. 1, lib. IV, disp. 25, no. 1, 807: "quia cum matrimonium, sit sacramentum, et contractus naturalis et politicus [...] at quatenus contractus est, ipsius est curare ut convenienter quieti et paci reipublicae celebretur: ergo potest statuere poenas aliter contrahenti".

89 Sánchez, *DSMS*, vol. 1, lib. IV, disp. 25, no. 5, 809: "id [i.e., such punishments] non posse efficere legem saecularem, sed ecclesiasticam, ad quam de matrimonio pertinet disponere: quae vult non tantum ne absolute impediatur libertas matrimonii contrahendi, sed ne minuatur".

90 Sánchez, *DSMS*, vol. 1, lib. IV, disp. 24, no. 15, 807: "Non l. 49 Tauri, quia loquitur de matrimonio clandestino, quale non reputatur, eo quod desit patris consensu". Compare to the original passage in the *Leyes de Toro*, l. 49: "Mandamos quel que contraxiere matrimonio que la yglesia tuviere por clandestino [...] que sea justa causa para quel padre y la madre puedan desheredar sy quisieren a sus fijas que el tal matrimonio contraxeren lo qual otro ninguno no pueda acusar sy no el padre y la madre muerto el padre".

91 See Sánchez, *DSMS*, vol. 1, lib. III, disp. 47, no. 13, 660: "Quare lege exhaeredantes filiam absque patris consensu nubentem, tanquam iuri canonico adversae, repelluntur: punientes vero clandestinum, tanquam ius canonicum imitantes, ipsumque coadiuvantes, admittendae sunt".

92 Domingo, "Tomás Sánchez", 231.

Despite his disagreement with Vitoria and Soto, however, it is crucial to note that Sánchez did not abandon the central Thomist-Aristotelian notion that the *filii* were under the governing power of their father. He, too, insisted that to ignore paternal commands was morally problematic if and insofar as this went against the demands of piety and charity. In their discussions of filial obedience, all the Iberian theologians complemented and contrasted the "thin" account of marriage that was so characteristic of their understanding of slave matrimony with a much "thicker" understanding of Christian duties, household power, and indeed of marriage itself. Upon closer inspection, then, the initially straightforward association between slaves and children starts to crumble.

According to the Iberian imperial theorists, the *liberi* were implicated in the broader teleology of political life. Children had the license to enter matrimony by their own volition, but their natural right was constrained by parental command, Christian duties, and civil legislation. Children's marriages affected the future, honor, and status of the family. And they posed a potential danger to the political fabric of the city in a way that slave marriages did not. Paradoxically, this meant that the liberty of free children was more constrained than that of unfree slaves.

2 The Politics of Slave Marriage

Thinkers from Aquinas to Sánchez, as we saw, understood enslaved persons' right to matrimony in essentially naturalistic terms. In their discussion of filial obedience, by contrast, they stressed the potential constraints of this freedom—constraints that stemmed not from nature but from the political status of children in the Christian *civitas*. Yet the will of the paterfamilias was not only relevant to free children. It was equally consequential for the enslaved members of the household, whose marriages could not be reduced to mere carnal necessity. Although procreation constituted the central pillar of the marriage contract, conjugal life also entailed the mutual administration of the household and the education of one's children. And it was precisely in view of these broader obligations that the master's consent had far-reaching consequences.

Already Aquinas insisted that "by allowing a slave to enter into marriage, it is understood that the master allows the slave to perform *all* the duties that marriage requires".[93] He insisted that this did not conflict with the status of

93 Aquinas, *Scriptum super Sententiis*, ed. Alarcón and Busa, lib. 4, dist. 36, q. 1, a. 2, ad 3,

slavery, since spousal responsibilities required devotion only "at fitting times", which left enough room to meet the demands of both roles.[94] But if an enslaved person's conjugal duties clashed with their obligations *qua* slave, the former took precedence.[95] In this sense, the master's consent effectively granted the slave all the privileges of marriage, including spousal obligations that extended beyond sexual reproduction.

Was this still true when masters remained silent or even opposed the marriage of an enslaved person? In that case, Aquinas posited, slaves were bound to privilege the master's will in conflicting calls of duty.[96] But he stressed that there were important exceptions to this general rule. In several circumstances, spousal duties still trumped the obligations toward slaveholders—above all, if the wife's chastity was "imminently endangered".[97] Yet without the master's consent, the marriage of an enslaved person was reduced to the bare minimum and thinned down to one basic purpose: the natural act of procreation.

Domingo de Soto and Miguel de Palacio, the two major 16th-century Iberian thinkers who had published a commentary on Book Four of the *Sentences*, agreed with this view. If the master gave his consent to his slave's marriage, Soto argued, "he is compelled by law to allow his slave to live with his wife",[98] even though this was to the detriment of his own claim in the slave.[99] And in the absence of the master's consent, as Palacio asserted, the master's will had to be obeyed more than the spouse's, unless the latter was about to commit

---

emphasis mine: "quia per hoc quod dominus concessit ut matrimonium servus contraheret, intelligitur ei concessisse omnia quae matrimonium requirit".

94 Aquinas, *Scriptum super Sententiis*, ed. Alarcón and Busa, lib. 4, dist. 36, q. 1, a. 2, ad 5: "sed vir tenetur uxori debitum reddere non semper, sed congruis temporibus".

95 Aquinas, *Scriptum super Sententiis*, ed. Alarcón and Busa, lib. 4, dist. 36, q. 1, a. 2, ad 3: "si servus volente domino matrimonium contraxit, tunc debet praetermittere servitium domini imperantis, et reddere debitum uxori".

96 Aquinas, *Scriptum super Sententiis*, ed. Alarcón and Busa, lib. 4, dist. 36, q. 1, a. 2, ad 3: "si autem matrimonium ignorante vel contradicente domino est contractum, non tenetur reddere debitum, sed potius domino obedire, si utrumque simul esse non possit".

97 Aquinas, *Scriptum super Sententiis*, ed. Alarcón and Busa, lib. 4, dist. 36, q. 1, a. 2, ad 3: "Sed tamen in his multa particularia considerari debent, sicut etiam in omnibus humanis actibus; scilicet periculum castitatis imminens uxori, et impedimentum quod ex redditione debiti servitio imperato generat, et aliis huiusmodi: quibus omnibus rite pensatis iudicari poterit cui magis servus obedire teneatur, domino, vel uxori".

98 Soto, *In quartum*, vol. 2, dist. 35, q. unica, a. 1, 243: "Unde si dominus servo facultatem faciat ineundi matrimonium cum ancilla [...] iure tamen cogitur, eum permittere cum uxore habitare [...] non obstante detrimento, quod sibi inde accrescat".

99 It is worth noting that the lack of cohabitation did not necessarily hinder the marriage of slaves in the urban domestic context, as recent studies have shown. See Bennett, *Africans in Colonial Mexico*, 87; and Velázquez Gutiérrez, *Mujeres de origen africano*, 249.

the sin of fornication.[100] At the end of the century, Pedro de Ledesma again restated this authentically Thomist position, foregrounding the critical importance of the master's consent for the enslaved person's use of matrimony.[101] But Ledesma also noted that even if the slaveholder had not agreed with the wedding, "he cannot prevent the use of marriage without a reasonable cause [...] so that slavery does not hinder the reasonable payment of the marital debt, which pertains to the essence of matrimony".[102]

In practice, many slave owners were sympathetic to the marriages of their enslaved subjects because married slaves were tied to the place and therefore less likely to escape.[103] Perhaps Tomás Sánchez was aware of this when, in the early 17th century, he made clear that he was "in no way convinced"[104] by what his contemporaries had discussed so far. In his opinion, the question of whether or not the master had given his approval was completely irrelevant. Instead, Sánchez sought to point out to his readers the fundamental difference between the two institutions in question: matrimony "proceeds and receives its force from the primeval law of nature",[105] whereas enslavement was framed by the *ius gentium*, which was not natural in itself.

Yet how was this conundrum resolved when both *coniux* and *dominus* simultaneously requested the service of their spouse or slave? In cases where servile and conjugal duties clashed, and both master and spouse were in equal necessity, Sánchez argued, the marital duties took precedence—"irrespective of whether the slave had married with or without the master's consent".[106] The notion that the spouse's imminent danger of concupiscence would always allow an enslaved person to prioritize conjugal duties over the master's command was neither new nor contested among the Iberian theorists. But the

---

100 Palacio, *Disputationes theologicae*, vol. 2, dist. 30, disp. unica, 672.

101 Ledesma, *De magno matrimonii sacramento*, q. 52, a. 2, 346: "quando contrahit cum eius voluntate [...] possit libere uti matrimonio caeterum quando non contrahit cum eius voluntate minime".

102 Ledesma, *De magno matrimonii sacramento*, q. 52, a. 1, 338: "dominus non potest impedire redditionem debiti rationabilem, et sine rationabili causa (ut infra dicemus) et ita servitus non impedit redditionem debiti rationabilem, quae pertinet ad essentiam matrimonii".

103 See McKinley, *Fractional Freedoms*, 84.

104 Sánchez, *DSMS*, vol. 2, lib. VII, disp. 21, no. 15, 151: "nulla tamen ratione mihi persuadere possum, aliquid discriminis inter matrimonium utrovis modo contractum interesse".

105 Sánchez, *DSMS*, vol. 2, lib. VII, disp. 21, no. 15, 151: "Quod proficiscatur, ac robus accipiat ex iure naturali primaevo [...] Quod quidem praefertur iuri gentium, ac prius illo est".

106 Sánchez, *DSMS*, vol. 2, lib. VII, disp. 21, no. 15, 151: "atque illi potius obsequendum esse, cuius necessitas magis urget. [...] at ubi caetera sunt paria [...] potiores esse coniugis partes, ut sibi redatur debitum postulanti sive convenienti, sive invito domino matrimonium initum sit".

"thick" conception of servile marriage featured in the theories of Soto, Palacio, and Ledesma was entirely absent from Sánchez's account. By denying the significance of the master's consent, Sánchez stripped the marital right of enslaved persons to its bare bones.

Not all Jesuits writing in the 17th century concurred with Sánchez's opinion. The Spaniard Juan Azor, for instance, returned to the earlier Dominican position. When a master endorsed a slave's marriage, Azor argued, "he implicitly or tacitly wanted his slave to return to his wife what she is due".[107] This underscores that there was no clear-cut divide between the Dominicans and Jesuits on this question. Another alternative view was later advocated by the Portuguese Jesuit Fagundez. He argued that a wide range of "most probable" opinions existed, not least those emanating from Sánchez, Aquinas, and Soto.[108] Rather than endorsing one particular solution, Fagundez argued that the upshot of this debate was that "the slave does not escape the law of slavery in marriage, and he neither becomes *sui iuris* but remains obliged to perform the usual services to his master".[109]

But the most important and influential mid-century Spanish Jesuit, Juan de Lugo, revived and revalidated the opinion of Tomás Sánchez. By agreeing to an enslaved person's wedding, Lugo elucidated, the master was doing nothing more than "allowing the slave to use his or her own right without impeding it".[110] The decisive point was that the master "can consent to his slave's marriage without giving up his own right".[111] For that reason, whether or not the master had consented to the matrimony was irrelevant. In neither case did the master make any concession to the slave that would prejudice his own right. In so arguing, Lugo reinforced Sánchez's critique of the "thick" understanding of servile matrimony articulated by Soto, Palacio, or Ledesma.

---

107 Azor, *Institutionum moralium*, vol. 2, lib. II, cap. 38, 148: "servus aut domini consensu uxorem duxit, aut ipso inscio, vel etiam invito. Si primum, magis debet uxoris ius suum reddere, quam domino obsequium praestare; quoniam eo ipso, quod dominus servi nuptias permisit, implicite, ac tacite voluit, ut servus suae uxori debitum solveret".

108 Fagundez, *In quinque praecepta decalogi*, vol. 1, lib. IV, cap. 14, no. 8–13, 575–576.

109 Fagundez, *In quinque praecepta decalogi*, vol. 1, lib. IV, cap. 14, no. 13, 576: "per matrimonium non effugere servum ius servitutis, nec effici sui iuris; sed adhuc teneri ad consueta domino obsequia exhibenda".

110 Lugo, *DIEI*, disp. 3, sect. 2, no. 39, 47: "solum permissive se habendo et nolendo impedire quod servus suo iure utatur".

111 Lugo, *DIEI*, disp. 3, sect. 2, no. 39, 47: "Quare cum dominus possit consentire absque concessione sui iuris [...]. posse facere dominum circa servum, qui post servitutem matrimonium contrahit, locum habebunt sive sciente et consentiente, sive ignorante aut contradicente domino, matrimonium factum sit".

2.1 *Marriage and Enslavement Reversed*

While much of the debate over the nexus of slavery and marriage centered on questions relating to slaves' capacity for matrimony vis-à-vis their master's power, the Iberian theologians also grappled with a different moral dilemma: what if the conjugal bond preceded the condition of servitude? In such cases, the tension was no longer between the master's ownership of the slave and the enslaved person's right to marry. Rather, the conflict emerged between conjugal obligations and individual liberty. Could freeborn spouses voluntarily commit themselves to servitude against the will of their wife or husband?

Thomas Aquinas approached this issue, noting that, in light of the natural necessity of marriage, the spouses were equal and mutually subject to each other.[112] Yet conjugal life, in the Thomist understanding, was not one of full-scale equality. On the question of the governance of the household, "the husband is the head of the wife and ought to chastise her, but the reverse is not the case".[113] For this reason, Aquinas affirmed that a free husband had the right to "voluntarily drive himself into slavery against the will of his wife".[114] Although he could not inflict any harm upon his wife and was bound to perform his conjugal duties "even against the master's will", he alone had this right of self-enslavement.[115] The wife, by contrast, would always need the approval of her husband as the head of the household.[116]

Following Aquinas, Domingo de Soto maintained that "in the same way that a slave can enter marriage against his master's will, so can a free man enslave himself against the will of his wife".[117] The key point about this analogy was that in Soto's view, both servile and conjugal subjection were limited and did not fully deprive man (*vir*) of his liberty. Like Aquinas, Soto restricted this privilege for the husband as *caput uxoris*.[118]

---

112 Aquinas, *Scriptum super Sententiis*, ed. Alarcón and Busa, lib. 4, dist. 36, q. 1, a. 3, corp.: "vir subditur uxori solum in his quae ad actum naturae pertinent, in quibus sunt aequales". See also Aquinas, *Scriptum super Sententiis*, ed. Alarcón and Busa, lib. 4, dist. 36, q. 1, a. 3, ad 3: "quod quamvis in actu matrimoniali et his quae ad naturam spectant, ad paria vir et uxor iudicentur".

113 Aquinas, *Scriptum super Sententiis*, ed. Alarcón and Busa, lib. 4, dist. 36, q. 1, a. 3, ad 3: "tamen quantum ad dispensationem domus, et ad alia huiusmodi superaddita, vir est caput mulieris, et debet corrigere, non autem e converso".

114 Aquinas, *Scriptum super Sententiis*, ed. Alarcón and Busa, lib. 4, dist. 36, q. 1, a. 3, corp.: "vir nolente uxore potest se alteri in servum dare".

115 Aquinas, *Scriptum super Sententiis*, ed. Alarcón and Busa, lib. 4, dist. 36, q. 1, a. 3, ad 2: "servus tenetur uxori reddere debitum, etiam nolente domino".

116 Aquinas, *Scriptum super Sententiis*, ed. Alarcón and Busa, lib. 4, dist. 36, q. 1, a. 3, ad 3.

117 Soto, *In quartum*, vol. 2, dist. 35, q. unica, a. 3, 247: "sicut servus nolente domino potest se in matrimonium tradere, ita et liber nolente uxore in servitutem mancipare".

118 See Soto, *In quartum*, vol. 2, dist. 35, q. unica, a. 3, 247: "in re domestica vir est caput uxoris. [...] atque adeo absque viri facultate obtenta nequit se in servitutem dedere".

In his earlier treatise *De iustitia et iure*, however, Soto had framed the right of voluntary enslavement in terms of necessity, and thus as a function deriving from the very same natural right of corporeal self-preservation that underpinned the right to matrimony.[119] How, then, was it possible to claim that it only pertained to the husband? The Dominican made a partial concession: although the husband's voluntary servitude did not violate the demands of justice, he nevertheless considered it morally problematic, for the status of slavery undermined the "thick" account of marriage—the mutual obligations beyond sexual intercourse—to which the spouses had originally committed. To enter into such a condition without the compulsion of necessity was, for Soto, "against charity".[120]

Miguel de Palacio went even further. He maintained that the husband's voluntary enslavement was not merely an issue of morality, but even contravened justice. "Nobody can alienate what he does not own without the possessor's license", Palacio argued, "and the husband's body belongs to the wife".[121] His argument hinged on a conception of conjugal subjection that mirrored enslavement as well. However, Palacio sharpened the analogy, emphasizing the coercive force of marriage and describing it in the very same language of ownership so characteristic of the discourse on slavery. Just like enslaved persons, Palacio implied, neither husband nor wife were altogether *sui iuris*, but possessed by each other. He thus circumvented the uneasy tension in Soto's account of self-enslavement as an expression of *natural* right, on the one hand, and as a *male* right, on the other.

Paradoxically, however, Palacio's understanding of marriage *qua* possession was itself implicated in the Thomist understanding of matrimony. As Vitoria put it in his lecture *De matrimonio*, the mutual obligation of the spouses entailed the exchange of *dominium* over each other's bodies: "the wife's body does not belong to the wife, but to the husband, and conversely".[122] And as we saw in the discussion of filial obedience, Soto viewed marriage as perpetual

---

119 See Soto, *DIEI*, lib. IV, q. 2, a. 2, 289.

120 Soto, *In quartum*, vol. 2, dist. 35, q. unica, a. 3, 247: "facit quidem contra charitatem, iusque subinde matrimonii violat, et fraus illa in suum ipsius caput refunditur, quia ex libero sit mancipium, nihilominius quia iure suo utitur, non peccat contra iustitiam, quam debet uxori". This point was later reiterated by Ledesma, *De magno matrimonii sacramento*, q. 52, a. 3, 348.

121 Palacio, *Disputationes theologicae*, vol. 2, dist. 30, disp. unica, 675: "siquidem nemo potest divendere quod non est suum, sine licentia domini, at corpus viri, est uxoris".

122 Vitoria, *De matrimonio*, in *Relectiones theologicae XII*, vol. 1, no. 1, 435–436: "ratione matrimonii constitit in mutua traditione corporis, et obligatione ad usum corporis […] per obligatione intelligo non solum ius, sed verum dominium […] corpus uxoris non est uxoris, sed viri, et contra".

slavery, and hence as a form of ownership, too. In this sense, Palacio disagreed with the Salamancan theologians by drawing on their very own theories of marriage and enslavement.

When Tomás Sánchez entered the discussion in the early 17th century, he confirmed the dictum that, despite the equality of the spouses in view of the "conjugal debt", the wife remained subject to her husband in all other things pertaining to the "government of the household and the family".[123] Consequently, he argued, the wife was unable to enslave herself against the will of her spouse.[124] Like Aquinas and Soto, Sánchez concluded that the husband's right was more extensive. As head of the household, he could voluntarily enter into slavery "in using his own right"[125] and without violating the nature of marriage. But Sánchez also concurred with Soto that this was detrimental to the "thick" conception of marriage and, therefore, morally problematic.[126]

The laws of Castile, however, did not confirm the sentence he had just defended, as Sánchez highlighted by way of an unusually lengthy quote. The *Siete Partidas* stated that if the husband enslaved himself against the wife's will,

> [...] this must not be valid and neither impedes the marriage for this reason. He must first solicit the consent of his wife, who can even remove him from slavery if she wants. This is so because she has a right in him, and because it would bring great dishonor on her, and on her children, if he did so.[127]

---

123 Sánchez, *DSMS*, vol. 2, lib. VII, disp. 23, no. 9, 1582: "Quia ultra obligationem reddendi debiti coniugalis, in qua coniuges sunt pares, subditur viro tanquam capiti, in reliquis, quae ad regimen domus et familiae attinent".

124 Sánchez, *DSMS*, vol. 2, lib. VII, disp. 23, no. 9, 158. In the posthumously published *Consilia moralia*, which was compiled on the basis of notes that Sánchez had left behind, this gendered account is absent. See Sánchez, *Consilia*, lib. I, cap. 1, dub. 4, no. 1, 4: "Quartus titulus, est quando ipsi sua voluntate se vendunt in servos [...] et id non cedat in alterius praeiudicium, ut quia sunt coniugati".

125 Sánchez, *DSMS*, vol. 2, lib. VII, disp. 23, no. 4, 158: "Quod iure suo utatur, nec in uxoris detrimentum cedat quoad debitum coniugale, ut docuit D. Thomas [...] ita docet Sotus".

126 Sánchez, *DSMS*, vol. 2, lib. VII, disp. 23, no. 4, 158: "At verius est non esse contra iustitiam, licet vir faciat in fraudem".

127 Sánchez, *DSMS*, vol. 2, lib. VII, disp. 23, no. 1, 157, original emphasis: "*non deve valere, ni se departira el casamiento porende; ante lo puede la muger demandar, e sacarle aun de la servidumbre, si quisiere. E esto es, porque ha derecho en el, è porque nace ende muy grand deshonra à ella, è à sus fijos, si los oviere*". Sánchez here quoted l. 4, tit. 5, partida 4 of the *Siete Partidas*.

This closely echoes Palacio's forceful attack on the Dominican line of reasoning. Did Sánchez, then, concur with Palacio after all? He did concede that the strict enactment of the *Siete Partidas* was licit and binding within the Spanish commonwealth. Universally speaking, however, Sánchez agreed with Aquinas and Soto in accordance with the "true" sentence of the *ius commune*.[128]

3 Breaking Marriage and Ending Slavery

The Iberian theorists' reflections on the intersection of enslavement and marriage featured a variety of different perspectives. Yet, despite the intricacies, tensions, and disagreements that we have encountered so far, the core idea underpinning the discussion as a whole was that slaves possessed a right to matrimony that lay beyond the authority of their owners. Against this backdrop, one question became particularly contentious: Could married slaves be sold to distant places?

As property, enslaved persons were subject to the dynamics of trade. However, selling married slaves to distant regions was morally problematic because it effectively invalidated their marriage. Recent research has revealed that enslaved people in the Spanish and Portuguese colonies often successfully appealed to the church to prevent the forced separation of a marriage through illegal sale, or to reunite married couples. Michelle McKinley has documented no less than 270 cases for 17th-century Lima alone, where enslaved wives, husbands, or couples appeared before ecclesiastical authorities to vindicate their marital unity. Married slaves, she shows, "were fully aware of their conjugal rights and acted swiftly to protect them".[129] The situation was similar throughout colonial Peru and New Spain.[130] What the Iberian theorists examined between the pages of their treatises, then, were not mere academic quibbles, but urgent real-world conflicts spanning the wider Iberian world. Some even explicitly pointed this out, as we shall see.

Thomas Aquinas had mentioned the issue only in passing, noting that a sale to a distant city was illicit if the enslaved person's wife was unfree herself and

128 Sánchez, *DSMS*, vol. 2, lib. VII, disp. 23, no. 8, 158: "Quamvis autem dicta circa viri venditionem, sint vera attento iure communi: at in hoc Hispaniae regno est servanda lex regia finalis, tit. 5. par. 4".

129 McKinley, *Fractional Freedoms*, 75.

130 See Bennett, *Africans in Colonial Mexico*, 127; Bowser, *The African Slave in Colonial Peru*, 261–262; Wisnoski, "'It is Unjust for the Law of Marriage to be Broken by the Law of Slavery'", 234–252.

could, therefore, not follow her husband, "especially since it is possible to sell one's slave everywhere at a just price".[131] Aquinas did not elaborate further on the subject, as the practical implications of the idea of long-distance sales of slaves were rather limited in his time. But when Domingo de Soto revisited the question, the transatlantic trade in enslaved persons was in full swing. Accordingly, he provided a more comprehensive account.

Soto emphasized, as we saw, that masters consenting to a slave's marriage had to allow the cohabitation of the spouses. The absence of the master's approval did not alter the moral problem posed by selling enslaved persons to remote places. "Such a sale is prohibited", he maintained, "because it corrupts the natural right of marriage".[132] He agreed with Aquinas that a sale to distant cities was problematic insofar as a married slave could be sold "everywhere at a just price".[133] For Soto, there was only one exception: if "the master is in good faith and forced to do so: for instance, if he is going abroad and takes along his slave, either to go to war or for another reason, and there sells the slave under the pressure of necessity".[134] Indeed, this was a real practical issue at the time when masters routinely undertook extensive journeys along with their enslaved subjects, often for several months.[135]

Domingo de Soto's interventions had a lasting impact on later Iberian imperial theorists. He posited that slaveholders were not permitted to sell away married slaves to distant places if they had previously consented to marriage. In Miguel de Palacio's view, however, there was a critical exception to this rule. If an enslaved person endangered the master's life or was about to steal the master's things, it was licit to "sell the slave to distant regions, because the master's consent to his slave's marriage does not include such sacrifices on the mas-

131 Aquinas, *Scriptum super Sententiis*, ed. Alarcón and Busa, lib. 4, dist. 36, q. 1, a. 2, ad 4: "dominus cogendus est ne servum vendat [...] praecipue cum non desit facultas ubique servum suum vendendi justo pretio". See also Aquinas, *Scriptum super Sententiis*, ed. Alarcón and Busa, lib. 4, dist. 36, q. 1, a. 2, arg 4.

132 Soto, *In quartum*, vol. 2, dist. 35, q. unica, a. 2, 243: "talem venditionem esse prohibendam, quia est in perniciem naturalis iuris matrimonii".

133 Soto, *In quartum*, vol. 2, dist. 35, q. unica, a. 2, 243: "Cui quidem sententiae impresentiarum Divus Thomas patrocinatur. Praecipue cum non desit facultas servum iusto pretio ubicunque atque adeo in propria patria vendendi".

134 Soto, *In quartum*, vol. 2, dist. 35, q. unica, a. 2, 243: "Adversaretur enim in primis talis venditio charitati et forsan iustitiae, nisi bona fide herus id compulsus faceret: ut si peregre proficiscens, vel ad bellum, vel aliqua de causa secum servum duceret, et illic egestate pressus illum venderet".

135 Bowser, *The African Slave in Colonial Peru*, 265–266; McKinley, *Fractional Freedoms*, 75 and 96.

ter's side".[136] Tomás Sánchez similarly insisted that an owner's right to preserve his life and property took precedence over the duty to protect a delinquent slave's marriage.[137] To ensure his own survival, the master could alienate all his possessions—including enslaved individuals, who, under these conditions, were reduced to the status of merchandise.

Soto's second major move was to allow the sale of enslaved persons if the master had not approved their marriage and was faced with necessity. Dominicans and Jesuits alike were in agreement. They added that a sale to distant cities was also justifiable if slaveholders were compelled by necessity *at home* and could not secure a "just price" for their human property locally.[138]

Two theologians, however, dissented. Soto's contemporary Miguel de Palacio deemed selling a married slave as indeed detrimental to their marriage. Yet this harm to the abandoned spouse, he argued, "is his or her very own fault, having married an enslaved person without the master's admission".[139] In Palacio's estimation, the master's refusal to sanction the marriage meant that he preserved the right to sell his slave "wherever he wants",[140] because he simply "uses his very own right".[141] He firmly rejected the idea that the natural right of matrimony trumped the non-natural right of slavery, so long as the slaveholder was not in necessity. For Palacio, the decisive factor was temporal priority: which ownership came first—the *dominium* of the master or that of the spouse. And if a person's enslavement preceded their marriage, then the right of slavery prevailed and could only be restricted by the owner of that right. This dictum was later revived by the Quito creole Juan Machado de Chavez (1594–1653), who was educated in Castile and once held the prime chair in canon law at Salamanca. In his *Perfecto confesor y cura de almas* of 1641, the most important manual for confessors of the 17th century, he wrote "that it is licit for the master to sell his slave to remote places whenever he wants, because a slave, who married with-

136 Palacio, *Disputationes theologicae*, vol. 2, dist. 30, disp. unica, 672: "Iudicarim hoc casu non obstante concessa ad coniugium licentia, posse tunc dominium illum distrahere longe quia illa licentia non est interpretanda cum tanta iactura domini".

137 Sánchez, *DSMS*, vol. 2, lib. VII, disp. 22, no. 10, 155.

138 For a Dominican example, see e.g., Ledesma, *De magno matrimonii sacramento*, q. 52, a. 2, 345. For a Jesuit example, see e.g., Sánchez, *DSMS*, vol. 2, lib. VII, disp. 22, no. 11, 155.

139 Palacio, *Disputationes theologicae*, vol. 2, dist. 30, disp. unica, 672: "coniux remanens sibi imputabit, quod acceperit servum in coniugem sine copia domini sui".

140 Palacio, *Disputationes theologicae*, vol. 2, dist. 30, disp. unica, 672: "Porro dominus tunc libere poterit vendere servum, vel ancillam suam quoquo voluerit [...] remanente nihilominus cuoniuge altero apud nos".

141 Palacio, *Disputationes theologicae*, vol. 2, dist. 30, disp. unica, 672: "Utitur namque ipse iure suo". Palacio pointed out that he was here following the argument of the 14th-century Dominican Durand de Saint-Pourçain.

out his master's consent, could not prejudice the right that the master had held before the slave's marriage".[142]

With the notable exceptions of Palacio and Machado de Chavez, however, virtually all the Iberian imperial theorists sided with Soto, noting that the absence of the master's consent did not grant a *carte blanche* to alienate married slaves to distant cities. This position was also shared by ecclesiastical authorities in the Americas, with whose aid enslaved persons often successfully prevented or revoked the long-distance sales of their spouses.[143] And yet, the Iberian theologians all agreed that a master, who did not intend for his enslaved subjects to enjoy the full benefits of conjugal life, was not obliged to uphold such a marriage under all conditions. Slavery was not a natural human condition and did not, therefore, confer authority over an enslaved person's natural acts. But when the survival of slaveholders was at stake, they fell under the law of nature with recourse to a different set of legal claims, and their natural right of self-preservation overrode the enslaved person's natural right of marriage. In this sense, the necessity of the master was constitutive of the slave's precarious status.

3.1 *Selling Slaves Reconsidered*

Yet this was not the end of the story. One of the most prominent Spanish Jesuits of the 17th century launched an ardent critique on how his colleagues approached the question of selling enslaved persons. In his *De iustitia et iure* of 1642, Juan de Lugo argued that if the right to *sell* a married slave was subject to moral and legal limits, then, by extension, the same constraints applied to the purchaser's right to *buy*.[144] None of his predecessors had considered this point. Lugo singled out Tomás Sánchez, the Iberian authority on marriage par excellence, noting that even he had failed to resolve this problem. "It does not therefore appear", Lugo charged, "that the said author argues logically".[145] Fol-

---

142 I am quoting from the 1646 edition: Machado de Chavez, *Perfecto confesor*, vol. 2, lib. VI, parte 7, tr. XII, doc. 10, no. 5, 523: "Pero otros muchos absolutamente defienden que es licito al señor venderle quando quisiere a partes remotas; porque el esclavo casandose sin consentimiento de su señor, no pudo perjudicar al que sobre èl tenia antes que se casasse, para venderle en las partes que gustare, y fuere su voluntad". Machado de Chavez presented clashing opinions and did not explicitly side with either—but the fact that he ended his exposition with the opinion quoted here suggests that he had a preference for this particular stance. Biographical information on Machado de Chavez is from Vargas, *Historia de la cultura ecuatoriana*, 115–117.

143 Seijas, *Asian Slaves in Colonial Mexico*, 184–186.

144 Lugo, *DIEI*, disp. 3, sect. 2, no. 23, 44.

145 Lugo, *DIEI*, disp. 3, sect. 2, no. 23, 44: "Non ergo videtur consequenter loqui ille auctor".

lowing Sánchez's own argument to its conclusion, Lugo noted that the buyer evidently committed "sins against justice in the very same way by keeping the slave near himself, if he knows that the slave's wife is in a place far away and cannot conveniently come to her husband".[146]

Why did Lugo place such considerable emphasis on a point that all the other Iberian intellectuals had considered irrelevant? The answer lay in the political and practical context of the discussion that Lugo emphasized:

> Day by day, prisoners of war are taken—enslaved Turks, Saracens, or other infidels—who in their native land have legitimate wives, who cannot come to their spouses. Nevertheless, the owners of these slaves are not obliged to send them back to their native land, so that they live with their spouses. Not only are they not sent back, but these slaves are actually sold to places even further away. [...] The slave, therefore, has no right by justice (*ius ex iustitia*) not to be sold to distant places, where he cannot enjoy the use of matrimony.[147]

Lugo's move to shift the focus of the discussion to the origin of enslavement had profound implications. From this perspective, the question was not whether slaves had married with or without their master's consent. Instead, Lugo highlighted that the "Turks and Saracens", who were now the slaves of Spaniards, had "legitimate wives" in their homeland. In this sense, Lugo made explicit what many of his predecessors had only implied: marriage was an institution rooted in nature, and therefore not limited to the Christian world.[148] What is less straightforward, however, is why Lugo's turn to the origin of servitude led him to deny enslaved persons a "*ius ex iustitia*", a right by justice, to an inseparable marriage.

Already in the 16th century, Portuguese missionaries in Brazil were grappling with a thorny question: should enslaved West Africans be allowed to remarry

---

146 Lugo, *DIEI*, disp. 3, sect. 2, no. 25, 44: "dominus peccat contra iustitiam distrahendo illum in loca remota; videtur quod eodem modo peccabit detinendo illum apud se, quando sciret uxorem esse in loco remoto, nec posse commode ad virum venire".

147 Lugo, *DIEI*, disp. 3, sect. 2, no. 26, 45: "Quotidie enim captivi, ac servi fiunt Turcae et Sarraceni, ac alii infideles, qui uxores legitimas in patria habent, quae ad ipsos venire non possunt: et tamen domini non tenentur eos ad patriam remittere, ut cum uxoribus habitent, nec solum non remittuntur, sed distrahuntur etiam ad loca magis remota. [...] Non ergo habet servus ius ex iustitia, ut non transferatur in loca remota, in quibus non possit coniugii usum habere".

148 On this point, see Sánchez, *DSMS*, vol. 2, lib. VII, disp. 19, no. 16–17, 137–138. The apostle Paul had already recognized this; see 1 Cor 7:12–15.

if their spouses had been left behind on the other side of the Atlantic?[149] This issue preoccupied the highest circles of the Society of Jesus. Cristóvão de Gouveia (1542–1622), appointed visitor of Brazil by the Superior General himself, was tasked to resolve the doubts of missionaries overseas. To that end, Gouveia paid a special visit to the University of Évora, where he consulted the expert opinions of theologians and lawyers. Among them was none other than Luis de Molina, who, along with his colleagues, insisted on the urgency of papal intervention. The appeals of the Portuguese Jesuits, as Charlotte Castelnau-L'Estoile has shown, eventually bore fruits. In 1585, pope Gregory XIII issued the bull *Populis ac nationibus* and licensed the re-marriages of converted slaves "from Angola, Aethiopia, Brazil, and other regions of the Indies", whose "infidel" spouses were left behind in their native cities.[150]

Lugo did not engage with this missionary debate about re-marriage in the Americas. Rather, his point was that "almost all the slaves" in Iberian hands had been "captured from a hostile commonwealth".[151] The global label "Saracens" encompassed not just "Turks" but all enslaved Muslims from the Iberian Peninsula to Manila. The prince's command had justified their enslavement in war, which simultaneously voided the enemy's right to the use of marriage. The same principle, Lugo explained, applied to criminals condemned to slavery by the public authority.[152] In both cases, the exercise of conjugal duties was interrupted by the coercive power of the commonwealth.

Lugo thus offered a novel lens through which to understand the issue, viewing it not as a clash of individual rights, but as a consequence of princely power. He did not challenge the established dictum that the marriage of enslaved persons was, in principle, exempt from the right of slavery. Rather, the perspective

149 This paragraph draws on Castelnau-L'Estoile, "Le mariage des infidèles au XVIe siècle", 115–118. Castelnau-L'Estoile has reconstruced the debate among Portuguese missionaries and university theologians on the basis of a late-16th century manuscript entitled "Cousas do Brazil", which consists of several hundred folios and is preserved in the Public Library of Évora.

150 Gregory XIII, "Populis ac nationibus" (1585), ed. Metzler, 1229–1230: "infideles post contracta gentili ritu matrimonia ex Angola, Aethiopia, Brasilia et aliis Indicis regionibus [...] concedimus facultatem dispensandi cum quibuscumque utriusque sexus christifidelibus incolis dictarum regionum et serius ad fidem conversis, qui ante baptisma susceptum matrimonium contraxerant ut eorum quilibet etiam superstite coniuge infideli et eius consensu minime requisito aut responso non expectato matrimonia cum quovis fideli alias tamen rite contrahere et in facie Ecclesie solennizare et in eis postea carnali copula consumatis quoad vixerint remanere licite valeant".

151 Lugo, *DIEI*, disp. 3, sect. 2, no. 26, 45: "Nam omnes fere servi, qui apud nos sunt, capti sunt a republica inimica".

152 Lugo, *DIEI*, disp. 3, sect. 2, no. 29, 45.

that Lugo provided justified the breach of matrimony with recourse to public authority rather than private right. The irony, of course, was that the "state" sanctioned breach of marriage made any subsequent sale by individual slaveholders just as legal.[153] Accordingly, Lugo cynically asked: "Who, then, are these slaves, whose master cannot sell them to remote places without violating their right?"[154]

If Iberian wars against non-Christians provided a powerful legal justification for overriding the right of matrimony, this logic did not apply to enslaved people who ended up in Iberian hands through purely commercial channels. Did this mean, then, that people from sub-Saharan Africa, Asia, or Brazil—who, as we saw in the previous chapter, had reputedly sold themselves to Iberian traders or been lured onto slave ship with false promises—were illegally separated from their spouses? Lugo cautiously avoided pursuing that line of reasoning. Instead, he asserted that even those who had voluntarily entered the condition of slavery "cannot prejudice the right that had already been acquired by the master".[155] In such cases, the master could sell the slave "wherever he pleases, when it is unavoidable or advantageous".[156]

The question of how enslaved persons came into Iberian possession thus had far-reaching consequences for assessing whether they could be justly resold across the Atlantic. Through this two-tiered approach, Lugo found a new legitimation for the sale of married, enslaved persons to the New World and beyond without moral qualms. For Lugo, therefore, Tomás Sánchez's objection that slaves should enjoy "a reasonable use of marriage" did not apply.[157] Enslaved persons, he acknowledged, retained a right to defend the integrity of their marriage. But, ultimately, Lugo concluded, this right was "vain and useless".[158]

153 Lugo, *DIEI*, disp. 3, sect. 2, no. 29, 45.

154 Lugo, *DIEI*, disp. 3, sect. 2, no. 26, 45: "Qui ergo sunt illi servi quos dominus distrahere non poterit in loca remota absque eorum iniuria?"

155 Lugo, *DIEI*, disp. 3, sect. 2, no. 30, 45: "Non potuit per subsequens matrimonium praeiudicare huic iuri, quod iam domino fuerat acquisitum". Lugo here anticipated Palacio's dictum that the temporal priority of slavery curtailed the slave's right to the integrity of marriage.

156 Lugo, *DIEI*, disp. 3, sect. 2, no. 30, 45: "non potuit auferre a domino ius, quod prius habebat vendendi eum et mittendi ad quaelibet loca, quando id necesse, vel utile domino fuisset".

157 Lugo, *DIEI*, disp. 3, sect. 2, no. 31, 45: "Nec obstat ratio, quam Sanchez supra relatus afferebat, propter quam dominus debet servo coniugato concedere usum rationabilem matrimonii".

158 Lugo, *DIEI*, disp. 3, sect. 2, no. 31, 45: "esset autem frustra et inutile illud ius".

3.2 *Marriage and Manumission*

The final central theme in the early modern Iberian discourse on marriage and slavery invites a markedly different perspective. Iberian theologians not only debated the circumstances under which the right of slavery could effectively nullify the marital bond, they also examined the reverse possibility: was marriage also a means of breaking free from slavery? The answer to this question centered on the interpretation of particular laws from the bodies of Roman and Castilian legislation. And it was the Salamancan canon lawyer Diego de Covarruvias y Leyva who provided a particularly influential account on the interface between matrimony and manumission.

In his treatise on marriage, Covarruvias began by affirming the standard assertion that the conjugal bond between enslaved and free persons was legitimate so long as the servile status was known.[159] The question he set out to investigate, however, was whether the marriage would be rendered invalid if the free spouse was unaware of their partner's condition. Aquinas had indeed suggested that it did. However, Covarruvias invoked the *Siete Partidas* to challenge the absolute validity of this notion. If a master gave a slave in marriage to a free person without revealing the enslaved person's status to them, this meant that he effectively relinquished his ownership, and the slave was *eo ipso* manumitted.[160] The laws of Castile, Covvarruvias explained, here restated an idea that went back to the *Novels* of Justinian.[161] This legal dictum was later abolished in Spanish America and constituted one of the major differences between Spanish slave law in the Old and New World.[162]

Interestingly, this tension between metropolitan and colonial legislation was neither addressed by Covarruvias nor by later commentators. But that did not render the stance of the *Siete Partidas* any less contentious. Covarruvias forcefully disagreed with the rationale of Roman and Castilian law, arguing that

> […] the marriage was concluded between a slave and a person ignorant of the spouse's condition, and the contract is not therefore valid at all. Indeed, if the slave gains his freedom in this way, it is possible for the other spouse to withdraw from this contract.[163]

159 Covarruvias, *In librum quartum Decretalium*, pars 2, cap. 3, §7, no. 1, 42.

160 Covarruvias, *In librum quartum Decretalium*, pars 2, cap. 3, §7, no. 1, 43. Covarruvias referred to the following laws in the *Siete Partidas*: l. 1, tit. 5, partida 4; l. 5, tit. 22, partida 4; and l. 5, tit. 11, partida 4.

161 Covarruvias refered to Nov. 22.10.

162 Colonial authorities blocked off this important route for social and cultural mobility as early as 1527. See Velázquez Gutiérrez, *Mujeres de origen africano*, 250.

163 Covarruvias, *In librum quartum Decretalium*, pars 2, cap. 3, §7, no. 1, 43: "Verumtamen est

If the slave only gained his or her liberty *through* marriage rather than beforehand, this meant that the wedding itself had been concluded between an enslaved and a free person, who had been unaware of the former's condition. This was, in other words, an *error conditionis*. As Covarruvias noted, this not only contravened the most fundamental teaching of canon law but also clashed with other provisions in the *Siete Partidas*.[164] Moreover, if the marriage rested on a faulty foundation, then the liberty derived from it was equally questionable. By drawing attention to the problematic temporal sequence from marriage to liberty, Covarruvias delivered a cogent critique of a key argument in Roman law.

How did Covarruvias's contemporaries react to his intervention? Domingo de Soto sidestepped the issue and simply restated the validity of the dictum in Justinian's *Novels*.[165] It was Miguel de Palacio, however, who made at least a tacit reference to the canon lawyer's stance. "There are those who say that the free spouse can withdraw from this contract", he explained.[166] But Palacio himself defended the rationale of Roman law. The master's consent to the marriage, he insisted, coupled with his silence about the condition of slavery effectively constituted the enslaved person's manumission.[167]

As historian Debra Blumenthal has shown, in late medieval Castile, this law served as the mechanism through which masters could shape and restrict marital choices of their slaves. Heads of households, Blumenthal argues, did so for the very same reason they intervened in the marriages of their children: enslaved persons were part of their owners' extended family, and slaveholders were therefore keen "to ensure that their former slave women were married off 'honorably'".[168] The 16th-century theologian Palacio, however, argued rather differently. Freedom through marriage was not a consequence of benevolent, tacit manumission. Rather than granting liberty *to* the enslaved person, Palacio insisted, the law was directed *against* the master: "he is punished [...] because his silence does great injustice to the free spouse".[169] What liberated the slave, then, was the master's deceptive silence about the true condition of servitude.

in hoc casu matrimonium cum servo contractum ab ignorante minime valere, etiam si ex hoc contractu servus efficiatur liber, potest nam ipsa ab hoc contractu discedere".

164 Covarruvias referred to X.4.9.4 and *Las Siete Partidas*, l. 4, tit. 5, partida 4.

165 Soto, *In quartum*, vol. 2, dist. 35, a. 2, 245.

166 Palacio, *Disputationes theologicae*, vol. 2, dist. 30, disp. unica, 673: "sunt qui dicant, quod tunc libera potest discedere a contractu illo".

167 Palacio, *Disputationes theologicae*, vol. 2, dist. 30, disp. unica, 673.

168 Blumenthal, *Enemies and Familiars*, 143.

169 Palacio, *Disputationes theologicae*, vol. 2, dist. 30, disp. unica, 673: "Hac enim mulctatur

More importantly still, Palacio insisted that such marriages were perfectly legitimate. There was no *error conditionis*, as Covarruvias had claimed, because it was mistaken to assume that marriage preceded manumission. In Palacio's view, both acts occurred simultaneously: "freedom is granted by law under the very same contract so that the spouses marry as free people, not as slaves, and the marriage is therefore valid".[170] Luis de Molina later confirmed this view.[171] And in the early 17th century, Tomás Sánchez again reaffirmed what had by then become the standard position among Iberian thinkers.[172] Explicitly following Palacio, he argued that the acts of marriage and of manumission coincided so that the enslaved person was freed "at the very moment in which marriage is being concluded".[173] For this reason, the condition of slavery "need not be considered at all, as it neither militates against the end of marriage nor does it bring about any of the disadvantages, on whose ground canon law would invalidate marriage in cases of initial ignorance of the condition of slavery".[174]

But not everyone agreed. The Portuguese Jesuit Fernão Rebello, Molina's colleague at the University of Évora, added an important qualification. Rebello argued that if the master was invincibly ignorant and did not intend to manumit the enslaved person, "he is not obliged in conscience to liberate the slave, even though he is bound to do so by the courts (*iudiciali*)".[175] At least some of the Iberian theologians were prepared to reopen a line of argument that

---

poena dominus quia tradens servum nutpiis cum libera ineundis tacet servilem conditionem servi, quae latet liberam, quia illi magnam ex hoc silentio infert iniuriam: unde ob hanc causam leges illum donant libertatem in authentica de nuptiis. §. Si vero". The reference is to Nov. 22.11.

170 Palacio, *Disputationes theologicae*, vol. 2, dist. 30, disp. unica, 674: "si dixeris, illam libertatem non provenire servo post contractum matrimonium, quia hic proventus libertatis non statueret matrimonium [...] at sub ipso contractu donatur a lege libertas, ideoque contrahunt liberi, et non servi, et matrimonium stat".

171 Molina, *DIEI*, vol. 1, tr. II, disp. 38, no. 5, col. 203–204.

172 See also Ledesma, *De magno matrimonii sacramento*, q. 52, a. 1, 339–340; and Azor, *Institutionum moralium*, vol. 2, lib. II, cap. 33, 138.

173 Sánchez, *DSMS*, vol. 2, lib. VII, disp. 20, no. 14, 149: "Quia cum statim eodem momento, quo perficitur matrimonium, maneat coniux servilis conditionis, effectus liber".

174 Sánchez, *DSMS*, vol. 2, lib. VII, disp. 20, no. 14, 149: "servitus illa est nullius considerationis, nec obstet matrimonii fini, nec affert incommoda, ob quae ius ecclesiasticum irritavit matrimonium cum errore conditionis initum".

175 Rebello, *Opus de obligationibus iustitiae*, pars 1, lib. I, q. 13, no. 6, 79: "si tamen dominus per ignorantiam invincibilem absque animo decipiendi, ita [...] ut non intenderet servo vel ancillae libertatem concedere, non teneretur in foro conscientiae eam concedere, licet in iudiciali ad id compellatur".

pointed in the direction of Covarruvias's earlier critique of a straightforward nexus of marriage and manumission.[176]

The second major point of contention among the Iberian intellectuals concerned whether the enslaved person would be liberated by marrying the master. Covarruvias explained that according to Roman law, the matrimony between master and slave did not *eo ipso* free the latter, so that an additional act of manumission was necessary.[177] The *Siete Partidas*, however, stated the exact opposite and "expressly affirm that the *ancilla* is freed by the very fact that her master takes her as his wife".[178] Interestingly, Covarruvias himself did not offer any further elaboration on this issue and refrained from judging which of the two laws was in accordance with true justice. And he was not alone. Domingo de Soto sidestepped this legal conflict entirely, solely pointing to the fact that if giving an enslaved person in marriage rendered them free, then marrying one's slave was "*a fortiori*" an act of manumission, "as is clear from the royal law in Spain".[179] Even Tomás Sánchez, who had previously privileged the authority of Justinian's *Novels* over the *Siete Partidas*, now refrained from siding with either Roman or Spanish civil legislation.[180]

Only Miguel de Palacio insisted that this issue needed a concrete solution. By drawing on Aristotle's *Nicomachean Ethics*, Palacio argued that the relationship between husband and wife was incompatible with that of master and slave, for only in the former could there be true friendship. Between master and slave,

176 Another example would be the Palermitan theologian Antonino Diana, who followed Rebello's argument. See Diana, *Resolutionum moralium*, tr. VII, resol. 14, 242.

177 Covarruvias, *In librum quartum Decretalium*, pars 2, cap. 3, § 7, no. 1, 43. Covarruvias pointed to Nov. 18.11.

178 Covarruvias, *In librum quartum Decretalium*, pars 2, cap. 3, § 7, no. 1, 43: "Regia tamen l. 5, tit. 22, par. 4 et l. 1, tit. 13, eadem par. expressim afferit ancillam liberam effici ex eo quod dominus eam in uxorem acceperit".

179 Soto, *In quartum*, vol. 2, dist. 35, a. 2, 245: "eo ipso, quod dominus ancillam ingenuo nuptum tradidit, eam manumittit, et libertate donat [...] Unde a fortiori si dominus ancillam suam propriam in uxorem duxerit, matrimonium tenet: quia eo ipso libertam facit. Et de hoc extat lex regia in Hispania". This was restated verbatim by Ledesma, *De magno matrimonii sacramento*, q. 52, a. 1, 340.

180 Sánchez, *DSMS*, vol. 2, lib. VII, disp. 20, no. 11–12, 145: "iure optimo ab hac opinione recedendum est, dicendumque iure communi attento eam ancillam minime effici liberam. [...] Attento autem iure regni Hispaniae ancilla ducta a domino, sit eo ipso libera". For the same argument, see also Molina, *DIEI*, vol. 1, tr. II, disp. 39, no. 1, col. 209–210; and Azor, *Institutionum moralium*, vol. 2, lib. II, cap. 33, 138.

he noted, friendship was impossible, “except insofar as the slave is a human being”.[181] This Aristotelian dictum, as we shall see in the final section of this chapter, led some of the Iberian imperial theorists to assert that enslaved persons retained the capacity to own certain things for themselves *qua homines*, although this was unthinkable insofar as they were slaves. But Palacio was making a completely different point. Rather than pondering the slave’s dual roles, he argued that the presence or absence of true friendship was indicative of the kind of rule that characterized the domestic relations. Marriage, too, was marked by the authority of the paterfamilias. But conjugal friendship was indicative of the fact that “the husband’s rule is *political*, since it is the rule over a free person, rather than a slave”.[182] Therefore, Palacio explained,

> [...] it is not obscure to conclude that Castilian law rightly establishes that when a master marries his slave, she is already free by that very fact; because of the friendship, partnership, and civil rule that result between them, which seem impossible if the wife remains a slave.[183]

Based on a close reading of Aristotle, Palacio ultimately defended the rationale of the *Siete Partidas* against the sentence of Roman law. At least implicitly, this also constituted an attack on what had by then become the standard legal practice in colonial Spanish America.[184] In Palacio’s view, it was simply impossible to be a spouse and a slave to the same person. No one could be ruled both politically and despotically—and be both free and unfree—at the same time. Consequently, marriage between master and slave justly liberated the latter.

181 Palacio, *Disputationes theologicae*, vol. 2, dist. 30, disp. unica, 675: “servi ad dominum nullam esse amicitiam, nisi quatenus servus est homo: at vero virum et uxorem est amicitia, 8. Ethicorum, cap. 7”. For the original passages in Aristotle, see his *Nicomachean Ethics*, ed. and trans. Crisp, lib. 8, cap. 7 and 11.

182 Palacio, *Disputationes theologicae*, vol. 2, dist. 30, disp. unica, 675, emphasis mine: “Quod dudum appellarat Aristoteles dominium civile, siquidem dominium viri ad uxorem est dominium politicum, quia est dominium ad liberam, non ad servam”.

183 Palacio, *Disputationes theologicae*, vol. 2, dist. 30, disp. unica, 675: “Ex quibus non est obscurum colligere regiam legem bene sanxisse si dominus acceperit in uxorem ancillam, vel hoc solo nomine iam esse liberam: ex amicitia, ex societate, ex dominio civili, quod resultat inter utrumque, quae videntur repugnare uxori si maneret ancilla”.

184 It is worth noting that the situation in colonial Spanish America gave rise to court cases of wives litigating against their husbands in their capacity as *slaves* litigating against their *master*. See Velázquez Gutiérrez, *Mujeres de origen africano*, 258–259; McKinley, *Fractional Freedoms*, ch. 5.

4 Enslavement, Marriage, and "Human Rights"

In conclusion, the meditations of Iberian imperial theorists on the marriage of enslaved persons allow me to revisit a question that has long been the subject of intense scholarly debate: Do these Spanish and Portuguese thinkers have a place in the history of human rights?

At first glance, this question may seem surprising, given the extensive rights Juan de Lugo and others granted to slaveholders. Yet scholars have repeatedly linked the Iberian imperial theorists to the "origins" of human rights because they insisted on the God-given natural rights of all humans, especially Indigenous peoples overseas, regardless of religion or race.[185] But is this position really tenable? And how do human rights and slavery fit together?

Philosophers such as Matthias Kaufmann and Danaë Simmermacher have offered a provocative answer to this question, which centers on an argument that Luis de Molina made in his *De iustitia et iure*. In Kaufmann's view, Molina was one of the first thinkers in Western history to ever speak of a right as a human being, and in so doing "sowed the seeds for contemporary human rights".[186] Similarly, Danaë Simmermacher emphasizes that "Molina may justly be considered as one of the forerunners of pre-political human rights".[187]

In fact, Molina argued, enslaved humans and all their possessions belonged entirely to their masters. But slaveholders could grant them rights to retain certain material and financial benefits of their labor, as well as personal gifts received from others, and their winnings from gambling.[188] Molina drew on

185 See e.g., Doyle, *Collected studies on Francisco Suárez*, ed. Salas, 355: "we can see in Suárez a recognition of basic human rights". See also Jansen, *Theologie, Philosophie und Jurisprudenz*, 40: "Vitoria, de Soto, oder Franciscus Suárez, haben das *dominium* folgerichtig als ein Freiheitsrecht verstanden, das grundsätzlich allen Menschen gleichermassen zukam [...] Damit implizierte dies Konzept eine menschenrechtliche Dimension *avant la lettre*". See also Moreira and Azevedo Alves, *De Salamanca a Coímbra y Évora*, 23: "La importancia de la aportación portuguesa [...] en la afirmación de la existencia de derechos humanos inalienables, independientemente de la raza y el credo". And see also Calafate and Balsas, "Apresentação", 763: "A recente celebração dos setenta anos da Declaração Universal dos Direitos Humanos [...] lança raízes nas reflexões filosóficas de teólogos ibéricos dos séculos XVI e XVII".

186 Kaufmann, "Slavery between Law, Morality, and Economy", 225.

187 Simmermacher, "'Non qua servus est, sed qua homo'", 7: "darf Molina zurecht als einer der Wegbereiter vorpolitischer Menschenrechte angesehen werden". The same is restated in her more recent *Eigentum als ein subjektives Recht bei Luis de Molina*, most forcefully at 180.

188 Molina, *DIEI*, vol. 1, tr. II, disp. 38, no. 5, col. 203: "si interveniat pactum inter ipsos et dominum, ut quotidie aut singulis hebdomadibus, mensibus, vel anis, certum quid ei

Aristotle's distinction between the slave *qua servus* and the slave *qua homo*: in the former sense, enslaved persons were mere tools to their owners. Still, Molina stressed that as human beings, masters and slaves could share true friendship and justice.[189] Based on that principle, he insisted that a master's concession gave rise to a proper contract, such that the enslaved person acquired full right of property.[190] Molina thus provided the theoretical justification for a widespread practice, and those writing in his vein agreed with him.[191] Enslaved persons could therefore hold the paradoxical status of both being and owning property.[192]

Molina's formulation of slaves' rights *qua homo* is catchy. It has led Matthias Kaufmann and Danaë Simmermacher to elevate the Spanish Jesuit to the jumping-off point of a forward-looking narrative that culminates in the modern understanding of human rights. But I hope to have shown that the way in which Molina and others understood the rights of human beings was fundamentally different from the legal discourse of our own time. "The terms of debate", as Richard Helmholz rightly warns, "were very far from those that would be accepted today. The starting point was not a recognition of human

solvant, reliquunt vero de suis laboribus ac lucris sibi reservent, aut aliud simile pactum. [...] si quid dominus tacite vel expresse donet suo servo, aut velit cum tanquam suum habere, sive ex alterius donatione, sive ex ludo, aut quacunque alia ratione".

189 Molina, *DIEI*, vol. 1, tr. II, disp. 38, no. 5, col. 203: "Licet enim domini comparatione servi, ea ratione qua servus est, neque amicitia, neque iustitia sit: ea tamen ratione, qua homo est, utrumque esse potest, ut Aristoteles 8. *Ethicorum, capitulum* 11. affirmat". For the original passage in Aristotle, see his *Nicomachean Ethics*, ed. and trans. Crisp, lib. 8, cap. 11, 1161b3–1161b11, 158.

190 Molina, *DIEI*, vol. 1, tr. II, disp. 38, no. 5, col. 203.

191 See e.g., Sánchez, *Consilia*, lib. I, cap. 1, dub. 1, no. 5–10, 2–3; Lugo, *DIEI*, disp. 3, sect. 3, no. 46–55, 49–51; Machado de Chavez, *Perfecto confesor*, vol. 2, lib. VI, parte 7, tr. XIII, doc. 5, no. 4–9, 528–529; and Diana, *Resolutionum moralium*, tr. VII resol. 29–32, 249–252. On enslaved humans' capacity to possess their own things, see also Martín Casares, *La esclavitud en la granada*, 445.

192 We find a similar argument in the manuscripts of Molina's contemporaries Pedro Simões and Fernando Pérez. See Simões, *Materia de restitutione*, ed. and trans. Maurício and Miranda, membrum 2, a. 4, 300: "expresso vel tacito domini consensu potest servus habere dominium aliquarum rerum [...] Probatur quia dominus potest cedere iure suo quod habet in servum [...] Licet enim servus, quia servus, incapax sit dominii, tamen qua ratione homo est capax etiam dominii". Pérez, whom Molina had accused of plagiarizing his writings, argued that slaves were *sui iuris* with regard to their bodily and spiritual health, so that such injuries had to be compensated to the enslaved person rather than to the slaveholder. See Pérez, "Non nulla ante materiam de restitutione", ed. and trans. Tarrío et al., disp. 13, 452: "illa solutio de qua loquimur est satisfactio iniuriae illatae servo, non ea ratione qua servus est domini, sed qua homo est, et sub ea ratione sui iuris".

rights".[193] Early modern Iberian theologians and jurists were concerned with negotiating and justifying the limits of human agency in conscience while accepting the fundamentally unequal and unstable legal status of human beings under the *ius gentium*.[194] They all endorsed slavery and problematized only the legitimacy of certain practices—in fact, this is also true of the supposed "proto-abolitionist" Bartolomé de Las Casas (1484/85–1566).[195] In early modern natural law, the only inalienable right was the right of self-preservation. And this was precisely *not* an exclusively human right. As Domingo de Soto had pointed out, animals had it too, because it was a consequence of natural instinct—not the uniquely human capacity to act with reason and foresight.[196]

This links up with the right of matrimony, which was likewise derived from natural human inclination to preserve one's species through procreation. It was a desire God had implanted in all creatures, and in this sense, it would be difficult to describe what early modern Iberians conceded to enslaved persons as a specifically "human" right. At the same time, both Aquinas and the Iberian imperial theorists complemented the natural necessity of procreation with what I have called a "thick" account of marriage to emphasize the political dimension.[197] Unlike the "*qua homo*-rights" to own material goods, enslaved persons could exercise their right to marry by their very own volition, even against their master's will. Indeed, in and through marriage, slaves partially abandoned their status as commodities and subjects of their owners. The insti-

193 Helmholz, "Diego de Covarrubias y Leyva", 185.

194 On this point, see Brett, "Human Rights and the Thomist Tradition", 98.

195 Kenneth Pennington's take on Las Casas is exemplary: he describes the Dominican monk as a "full-throated, if a bit rambling, abolitionist" because he had campaigned against the enslavement of Indigenous peoples in the New World. At the same time, however, Pennington admits that Las Casas was a staunch supporter of the Portuguese trade in enslaved people from West Africa for most of his life and never questioned the idea of enslavement in "just wars". See Pennington, "Bartolomé de Las Casas", 108. For the Iberian imperial theorists who are the subject of this book, Las Casas was not a relevant interlocutor because his concern lay not with legal-theological justifications for slavery, but with translating his own personal convictions into pointed and polemical instructions for the Spaniards overseas. See Birr, "Recht als Argument in Bartolomé de Las Casas' *Tratado sobre los indios*", 123.

196 On this point, see also Brett, "Doing Without an Original", 64–66. On animal rights in early modern natual law thinking more broadly, see Brett, "Rights of and over Animals in the *Ius naturae et gentium*", 257–261.

197 *Pace* Haar, who argues that marriage was only political for the later, especially Jesuit, theologians. See Haar, *Natural and Political Conceptions of Community*, 198 and Chapter 4, *passim*.

tution of marriage opened the door to the world of political agency, rights, and mutual contractual obligations.

The tension between these two ways of thinking about marriage, however, did not lie in a contrast between a male-dominated natural conception of marriage and a more egalitarian political notion of matrimony, as Christoph Haar suggests in his study of the household community in early modern Jesuit thought. If anything, the reverse was true. The Iberian theologians emphasized equality between the spouses in regard to the natural act of procreation, while maintaining that the wife was subject to her husband in matters concerning the "government of the household and the family", as Tomás Sánchez put it.[198] And yet, a rigid juxtaposition between the hierarchical and the political side of marriage would be misleading. Consider Domingo de Soto's observation that domestic governance involved both spouses, or Miguel de Palacio's assertion that conjugal rule was political. Luis de Molina similarly argued that the wife was her husband's "accomplice" in the joint administration of the household, so that "the right that each of the spouses has entitles the other to be superior in those tasks and all that which is necessary for the sustenance and management of the family".[199] In this sense, the natural and political dimensions of marriage were not opposed—they were intimately linked and embedded within a broader teleology of political life that ran through the city.

And yet the rights of enslaved persons were utterly vulnerable and unstable in the end. The fact that the legal status of slaves oscillated between object and agent gave the Iberian imperial theorists enormous flexibility and latitude to make arguments about slavery. While the natural right of marriage was technically beyond the master's power, the early modern theologians and jurists found loopholes to get around this dictum. For Palacio, it was the temporal priority of enslavement over matrimony that could be cited against it. In Lugo's account, it was war and the prerogatives of public authority which ultimately overrode the rights of individuals. And virtually all authors conceded that, in situations of extreme necessity, the master retained the right to sell his slave like any other item of property.

---

198 Sánchez, *DSMS*, vol. 2, lib. VII, disp. 23, no. 9, 158: "Quia ultra obligationem reddendi debiti coniugalis, in qua coniuges sunt pares, subditur viro tanquam capiti, in reliquis, quae ad regimen domus et familiae attinent".

199 Molina, *DIEI*, vol. 4, tr. III, disp. 2, no. 1, col. 515: "Et enim uxor adiutorium viro datum, non solum ad generationem opus, sed etiam ad familiae administratione, ut *Genesis* 2 habetur, ac proinde ius unicuique eorum competit in alium, ut alter eas operas idque praestet, quod ad familiae sustentationem et administrationem tenetur".

What conclusions can we draw? Social and legal historians have rightly emphasized the agency of enslaved persons in the early modern Iberian world. But the agency of slaveholders, as the writings examined here show, was far greater. With their legal loopholes, the Iberian imperial theorists pushed the limits of moral agency to the extreme in favor of those who owned and traded enslaved people as merchandise. Marriage was based on natural law and thus more fundamental than the law of slavery. But the Iberian thinkers found ways to justify the separation of enslaved spouses and pacify the conscience of those who sold a married slave across the Atlantic, even if her husband was left behind in the Old World. Juan de Lugo was most outspoken on this point. He bluntly admitted that the marriage right of slaves was, in fact, “vain and useless”.

CHAPTER 5

Punishment, Power, and Care

In the previous chapter, we saw that even if enslaved persons belonged to their masters, both as property and domestic subjects, the bond of marriage placed them at the head of their own household community. But marriage was only one aspect of a broader discourse about the power relations between masters and slaves. At the heart of this discussion were both the question of the limits of masters' authority and their duty of care toward enslaved subjects. Slave rule was a double-edged sword of rights and responsibilities, and the implications of this duality led to intense debates among early modern Iberian thinkers.

Social and legal historians have shown the close bonds between enslaved persons and their owners. Debra Blumenthal, one of the foremost historians of slavery in late-medieval Spain, emphasizes the "'paternal' responsibilities" of slaveholders and maintains that "masters and slaves formed a 'family' linked by mutual obligations".[1] A similar thrust pervades recent scholarship on domestic enslavement in colonial Mexico and Peru.[2] At the same time, historians have equally highlighted the "almost limitless powers of coercion"[3] and the "brutal violence"[4] exerted by masters. "Corporal punishment", as one historian put it, "was at the very base of relationships between master and slave".[5]

The realities of slaving in the wider Iberian world gave rise to pressing questions. Could enslaved persons be detained in so-called "private prisons"? Was it just for heads of households to punish their slaves? And if so, what was allowed and what was not? In responding to these issues, early modern Iberian thinkers gave extensive consideration not just to the morality of what occurred on the ground. They also confronted the question of how private right related to public authority. In principle, the answer was straightforward: only the prince was vested with coercive power, whereas subjects had no such power over fellow citizens. Yet the discourse on disciplining slaves put pressure on this supposedly clear-cut boundary.

---

1 Blumenthal, *Enemies and Familiars*, 141 and 149.

2 See e.g., McKinley, *Fractional Freedoms*, 110; Velázquez Gutiérrez, *Mujeres de origen africano*, 133; Bowser, *The African Slave in Colonial Peru*, 228–229.

3 Phillips, *Slavery in Medieval and Early Modern Iberia*, 86.

4 Bono, *Schiavi*, 141.

5 Bowser, *The African Slave in Colonial Peru*, 231.

Moreover, the Iberian thinkers' accounts of slave rule also negotiated the relationship between rights and broader moral obligations. Slavery was not a purely legal relationship, for masters had an obligation to provide for the temporal and spiritual well-being of domestic subjects. The Iberian intellectuals advocated a vision of slave rule as guardianship, in which care and punishment were two sides of the same coin. And as we will see in the final part of the book, a strikingly similar mode of protection also characterized Iberian visions of the status of Indigenous vassals in the Spanish empire in the Americas.

The effects of these entanglements between public and private, and between the strictly juridical and the non-juridical, were ambiguous and explosive. For this reason, turning our attention to the place of slavery in the household more broadly reveals one of the most innovative strands of the Iberian theorists' political thought. The intersection of power and care raised fundamental questions about the political and legal dimensions of human relations, about the boundary between domestic and public power, and ultimately about human nature itself.

1 *Dominium* and Human Life

Let us begin with the question of the limits of the power over slaves. In the eyes of early modern Iberians, the quintessential rationale that justified the passage from freedom to enslavement was the idea that preserving human life warranted the loss of natural liberty. The power over life itself, however, was a rather different matter. In the *Secunda secundae*, Thomas Aquinas had argued that "the judgment of life and death belongs to God alone, according to Deuteronomy 32, *I kill, and I make alive*".[6] But Aquinas also insisted that "if it is expedient for the health of the whole human body to cut off any member, for instance, because it is decayed or corrupts other members, it is laudable and advantageous to one's health to have it cut away".[7] Human beings were merely guardians of their life and were permitted to remove "decayed" members insofar as it was indispensable to their survival.

6 Aquinas, *Summa*, ed. Alarcón and Busa, 2a2ae, q. 65, a. 5, corp.: "vita est quoddam donum divinitus homini attributum, et eius potestati subiectum qui occidit et vivere facit. [...] Ad solum enim Deum pertinet iudicium mortis et vitae, secundum illud Deut. XXXII, *ego occidam, et vivere faciam*".

7 Aquinas, *Summa*, ed. Alarcón and Busa, 2a2ae, q. 64, a. 2, corp.: "Et propter hoc videmus quod si saluti totius corporis humani expediat praecisio alicuius membri, puta cum est putridum et corruptivum aliorum, laudabiliter et salubriter abscinditur".

According to Aquinas, the same logic also applied to political bodies. As he went on to explain, this meant that "if any human being is dangerous for the community and corrupts it on account of a given sin, it is laudable and advantageous to the health of the community that this person be killed, so that the common good may be preserved".[8] Although capital punishment might appear incompatible with the belief that God alone holds power over life and death, Aquinas maintained that the execution of a malefactor was just. And although this was "against the particular nature of the person whose body is maimed", he noted, "it is nevertheless in accordance with natural reason with regard to the common good".[9]

The early modern Iberian followers of Aquinas all agreed with this position.[10] Francisco de Vitoria, for instance, argued that in view of the body and life, "man is specifically the slave of God".[11] And his Salamancan contemporary Soto explained that God had retained the *dominium* of human life for himself, since he was "its author".[12] The power and right to kill could be entrusted only to magistrates, since the judgment of those personally wronged by a violation of right would stem from their "irascibility" (*iracundia*) rather than from "reason" (*ratio*).[13] Yet Soto underlined that while executing malefactors was just if carried out by public authority, this did not imply that the commonwealth possessed any *dominium* over the lives of its citizens: "for the prince can by no means kill innocents at will like God can [...] but only insofar as he is the defender of the commonwealth, and the guardian of what is just".[14]

---

8 Aquinas, *Summa*, ed. Alarcón and Busa, 2a2ae, q. 64, a. 2, corp: "Quaelibet autem persona singularis comparatur ad totam communitatem sicut pars ad totum. Et ideo si aliquis homo sit periculosus communitati et corruptivus ipsius propter aliquod peccatum, laudabiliter et salubriter occiditur, ut bonum commune conservetur".

9 Aquinas, *Summa*, ed. Alarcón and Busa, 2a2ae, q. 65, a. 1, ad. 1: "etsi sit contra naturam particularem corporis eius qui mutilatur, est tamen secundum naturalem rationem in comparatione ad bonum commune".

10 As observed in Brett, *Changes of State*, 164.

11 Vitoria, *De homicidio*, in *Relectiones theologicae XII*, vol. 2, 138, no. 23: "non est autem ita dominus, aut corporis, aut vitae propriae. Est enim solus Deus dominus vitae et mortis, et quantum ad hoc homo peculiariter est servus Dei".

12 Soto, *DIEI*, lib. IV, q. 2, a. 3, 292: "Cum vita [...] homo non per se acquirit, sed Dei beneficio parentumque opera recipit: non decuit illi concedi eius dominium, sed ut Deus eius autor id retineret".

13 Soto, *DIEI*, lib. V, q. 1, a. 3, 389.

14 Soto, *DIEI*, lib. V, q. 1, a. 5, 395: "Nempe rempublicam non proprie habere dominium vitae civium, sicuti Deum. Haud enim princeps pro libito, veluti ille, potest innocentem in mortem adigere [...] sed tantum ut reipublicae propugnator, iustique custos". Daniel Schwartz similarly gestures to the limits of the body/member—city/citizen analogy but does not discuss this crucial point. See Schwartz, *The Political Morality of the Late Scholastics*, 146.

1.1 *Owning the Lives of Enslaved Persons*

What consequences did this have for the Iberian thinkers' understanding of slavery? Above all, it meant that the transfer of rights in the passage from freedom to slavery was inherently limited. No human being was the master of their life, and for that reason, it could not be alienated. The bodily integrity of enslaved persons was expressly excluded from the contract of slavery. As Domingo de Soto made clear, "a master cannot kill his slave, because only God is the *dominus* of life".[15] Whereas Vitoria understood God's power over human life in terms of enslavement, Soto pointed to the crucial difference between the authority of the divine master of creation and the power of human masters of slaves.

Later Jesuits affirmed this basic principle, while introducing some important additions. Luis de Molina, for instance, emphasized that the limits of slavery not only concerned the bodily integrity of enslaved persons, but also their "spiritual health".[16] Francisco Suárez similarly warned that masters did not have the right to use a slave in any way that was "contrary to the other's natural law and honor".[17] The Portuguese Fernão Rebello even went as far as to suggest—in a manner reminiscent of Palacio—that "the slave does not belong to the master in all respects, but is to some extent *sui iuris*".[18]

This same point was powerfully asserted by Estevão Fagundez in his treatise *On Justice and Contracts*. He argued that the reason why a master did not possess absolute *dominium* over a slave in the way that he owned "a mule" lay in the fact that "the slave is not only to be considered in his servile condition but equally in his human nature, which is in the slave in the same way that it is in the master".[19] In this sense, Fagundez provided a particularly powerful iteration

---

15 Soto, *DIEI*, lib. IV, q. 1, a. 1, 279: "quicquid est, totum est domini […] nisi quod servus occidi non potest: quia solus Deus est vitae dominus".

16 Molina, *DIEI*, vol. 1, tr. II, disp. 38, no. 2, col. 201–202: "ius dominorum in servos […] non tamen se extendit ad eorum vitam […] Et multo minus se extendit ad salutem illius spiritualem, quasi aliquid praecipere ei, aut ab eo exigere possint, quod cum spirituali illius salute pugnet".

17 Suárez, *Commentariorum ac disputationum*, vol. 3, disp. 25, sect. 4, 265: "Nam licet verum sit, non posse dominum uti servo ad omnem usum pro suo arbitrio, quando in illo usu est aliquid contrarium alterius naturali legi seu honestati".

18 Rebello, *Opus de obligationibus iustitiae*, pars 1, lib. I, q. 9, no. 2, 67: "nec enim […] servus est domini, quoad omnia, sed quoad aliqua, est sui iuris".

19 Fagundez, *De iustitia*, lib. II, cap. 5, no. 1, 154: "in servo non solum consideranda est conditio servilis, sed etiam natura humana, quae est in servo, et in domino, una eademque, non licet domino uti servo sicut iumento". A similar argument had previously been put forward by Molina, *DIEI*, vol. 1, tr. II, disp. 38, no. 1, col. 201. On animal righs in early modern natural law thinking, see Brett, "Rights of and over Animals in the *Ius naturae et gentium*".

of the dictum that the ownership of enslaved persons differed in quality from the mastery of animals and inanimate things.

It is worth noting, however, that the arguments we have encountered so far sidestepped a major body of authorities that featured centrally in the moral and political reasoning of early modern Iberian thinkers: Roman law. As the canon lawyer Diego de Covarruvias pointed out, Justinian's *Institutes* specifically stated that masters had the very same *dominium* over slaves that they had over their "fields and farms".[20] But slaveholders were bound to use this right "benevolently rather than severely or cruelly, as Augustine rightly admonishes in *The City of God*, Book 19, Chapter 16, and as is stated in Roman law".[21] In so arguing, Covarruvias revived a crucial tension at the heart of the slave laws in Justinian's *Institutes*: on the one hand, enslaved persons fully belonged to their owners like any other thing (Inst. 1.8.1). But on the other, the recourse to this right was limited (Inst. 1.8.2).

The most comprehensive treatment of this issue came from the pen of the Jesuit Juan Azor, the most distinguished Roman law expert among the Iberian theorists.[22] Azor explained the apparent contradiction between these two laws by revisiting the legal history: the latter provision had been enacted by Emperor Antoninus Pius in the 2nd century A.D. to moderate the former.[23] From that point onwards, Azor argued, the once "inhuman power of masters over slaves was made more clement so that masters could not licitly kill their slaves with impunity unless the latter committed a crime, which had been juridically examined".[24] This meant that a slaveholder could take the life of an enslaved person only "as a minister" of the prince, thus carrying out the execution with the license of public authority.[25] However, he argued, to entrust the power over

20 Covarruvias, *In regula peccatum*, pars 2, § 11, no. 3, in *Opera omnia*, vol. 1, 567: "Unde dominus in servos naturali ratione dominium habet, sicut et in agros et fundos qui ad eum pertineant".

21 Covarruvias, *In regula peccatum*, pars 2, § 11, no. 3, in *Opera omnia*, vol. 1, 567: "Uti tamen debent domini hoc iure, quod in servos habent benigne, non severe, et crudeliter, quod admonet Divus Augustinus lib. 19 de civi. Dei c. 16 et iure civili statutum est [...] de his qui sui vel ali. iur § in potestate et § sed". Covarruvias here referred to Inst. 1.8.1 and 1.8.2.

22 This becomes clear from the title of his treatise already, which Azor called "Moral Institutions" and which points to his synthesis of moral theology and Justinian's *Instiutes*. On Azor and Roman law, see also Decock, "Spanish Neo-Scholasticism", 327.

23 Azor, *Institutionum moralium*, vol. 2, lib. 11, cap. 34, 139. The reference was to Inst. 1.8.2.

24 Azor, *Institutionum moralium*, vol. 2, lib. 11, cap. 34, 139: "Postea vero tam immanis dominorum in servos potestas mitior est facta, ut non nisi ob crimen a servo commissum, et causa cognita, dominis liceret servos impune interimere".

25 Azor, *Institutionum moralium*, vol. 2, lib. 11, cap. 34, 139: "Certe quamvis auctoritate Reipub-

life and death to masters without proper juridical inquiry and judgment would be "barbarous, and indeed savage and cruel".[26]

Although Azor neither pointed to Scripture nor to the arguments proposed by his intellectual predecessors, he eventually reached the same conclusion. By pointing to the historical evolution of Roman law, as mediated in and through Justinian's *Institutes*, Azor argued that the right of masters over the lives of their slaves had been abolished at a specific point in time in the past. In this sense, he tacitly pushed back against Covarruvias's argument of the simultaneity of a law that granted masters extensive power (Inst. 1.8.1) and another law that limited the actual scope of the former (Inst. 1.8.2).

But Azor went further. In his estimation, the older law was illegitimate to begin with, since the right to kill slaves stemmed solely from the *ius gentium*.[27] "By the law of war", Azor maintained, "enemies are slaughtered in combat. But after the end and completion of the war, the vanquished cannot be justly killed unless they commit a new atrocity".[28] He borrowed this point from Luis de Molina, who had previously argued that enslaved enemies—*mancipia*—could be lawfully killed only during wartime, and only by the authority of the commonwealth.[29] And it was this principle that the earlier Roman dictum violated. As the Sicilian Antonino Diana later put it, the law in question violated the principles of natural law, according to which "homicide is intrinsically evil".[30] This completes the arc of the argument and brings us back to Aquinas's position: the commonwealth alone holds legitimate power to end human life, insofar as it is necessary for preserving the common good.

---

licae, vel Principis concedi queat, ut dominus tanquam minister ad id constitutus servum occidat propter ea crimina".

26 Azor, *Institutionum moralium*, vol. 2, lib. II, cap. 34, 139: "nec negari potest esse barbarum, utpote immane et crudele, penes dominos esse ius occidendi servos arbitratu suo [...] noxa gravitate non satis cognita".

27 This point is also noted in Höpfl, *Jesuit Political Thought*, 197 fn. 42.

28 Azor, *Institutionum moralium*, vol. 2, lib. II, cap. 34, 139: "iure belli trucidantur hostes in ipsa belli pugna; victi vero finito perfectoque bello, iure interfici nequeunt, nisi novum scelus admiserint".

29 See Molina, *DIEI*, vol. 4, tr. III, disp. 33, membrum 5, no. 8, col. 692–693.

30 Diana, *Resolutionum moralium*, tr. VII, resol. 4, 234: "Licet enim illa olim fuerit summa, hoc est, licet dominus potuerit servum suum sine causa impune occidere [...] quae quidem olim procedebant de iure civili, nam de iure naturae contrarium dicendum, cum homicidium sit intrinsece malum".

2 Punishment and Incarceration

Although masters could not rightfully kill their slaves, this did not imply a complete absence of power over the bodies of enslaved individuals. Central to the debates among early modern Iberians were two fundamental questions: whether masters could lawfully flog their slaves and whether they had the right to imprison them. These issues were particularly salient because they had prominently featured in Thomas Aquinas's *Secunda Secundae*.

Aquinas argued that "a father and a master can licitly flog their son and slave, respectively, for the sake of correction and discipline".[31] In so arguing, he drew a contrast between the city and the household, and between the coercive authority of the prince and the kind of power natural to the domestic sphere:

> […] the father and master who is in control of the family and household, which is an imperfect community, has the imperfect coercive power to inflict milder penalties, which do not cause irreparable harm. And flogging belongs to this kind of power.[32]

According to Aquinas, princes could kill and mutilate because they had coercive power. But heads of households could only inflict transient punishments.

When Francisco de Vitoria revisited the issue in his lecture course on Aquinas's *Secunda secundae* in the 1520s, he followed the rationale outlined in the treatise he was commenting on. He argued that whipping was legitimate insofar as it stemmed from the power to "govern" and "punish" inferiors.[33] Like Aquinas, he also insisted on the qualitative difference between forms of mutilation that "militate against the integrity of the body" and the merely "transient" harm that masters and fathers could justly inflict on their slaves and sons.[34] And finally, he admonished that resorting to the "stick" for "correc-

---

31 Aquinas, *Summa*, ed. Alarcón and Busa, 2a2ae, q. 65, a. 2, corp.: "licite potest verberare pater filium et dominus servum, causa correctionis et disciplinae".

32 Aquinas, *Summa*, ed. Alarcón and Busa, 2a2ae, q. 65, a. 2, ad 2: "Pater autem et dominus, qui praesunt familiae domesticae, quae est imperfecta communitas, habent imperfectam potestatem coercendi secundum leviores poenas, quae non inferunt irreparabile nocumentum. Et huiusmodi est verberatio".

33 Vitoria, *Comentarios a la Secunda secundae*, ed. Beltrán de Heredia, vol. 3, q. 65, a. 2, no. 1, 314: "Verberare aliquem absolute loquendo, id est nisi quis habeat potestatem super illum, nullo pacto licet alicui. […] quia habent potestatem super illos castigandi et gubernandi illos: ergo licet illis verberare illos".

34 Vitoria, *Comentarios a la Secunda secundae*, ed. Beltrán de Heredia, vol. 3, q. 65, a. 2, no. 1–2, 314–315: "mutilare est contra integritatem corporis, non tamen verberare. […] quia ver-

tion and discipline" was only licit when it was impossible to accomplish the task of governing children and enslaved persons through "good counsel, good teaching, and reproachful words" because the subject in question was "stiff-necked".[35]

The originally Thomist understanding of punishment as a distinctive element of rule in the household, grounded in the rationale of disciplining domestic subjects, was emphasized consistently by all Iberian theologians. It is therefore inaccurate to claim that Aquinas, and the tradition that followed him, completely turned against what Michel Senellart has called the medieval *regimen animarum*, that is, an Augustinian understanding of the end of political rule centered on the correction of human beings.[36] At least when it came to the rule of children and enslaved persons—and to some extent wives as well—the punitive element inherent in the nexus of *regere* and *corrigere* was and remained a defining feature of Catholic natural law thinking.

2.1 *Punishment, Oeconomic Power, and the "Household Republic"*

The line between just punishment and unjust killing was, at times, treated with remarkable flexibility. In late-medieval Genoa, for instance, a master who unintentionally killed a slave—such as by using a stick rather than a sword—escaped the charge of homicide. As Steven Epstein has shown, in such situations "it was presumed that the intent was to correct [...] even if the slave died".[37] The Iberian imperial theorists did not ponder this specific question. But confronting the historical evolution of Roman law compelled them to revisit the question of whether the masters could, at least in principle if not in fact, take the life of and mutilate the subjects of their household.

Juan Azor, as we saw, forcefully rejected the legitimacy of such acts. But where none of the Iberian thinkers was prepared to concede this right to masters in the present, not all refuted the rationale of Roman law as such. In the early 16th century, Francisco de Vitoria argued that it "is not absolutely against

beratio est nocumentum et correctio per modum transeuntis sine laesione et nocumento corporis".

35 Vitoria, *Comentarios a la Secunda secundae*, ed. Beltrán de Heredia, vol. 3, q. 65, a. 2, no. 4, 315–316: "causa correctionis et disciplinae liceat [...] si pueri sint bonae indolis, sufficiunt bona consilia, bona doctrina, et verba increpatoria. [...] si vero filii sint durae cervicis, opus est virga".

36 For Senellart, the shift with Aquinas was from a punitive towards a directive end and understanding of political rule. See Senellart, *Les arts de gouverner*, 65–83 and 157–164. It is important to note, however, that Iberian theorists did not legitimate the need for (domestic) discipline primarily with reference to the fallen state of human nature.

37 Epstein, *Speaking of Slavery*, 101.

natural and divine law" for fathers to mutilate their children.[38] With an implicit reference to Justinian's *Institutes*, Vitoria explained that

> [...] among the Romans, parents had the power to flog and mutilate their sons [...] and at least insofar as this was bound up with the preservation of the commonwealth, they preserved a great part of the law of nature. And with this, they mutilated their sons, because parents had such great power over their children like judges, and it was not only just for them to mutilate but also to kill.[39]

Vitoria refrained from explicitly claiming that mutilation or killing fell under paternal power *by* natural law. Nevertheless, he defended the pre-Antonine stance of Roman law, emphasizing its compatibility with the law of nature. When framed through the lens of the common good, Vitoria was prepared to locate the right to mutilate and kill within the household. To be sure, he acknowledged that these laws were no longer in force.[40] Yet Vitoria deemed it acceptable that Roman law had granted proper coercive authority to heads of households, viewing them as judges.[41]

Domingo de Soto was well aware of the bold move made by his fellow Salamancan theologian. He took Vitoria's insistence seriously and pondered its implications:

---

38 Vitoria, *Comentarios a la Secunda secundae*, ed. Beltrán de Heredia, vol. 3, q. 65, a. 2, no. 2, 314: "Non ergo est absolute contra jus naturale et divinum mutilare filium".

39 Vitoria, *Comentarios a la Secunda secundae*, ed. Beltrán de Heredia, vol. 3, q. 65, a. 2, no. 2, 314: "Item, quia inter romanos, parentes habebant potestatem et verberandi et mutilandi filios, et concedebatur illis per antiqua jura. Et tamen quantum ad conservationem reipublicae servabant magnam partem juris naturalis, et cum hoc mutilabant illos, quia tantam potestatem habebant super filios quantam judex, et non solum licebat mutilare, sed occidere." Note that in his earlier 1528 *relectio De potestate civili*, Vitoria had not made this point and instead argued that the power to mutilate (and kill) was a function of civil power, which the commonwealth received directly from God. See Vitoria, *De potestate civili*, q. 1, a. 3–5, in *Political Writings*, trans. Pagden and Lawrance, 10–17.

40 Vitoria, *Comentarios a la Secunda secundae*, ed. Beltrán de Heredia, vol. 3, q. 65, a. 2, no. 2, 314–315: "Dico nunc non licet mutilare illos, taliter quod si pater mutilasset filium vel etiam dominum servum, peccaret mortaliter, quia jura dantia et adimentia jus in foro conscientiae abstulerunt a patribus hanc potestatem."

41 *Pace* Haar, who argues that "Vitoria also failed to introduce any innovations concerning the husband's power to punish" and that the Roman law notion of paternal coercive power "was unacceptable" to him (Haar, *Natural and Political Conceptions of Community*, 104).

> It appears that, by natural law, parents are not only free to beat their children, but also to mutilate them, and if it is necessary, to punish them with murder. [...] in the primordial world there was no other commonwealth than the domestic. For as long as Adam's family alone held possession of the world, and since a public punishment of crimes was necessary, it follows that this duty fell to the father.[42]

If fathers ever had a right to inflict such punishments by natural law, Soto suggested, this could only be explained with reference to the state of humanity in Eden, when household and commonwealth were one and the same.[43]

But in contrast to Vitoria, Soto argued that heads of households in the postlapsarian world never held the authority to kill. "Once humankind multiplied and the world was divided by the families under the *ius gentium*", he asserted, "every one of them came to have their own prince".[44] Digressing into sacred history, Soto not only illustrated his disagreement with Vitoria but also refined Aquinas's original account. The power of fathers and masters was neither properly public, as Vitoria suggested, nor was it an "imperfect coercive power" along the lines of Aquinas's understanding. In contrast to his intellectual predecessors, Soto carved out the theoretical space for a third, novel kind of authority that he called "oeconomic power" (*potestas oeconomica*).[45] Where princely authority was concerned with the vindication of the common good, the oeconomic power of the head of household was directed toward the good, government, and correction of the person.[46] In this sense, it was a kind of power that was both inter-individual and involved a broader, vertical dimension.

---

42 Soto, *DIEI*, lib. v, q. 2, a. 2, 413: "Apparet enim iure naturae liberum esse patribus, non solum verbere, sed etiam mutilatione, et si opus esset, caede etiam in filios animadvertere. [...] in mundi primordiis non erat alia respublica quam domestica: nempe dum sola familia Adae orbem possidebat: tunc ergo cum necessaria esset publica scelerum vindicatio, consequitur ut patri id incumberet munus".

43 The idea that there was proper political, coercive power in Eden was not novel and dated back to Aquinas. On this point, see Markus, *Saeculum*, 224; and Aquinas, *Summa*, ed. Alarcón and Busa, 1a, q. 96, a. 4, corp.

44 Soto, *DIEI*, lib. v, q. 2, a. 2, 413: "aucto vero mortali genere, orbeque iure gentium per familias distributo, una quaeque habuit suum principem".

45 Soto, *DIEI*, lib. v, q. 2, a. 2, 414: "Nam praelati habent publicam potestatem ac iurisdictionem cum vi coerciva: parentes vero ac reliqui non nisi oeconomicam".

46 Soto, *DIEI*, lib. v, q. 2, a. 2, 413–414: "Publica enim potestas, ut supra dictum est, non tam reo ad emendam consulit, quam communi bono ad vindictam: patri vero, ac domino, et paedagogo non alia ratione verberare suos fas esse, nisi quo ad eius emendationem salubrius ei consulitur". On the interplay between physical (coercive) and moral (directive) force, see also Brett, *Changes of State*, 130, and Höpfl, *Jesuit Political Thought*, 208–212.

Soto's account of oeconomic power also led to broader reflections on the scope of punishment within the household. In his view, the right to flog domestic subjects was vested with the head of the household, "primarily" as father in relation to his children and "secondarily" as master with respect to enslaved persons.[47] But based on the assertion that the husband was the *caput uxoris*, Soto also argued that the "right to whip the wife cannot be denied to the husband".[48] This was a troubling claim, even from within the logic of Soto's treatise. While it followed logically from his theory of domestic authority, it appeared to contradict Soto's vision of marriage laid out in the previous chapter, in terms of mutual spousal governance. Soto himself was keenly aware of the problematic nature of this idea and stressed that it was "shameful for husbands to use this right and indeed illicit unless they are overtaken by the gravest necessity. For those who make use of their wives as slaves are barbarians, as Aristotle says in *Politics* I".[49] Yet he could not avoid the implications that his theory of oeconomic power carried for *all* household relations.

At the end of the 16th century, Luis de Molina put forward a remarkably similar vision of domestic authority he called the *ius patrisfamilias*. This right allowed the paterfamilias to impose moderate punishments on all members of the household community, "whether they are free or slaves".[50] Like Soto, Molina conceded that the husband could whip his wife "to remind her of her crimes and excesses", while insisting that this was a "shameful" act because the wife was her husband's "ally and subject to him as the mother of the family".[51]

---

47 Soto, *DIEI*, lib. v, q. 2, a. 2, 413.

48 Soto, *DIEI*, lib. v, q. 2, a. 2, 414: "De marito autem utrum uxorem verberandi ius habeat, respondetur non esse illis denegandum: quandoquidem vir […] caput uxoris sit".

49 Soto, *DIEI*, lib. v, q. 2, a. 2, 414: "Uti tamen eodem iure dedecus est, atque adeo nefas, nisi gravissima ingruente necessitate. Sunt enim barbari qui uxoribus ut mancipiis utuntur, ut I Politica autor est Aristoteles".

50 Molina, *DIEI*, vol. 1, tr. II, disp. 228, no. 25–26, col. 999–1000: "ius patrisfamilias […] Hic tamen effectus, licet patribus […] liberorum, qui sunt sub eorum potestate […] etiam convenit in reliquos qui de sua familia sunt, sive liberi sint, sive servi".

51 Molina, *DIEI*, vol. 4, tr. III, disp. 2, no. 20, col. 523: "etiam usque ad verbera, et alias non atroces percussiones, si ita opus sit, commemoranturque delicta et excessus illius [i.e., the wife's]. […] Nefas tamen erit marito eam tractare ut servam, aut ancillam, sed sociam, ac matrem familiae ipsi tamen subditam. Est autem deducus viris punire uxores". Yet as Sibylle Schnyder has shown, the early modern Iberian theologians argued that a husband, who caught his adulterous wife *in flagranti* and then killed her, though he sinned, was not a murderer and went unpunished. In so arguing, the Iberian theorists sought to offer theological reasoning that was in accordance with contemporary Spanish civil legislation. See Schnyder, *Tötung und Diebstahl*, 129–131.

But Molina intervened in the ongoing debate about the scope of coercive authority entailed within domestic power. Soto maintained that only Adam ever ruled a household with public authority, while in the postlapsarian world of divided commonwealths, the power to kill and mutilate was the prerogative of princes. But Molina offered a vigorous rebuttal. Even in the political state of humanity after the Fall, he explained, not all people lived in full-fledged polities:

> [...] if any nation is so barbarous that it does not have a superior, but only two single families; or if two villages are divided from each other so that they do not have a common superior—which seems to be happening in the region of Brazil—it is licit for each family or village to impose, by their own authority, a vindication and penalty for the violation of right and harm that they suffered from the other family or village.[52]

Molina did not claim that the Brazilians lacked true mastery over their affairs, nor did he offer a veiled apology for Portuguese imperial domination. While he acknowledged that the Brazilians might not live in fully developed commonwealths, the authority he ascribed to their domestic rulers was nonetheless quasi-princely. They held *internal* coercive authority over their own subjects and could defend the community against *external* enemies.[53] In that sense, they functioned as "household republics".

But what of households situated within a commonwealth? Molina addressed this question in the Third Tractate of his *De iustitia et iure*, turning to yet another example from the wider world: in Japan, heads of household exercised extensive power "within their own families" and this was legitimate "as long as they are not forbidden to do so by the commonwealth".[54] By highlight ing the diversity of human communities in the "West" and "East Indies", Molina

---

52 Molina, *DIEI*, vol. 1, tr. II, disp. 100, no. 6, col. 411: "si tam barbara sit aliqua natio, ut superiorem non habeat, sed singulae duae familiae, aut duo pagi ita ab invicem sint divisi, ut communem non habeant superiorem, quod in Brasilica regione evenire videtur, fas sit uni familiae, aut pago, propria authoritate sumere iustam vindictam et satisfactionem de iniuriis ac damnis ab altera familia aut pago illatis. Respondendum est, posse".

53 This passage of Molina's is also mentioned in Costello, *The Political Philosophy of Luis de Molina*, 46; Höpfl, *Jesuit Political Thought*, 200; and Haar, *Natural and Political Conceptions of Community*, 110–111.

54 Molina, *DIEI*, vol. 4, tr. III, disp. 2, no. 19, col. 523: "Quare condemnandi non sunt Iaponenses, aut si qui alii sunt similes, qui in propriis familiis more ipsis permisso, longe maiorem exercent potestatem, quam hactenus explicatam, interim dum per rempublicam totam, cuius familiae illae sunt partes, id illis non prohibetur".

ultimately agreed with Vitoira that domestic power was naturally coercive. The limited authority of *patresfamilias* within the Christian-Roman world, he concluded, was therefore a consequence of human law and institution.[55]

However, he located a crucial difference between the "household republics" in Brazil and the domestic communities in Japan. While the latter held extensive power "within their own families", they were embedded in a commonwealth and did not, therefore, possess any authority vis-à-vis other domestic rulers.[56] It was only in the absence of a common superior that heads of households could justly punish external enemies. As Molina explained elsewhere in the *De iustitia et iure*,

> [...] if the power to kill external malefactors arises in the family by the nature of things, and that power does not exist in the individuals of the family—insofar as they are individual and private persons—why, then, does a similar power not arise in the whole commonwealth, which was not given to it by the parts of which it consists? Indeed, one cannot give any reason.[57]

Molina pushed back against the notion that the commonwealth received its jurisdiction from its constituent households. The idea of such a transfer of power was as unthinkable to him as it had been for his Dominican predecessors, and it seems strange to cast Molina's position on this point as "not entirely clear".[58] Princes as well as those who governed a "household republic" were vested with a kind of authority that had naturally arisen in their respective communities as a whole.[59]

55 Molina, *DIEI*, vol. 4, tr. III, disp. 2, no. 19, col. 523: "Quo fit, ut potestatem patrum familias in suos subditos, coarctatam esse, ut hodie est in provinciis, quae iure Romanorum utuntur, pendeat a iure humano, ut Victoria asservit".

56 See the quote in the footnote before the last.

57 Molina, *DIEI*, vol. 1, tr. II, disp. 22, no. 9, col. 115: "Praeterea, qua ratione in familia ex natura rei consurgit potestas occidendi externos malefactores, quae potestas non est in singulis de familia, quatenus singulares, privataeque personae sunt, cur etiam non consurget similis potestas in tota Republica, quae a partibus, quibus constat, communicata illi non sit? Profecto nulla potest reddi legitima ratio".

58 See Haar, *Natural and Political Conceptions of Community*, 111: "Molina said, even if this (public) power existed by nature in the family, then one might ponder along the same lines why it should not reside in the same way—namely by nature—in the political community as well. In any case, this particular issue was not entirely clear, he claimed".

59 On this point, see also Brett, "Luis de Molina on Law and Power", 169–170; and Höpfl, *Jesuit Political Thought*, 194.

This point was later confirmed by Juan de Lugo, who conceded that life in dispersed and politically isolated households was possible, both theoretically and practically.[60] However, if these households, at any point, decided to come together and form a community, they would have to relinquish their "right of superiority; in the same way that he who turns himself into slavery *eo ipso* gives to his master the right to govern him, and to correct his crimes".[61] By comparing the formation of political society to the process of enslavement, Lugo offered a sophisticated explanation for why the theory of the "household republic" was compatible with the idea of civil power being derived solely from God and natural law. To say that households could be quasi-cities in the absence of a prince was merely an addition, rather than a contradiction, to the established theories that Vitoria and Soto had developed in the 16th-century lecture halls of Salamanca.

2.2 *Whipping and Branding Slaves*

A central question that we have not yet addressed is the scope of slave punishment in the households of the Iberian empires. The Salamancan Dominicans, as we know, were primarily concerned with the fundamental, but largely abstract, distinction between the domestic power of flogging and public punishments that affected bodily integrity. However, Luis de Molina inquired into concrete forms of domestic punishment to determine what kinds of retributions the paterfamilias could legitimately inflict.

His meditation homed in on the legal validity of two of the most contentious forms of slave punishment in the 16th-century Iberian world. Firstly, Molina argued that he "did not dare condemn" that masters could justly "scorch their slaves with drops of pork fat, or wax" if they were "crude and incorrigible".[62] Secondly, he maintained it was licit to brand enslaved persons in the face "without any previous offense of the slaves", simply to prevent their "loss".[63] Molina considered facial branding legitimate under three circumstances: "if

60 Lugo, *DIEI*, disp. 10, sect. 2, no. 74, 268.

61 Lugo, *DIEI*, disp. 10, sect. 2, no. 75, 268: "Possent ergo homines non facere communitatem, sed vivere seorsim; eo tamen ipso quod faciunt communitatem, dant illi ius superioritatis; sicut qui se facit servum, eo ipso dat ius domino, ut eum gubernet, eiusque delicta corrigat".

62 Molina, *DIEI*, vol. 4, tr. III, disp. 2, no. 14, col. 521: "Utrum autem licitum sit adurere mancipia gutta suila, aut cera [...] Non auderem id damnare [...] quando delictum esset tanta poena dignum, aut mancipium adeo esset durum ac incorrigibile".

63 Molina, *DIEI*, vol. 4, tr. III, disp. 2, no. 14, col. 521: "Utrum ite sit licitum, signare mancipia in facie. Affirmante est respondendum, esto nulla illorum antecedat culpa, quando periculum est amissionis illorum, nisi ita signentur".

nobody thought that they were slaves; if they were fugitives, as a punishment; and to curb them from escaping and find them more easily".[64] He concluded with the forceful assertion that, should these circumstances arise, "reason itself demands that they be branded".[65]

Historians have shown that branding and *pringar*, as the dropping of hot fat or wax onto the body of enslaved humans was called in the vernacular, were widely used in practice and constituted pivotal manifestations of the master's power over the slave's body.[66] A common way of branding enslaved persons in the Spanish empire was to mark their faces with the letter "s" and the image of a nail (Spanish: *clavo*). Put together, this made up the word slave: *es-clavo*.[67] Branding was quite literally the process of impressing the servile status onto the slave to mark one's own property.[68] This practice was also described and defended by Juan de Solórzano y Pereira, who in his *Política indiana* of the mid-17th century similarly pointed to "the letters, or marks with which the faces of slaves were tagged".[69] Facial branding was rarely imposed upon enslaved persons of sub-Saharan origin, as their skin color itself came to be regarded as a marker of servile status.[70] This, in turn, resonates with Molina's argument that slaves were branded "if nobody thought that they were slaves". It was a means to suppress the resistance of enslaved persons and a pervasive form of punishment, executed by owners whose slaves had tried to run away, both in Iberia and the wider Mediterranean world.[71]

---

64 Molina, *DIEI*, vol. 4, tr. III, disp. 2, no. 14, col. 521: "Eo quod eiusmodi sint, de quibus nullus praesumet ea esse mancipia; aut quando fugitiva sunt atque in poenam, et ut coerceantur a fuga meliusque inveniantur".

65 Molina, *DIEI*, vol. 4, tr. III, disp. 2, no. 14, col. 521: "ratio ipsa postulat, ut signentur". Molina's line of argument was later restated by Machado de Chavez, *Perfecto confesor*, vol. 2, lib. VI, parte 7, tr. XII, doc. 2, no. 1–4, 518–519; and Diana, *Resolutionum moralium*, tr. VII, resol. 22, 246.

66 Phillips, "Slavery in the Atlantic Islands", 343. The notion of *pringar* is also mentioned, for instance, by Machado de Chavez, *Perfecto confesor*, vol. 2, lib. VI, parte 7, tr. XII, doc. 2, no. 2, 519.

67 Martín Casares, *La esclavitud en la Granada*, 392; Seijas, *Asian Slaves in Colonial Mexico*, 165–166.

68 Martín Casares, *La esclavitud en la Granada*, 392. This also applies to colonial Spanish America. See Velázquez Gutiérrez, *Mujeres de origen africano*, 133.

69 Solórzano, *Política indiana*, ed. Ochoa Brun, vol. 1, lib. II, cap. 1, no. 33, 140: "Por donde comunmente solian ser llamados *Stichos*, *Stigmaticos*, ó *Stigmatosos* por las letras, ó marcas con que les señalaban el rostro".

70 Martín Casares, *La esclavitud en la Granada*, 396. Tatiana Seijas notes, however, that enslaved Africans in colonial Mexico were sometimes branded on their arms or chest in order to associate them with the traders who had brought them overseas, to facilitate the calculation of taxes for asiento holders. See Seijas, *Asian Slaves in Colonial Mexico*, 165.

71 Martín Casares, *La esclavitud en la Granada*, 94. The practice of branding fugitive slaves

Even though facial branding was widespread, Molina's defense of the practice was striking. For according to the *Siete Partidas*, facial branding was considered a form of mutilation. Furthermore, it was illicit even as public punishment "because God made the face of man in his image: and therefore no judge is allowed to apply punishments to the face".[72] In his gloss, Gregorio López noted that the sentence of the *Partidas* was compliant with Roman law. For indeed, after his turn to Christianity, emperor Constantine had decreed that the face be exempt from branding due to its resemblance to "celestial beauty".[73] But López went on to explain that Alfonso X, the author of the *Partidas*, had overlooked the fact that medieval canon law did not exempt the face. Commentators of the *Liber Extra*, as López highlighted, expressly allowed that clerics who faked the king's seal could be punished with facial branding.[74] In the curia's understanding, this served the dual purpose of punishment and reconciliation. A branded face was a mark of transgression. But as Valentin Groebner has shown, "by way of analogy with the biblical mark of Cain, [it] also recorded the particular status of those who had been punished and to whom God therefore had accorded special protection".[75] In this sense, late-medieval canon law offered a rock-solid vindication of facial branding from a Christian perspective. It allowed López to defend the morality of a widespread contemporary practice against a fundamental dictum in force since the time of Constantine, the first Christian Roman emperor.

Luis de Molina justified facial branding without any reference to legal or theological authorities, thus choosing to circumvent this debate. However, he likewise granted slaveowners the authority to inflict permanent bodily injury. And in doing so, he blurred the line between domestic and public power.

was also licensed under late-medievel Genoese law (see Epstein, *Speaking of Slavery*, 119). On branded, enslaved "Tartar" women in later *trecento* Florence, see Groebner, *Who Are You?*, 108–110. On the practice of tattooing enslaved persons in precolonial central America, especially among the Mayas and Aztecs, see the discussion in Zeuske, *Sklaverei*, 58.

72 *Las Siete Partidas*, l. 6, tit. 31, partida 7: "Pero algunas maneras son de penas, que las non deven dar a ningun ome, por yero que aya fecho: assi como señalar a alguno en la cara, quemando le con fuego caliente [...] Esto es porque la cara del ome fizo Dios a su semejança: e porende ningun juez, non debe penar en la cara".

73 C.9.47.17: "minime in eius facie scribatur [...] quo facies, quae ad similitudinem pulchritudinis caelestis est figurata, minime maculetur". On the Christian context of Constantine's law from 319 AD, see Epstein, *Speaking of Slavery*, 63.

74 *Las Siete Partidas*, l. 6, tit. 31, partida 7, gloss López, verb. *en la cara*: "fallit tamen in casu a. *ad audientiam, de crimi. fal.* ubi vide per Inno. et docto. ibi tamen non exprimitur de facie [...] videntur velle, quod etiam in facie possit fieri in casu illo in odium criminis illius". For the respective passage in the *Liber Extra*, see X.5.20.3.

75 Groebner, *Who Are You?*, 104.

2.3 *Incarceration, Domestic Detainment, and "Private Prisons"*

The relationship between slave rule and political rule was further complicated by yet another hotly debated question: did masters also have a right to imprison their slaves? In Aquinas's understanding, each individual could "detain a human being temporarily and immediately so that he does not carry through an illicit deed".[76] But pre-emptive detainment was not the same as proper incarceration. The power to lock someone up was the sole privilege of the person "who has the power to universally dispose of the acts and the life of the other, because this not only prevents the person from committing evil deeds but also from doing *good*".[77] Aquinas did not explicitly point to the power of heads of households in this context. But as explained, he previously insisted that the paterfamilias held no right over the lives of domestic subjects, making it clear that imprisonment was an exclusively public intervention.

In their 16th-century commentaries on the *Summa*, the theologians of the School of Salamanca sought to offer further elaborations on these issues. Domingo de Soto argued that the right to incarcerate another solely lay in the hands of the commonwealth and did not extend to fathers or masters.[78] What is more, he distinguished between two kinds of public rationales for imprisonment. The first was *civil* and served the function of "keeping malefactors unharmed while their trial proceeds and is being decided", whereas the purpose of incarceration by *ecclesiastical* authority was "punishment".[79] The reason for this distinction was that the church could not inflict the corporal punishment of whipping upon those who violated its law and hence made "great use of this power", as Soto emphasized.[80] From a canon law perspective, therefore, imprisonment was a form of public punishment. In civil jurisdiction, by contrast, prison was merely a stopover on the way to corporal punishment.

---

76 Aquinas, *Summa*, ed. Alarcón and Busa, 2a2ae, q. 65, a. 3, ad 3: "detinere hominem ad horam ab aliquo opere illicito statim perpetrando, cuilibet licet".

77 Aquinas, *Summa*, ed. Alarcón and Busa, 2a2ae, q. 65, a. 3, ad 3, emphasis mine: "Sed simpliciter aliquem includere vel ligare ad eum solum pertinet qui habet disponere universaliter de actibus et vita alterius, quia per hoc impeditur non solum a malis, sed etiam a bonis agendis".

78 Soto, *DIEI*, lib. V, q. 2, a. 3, 415: "Concedens est, ut eidem soli reipublicae sit deputatum, penes quam potestas est vitae et mortis. Quocirca neque parentibus neque dominis id licet".

79 Soto, *DIEI*, lib. V, q. 2, a. 3, 415: "Hinc sit carcerum duplicem esse usum in republica. Serviunt nanque et ad conservandum malefactores dum eorum causae tractantur ac deciduntur, et praetera in poenam".

80 Soto, *DIEI*, lib. V, q. 2, a. 3, 415: "Qua plurimum ecclesiastica potestas utitur, dum ad verbera procedere non potest".

Soto also followed Aquinas's argument that temporary detainment was licit for individuals, insofar as it prevented an imminent evil.[81] The more difficult question, however, was whether a middle ground existed between this private right, on the one hand, and the commonwealth's power to imprison, on the other. Francisco de Vitoria suggested that it did, in fact, exist. He argued that heads of households could justly "detain their son or slave, because they are responsible for their care, and because this is convenient to manage their business".[82] Soto, too, acknowledged the paterfamilias' right of detention. But unlike Vitoria, who had not further elucidated how this related to public, coercive incarceration, Soto made an important addition. Enslaved persons and children could be locked up for shorter periods of time, "either as a form of punishment or to keep them in check, because this kind of confinement does not have the rationale of a prison".[83]

And yet, this understanding of domestic detainment came remarkably close to the logic of incarceration by ecclesiastical power. Moreover, heads of households had this right in addition to the authority to inflict the corporal punishment of flogging—a right that ecclesiastical authorities lacked. In this sense, the boundaries between domestic and public forms of imprisonment in Soto's account were anything but sharp.

∴

According to the *Siete Partidas*, the purpose of the prison was to prevent those accused of serious crimes—punishable by death or mutilation—from fleeing or going into hiding until their trial.[84] The principle that prisons should be places of detainment rather than punishment entered medieval Castilian law via the Roman *Digest*, and it remained a prominent tenet into the early modern period.[85] Gregorio López and the equally widely read and quoted jurist

81 Vitoria, *Comentarios a la Secunda secundae*, ed. Beltrán de Heredia, vol. 3, q. 65, a. 3, no. 4, 318–319; Soto, *DIEI*, lib. v, q. 2, a. 3, 416.

82 Vitoria, *Comentarios a la Secunda secundae*, ed. Beltrán de Heredia, vol. 3, q. 65, a. 3, no. 3, 319: "licitum est de se patri et domino tenere illum, quia et pater habet curam illorum et dominus servorum, quia hoc est commode gerere negotium eorum".

83 Soto, *DIEI*, lib. v, q. 2, a. 3, 416: "solummodo parentes retinere filios possunt, ac domini servos occlusos in parum tempus, tam in poenam, quam ad eos cohibendos: nam inclusio illa non habet rationem carceris".

84 *Las Siete Partidas*, l. 4, tit. 31, partida 7: "Ca la carcel non es dada para escarmentar los yerros: mas para guardar los presos tan solamente en ella, fasta que sean judgados". See also the preface of tit. 29, partida 7.

85 The locus was D.48.19.8.9. See also Ramos Vázquez, "Detenciones cautelares, coactivas o punitivas", 750.

Jerónimo Castillo de Bobadilla confirmed this anew.[86] Just as Soto had put it, they argued that the purpose of the civil jail was to detain those accused of committing crimes, while the church alone possessed the power to impose the "punishment of perpetual prison".[87]

Yet a closer look at the theological and juridical discourse of the time calls into question the idea that Spain's early modern prisons were merely places of detainment—an idea also widespread in modern scholarship on the topic.[88] As Luis de Molina noted in his classification of public retributions, the civil prison was not only a place to detain criminals, who were awaiting their trial. It was also a punishment in its own right.[89] An example of this kind of prison sentence, as Molina explained elsewhere in his treatise, was the commutation of pecuniary punishments for those guilty of "trivial thefts" and unable to pay the sum to which they were sentenced.[90] This notion of the debtor's prison, the so-called *prisión por deudas*, had existed in Castile since the medieval period.[91] Drawing on Gregorio López's gloss, Molina explained that the duration of such prison punishments usually ranged from a few days to few months, depending on the amount owed.[92]

---

86 On Bobadilla's life and work, see the excellent overview in Danwerth, "*Política para Corregidores*", 144–148.

87 *Las Siete Partidas*, l. 4, tit. 31, partida 7, gloss López, verb. *a ome libre*: "poena perpetui carceris imponitur a iure canonico illis casibus, quibus de iure civili imponitur poena mortis. […] non potest quis damnari ad perpetuam custodiam carcerum, licet tamen de iure canonico haec poena permittatur". The same point was also made by Bobadilla, *Política para corregidores*, lib. III, cap. 15, no. 3.

88 See e.g., Pike, *Penal Servitude in Early Modern Spain*, 3; Heras Santos, *La justicia penal*, most forcefully at 265; and Spierenburg, "Prison and Convict Labour in Early Modern Europe", 112–113. The notable exeption is Isabel Ramos Vázquez's excellent work: See Ramos Vázquez, "Detenciones cautelares, coactivas, o punitivas"; and Ramos Vázquez, *Arrestos, cárceles y prisiones*, 101–149.

89 Molina, *DIEI*, vol. 4, tr. III, disp. 2, no. 13, col. 520: "constat rempublicam, et potestates laicas ab ea ad id derivatas, procedere posse usque ad mortis poenam, si delictum ea sit dignum; et longe maiori cum ratione posse procedere ad membri mutilationem, ad poenam flagellorum, exilii, ad inclusionem in carcerem, tum ad reorum custodiam, tum etiam in eorundem poenam".

90 Molina, *DIEI*, vol. 3.2, tr. II, disp. 695, no. 12, col. 90–91: "Quare eiusmodi levia furta hodie vel poena pecuniaria […] erunt punienda, vel, si reus non sit solvendo, punienda erunt detentione illius in carcere aliquibus diebus, aut mensibus […] ut supra cum Greg. Lopez est dictum". See also *Las Siete Partidas*, l. 18, tit. 14, partida 7, gloss López, verb. *matar ni cortar miembro*: "Si tamen ista tria furta essent parva […] vidi condenare in pecunia, vel ad standum per aliquod tempus, puta duorum, vel trium mensum in carceribus".

91 Ramos Vázquez, "Detenciones cautelares, coactivas, o punitivas", 710.

92 See the quote in the footnote before the last. Despite his forceful argument against the

With the promulgation of the *Nueva recopilación*, Spain's legal code of 1566, it became permissible to punish lesser crimes with short-term prison sentences.[93] López's commentary on the *Partidas*, published a decade earlier, did not address this point. But Spain's most influential juridical commentator of the later 16th century, Jerónimo Castillo de Bobadilla, explicitly emphasized this legal innovation. As he wrote in his *Política para corregidores* (1597), the civil prison had become an institution with multiple functions. It still served to detain those awaiting their trial and press debtors to pay their dues. But it had also become a place of punishment for blasphemers, gamblers, or those who resisted judicial authorities.[94]

While Molina made a similar point, his real move was to challenge the idea of a mutually exclusive understanding of punishment and imprisonment by the church and civil authorities, respectively. Domingo de Soto, as we saw, insisted that ecclesiastical judges resorted to the punishment of incarceration because they could not licitly impose the punishment of whipping on malefactors. But Molina strongly disagreed. On the one hand, he conceded that canon law did indeed prohibit the imposition of punishments that involved the shedding of blood. So-called *penas de sangre* were beyond the power of the church.[95] However, Molina maintained that this did not amount to a prohibition of flogging, as Soto had claimed. "It is manifest", Molina insisted, "that ecclesiastical and monastic prelates may go as far as to lock up their subjects in prisons, to whip them, or to inflict other punishments laid down by canon law".[96] In so arguing, Molina emphasized the close relationship between civil and ecclesiastical jurisdiction, and between punishment and imprisonment.[97]

---

idea that civil authorities could sentence malefactors with *perpetual* incarceration, López did not therefore refute the idea of prison punishments *tout court*.

93 Ramos Vázquez, "Detenciones cautelares, coactivas, o punitivas", 752–754.

94 Bobadilla, *Política para corregidores*, lib. III, cap. 15, no. 8. See also the discussion in Ramos Vázquez, "Detenciones cautelares, coactivas, o punitivas", 753–757.

95 Molina, DIEI, vol. 4, tr. III, disp. 2, no. 13, col. 520: "Poenam sanguinis exercere non possunt praelati".

96 Molina, DIEI, vol. 4, tr. III, disp. 2, no. 13, col. 520: "De praelatis ecclesiasticis, et de praelatis religiosorum, manifestum etiam est, procedere adversus sibi subditos posse usque ad inclusionem in carcerem, et usque ad verbera, et alias poenas iure canonico statutas". The jurist Bobadilla later even went so far as to argue that flogging was a licit ecclesiastical punishment if "some drops of blood" were going to be shed in the process of doing so. See Bobadilla, *Política para corregidores*, lib. II, cap. 17, no. 29: "Podra el obispo, inquisidores, o iurez ecclesiastico, mandar [...] açotes (los quales se davan por pena de derecho divino) y aunque dellos saliesse alguna gota de sangre, no se incurrirà la irregularidad". On ecclesiastical punishments in 16th-century Spain, see also Schnyder, *Tötung und Diebstahl*, 144–148.

97 Ramos Vázquez argues that in 16th-century Spain, the nexus between civil and ecclesias-

∴

Where Molina disagreed with Soto on the issue of public incarceration, the question arises as to whether he also challenged the Salamancan understanding of domestic detainment. "Parents and masters", he explained, "are allowed to lock up their sons or slaves in a private prison, either as a punishment or to repress their malicious customs".[98] Molina was well aware that his interpretation seemed incompatible with the Thomist position. "Aquinas", he noted, "perhaps did not understand the notion of prison in this way".[99] How, then, did Molina justify his fundamental departure from the established view? He argued that "the common good demands" that heads of households have this power over slaves and sons, and "by *epikeia* one must suppose that the private prison is exempt from the above-mentioned laws, and its use is accepted everywhere with impunity".[100]

The full force of Molina's argument becomes apparent against the understanding of what "private prison" meant in the legal discourse of his time. Up to the 13th century, it had been a common practice for princes to delegate the authority to imprison malefactors to individual lords. However, with the growing influence of the Roman legal understanding of the civil prison as a place of detainment rather than punishment, so-called "private" or "particular prisons" (*cárceles privadas* or *particulares*) were gradually abolished and came to be seen as an attack on the monarch's power.[101] Accordingly, Alfonso X's *Siete Partidas* categorically prohibited the delegation of the public right of punishment, declaring that those who imprisoned others on their own authority were going to be punished by death. This prohibition of private prisons remained a cen-

tical rationales of punishment was most apparent insofar as women of particularly distinguished social status (*mujeres honradas*) were exempt from corporal punishment and sent to monasteries for expiation of grave crimes. She understands this as the importation of an ecclesiastical punishment into the civil realm ("Detenciones cautelares, coactivas, o punitivas", 750–752). Gregorio López, however, argued that this was a specifically medieval practice that was no longer in use in the 16th century. See *Las Siete Partidas*, l. 4, tit. 29, partida 7, gloss López, verb. *monasterio*.

98 Molina, *DIEI*, vol. 4, tr. III, disp. 2, no. 18, col. 522: "parentibus tamen ac dominis permittitur includere in privato carcere filios, aut servos, ut eos puniant ac coerceant ab aliquibus moribus sinistris".

99 Molina, *DIEI*, vol. 4, tr. III, disp. 2, no. 18, col. 522: "Forte Divus Thomas non intellexit de hoc modo carceris".

100 Molina, *DIEI*, vol. 4, tr. III, disp. 2, no. 18, col. 522: "bonum commune postulat, atque per epicheiam censendus est exceptus [i.e., the private prison] a praedictis iuribus, usuque impune omnino est receptus".

101 Vázquez, "Cárceles públicas y privadas", 376; Heras Santos, *La justicia penal*, 266.

tral tenet of Castilian civil law into the early modern period, as López's gloss underscores.[102]

In light of this, Molina's audacious justification of an institution prohibited *tout court* appears striking. He could have simply reiterated the opinion of his Dominican predecessors, who had managed to carve out a legal space for domestic detention, which was extensive and yet formally distinct from public imprisonment. But Molina's justification of the private prison was not entirely beyond the legal discourse of his time. Notably, the same law in the *Partidas* that outlawed private prisons nevertheless also declared that it was permissible "without any mandate of the king, to make traps in one's house to guard one's captive Moors [...] over whom one has dominion so that they do not flee to the lands of the Moors".[103] Alfonso X's original wording testifies to the fact that this law was enacted in the context of the *Reconquista*. But Gregorio López emphasized the general validity of this dictum by pointing to its roots in Roman law.[104]

It is important to note, however, that neither Alfonso X nor his early modern glossator López associated domestic detainment with the concept of the private prison. Like Domingo de Soto, they understood the right to "guard" children and enslaved persons as a function of household authority. López pointed out explicitly that "the domestic *prison* is not allowed".[105]

---

102 See *Las Siete Partidas*, l. 15, tit. 29, partida 7, gloss López, verb. *fazer carcel*: "habere carcerem est publici iuris, et meri imperii, et non convenit privatis: neque est concessibile".

103 *Las Siete Partidas*, l. 15, tit. 29, partida 7: "Pero si algunos quisieren fazer cepos en sus casas para guardar sus moros cautivos, bien lo pueden fazer sin mandado del rey [...] pues que lo fazen para guardar sus cautivos en que han señorio, e lo fazen porque non se fuyan a tierra de moros".

104 *Las Siete Partidas*, l. 15, tit. 29, partida 7, gloss López, verb. *guardar sus moros*: "de patre quo ad filium cum sit ad correctionem morum l. 1. C. de emen. servo. & l. 1. C. de emen. propinquo". López here referred to D.9.14.1 and D.9.15.1.

105 See *Las Siete Partidas*, l. 15, tit. 29, partida 7, gloss López, verb. *guardar sus moros*: "Et nota quod carcer domesticus non permittitur, nisi in casibus expressis in iure l. divus. de offi. praesid. Bal. in. l. imperium, prima lectura, colum. 4. ff. de iuris. omnium. iudi". López here pointed to Baldus de Ubaldis's commentary on D.1.1.18, where it was stated that the only case in which private imprisonment was licit was if a madman, who was entirely devoid of his intellect, killed another person. In that case, he was locked up merely for the protection of others, for it was thought that his insanity was punishment enough. Baldus, in his commentary, stressed that this form of domestic imprisonment did not involve any form of private jurisdiction. See Baldus, *Commentaria in primam digesti*, lib. I, De iurisdictione omnium iuridocum, l. 2, additio 9, 73: "Quartus carcer est domesticus, quod non est licitus nisi in casibus expressis a iure, ut statutum de off. prae. l. divus & ille carcer non est sub aliquo gradu iurisdictionis, quam competiti privato".

Molina, however, took a markedly different stance. He argued that the paterfamilias could legitimately confine children and enslaved persons in a *carcer privatus*. To be sure, this does not represent a rupture from his intellectual predecessors, who likewise understood domestic punishment as a means of correction within the household, distinct from the public vindication of the common good with attendant rights to kill or maim. Molina himself conceded that when compared with the ecclesiastical power of perpetual imprisonment, the authority of fathers and masters amounted solely to the punishment of "imperfect jail".[106]

And yet, Molina's invocation of the term "private prison" was fundamentally beyond the theological and legal discourse of his time. Steeped in the language of public authority, it implied that coercive power extended into the household. Molina emphasized that the private prison was not only necessary for maintaining order in the domestic community but also indispensable for the common good. This was not quite the same as claiming that masters had received this power by actual delegation of the monarch.[107] But Molina's concept of private prison constituted a space in which a mediated form of public authority was exercised within the domestic sphere and enacted upon the body of the child and slave.

3 Care and Carelessness

As we saw in the previous section, Thomas Aquinas's discussion of punishment and imprisonment had a lasting influence on early modern Iberian debates about the authority of masters over slaves. But it is equally important to note that theologians and jurists writing in the late 16th and early 17th centuries departed in important ways from the structure and scope of Aquinas's account. This is especially true when it comes to questions about the duties of slaveholders toward their slaves.

The most comprehensive treatment of the relationship between slavery and care stems from the writings of Luis de Molina. He emphasized that the domestic rule of enslaved persons exceeded the scope of discipline and punishment.

---

106 Molina, *DIEI*, vol. 4, tr. III, disp. 2, no. 18, col. 522: "Unde carcer perpetuus, et exilium, mors civilis nuncupatur. Sicut autem domini ac parentes uti possunt carcere imperfecto".

107 It is noteworthy that this account of delegated public power not only corresponded to the medieval Castilian understanding of private imprisonment, but also to the way in which slaveholders received their right of punishment in the British Empire in the early 19th century. On this latter point, see Benton and Ford, *Rage for Order*, 45.

Invoking Aristotle's *Politics*, he underscored that the government of slaves also involved broader moral obligations. On the one hand, as Molina argued, "the rule of slaves chiefly concerns the good of the master and the benefit of the family".[108] Yet on the other, the relationship between master and enslaved person was also one of the "three relations of persons who mutually care for each other".[109] This emphasis on care is relevant, as it reveals that, in Molina's view, slave government reflected a broader Aristotelian understanding of reciprocal responsibility. "Reason itself", he insisted, "demands that masters, through their rule, make an effort and care for the good of the slaves".[110]

The theologians writing after Molina reiterated this emphasis on the obligations of masters toward their slaves.[111] Juan Azor emphasized a tripartite duty to provide enslaved persons with food, clothing, and shelter.[112] The Portuguese Fernão Rebello stressed that this also applied to elderly slaves, who were no longer able to work but had served their master faithfully throughout their lives.[113] And the Quiteño Creole Machado de Chavez reminded his readers of Seneca's dictum that "the master should imagine himself as a slave, and how he would like to be treated by his master [...] and he should treat his slave in this way".[114]

---

108 Molina, *DIEI*, vol. 1, tr. II, disp. 22, no. 7, col. 113: "Servorum autem regimen, domini bonum, familiaeque commodum praecipue respicit".

109 Molina, *DIEI*, vol. 1, tr. II, disp. 22, no. 3, col. 111: "Porro perfecta familia, *autore Aristotele loco citato*, ex tribus personarum se mutuo respicientium complicationibus coalescit. [...] Tertia dominorum cum servis". Molina here referred to Aristotle, *Politics*, ed. Everson and trans. Jowett, lib. I, 1253b1–1253b14.

110 Molina, *DIEI*, vol. 1, tr. II, disp. 22, no. 7, col. 113: "quamvis ratio ipsa postulet, ut domini, quorum commodi servi, voluntatique inserviunt, vicissim illorum bonum, in suo ordine et gradu, regimine suo curent et intendant". On this point, see also Brett, "Luis de Molina on Law and Power", 167–168.

111 An exception is Fernando Pérez. While pointing to the limits of the master's power over slaves, he insisted that the use of one's slave was solely for the master's advantage and in that sense comparable to the use of a horse. See Pérez, "De acquisitione dominii in homines", ed. and trans. Tarrío and Brito, dubitatio 5, 350: "Etiamsi homo sit dominus sui servi non quo ad servi utilitatem sed quo ad suam propriam, sicut est equi et aliorum, magnum tamen est discrimen inter dominium servi et aliarum rerum, quia cum sit in hominem ex obiecto et nobilius et non est dominium quo ad omnem usum, sicut dominium aliarum".

112 Azor, *Institutionum moralium*, vol. 2, lib. 11, cap. 38, 147: "Nempe, victum, vestitum, habitatione: quae tria nomine alimentorum comprehendantur".

113 Rebello, *Opus de obligationibus iustitiae*, pars 2, lib. XIII, q. 18, no. 12, 763: "potest cogere dominos, ad alendos eos servos, et famulos, qui exacta ferme vita in dominorum obsequio, iam pare senio laborare nequeunt".

114 Machado de Chavez, *Perfecto confesor*, vol. 2, lib. VI, parte 7, tr. 12, doc. 6, no. 1, 521: "considere pues el señor si fuera esclavo, como quisiera ser tratado de su señor; y pues Dios le

3.1 *Beyond Good Government*

Discussions of the duty to care and provide for enslaved persons occupied a prominent place in the writings of early modern Iberian thinkers. Many more pages, however, were filled with reflections on the consequences of the master's transgressions of power. In a crucial passage of his *De iustitia et iure*, Molina explained the following:

> [...] if their masters snatch away the life or members of slaves, or if they harm their bodies by immoderate labor, starvation, nudity, unjust suffering, any other undue reason, or anything that exceeds the coercive power of masters over slaves; or if they harm their health or body, command anything against the slaves' spiritual health, or violate their rights in any other way, then the masters certainly commit a mortal sin.[115]

The implications of this dense quote are manifold. It directly links up with the established discourse on homicide and mutilation examined in the previous section. Notably, Molina expressly located coercive authority within the household. At the same time, he also elaborated more fully on the limits of authority over enslaved subjects. Any act that compromised the bodily integrity or the spiritual well-being of the enslaved was not just morally problematic. Molina emphasized that inflicting starvation, unnecessary suffering, or other forms of abuse upon enslaved persons also constituted an *iniuria*—a violation of their rights.

But what were the consequences when masters abused their power? "If the ferocity of masters seems intolerable", Molina argued, "then the prince is bound to coerce them to sell their slaves on good conditions"—and those who killed enslaved persons under their authority had to be "punished as murderers".[116]

hizo tanta merced de hazerle señor, trate de essa manera a su esclavo: que dotrina es de un filosofo gentil [...] *Sic cum inferiore vivas, quemadmodum te eum superiorem velis*". The reference was to Seneca, Epistle XLVII, in *Epistles*, ed. and trans. Gummere, 306.

115 Molina, *DIEI*, vol. 1, tr. II, disp. 38, no. 3, col. 202: "Quare, si eorum domini, vel vitam, vel membrum ab eis eripiant, vel immoderatis laboribus, inedia, nuditate, vel iniusto supplicio, aut aliqua alia ratione indebita, et quae vim coercivam dominorum in servos excedat, valetudini aut corpori eorum noceant, vel aliquid, quod contra eorum spiritualem sit salutem illis praecipiant, aut quocumque alio modo iniuria eos afficiant, sane et lethaliter peccant".

116 Molina, *DIEI*, vol. 1, tr. II, disp. 38, no. 3, col. 202: "Quod si dominus servum suum interficiat tanquam homicida est puniendus, non secus ac si alienum servum interficeret, ut habetur *Inst. De iis qui sunt sui vel alieni iuris*, ubi scriptum legimus. Praecipit princeps, ut si intolerabilis videatur saevitia dominorum, cogantur servos suos, bonis conditionibus vendere". For the original passage in Roman law, see Inst. 1.8.2.

The Iberian theorists writing after Molina added that if sick and enfeebled slaves were abandoned or denied food by their masters, public authorities were obligated to intervene and effect their manumission.[117] These statements illustrate that slavery did not operate in a legal vacuum. What occurred within the household was not purely a private matter, but intimately connected to the political order of the community.

At the same time, enslaved persons were not entirely without agency. As numerous recent studies show, they engaged the legal system and often succeeded in leveraging it to their advantage.[118] This was also emphasized by the early modern Iberian theorists. Although slaves could not formally sue their master in court, Molina explained, they could nevertheless "go to the judge and report the injustice and damage suffered at the hands of the master".[119] Enslaved women who were victims of sexual abuse by owners could either seek refuge in the church, where they would be freed by the bishop, or they could rightfully flee their abusive masters.[120]

However, Molina also noted that lesser violations of rights were "neither punished nor heard in the external forum".[121] The responsibility for restitution and compensation was therefore partly delegated to the masters themselves. It hinged on whether or not they were prepared to rectify their malfeasance—for instance, by reducing work obligations or by providing better food and clothing.[122] In this context, the role of confessors was critical. They were bound to impose upon masters the duty of "making an appropriate satisfaction to the slaves", Molina insisted, "so that these poor human beings do not lack every aid with the damages and violations of rights unjustly inflicted upon them".[123] The duty to restore justice to enslaved persons was, above all, a matter of con-

117 See e.g., Sánchez, *Consilia*, lib. I, cap. 5, dub. 4, no. 3, 49; Azor, *Institutionum moralium*, vol. 2, lib. II, cap. 33, 138; Rebello, *Opus de obligationibus iustitiae*, pars 1, lib. I, q. 13, no. 1, 78.

118 See the studies discussed in the introduction of Chapter 4.

119 Molina, *DIEI*, vol. 1, tr. II, disp. 38, no. 3, col. 202: "permittitur tamen ei recurrere ad iudicem, eique denunciare iniurias et damna, quae a domino suo patitur".

120 See e.g., Molina, *DIEI*, vol. 1, tr. II, disp. 38, no. 3, col. 202–203; Azpilcueta, *Manual de confessores*, cap. 16, no. 22, 171; Sánchez, *Consilia*, lib. I, cap. 1, dub. 9, no. 1, 8; Fagundez, *De iustitia*, lib. II, cap. 4, no. 1, 151; Lugo, *DIEI*, disp. 6, sect. 4, no. 30, 138.

121 Molina, *DIEI*, vol. 1, tr. II, disp. 38, no. 3, col. 202: "Leviora autem damna et iniuriae, quae in exteriori foro, nec punientur, nec audientur".

122 Molina, *DIEI*, vol. 1, tr. II, disp. 38, no. 3, col. 202.

123 Molina, *DIEI*, vol. 1, tr. II, disp. 38, no. 3, col. 202: "Estque illis a confessariis iniungenda pro eiusmodi iniuriis debita satisfactio mancipiis facienda, quando per potestates publicas iniuria punita non fuerit, ne miseri homines omni subsidio careant in damnis et iniuriis, quibus a dominis iniuste afficiuntur".

science. In Molina's words, it was a moral demand "by the law of nature [...] insofar as slaves are human beings and our neighbors".[124]

Yet the boundary between illicit harm and just punishment was fluid. Juan Azor, for example, argued that slaveholders could legitimately "diminish" slaves' provisions as a form of punishment so long as they did not die as a result.[125] The Sienese Jesuit Vincenzo Filliucci, who held the prestigious chair of theology at the Roman College in the early 17th century, observed that masters would sin if they were "negligent" in correcting the moral transgressions of their slaves.[126] Once again, this proves the striking resemblance between the way early modern Iberian thinkers envisioned the government of enslaved persons and the kind of political power that Michel Senellart calls the medieval *regimen animarum*: both forms of rule centered on the intimate nexus of care, correction, and punishment.[127]

In contrast to the debates over slavery and marriage, the shifting status of slaves between property and person was far less important in Iberian discussions of the punishment and imprisonment of slaves—but it was not entirely irrelevant. This is most evident in the work of Juan Azor. His intervention centered on the question of what happened to enslaved humans who were abandoned. Sick and elderly slaves, as shown above, were *eo ipso* liberated as a result of such neglected care. But what if the abandoned slave was neither old nor ill? Azor turned to the Roman *Digest* to argue that, in such instances, the slave did not become a "free human being" but a "derelict thing"—and like any other thing without an owner, the slave became "the property of the one who occupies him".[128] The only way for such "derelict" slaves to gain their liberty, Azor

---

124 Molina, *DIEI*, vol. 1, tr. II, disp. 38, no. 3, col. 203: "teneturque hodie naturae iure, qui similia crimina in servos suos commiserint, satisfactionem competentem servis ipsis efficere, qua homines ac proximi sunt". This argument was reiterated by Juan de Lugo, *DIEI*, disp. 3, sect. 2, no. 19, 43.

125 Azor, *Institutionum moralium*, vol. 2, lib. II, cap. 38, 149: "quamvis ea ex parte minuere: ita ut servus non inedia absumatur et pereat, sed attenuato et diminuto victu castigetur". This argument was restated, for instance, by Machado de Chavez, *Perfecto confesor*, vol. 2, lib. VI, parte 7, tr. XII, doc. 6, no. 3, 521; and Antonino Diana, *Resolutionum moralium*, tr. VII, resol. 46, 259.

126 Filliucci, *Moralium quaestionum*, vol. 2, tr. XXVIII, cap. 4, no. 79, 77: "In quibus peccare possit dominus contra servum [...] Secundo, si sint negligentes in corrigendis eorum peccata".

127 Senellart, *Les arts de gouverner*, 65–83 and 157–164. The comparison is limited, however, because for the early modern Iberiain theorists, domestic rule was not primarily legitimated by the need to come to terms with human nature after the Fall.

128 Azor, *Institutionum Moralium*, vol. 2, lib. II, cap. 36, 146: "Quaeres, an servus, quem dominus pro derelicto habet, eo ipso fiat sui iuris, hoc est, liber homo? Ratio dubitandi est [...] scilicet si alius sciens eum [i.e., the slave] pro derelicto habitum a domino, statim

argued, was by prescription: if they managed to live as free persons for at least a decade, without being seized by anyone during that period.[129]

To illustrate the force of this move, it is worth noting how Iberian theologians had previously invoked the Roman notion of occupation. Vitoria and Soto had famously imported this originally private legal concept into the realm of public power, arguing that the Indigenous Americans had rightfully "occupied" their lands before the Spanish arrival.[130] But in fact, they had both invoked the law *ferae bestiae* from Justinian's *Institutes*. And what could be occupied according to this law were "wild beasts, birds, and fish", and thus "animals" rather than human beings.[131] But Juan Azor followed the reasoning of the law *De stipulatione servorum* in the *Digest*, arguing that enslaved persons were subject to the same logic of ownership as any other goods.[132]

This maxim was also adopted by Tomás Sánchez, who concurred with Azor that abandoned slaves could justly be "left to the one who occupies them".[133] The principle endured, at least implicitly, in the treatises of the major mid-century theologians Juan de Lugo and Antonino Diana. Both emphasized that the law of occupation did not apply to enslaved children and those who were sick, tacitly leaving it to their readers to conclude that the opposite might apply to healthy adults.[134] This illustrates the precarious status of enslaved persons

apprehendat tanquam pro derelicto omissum, hac enim ratione res pro derelicta a domino habita, occupantis sit propria, tunc enim ut in l. Quod servus, superius allegata dicitur". The reference was to D.45.3.36.

129 Azor, *Institutionum Moralium*, vol. 2, lib. 11, cap. 36, 146: "Hinc etiam sit, ut servus, quem pro derelicto dominus habet, possit seipsum liberum efficere, nimirum si pro libero diu se gerat, videlicet per decennium, inter praesentes, et per viginti inter absentes, ita ut a nullo alio apprehendatur".

130 Vitoria, *De indis*, in *Political Writings*, trans. Pagden and Lawrance, q. 2, a. 3, 264–265; Soto, *Relección "De Dominio"*, ed. Brufau Prats, 120–122 and 162. See the discussion in Benton and Straumann, "Acquiring Empire by Law", 21–24.

131 Inst. 2.1.12: "Ferae igitur bestiae et volucres et pisces, id est omnia animalia quae in terra mari caelo nascuntur, simulatque ab aliquo capta fuerint, iure gentium statim illius esse incipiunt: quod enim ante nullius est id naturali ratione occupanti conceditur".

132 D.45.3.36: "Quod servus stipulatus est, quem dominus pro derelicto habebat, nullius est momenti, quia qui pro derelicto rem habet, omnimodo a se reiecit nec potest eius operibus uti, quem eo iure ad se pertinere noluit. Quod si ab alio adprehensus est, stipulatione ei adquirere poterit: nam et haec genere quodam donatio est".

133 Sánchez, *Consilia*, lib. 1, cap. 5, dub. 4, no. 3, 49: "si servis sanis dominus negat alimenta, non fiunt liberi, sed pro derelictis videntur haberi, et conceduntur occupanti, *l. quod servus. ff. de stipulat. servorum*, secundum Azorem, *ubi infra*". The reference was again to D.45.3.36.

134 Lugo, *DIEI*, disp. 6, sect. 4, no. 29, 138: "si dominus [...] infantem servum exponat, quod idem est, si aegrotum servum derelinquat [...] in quibus casibus non incidit servus in

within the household. The paterfamilias bore a general duty to care for all his domestic subjects. But for slaves, the bond of belonging was tenuous at best. Their ambivalent position between subject and commodity put them in perpetual danger of losing their status as members of the domestic community.

4 Spiritual Care for Enslaved Children

In the remainder of this chapter, I wish to draw attention to a dimension of domestic power that we have not yet fully explored: the master's duty to provide *religious* tutelage to enslaved persons within the Christian commonwealth. As Estevão Fagundez wrote in his commentary on the first five of the Ten Commandments: "The master of a neophyte slave who fails to attend to the latter's instruction in the Christian doctrine sins mortally".[135] For Fagundez, this was not merely an issue of charity but also of justice. Slaveholders bore legal obligation to ensure that the enslaved persons under their authority would "not become accustomed to a corrupt life, to swearing falsely, or to condemning the precepts of God and the church".[136] The strong emphasis Iberian intellectuals placed upon the master's responsibility for spiritual rule and education was no coincidence. Since Christians did not enslave one another, enslaved persons in Iberian households were primarily Christian*ized* slaves. While baptism did not free "infidels" from servitude, it raised pressing question about the conditions under which they accepted the Christian faith in the first place.

As the Iberian theorists saw it, the conversion process could not be accelerated by force. Compelled conversion, according to Vitoria, was not just illicit but also counter-productive, as it would lead to *scandalum* and hatred rather than foster love and affection for Christianity.[137] Experience, he claimed, confirmed this: "we see that Saracens never become Christians; no indeed, *tan moros son*

dominium illius, qui eius derelicti, vel expositi curam suscipit". The same was later restated verbatim by Diana, *Resolutionum moralium*, tr. VII, resol. 16, 243.

135 Fagundez, *In quinque praecepta decalogi*, vol. 1, lib. IV, cap. 14, no. 1, 574: "Hinc est, quod dominus, qui servum neophitum habet, et non curat eum doctrina christiana instruere, peccet lethaliter". Fagundez made this comment in the context of his commentary on the Fourth Commandment ("honor thy father and thy mother"), into which he inserted a discussion of the mutual obligations between masters and slaves.

136 Fagundez, *In quinque praecepta decalogi*, vol. 1, lib. IV, cap. 14, no. 1, 574: "tenentur domini non solum ex charitate; sed etiam ex iustitia curare, ne servi prave vivere assuescant, peierare, Dei praecepta, et Ecclesiae contemnere".

137 Vitoria, "Lecture on the Evangelization of Unbelievers", in *Political Writings*, trans. Pagden and Lawrance, 341–342.

agora como antes".[138] Subsequent writings echoed this position, emphasizing that faith had to be embraced voluntarily rather than by force.[139] The Iberian theologians and jurists largely sidestepped the role that slaveholders had in the process of conversion. However, one specific issue concerned them a great deal: did masters have the power to baptize enslaved children against the will of their parents?

This was yet another question that early modern intellectuals inherited from the late-medieval tradition of commentary on Peter Lombard's *Sentences*. But this time, they were faced with a difficulty that resulted from the contrasting opinions between Thomas Aquinas and the French Dominican Durand de Saint-Pourçain, who had been writing in the early 14th century. In Aquinas's view, it was illicit to baptize the offspring of "infidels". Children were "under the care of their parents" before reaching the age of reason, he argued, and it was "against natural justice to baptize such children against parental will".[140] The benefits of conversion to their spiritual salvation did not justify overriding parental power, which was derived from the law of nature.[141] Yet, as the Iberian theorists were well aware, Durand had made an important addition to the Thomist stance. He singled out the special case of *enslaved* children. Since they were subject to the power of the master, Durand argued, such children could justly be separated from their parents and baptized.[142]

Domingo de Soto was the first to confront Durand's opinion directly. He began by arguing that children were "included in their parents' spiritual womb, as it were, just as when they were carried in their mother's womb".[143] This

---

138 Vitoria, "Lecture on the Evangelization of Unbelievers", in *Political Writings*, trans. Pagden and Lawrance, 344, original emphasis. The latter phrase featured in Spanish in Vitoria's otherwise Latin commentary and translates as follows: "they are as much Moors now as they were before".

139 See e.g., Soto, *In quartum*, vol. 1, dist. 5, q. unica, 267; and Suárez, *Commentariorum ac disputationum*, vol. 3, disp. 25, sec. 4, 264.

140 Aquinas, *Summa*, ed. Alarcón and Busa, 3a, q. 68, a. 10, corp.: "Si vero nondum habent usum liberi arbitrii, secundum ius naturale sunt sub cura parentum, quandiu ipsi sibi providere non possunt. [...] Et ideo contra iustitiam naturalem esset si tales pueri, invitis parentibus, baptizarentur".

141 Aquinas, *Summa*, ed. Alarcón and Busa, 3a, q. 68, a. 10, ad. 1.

142 Durand de Saint-Pourçain, *In quatuor libros sententiarum*, lib. IV, dist. 4, q. 6, 341: "filius est sub cura parentum non est eripiendus ut liberetur a periculo mortis eterne. [...] Hoc autem esset si filius infidelis liberi baptisaretur invitis parentibus quorum cure subest de iure naturali et divino: Secus autem est de filio infidelis servi, quia res domini est et potest eum subtrahere cure parentum".

143 Soto, *In quartum*, vol. 1, dist. 5, q. unica, 273: "filius autem quandiu usu rationis non viget, sub parentum cura continetur, quasi quodam spirituali utero inclusus, quemadmodum quando in matris ventre gestabatur".

striking metaphor epitomized the authentically Thomist idea that the *potestas* of parents was rooted in nature. Yet Soto also claimed that "if children have justly or unjustly been separated from their parents so that the latter cannot agree, then it is licit to baptize them without parental consent".[144] Since children before the age of reason necessarily had to be "governed by somebody's will, the master or church can baptize them" in the absence of the parents.[145] As Soto went on to explain, this meant that whoever "snatched away the children of the unbelievers of Africa or the Indies by theft or violence", could justly subject them to the Christian faith.[146]

Despite this striking argument, Soto avoided addressing the central issue that Durand had raised: did slaveholders also possess the power to *break* the natural bond between enslaved parents and their children, as Durand had suggested? Or was the natural right of parents immune to the right of slavery, which rested solely on the *ius gentium*?

A set of preliminary answers to this crucial question of conscience were put forward by Miguel de Palacio and Juan Azor. Palacio argued that it was just to remove enslaved children from their parents to then "plunge them into the holy water of baptism".[147] Azor, by contrast, claimed that "children cannot be justly baptized against the will of their parents", not even under the yoke of slavery.[148]

The most comprehensive discussion of this issue, however, came from Francisco Suárez, who addressed the matter in his commentary on the *Tertia pars* of Aquinas's *Summa*.[149] Suárez realized that there were two distinct questions

144 Soto, *In quartum*, vol. 1, dist. 5, q. unica, 274: "Quando vero sic separatus ab illis est sive iure sive iniuria, ut non possint conveniri: tunc licitum est sine eorum consensu ipsum baptizare".

145 Soto, *In quartum*, vol. 1, dist. 5, q. unica, 274: "parvulus semper sit censendus alicuius arbitrio gubernari, quando longe distat a parentibus, seu liberis, seu servis: quia iam non regitur eorum arbitrio, tunc dominus et ecclesia ipsa potest eum baptizare".

146 Soto, *In quartum*, vol. 1, dist. 5, q. unica, 274–275: "Quare licet quis vel furtum vel violenter ab infidelibus, qui sunt in Africa, vel in India liberi, suos parvulos surriperet, possent elongati a suis parentibus baptizari".

147 Palacio, *Disputationes theologicae*, vol. 1, dist. 4, disp. 5, 119: "authores Theologi [...] quod ispi et nos tradimus est huiusmodi filium fas esse subducere a cura patria, et subductum lustrali intingere baptismi aqua".

148 Azor, *Institutionum moralium*, vol. 1, lib. 8, cap. 25, col. 1033: "salus spiritualis ad patris non ad domini curam spectat. [...] haec omnia probant, eiusmodi infantes invitis parentibus ad baptismum afferri iure non posse". But note that Azor also restated Soto's argument that infidel children, who were stolen from their parents, could justly be baptized (see Azor, *Institutionum moralium*, vol. 1, lib. 8, cap. 25, col. 1032).

149 Scholars have suggested that Suárez first addressed the theme of baptism in his commentary on questions 60–83 of the *Tertia* pars of Aquinas's *Summa*, which was published in Salamanca in 1595. Unfortunately, this work is no longer available. We therefore do not

his predecessors had blurred: first, whether masters could separate enslaved children from their parents in order to baptize them; and second, whether masters could do so while parent and child remained in the same household under the same master. Let us begin with the latter, which is also the specific case on which Azor's critique had focused. Suárez explained that despite the father's presence near his child, the latter was no longer under parental care. "By the force of captivity", the father's right appeared to have been transferred to the master, who now "has the power to rule and govern the slave in all things that pertain to him".[150] To illustrate the legitimacy of this view, he compared the enslaved father's parental right to a war prisoner's right to escape. Although the captive could justly run away, the master nevertheless had a right to hinder his flight "with force, for the slave does not remain the absolute master of his liberty".[151] Similarly, although a servile father "in a way retains his paternal power over the child, the master can justly prevent him from using that very power".[152]

But Suárez also agreed with Miguel de Palacio that slaveholders could separate an enslaved father from the child, and only *then* administer baptism to the latter. While this seemed incompatible with the idea that enslaved fathers had a natural right in their children, Suárez offered another analogy to explain his reasoning:

> [...] the exercise of the conjugal act cannot be prohibited. [...] For these acts are deeply intrinsic and innate so that strictly speaking, a human

know the extent of the changes Suárez made between the first and the 1619 edition, from which I am quoting. See Doyle, *Collected studies on Francisco Suárez*, ed. Salas, 336–337; and Robert Fastiggi, "Fransico Suárez as Dogmatic Theologian", 149.

150 Suárez, *Commentariorum ac disputationum*, vol. 3, disp. 25, sec. 5, 268: "ex vi captivitatis [...] videtur ius paternum translatum in dominum: nam iure dominii habet potestatem in servum ad regendum et gubernandum illum in omnibus, quae ad ipsum pertinent".

151 Suárez, *Commentariorum ac disputationum*, vol. 3, disp. 25, sec. 5, 268: "Quod servus quantumvis, sit legitime bello captus, habet ius fugiendi, si potest occulte et absque vi, quamvis, quia absolute non manet dominus suae libertatis, non possit per vim resistere domino eum impedimenti, ne fugiat."

152 Suárez, *Commentariorum ac disputationum*, vol. 3, disp. 25, sec. 5, 268: "Sic ergo in praesenti, etiamsi parens simul cum filio maneat, et potestatem paterman aliquo modo in filio retineat, tamen a domino poterit iuste impedire, ne illa potestate utatur". A similar argument was made by his fellow Jesuit Gabriel Vázquez (1549–1604), who has been called "Suárez's personal bête noire" (Brett, *Changes of State*, 86). See Vázquez, *Commentariorum ac disputationum*, disp. 155, cap. 4, no. 50, 115: "nullamque in ea iniuriam parentibus servis irrogare, si parvuli adhuc existentes sub ipsorum cura a domino baptizentur, aut eos baptizari permittat".

> being is not deprived of them because of enslavement, although one can be deprived of them accidentally because of spatial distance. So it seems to be so in our present case. In fact, the father's right in his son is deeply inherent by nature and intrinsic, and so are his actions that follow from this right. Therefore, he cannot be completely deprived of it, although this is possible through separation and spatial distance.[153]

Just as the natural right of marriage could be compromised by viewing slaves as objects of commercial exchange, so too did a shift in perspective from subject to object allow Suárez to undermine an enslaved father's right in his son. He concluded that, ultimately, "the father's right in his child is not so intrinsic that he could not be deprived of it by punishment through the right of slavery".[154] This reasoning underscores yet again how Iberian imperial theorists affirmed the humanity of slaves even as they placed them under the transactional regime of commutative justice whenever it suited their purposes.

---

153 Suárez, *Commentariorum ac disputationum*, vol. 3, disp. 25, sec. 5, 268–269: "prohiberi non potest, quominus matrimonii actus cum coniuge exerceat [...] Nam hae actiones sunt valde intrinsecae, et connaturales, quibus per se loquendo, non privatur homo ratione servitutis, quamvis per acidens privari possit propter locorum distantiam. Ita ergo videtur esse in praesenti casu, de quo agimus. Nam ius etiam patris erga filium est valde connaturale, et intrinsecum, et eiusdem rationis sunt actiones, quae ab illo manant. Non ergo potest per se omnino illis privari, quamvis per accidens possit media separatione et distantia loci".

154 Suárez, *Commentariorum ac disputationum*, vol. 3, disp. 25, sec. 5, 269: "Nec ius, quod pater habet in filium, tam est intrinsecum, ut non possit illo privari in poenam, iure servitiutis".

PART 3

Slavery and Labor Coercion in the Americas

Introduction to Part 3

So far, the analysis has centered on how theologians and jurists from Spain and Portugal approached the question of slavery. In their examinations of enslavement across continents and contexts, ranging from the Morisco revolt in Spain to Mediterranean piracy and the Portuguese slave trade, Iberian thinkers shaped the juridical imagination of slaves and their position in society. The problem of slavery, as they cast it, intersected with broader questions of "human rights" and the boundaries of political power. The final part of this book, however, moves beyond the intellectual milieu of the European lecture halls. The following two chapters focus on writings by theologians, missionaries, and imperial administrators who penned their polemics in the Americas. The realities these thinkers encountered overseas, and the distinctly colonial issues they faced, left a deep imprint on their literary production.

Iberian intellectuals in colonial Peru confronted the troubling reality that formally free vassals were forced to work in the deadly mines of the Andean highlands. The treatment of Indigenous peoples resembled that of slaves rather than that of political subjects. The fundamental inequality between settlers and Natives posed both a conceptual and practical problem: it threatened the unity of the colonial body politic, and the countless deaths of Indigenous subjects undermined the very foundation on which the economy of the Spanish empire in the Americas was built.

Some European observers from the New World made analogous arguments regarding the transatlantic slave trade. Missionaries who witnessed the brutal realities of slavery firsthand emphasized the grave practical consequences of the Iberian imperial theorists' justification of the trade in enslaved Africans. They cautioned that the exploitation of sub-Saharan Africans would ultimately be punished by God and jeopardize the stability of the empire—unless it was stopped immediately. By insisting on the incompatibility of slavery and salvation, these voices redefined the complex relationship between humanity, freedom, and the Christian faith. The final part of this book traces these debates about coercion and slavery, revealing novel understandings of what constitutes political relations.

DOI:10.1163/9789004760592_009

CHAPTER 6

Forced Labor and the Politics of Empire

In the first decades of Spanish colonization in the Americas, conquistadors and early settlers were granted official rights and privileges over Indigenous people, with the right to exploit their labor, the so-called *encomiendas* or *repartimientos*. The Castilian crown had already tested an early form of this *encomienda* system in the context of the (re)colonization of the Iberian Peninsula, and on both sides of the Atlantic, the principal purpose of *encomiendas* was to extend and accelerate Castilian control over conquered lands and people.[1] But the *encomenderos*, the holders of these grants, soon became a thorn in the emperor's side. They grew increasingly powerful, forming a colonial elite that risked eluding the crown's control. What is more, they failed in their duty to instruct the Indigenous people under their authority in the Christian faith. As the Dominican friar Bartolomé de las Casas famously protested, the "*indios*" were held in outright slavery.[2] With the New Laws of 1542, Charles v sought to put an end to these developments. In Spanish America—unlike in Brazil—Indigenous peoples were recognized as free vassals of the Crown of Castile, and it became increasingly difficult to legitimize their enslavement outside the contexts of war and rebellion discussed in Chapter Two. Although the monarch's plans to reform the *encomienda* were met with fierce local resistance, the formal abolition of Indigenous slavery paved the way toward a new system of labor coercion.[3]

The rise of forced labor was closely linked to the expansion of silver mining in colonial Peru. In the late 16th century, the Andean highland city of Potosí became "the unrivalled centre of the Spanish Empire in South America"[4] and a

1 The best recent study of the *encomienda* and its significance for the political economy of conquest is Huber, *Beute und Conquista*. See also Puente Brunke, *Encomienda y encomenderos en el Perú*, 14–25 and *passim*; Elliott, *Empires of the Atlantic World*, 40; and Brading, *The First America*, 68.

2 See Birr, "Recht als Argument in Bartolomé de Las Casas' *Tratado sobre los indios*"; and Pennington, "Bartolomé de Las Casas".

3 Spanish authorities also policed Indigenous slavery in Castile. In 1543, the jurist Gregorio López—the later commentator of the *Siete partidas* who was a councilor of the Indies at the time—was personally responsible for overseeing an inspection in Seville that led to the liberation of more than one hundered enslaved "*indios*" (who were subsequently still obliged to work for their former master). See Van Deusen, *Global Indios*, 99–102; and Birr, "Tradition and Innovation in Knowledge Production", 80.

4 Gil Montero, "Free and Unfree Labour in the Colonial Andes", 309.

metropolis of world-historical significance. Silver from the Cerro Rico, the "rich hill", boosted Europe's textile production and traveled as far as Mughal India and Ming China. Until the mid-17th century, the "money mountain" at Potosí supplied roughly half of all silver in global circulation.[5] But this boom came at a tremendous cost. From a vast region between northern Argentina and the former Inca capital of Cusco, thousands of Indigenous tributaries were forced to leave their homes to work in the depths of the mines. Many never returned. The deadly labor in the Cerro Rico was "the stuff of the Black Legend of Spanish colonialism".[6]

Historians have come to describe the shift from *encomienda* slavery to labor coercion as largely rhetorical.[7] Andrés Reséndez argues that colonial authorities simply created "newfangled terms and practices to retain control of Native Americans when formal enslavement was no longer possible".[8] Similarly, Nancy van Deusen speaks of "thinly disguised slavery".[9] And according to Nicholas Robins, the difference between forced labor and slavery was "almost meaningless".[10] What has been overlooked, however, is that the alarmingly close connection between coerced work and enslavement was already a subject of intense debate in the early modern period. On what basis could free subjects be compelled to work in the Andean mines if the Romans had imposed such burdensome labor only on slaves? And how could such services be imposed on Indigenous vassals while Spanish subjects overseas were exempt?

Forcible mining in the Andes thus became a pivotal issue of justice, conscience, and imperial order, engaging colonial officials as much as missionaries and theologians in the Peruvian viceroyalty. Intellectuals in the Indies—much like their counterparts in Iberia—drew upon shared modes of thinking and arguing.[11] Among Anglophone scholars, the jurist Juan de Solórzano y Pereira (1575–1655) is perhaps the most familiar figure, famous for reinvigorating the

5 Lane, *Potosí*, xiv–xv and 8. The locution "money mountain" is from Ferguson, *The Ascent of Money*, 19.

6 Mahoney, *Colonialism and Postcolonial Development*, 70.

7 A different perspective is offered by José Antonio Piqueras, who, by reconstructing and following the logic of contemporary legal norms, insists on a categorical distinction between slavery and other forms of coerced labor. See Piqueras, *Derecho antiguo y esclavitud moderna*, 234.

8 Reséndez, *The Other Slavery*, 10.

9 Van Deusen, *Global Indios*, 6–7.

10 Robins, *Santa Bárbara's Legacy*, 85.

11 See Tau Anzoátegui, *El jurista en el Nuevo Mundo*, 8–12; Duve, "Salamanca in Amerika"; and Egío García, "La consolidación del estatuto teológico-político del pagano amerindio", 38–39.

controversy about the justice of the Spanish conquest from overseas, more than a century after its inception in the Iberian lecture halls.[12] And as we shall see, Solórzano's writings also left a deep imprint on the contested discourse surrounding forced Native labor. Importantly, however, a range of equally innovative and influential contributions have yet to receive their due place in the histories of their era. This chapter also includes the works of the theologian Miguel de Agia, a close advisor of the Peruvian viceroy Luis de Velasco (r. 1596–1604); the Franciscan missionary Juan de Silva, who voiced his opinion on the matter of mining in a series of memorials to the king; and the Jesuit Diego de Avendaño (1594–1688), who addressed the problem of forced labor in his academic, moral theological writing. By examining the works of these figures, the present chapter contributes to recent research on the role of colonial intellectuals in the production of social, political, and legal knowledge in Spanish America.[13]

Among historians of colonial Latin America, it is widely recognized that the Spaniards legitimated the hierarchy between Indigenous vassals and Spanish settlers by dividing the colonial society into a *república de indios* and a *república de españoles*.[14] It is undoubtedly true that the Spanish developed a distinctive understanding of "Indianness", whose principal purpose was to legitimate the continued conversion efforts and deferment of the prospect for full integration of Indigenous peoples into the Christian community.[15] Yet I will argue that the notion of "two republics or political communities",[16] which dominates the present-day historiographical imagination, does not reflect how historical actors understood colonial society. Their solution to the problem of a deeply uneven political community was not to distinguish a "republic of *indios*" from a "republic of Spaniards".[17] Rather, I show that Spanish voices overseas articulated the vision of what I call a "composite commonwealth": a unified political body forged from unequal parts.

12 See e.g., Fitzmaurice, *Sovereignty, Property, and Empire*, 73–79; Muldoon, *The Americas*, *passim*; and Pagden, *Lords of all the World*, 89–90. For my own perspective, see Allemann, "After Vitoria".

13 For a recent example, see Duve and Danwerth (eds.), *Knowledge of the Pragmatici*.

14 See e.g., Puente Luna, *Andean Cosmopolitans*, 15 and 159–160; Martínez, *Genealogical Fictions*, 5–6 and ch. 4; Herzog, *Defining Nations*, 45–48 and 157; and Levaggi, "República de indios y república de españoles", 419–428.

15 Estenssoro Fuchs, *Del paganismo a la santidad*, 97–98.

16 Seijas, *Asian Slaves in Colonial Mexico*, 3 and 146.

17 For a related critique of the two-republics concept based on 16th-century colonial decrees and petitions, see Masters, "The Two, the One the Many, the None".

In a thought-provoking study, Orlando Bentancor recently suggested that the ideology of forced native mining rested on the notion that "indigenous people are considered an imperfect matter that needs to be modeled by the imposition of superior cultural forms".[18] Bentancor argues that Spanish theorists of empire considered "both nature and humans as malleable material", tracing the origins of this "instrumentalist" understanding in the thought of Thomas Aquinas and the School of Salamanca.[19] His reading echoes Giorgio Agamben's characterization of the early modern period, as marked by a sharp divide between a purely natural life (*zoé*) and a properly political life (*bios*).[20] Equally, it mirrors Michel Foucault's argument that the 16th century saw the birth of new art of government, with princes manipulating their subjects in the same way that craftsmen molded material objects.[21] Indeed, Bentancor asserts that Spanish thinkers regarded Indigenous peoples as "raw and defective material" of nature that "had to be dominated from above and directed to a higher end".[22]

However, the notion of a stark binary between raw nature and artificially perfected politics is not reflected in early modern writings. As Annabel Brett has shown, Aquinas and his early modern followers in Iberia had a far more sophisticated understanding of the interplay between nature and politics.[23] The same holds true, I will contend, of those who shaped the emerging ideology of Indigenous labor coercion in colonial Peru. Spanish imperial thinkers envisioned a deeply hierarchical juxtaposition between politically sophisticated settlers and passion-driven, rustic Andeans. Yet they did not imagine Indigenous individuals as pre-political "matter". On the contrary, colonial jurists and theologians emphasized their status as vassals and subjects of the Spanish empire in the Americas. It was precisely by assigning the "*indios*" a place within the political community that it was possible to insist on their duty to perform a set of tasks commensurate with their supposedly inferior condition. Native labor, according to this logic, was an enforceable contribution to the maintenance of a sharply stratified, composite commonwealth of "*indios*" and Spaniards.

---

18 Bentancor, *The Matter of Empire*, 346–347.

19 Bentancor, *The Matter of Empire*, 2 and *passim*.

20 Agamben, *Homo sacer*, introduction and *passim*. It is astonishing that Bentancor does not cite Agamben's work.

21 Foucault, *Sécurité, territoire, population*, leçon du 22 février, 168; and Foucault, *Sécurité, territoire, population*, leçon du 8 mars, *passim*. See also Bentancor, *The Matter of Empire*, 277–281.

22 Bentancor, *The Matter of Empire*, 1 and *passim*.

23 See especially Brett, *Changes of State*.

In what follows, I reconstruct debates over the justice of forced Indigenous labor during the rise and heyday of silver mining in the Andes from the mid-16th to the mid-17th centuries. The writings examined here reveal that the scope of political and legal authority over Spain's vassals in the New World was contested, and that early modern thinkers understood "law as a flexible framework for negotiation and conflict rather than an assemblage of sets of norms or rules".[24] In this sense, exploring the debate over forced Indigenous labor in colonial Peru demonstrates how the study of jurisdictional politics can contribute to "new narratives about historical moments when empires and states moved to assert power over multi-jurisdictional orders and, in the process, transformed regional regimes and global legal order".[25]

Potosí serves both as a point of departure and a guiding thread to explore how thinkers legitimized and challenged the variegated realities of forced labor that emerged from the major social and economic transformations in colonial Peru. Beyond mining, this system of forced labor also encompassed domestic services provided in the homes of Spanish settlers or the use of "*indios*" as human carriers on Andean highland routes impassable to pack animals. These practices raised broader questions about the fraught interface between slavery and political subjection, the boundaries between human and animal bodies, and the ideological foundations of the Spanish empire in the Americas.

1 The Rise of Forced Labor

In 1545, the Spaniards discovered a vast deposit of silver ore in the Andean highland city of Potosí, located over 4,000 meters above sea level in what is today Bolivia. The potential for profit was immediately apparent to Spanish settlers, and many began to send Natives into the newly encountered mines. From the outset, however, this practice was contested. As early as 1550, Domingo de Santo Tomás (1499–1570), head of the Dominicans of Lima, criticized *encomenderos* for showing little concern for the perilous work forced upon Indigenous people inside the Cerro Rico. In a letter to Emperor Charles v, he famously described the mines of Potosí as a *boca del infierno*, a "mouth of hell".[26]

Yet the deposits soon appeared depleted, and Andean mining entered a period of crisis. Its true resurgence began in the 1570s with the introduction

24 Benton and Clulow, "Interpolity Law and Jurisdictional Politics", 199.
25 Benton and Clulow, "Interpolity Law and Jurisdictional Politics", 201.
26 An excerpt of Santo Tomás's letter is available in English translation in Lane, *Potosí*, 198–199.

of a new technique for silver extraction using poisonous mercury amalgam.[27] "Overnight", as David Brading puts it, "the entire structure and pace of production of the industry was transformed".[28] This technical innovation coincided with a profound social, political, and economic reorganization in Peru under the reign of viceroy Francisco de Toledo (r. 1569–1581).

A central pillar of the Toledan reform program was the implementation of large-scale resettlement.[29] Andean communities had traditionally been organized around kinship rather than territory and governed by members of the nobility, the *caciques* (or *kurakas* in Quechua). From the beginning of Spanish colonization in Peru, these communities had come under the authority of the monarch's representatives overseas, the infamous *encomenderos*. It was only under Toledo, however, that the previously dispersed kinship groups were driven into small, Spanish-style towns defined by place rather than lineage, which aimed to disrupt Indigenous forms of social organization.[30] These so-called *reducciones* in part facilitated the collection of tributary payments and allowed tighter control over the process of evangelization. But first and foremost, they were intended to supply the workforce for a new socioeconomic system that was built on large-scale coercion of Native labor.

The success of Andean mining depended in large part on Toledo's revival and expansion of the pre-Hispanic system of rotational forced labor that the Incas had called *mit'a* (Hispanicized as *mita*). It is hard to imagine how the Spaniards could have successfully "summoned thousands of peasants to travel long distances for work on imperial projects" without relying on established structures.[31] Each year, at least one-seventh of the male adult population from every *reducción* was compelled to work for the viceroyalty as a form of tributary service. A significant proportion ended up in Potosí, where people labored in the mines or nearby mills, crushing the raw ore and refining it with mercury.[32]

27 González Casanovas, *Las dudas de la corona*, 35. For a detailed technical explanation of the process, see Robins, *Mercury, Mining, and Empire*, 3–4.

28 Brading, *The First America*, 136.

29 This paragraph draws on Mumford, *Veritcal Empire*, 28–29 and 119–121; Brading, *The First America*, 133–134; and Mahoney, *Colonialism and Postcolonial Development*, 69–71.

30 On the complex relationship between *repartimiento* and *reducción*, see Mumford, *Vertical Empire*, 119–121; and Puente Brunke, *Encomienda y encomenderos en el Perú*, 174–176.

31 Mumford, *Vertical Empire*, 138. On the Toledan revival of Inca institutions, see also Mumford, *Vertical Empire*, ch. 7.

32 Lane, *Potosí*, 69–71. In some parts of colonial Peru, however, the *reducciones* were completely exploited, and the idea of "only" assigning one seventh of the tributary population to *mita* mining disregarded. See e.g., Zamora, who makes this point with regard to San Miguel de Tucumán in northern Argentina (*Casa poblada y buen gobierno*, 54).

The liquid metal was itself a product of mining. Deposits at Almadén in Spain had been supplying smaller silver mines in Mexico since the middle of the century.[33] In the 1560s, the Spaniards also discovered mercury deposits a four-day hike from Lima. In the Santa Bárbara mines of Huancavelica, up to three thousand Andeans at a time extracted the poisonous quicksilver to be transported to Potosí.[34] The death and suffering that followed from exposure to the mercury dust, as we shall see, troubled even the most ardent defenders of *mita* mining.

1.1 *The Revival of Natural Slavery*

Juan de Matienzo (1520–1579), one of the first to address the problem of Indigenous labor coercion in a sustained way, studied law at Valladolid and subsequently joined the Castilian royal service as a clerk in the high tribunal in the same city.[35] He arrived in the New World in 1561 to assume the position of a judge (*oidor*) at the newly established Audiencia of Charcas, one of the high courts of the Peruvian viceroyalty, which also exercised important governmental functions and oversaw large parts of the Spanish territories between Cusco and Buenos Aires.[36] It was during this period that Matienzo composed the *Gobierno del Perú* (1567), a treatise on the administration of colonial Peru, described as the intellectual "blueprint" of viceroy Toledo's social and economic reforms.[37]

Matienzo was well-aware of the dangers of Andean mining. He pointed to the lack of well-constructed ladders, which made descending into the mountains a dangerous undertaking, with human bodies "breaking into pieces".[38] Yet Matienzo was quick to suggest that this problem could be solved, quite simply by building "good ladders".[39] He maintained that the business of mining was vital to the preservation of the Spanish empire in the Americas, and some danger was therefore acceptable. This was evident in a broader comparative

---

33 Pike, *Penal Servitude in Early Modern Spain*, 27.

34 Lane, *Potosí*, 71–72.

35 Biographical information on Mationzo is from Tau Anzoátegui, *El jurista en el nuevo mundo*, 47–48.

36 The Audiencia of Charcas was one of six jurisdictional and governmental units that were established in the Peruvian viceroyalty over the course of the 16th century. See Muldoon, *The Americas*, 8; and Brading, *The First America*, 215–216.

37 Brading, *The First America*, 139. The *Gobierno* was not published in the early modern period but, much like Vitoria's relections, circulated widely in manuscript form.

38 Matienzo, *Gobierno del Perú*, ed. Lohmann Villena, parte 1, cap. 40, 135: "Decir que caen en las minas abaxo ochenta o cien estados y se hacen pedazos".

39 Matienzo, *Gobierno del Perú*, ed. Lohmann Villena, parte 1, cap. 40, 135: "ésto es tan pocas veces que no se ha de traer en consecuencia, mayormente que esto [...] se puede dar remedio haciendo buenas escaleras".

perspective, Matienzo sought to show. Similarly indispensable types of work in his native Spain, he argued, involved much greater risk: "it has been observed more commonly that somebody falls from a roof, a high wall, or a wooden building [...] and one does not therefore have to give up on such trades".[40] By likening mining to carpentry, Matienzo effectively downplayed the supposedly exceptional danger of mining and reframed, even normalized, what was otherwise perceived as a distinctly colonial issue.

A more fundamental question concerned why mining and other forms of forced labor—including the construction of public buildings and roads, agricultural works on fields and estates, labor in textile workshops, or messenger services—were imposed exclusively on Indigenous subjects. Matienzo argued "there are no Blacks (nor is it suitable that there be any), which could perform the works in cities, sow seeds, or extract silver and gold from the mines".[41] Moreover, he insisted that enslaved Africans would not endure the rough climate of the Andean altiplano, a widespread belief at the time.[42] Yet as we know today, enslaved Black Africans in Potosí were notably present in Spanish households or pressing coins in the royal mint.[43] And the scarcity of Black slave laborers in the mines had economic reasons, since it was far cheaper to impose this labor on the Native tributaries under the *mita* system than rely on enslaved Black Africans.[44]

The very fact that Matienzo compared the *mita* to slave labor highlights that the tension between freedom, slavery, and political subjection that was at the heart of the debate. His own approach to this puzzle drew on the revival of an infamous idea: natural slavery.[45] According to Matienzo, the "*indios*" were

---

40 Matienzo, *Gobierno del Perú*, ed. Lohmann Villena, parte 1, cap. 40, 135: "Si esto se hubiese de considerar para impedir lo en que va tanto para se poder conservar el Reino, también se había de vedar en España [...] Otras cosas hay en que hay más peligro, como es el trastexar, el hacer tapias altas, la carpintería, porque se ha visto más ordinariamente caer de un texado, de tapias altas, de algún edificio de carpintería [...] mas por eso no se han de dexar de usar semexantes oficios".

41 Matienzo, *Gobierno del Perú*, ed. Lohmann Villena, parte 1, cap. 9, 32: "como los españoles no trabaxan en esta tierra por sus personas, ni hay negros (ni convenga que los haya), que puedan hacer las obras en las ciudades, ni las sementeras, ni que saquen plata u oro de las minas, se suele en este Reino mandar que en cada ciudad y en cada asiento de minas vengan indios de los repartimientos".

42 Matienzo, *Gobierno del Perú*, ed. Lohmann Villena, parte 1, cap. 40, 132.

43 This important corrective to scholarship has been offered by Lane, *Potosí*, 103–105 and 128.

44 Elliott, *Empires of the Atlantic World*, 101.

45 Matienzo also drew on classical temperament theory to justify the subjection of the Natives with reference to their "nature". See Morong Reyes, "Saberes hegemónicos y proyecto de dominio colonial".

"naturally born and raised to serve, and it is more advantageous for them to serve than to give orders [...] nature created them with stronger bodies and gave them less understanding".[46] The central crux, he went on to explain, was that they only

> [...] participate in reason in order to feel it, but not to have it or to follow it. In this they are no different from animals, who do not even feel reason, but are governed by their passions. And this is obvious because for them there is no tomorrow, and they concentrate only on what they need to eat and drink this week, and after that they concentrate on the next week.[47]

For Matienzo, Indigenous people were "natural slaves", whose perceived lack of reason and foresight rendered them incapable of participating fully and independently in political life. Importantly, however, he did not invoke this concept as an interpolitical justification for conquest, but rather as an intrapolitical argument in support of political hierarchy.[48] Matienzo started from the premise that Andeans were already Castilian subjects; thus portraying them as "natural slaves" served to define their subordinate role *within* the emerging colonial society:

> They are enemies of work and friends of idleness unless they are forced to work. [...] Out of fear they obey their superiors well, and therefore it is expedient—for whoever orders, rules, and governs them—to make them work, serve, and to keep them busy with something, lest they commit the many excesses that spring from their idleness and drinking.[49]

---

46 Matienzo, *Gobierno del Perú*, ed. Lohmann Villena, parte 1, cap. 4, 17: "naturalmente fueron nacidos y criados para servir, y les es más provechoso el servir que el mandar [...] según dice Aristóteles a estos tales la Naturaleza les creó más fuertes cuerpos y dió menos entendimiento".

47 Matienzo, *Gobierno del Perú*, ed. Lohmann Villena, parte 1, cap. 4, 17–18: "Son partícipes de razón para sentilla, e no para tenella o seguilla. En esto no difieren de los animales, que ni aun sienten la razón antes se rigen por sus pasiones, y vése esto claro pues no hay para ellos mañana, antes se contentan con lo que han menester para comer y beber aquella semana, y acabado aquello, buscan para otra".

48 On the invocation of "natural slavery" as a possible justification for the Spanish conquest, see Chapter 1 Section 1 above. Matienzo justified Spain's imperial venture by arguing that the Spaniards had liberated the Andeans from Inca tyranny. This claim drew on the established notion that protecting the innocent warranted war against foreign rulers. See Matienzo, *Gobierno del Perú*, ed. Lohmann Villena, parte 1, cap. 1–2.

49 Matienzo, *Gobierno del Perú*, ed. Lohmann Villena, parte 1, cap. 4, 18: "Son enemigos del trabaxo y amigos de la ociosidad, si por fuerza no se les hace trabaxar. Son amigos de beber

For Matienzo, the doctrine of natural slavery provided the justification for coercing Indigenous labor. He was careful to emphasize, however, that the "*indios*" were neither legally enslaved nor categorically distinct from Spanish subjects in the Old World. There, too, he argued, similar coercion would be necessary if agricultural laborers did not work the fields voluntarily, since they "were born for this" and yet "they are not slaves, but free".[50] This comparison between "*indios*" and Spanish peasants had already been invoked by Vitoria: "Even among ourselves", the Salamancan had argued, "we see many peasants (*rustici*) who are little different from brute animals".[51] For Vitoria, however, this condition was ultimately due to their lack of education.[52] Matienzo, by contrast, argued otherwise and took the "natural" in natural slavery quite literally, arguing that farmers and Andeans were *born* to serve.

At the same time, Matienzo emphasized that labor coercion was a function of political power. If Indigenous people were unfit for political rule, this did not exempt them from their obligations as subjects of the crown of Castile. To illustrate this point, Matienzo again drew a comparison between the position of Spain's vassals in the New World and the status of subjects in Iberia. "If the Turks moved in on Spain", he asked, "isn't it clear that this would force all the Spaniards to go to war, without excusing anybody?" The answer was, of course, affirmative: "insofar as it concerns the common good and the preservation of the kingdom, its citizens and inhabitants can be compelled to serve in war".[53] For Matienzo, the practice of compelling subjects to safeguard the commonwealth was both just and well-established.[54] In Europe as well as in

---

y emborracharse y idolatrar, y borrachos cometen graves delitos [...] Por temor obedcen muy bien a sus mayores, y ansí es menester quien les mande, rija y gobierne, para que les haga trabaxar e servir e ocuparles en algo, para que no hagan tantos excesos como de la ociosidad y borracheras nacen".

50 Matienzo, *Gobierno del Perú*, ed. Lohmann Villena, parte 1, cap. 40, 136: "También por la mesma razón, si los labradores de Castilla, o de otro reino, no quisiesen trabaxar ni sembrar ni coxer pan, sino darse a otras cosas, claro está que le compelerían a arar y cavar, pues nacieron para aquello [...] Pues los labradores de España no son esclavos, sino libres".

51 Vitoria, *De indis*, in *Political Writings*, trans. Pagden and Lawrance, q. 1, a. 6, 250.

52 This becomes clear from the sentence that immediately preceds the one quoted above: "Thus if they seem to us insensate and slow-witted, I put it down mainly to their evil and barbarous education" (Vitoria, *De indis*, in *Political Writings*, trans. Pagden and Lawrance, q. 1, a. 6, 250).

53 Matienzo, *Gobierno del Perú*, ed. Lohmann Villena, parte 1, cap. 40, 136: "Si el turco viniese sobre España, ¿no está claro que compelerían a todos los españoles a ir a la guerra, y nenguno se escusaría?"

54 Matienzo, *Gobierno del Perú*, ed. Lohmann Villena, parte 1, cap. 40, 136: "no es cosa nueva compeler a algunos que trabaxen, antes es cosa lícita y justa cuando hay necesidad de su trabaxo para conservación de la república".

the Americas, the demands of the political whole took precedence over those of its parts.[55]

1.2 *A Composite Commonwealth*

Ten years after Matienzo completed his *Gobierno*, another Spaniard in colonial Peru entered the debate: the Jesuit José de Acosta (1539–1600). He is best known for his vernacular *Natural and Moral History* (1590), which earned him the reputation of a great Renaissance historian.[56] But Acosta wore many hats. He also served as provincial of the Jesuit order, played a leading role in the Third Council of Lima (1582–1583), and held the chair of theology at the University of San Marcos in Lima.[57] And it was in a text that betrays his theological learning that Acosta confronted the question of Indigenous labor coercion.

In 1577, when the Toledan reform program was already in full swing, Acosta penned a treatise on how to attend to the salvation of the "*indios*".[58] In what was later published as the *De procuranda indorum salute* (1588), he noted that the relationship between freedom and coercion remained utterly contested. On the one hand, Indigenous subjects were "absolutely free and *sui iuris*".[59] But on the other, they were forced to certain tasks to keep the empire up and going. In the eyes of many, he explained, this was untenable: "if a free human is coerced, he is not free, and indeed, whoever forces another to work against his will seems to be committing a grave violation of right, for it is servile to endure force".[60] Yet, Acosta explained, an equally widespread opinion was that "if we are to be lenient with those who are barbarous in nature and will, no works will ever be accomplished, and no job will ever get done".[61] The Spaniards themselves were unwilling or unable to perform "laborious" and "dirty" jobs such as

---

55 I therefore do not agree with Orlando Bentancor that "the central axiom of Spanish imperial idology" can be reduced to the notion that "everything must be subordinated to the common good, whose measure is money" (*The Matter of Empire*, 243).

56 Grafton, "José de Acosta", 170 and *passim*.

57 Biographical information on Acosta is from Grafton, "José de Acosta"; Pagden, *The Fall of Natural Man*, 147–148; Brading, *The First America*, 184–185; and from the entry on Acosta on *Scholasticon*.

58 Grafton, "José de Acosta", 178.

59 Acosta, *De procuranda*, ed. Pereña, vol. 1, lib. III, cap. 17, no. 1, 506: "Atque in primis indos non esse servitute mulctatos sed liberos prorsus et sui iuris".

60 Acosta, *De procuranda*, ed. Pereña, vol. 1, lib. III, cap. 17, no. 5, 512: "Movet enim non parum hinc quod liber homo si cogitur, liber non est atque adeo qui ad opus invitum trahit, non levem facere videtur iniuriam, servile enim est pati vim".

61 Acosta, *De procuranda*, ed. Pereña, vol. 1, lib. III, cap. 17, no. 5, 512: "Inde vero non parum quoque urget quod si barbarum ingenio et voluntati indulgendum est, nihil operis unquam fiet, nihil negotii conficietur".

"turning over the soil, carrying out pieces of raw ore, gathering bricks, conducting mules, bearing loads, and other servile tasks which, if absent, quickly lead to the demise of any commonwealth".[62]

What was Acosta's solution to this impasse? He conceded that, in principle, servile jobs such as mining or farming could also be carried out by Spaniards. These tasks, he noted, "are not greatly inconsistent with their birth and education".[63] Yet Acosta offered a long list of arguments in favor of imposing such labor on Indigenous subjects instead. First, the Indigenous population vastly outnumbered the Spanish settlers. Second, abolishing Indigenous labor coercion would be tantamount to "extinguishing the light of religion", since the Spaniards would abandon these lands if their hopes for material wealth were not fulfilled.[64] Under the condition they received fair compensation for their labor, their health was minimally damaged, and the burden was shared equally among them, Acosta maintained that "the multitude of *indios* should be assigned to these necessary tasks and, if they do not want to obey, forced to it".[65] Moreover, as he pointed out, the *mita* was "a very ancient custom" that the Incas had introduced many centuries before the name of Christ first reached the Americas.[66]

Acosta's most important intervention, however, lay in his new vision of the imperial polity. "Natural law", he argued, "holds that the necessary parts of the family or city can be ordered to work for the preservation of the whole body. However, one must not order an eye to tread on the ground or a head of house-

62 Acosta, *De procuranda*, ed. Pereña, vol. 1, lib. III, cap. 17, no. 5, 512–514: "sint multa quae nullo modo hispani in his locis per se faciant praeterea quod vel laboriosa vel sordida ducunt et ut quam maxime velint, non possunt tamen tanta perficere, quale est humum effodere, rudera egerere, lateres cogere, onera baiulare, iumenta agere, caeteraque servilia quae si desint, brevi omnis civitatis deleatur".

63 Acosta, *De procuranda*, ed. Pereña, vol. 1, lib. III, cap. 17, no. 6, 514: "Nam ut demus ex hispanis non paucos posse servilia ista tractare, propterea quod natalis educatioque non admodum abhorrent".

64 Acosta, *De procuranda*, ed. Pereña, vol. 1, lib. III, cap. 17, no. 6, 514: "lucri spes potest fortassis excitare; tamen quota ista portio est hominum prae multitudine necessaria? Iubere autem vel ista cessare vel nostrates ad sua remeare, quis no videt quam sit fidei et religionis lumen extinguere?"

65 Acosta, *De procuranda*, ed. Pereña, vol. 1, lib. III, cap. 17, no. 6, 514: "Quamobrem non est improbandum quod civitates omnes institutum tenent et servant, ut indorum ad ista necessaria multitudo deputetur parereque si nolit, cogatur, dummodo et conveniens, ut dixi supra, merces labori retribuatur et cum minimo salutis fortunarumque suarum incommodo ab indis ista exigantur, tum etiam inter ipsos iusta oneris vicissitudo servetur".

66 Acosta, *De procuranda*, ed. Pereña, vol. 1, lib. III, cap. 17, no. 6, 514: "Deinde ipsorum barbarorum consuetudo perantiqua ab ipsis ingarum regum exordiis ante christianum nomen auditum multis saeculis conservata".

hold to administer the affairs of the kitchen".[67] Drawing on the traditional metaphor of the political community as a human body, Acosta articulated a highly hierarchical understanding of colonial society in Peru. Yet, he simultaneously argued that "the universal multitude of *indios* and Spaniards must already be considered as one and the same commonwealth, not as two that are separate from each other".[68] Consequently, the labor demanded of the Indigenous people by the Spaniards was not that owed by strangers, but rather by "fellow citizens".[69]

The difficulty of Acosta's vision was that it centered on unity and difference at the same time. How could these two strands, which so obviously pulled in opposite directions, be brought together? One solution was the strategy of resorting to Aristotle's notion of natural slavery. This had been Matienzo's tactic, and Acosta followed in his footsteps. In every commonwealth, he argued, some were naturally fit to work while others had what it takes to rule. This was what the "great architect of the city" had posited in his *Politics*.[70] Acosta was keen to stress that the fundamentally unequal composition of the commonwealth did not amount to faction or division. In his view, the disparate parts of the body politic complemented one another: "they helped each other out, one lending the eyes to see and the other lending the feet to walk".[71]

To reinforce this point, Acosta turned to a different image from the Book of Daniel: the statue featured in Nebuchadnezzar's dream.[72] Its golden head, arms and chest made of silver, a belly and thighs of brass, iron legs, and feet in part iron and in part of clay made it an apt metaphor for unequal political bodies.[73] Acosta was not the first to realize this. In the 1540s, the Salamancan

67 Acosta, *De procuranda*, ed. Pereña, vol. 1, lib. III, cap. 17, no. 6, 514: "Postremo ius naturae hoc habet, ut ad totius corporis, familiae civitatisve conservationem necessariae partes laborare iubeantur. Neque enim oculus calcare terram iubendus est vel culinariam paterfamilias exercere".

68 Acosta, *De procuranda*, ed. Pereña, vol. 1, lib. III, cap. 17, no. 7, 516: "Universa porro indorum atque hispanorum multitudo una eademque respublica habenda iam est, non duae quaedam inter se disiunctae [...]."

69 Acosta, *De procuranda*, ed. Pereña, vol. 1, lib. III, cap. 17, no. 7, 516: "siquidem et rege et lege utuntur iisdem utrique et utrisque tribunal et ius non aliud atque aliud sed idem certe. Quare quae ab indis nostris hominibus operae impenduntur, non exteris et alienis collocari putandae sunt, quod fortassis fallit nonnullos, sed suis potius civibus".

70 Acosta, *De procuranda*, ed. Pereña, vol. 1, lib. III, cap. 17, no. 7, 516.

71 Acosta, *De procuranda*, ed. Pereña, vol. 1, lib. III, cap. 17, no. 7, 516: "dummodo alii aliis adiumento sint oculosque alter ad videndum, pedes alter ad ambulandum mutuet".

72 *Pace* Bentancor, who mistakenly argues that "Acosta is clearly employing here Aristotle's metaphor of the social body as a statue" (*The Matter of Empire*, 171).

73 Daniel 2:31–33.

Domingo de Soto had invoked it to caution against the oppression of the poor in his famous defense of mendicancy. By casting beggars as the feet and foundation of the city, he maintained that their destruction would tear down the whole body politic.[74] Yet Acosta's analogy was less concerned with the statue as a whole than with foregrounding the specifically composite character of its feet: "although clay badly adheres to iron", he wrote, "according to the prophetic prophecy, the two nevertheless compose the very feet of this statue".[75] In the biblical account, these feet symbolized a disjointed kingdom, an uneasy union made up of separate parts. And Acosta's point was that "*indios*" and Spaniards were united in the same way: despite their fundamental difference, they constituted one political whole.

The relationship between these parts was hierarchical: iron stood for strength and clay for weakness.[76] "One should not be bewildered", Acosta thus concluded, "if the clay is sometimes oppressed by the iron, but one should rather desire that it will not be entirely shattered and destroyed".[77] This was ultimately the statue's fate in Nebuchadnezzar's dream. Acosta's warning epitomized that the composite commonwealth of "*indios*" and Spaniards was fraught with danger.

1.3 *The Limits of Forced Labor and the Limits of Political Authority*

Proponents of the new regime of labor coercion were careful to distinguish it from legal slavery. Acosta, for instance, emphasized that it had been "introduced by public authority".[78] And Matienzo stressed that *encomenderos* could no longer claim any authority over Indigenous subjects.[79] They were bound to reside outside the newly formed *reducciones*, in exclusively Spanish towns.[80] Under the new regime, as Matienzo made clear, the sole role and right of

74 Soto, *In causa pauperum deliberatio*, cap. 12, 76 [mislabeled as 71]. See also the discussion in Schwartz, *The Political Morality of the Late Scholastics*, 73.

75 Acosta, *De procuranda*, ed. Pereña, vol. 1, lib. III, cap. 17, no. 7, 516: "Quoniam etsi testa ferro male cohaeret iuxta propheticum vaticinium, tamen eosdem statuae huius pedes ambo componunt".

76 Acosta, *De procuranda*, ed. Pereña, vol. 1, lib. III, cap. 17, no. 7, 516.

77 Acosta, *De procuranda*, ed. Pereña, vol. 1, lib. III, cap. 17, no. 7, 516: "Itaque mirandum non est, si testa ferro prematur interdum, illud potius optandum, ne penitus comminuatur ac dissipetur".

78 Acosta, *De procuranda*, ed. Pereña, vol. 1, lib. III, cap. 17, no. 9, 518: "At personalia servitia quae diximus, publica auctoritate inducta sunt".

79 Matienzo, *Gobierno del Perú*, ed. Lohmann Villena, parte I, cap. 31, 106: "Que a ningún cacique se le quite el dominio de sus tierras e indios vasallos que tienen". See also cap. 30, 101; and cap. 31, 104.

80 Matienzo, *Gobierno del Perú*, ed. Lohmann Villena, parte I, cap. 33, 113.

encomenderos was to oversee the collection of tributary payments and to control Native vassals' instruction in the Christian faith and political life.[81] In so arguing, he backed the official policy of the crown.[82]

Yet one of Matienzo's arguments threatened to erode the distinction between labor coercion and *encomienda* slavery. For in his view, the "*indios*" could still be forced to work in the households of Spanish settlers as part of the *mita*.[83] This was indeed a routine practice in the viceroyalty of Peru.[84] How, then, was this any different from the formally forbidden practice of keeping Indigenous slaves?

Matienzo himself offered no answer, but the theologian José de Acosta addressed this issue in his *De procuranda indorum salute*. In principle, he argued, those who forced free subjects to work for their own will and benefit "establish a kind of slavery" and "think that it is their right to violate the rights of others".[85] Yet Acosta went on to argue that "one must not find fault with the fact that for special reasons, *indios* are assigned to domestic services in certain places, such as in hospitals, in the houses of monks, and furthermore in the houses of office holders or noblemen".[86] For Acosta, the inclusion of forced labor in Spanish households under the rubric of *mita* labor did not contradict the claim that it was a public institution. Just as many contemporary thinkers in Iberia had insisted on the political character of the household, Acosta cast the domestic sphere as more than merely "private". In his estimation, it was the public offices of imperial administrators and *encomenderos* that legitimized forced Indigenous labor in Spanish households in colonial Peru.[87]

If domestic labor stretched the scope of public power to the utmost, another form of forced labor seemed to transgress the limits of political authority altogether: the use of Indigenous carriers as substitutes for pack animals. Juan de

---

81 Matienzo, *Gobierno del Perú*, ed. Lohmann Villena, parte I, cap. 29, 98.

82 On this point, see also Elliott, *Empires of the Atlantic World*, 40–41.

83 Matienzo, *Gobierno del Perú*, ed. Lohmann Villena, parte I, cap. 10, 35: "los indios de los repartimientos […] otros para servir a españoles en sus casas […] y otros, venir a servir a sus encomenderos en sus casas".

84 Zamora, *Casa poblada y buen gobierno*, 52–54.

85 Acosta, *De procuranda*, ed. Pereña, vol. 1, lib. III, cap. 16, no. 2, 502: "alii inhumana atrocique contentione servitutis genus educunt, ut tamdiu laborare cogantur quoad ipsorum arbitrio sit satisfactum […] ius suum iniuriam aliorum putent".

86 Acosta, *De procuranda*, ed. Pereña, vol. 1, lib. III, cap. 17, no. 8, 518: "Neque illud vituperandum quod peculiares ob causas ad domestica ministeria quibusdam locis attribuuntur, ut in xenodochiis, in religiosis domibus, tum etiam publicorum nobiliumve hominum".

87 On the *encomenderos* as public office-holders, see also Acosta, *De procuranda*, ed. Pereña, vol. 1, lib. III, cap. 11, no. 5, 468: "sunt alia etiam publicae utilitatis officia quibus cum addicuntur nobiles homines, iure renumerandi sunt".

Matienzo explained to his readers that this was an ancient practice dating back to the Incas. Alongside the main strategic roads of their empire, the Incas had set up inns, so-called *tambos*, which supplied travelers not only with food and shelter but also with manpower. The Spaniards revived this institution. As part of the *mita*, a proportion of Indigenous tributaries was assigned to these inns in order "to carry hay and firewood for travelers, and to carry loads from one *tambo* to another".[88] This service was especially indispensable in the Sierra, where many Andean roads could only be traveled on foot and were too narrow and steep for pack animals. Yet even where beasts of burden could pass, Matienzo emphasized, the use of "*indios*" was indispensable. The *tambos* often lacked provisions and beds, forcing travelers—especially confessors visiting *reducciones*—to haul all their belongings. Since not even a rich man could find enough horses for this purpose, Matienzo concluded, Spanish settlers resorted to native carriers: so-called *indios de carga*.[89]

The substitution of animal with human bodies was contested from the early years of Spanish colonization. Matienzo pointed to a piece of legislation that Cristóbal Vaca de Castro, the first governor of Peru, had promulgated as early as 1543. In his ordinances on the *tambos*, he had prohibited the use of Andeans as pack animals without demonstrable necessity and the express license of a judge.[90] This principle was still in effect when Matienzo was writing, much to his chagrin. He emphasized that in Spain, many casual laborers offered similar services to make a living.[91] Matienzo stressed that the precise number of

88 Matienzo, *Gobierno del Perú*, ed. Lohmann Villena, parte I, cap. 10, 35: "*Mitayos* de *tambos* son los que se dan para traer yerba e leña a los pasaxeros e para llevar cargas de un *tambo* a otro. [...] conforme a las del Inga, que hasta hoy se guardan, en que repartió los pueblos que habían de servir en cada *tambo* en los caminos reales".

89 Matienzo, *Gobierno del Perú*, ed. Lohmann Villena, parte I, cap. 10, 36: "aunque están abiertos los caminos y pueden pasar bestias de cargas, mas hay otra mayor dificultad para no poderse escusar las cargas, y es que como no hay en los más tambos comida para que el pasaxero la pueda comprar, ni camas en qué dormir [...] no puede escusarse de llevar todo consigo [...] y aunque sea rico, si pasa toda su casa de una ciudad a otra, no podrá hallar tantos caballos para que la lleve toda en ellos, hasta que se vaya puniendo la tierra en más orden. Mayormente esto es inpusible a los clérigos y frailes que andan en las dotrinas". For the locution *indios de carga*, see Matienzo, *Gobierno del Perú*, ed. Lohmann Villena, parte I, cap. 10, 37.

90 Matienzo, *Gobierno del Perú*, ed. Lohmann Villena, parte I, cap. 10, 36. A transcription of the original manuscript at the Biblioteca de la Real Academia de la Historia in Madrid is available in Vaca de Castro, "Ordenanzas de tambos".

91 Matienzo, *Gobierno del Perú*, ed. Lohmann Villena, parte I, cap. 10., 37. This practice was already reflected in the late medieval *Siete Partidas*, as Solórzano later explained. See Solórzano, *Política indiana*, ed. Ochoa Brun, vol. 1, lib. II, cap. 13, no. 13, 243; and *Las Siete Partidas*, l. 8, tit. 8, partida 5.

indios de carga needed often depended on unforeseen circumstances. If a horse died on the spot, for instance, this required quick action. The idea that Spanish travelers should previously seek the approval of a judge was therefore "impossible".[92]

The explosive nature of this claim was recognized by José de Acosta. The real question, he explained, was whether it was "sometimes licit to force unwilling barbarians to advantageous works by *private* authority".[93] This was a provocative question because, as Acosta and others viewed it, what distinguished Indigenous labor coercion from slavery was precisely its grounding in public authority. How, then, could it be just to forcibly recruit Indigenous carriers by private authority?

By the time Acosta was writing, the institution of *indios de carga* had been temporarily outlawed, making it even more difficult to legitimize.[94] One way around this problem was to emphasize that the practice of carrying goods on one's shoulders was a long-standing Inca tradition. Laws that prohibited a customary social reality could therefore be violated, in Acosta's view. As long as the Indigenous carriers were fairly paid and not overburdened, no one needed to fear for their conscience.[95] In so arguing, Acosta approached the issue from a new perspective, suggesting that the Spaniards and *indios de carga* could enter into voluntary agreements.

Yet what if this option failed as well? Acosta explained that if a Spaniard in need was unable to reach an agreement with his or her Andean counterpart, they should consult a local magistrate "who may coerce with public authority".[96] However, Acosta went on,

---

92 Matienzo, *Gobierno del Perú*, ed. Lohmann Villena, parte I, cap. 10, 37: "Haber de preceder licencia de juez, con conocimiento de causa, para las cargas, si es para los caminantes, es inpusible, porque no hay jueces en el camino que la puedan dar, y menos al salir de las ciudades, porque acaece en el camino morírseles un caballo y haber menester más indios de carga que al principio".

93 Acosta, *De procuranda*, ed. Pereña, vol. 1, lib. III., cap. 17, no. 9, 518, emphasis mine: "At personalia servitia quae diximus, publica auctoritate inducta sunt. Privata vero an fas sit aliquando barbaros nolentes ad opera opportuna compellere".

94 On the legal situation in the later 16th century, see Burciaga Campos, "Corona española, política económica e indígenas", 970–971.

95 See Acosta, *De procuranda*, ed. Pereña, vol. 1, lib. III, cap. 17, no. 11, 524: "Lex vero quatenus obliget consuetudine contra obtinente, nihil habet hic propriae difficultatis sed commune est cum aliis plerisque. [...] Itaque gentes indorum apud nos baiulandis oneribus perassuetae si aequo plus non urgeantur, neque iniuriae neque incommodi quidquam subeunt".

96 Acosta, *De procuranda*, ed. Pereña, vol. 1, lib. III, cap. 17, no. 9, 520–522: "Primum, si potest pactione transigi, id multo prius ac melius. Ubi non potest, si commode conveniri potest magistratus aliquis qui publica auctoritate cogat, adeundus est".

> […] if this fails too, for magistrates are absent very often, and if the weight of the matter is urgent, one can teach nothing other, neither shorter nor plainer, than to follow the laws of necessity; that you should strive for what is necessary for you, with minimal detriment to your neighbor.[97]

The upshot of Acosta's argument was that necessity legitimized the idea that Spaniards could coerce Indigenous people to labor for their very own benefit and by their own right. When faced with urgent need, he concluded, "one can certainly use some morally right force and compulsion, and some indication of terror, just as it is done to the child that disregards what is just and suitable".[98]

Here Acosta drew on a classic locus of Catholic moral theology, importing the argument of necessity into the colonial context. His intellectual predecessors in Iberia had also argued that a threat to one's life pushed the boundaries of what was morally right and legally permissible: in a state of necessity, an individual could take another's property, which would otherwise be theft. Acosta's vision, however, set in motion a very different mechanism. For him, necessity did not reintroduce a state of common property under natural law. Instead, it actualized the full implications of the natural hierarchy between Spanish and Indigenous subjects, which lay at the heart of his understanding of the imperial order.

The institution of *indios de carga* remained a controversial issue well into the 17th century. The jurist Juan de Solórzano later observed that among the many royal decrees on the subject, some strongly condemned it while others tolerated and re-legalized the use of native carriers as a necessary evil.[99] Without discrediting the institution *tout court*, Solórzano conceded that the idea of using humans for "offices of beasts" was and remained deeply problematic.[100] Like the university theologians in Iberia, he insisted that even slaves could not be owned in the same way as animals.[101] Solórzano's concern, however, was not

---

97 Acosta, *De procuranda*, ed. Pereña, vol. 1, lib. III, cap. 17, no. 9, 522: "Hic quoque si desit, ut deest persaepe ac negotii gravitas urget, nihil aliud praecipi potest neque brevius neque planius quam ut leges necessitatis observes, quae tibi necessaria sunt quaerens cum quam minimo proximi detrimento".

98 Acosta, *De procuranda*, ed. Pereña, vol. 1, lib. III, cap. 17, no. 9, 522: "Honesta certe aliqua vis et compulsio afferri potest et terroris quaedam significatio tanquam puero alicui iusta et commoda contemnenti".

99 Solórzano, *Política indiana*, ed. Ochoa Brun, vol. 1, lib. II, cap. 13, no. 15 and 22–27, 243–247.

100 Solórzano, *Política indiana*, ed. Ochoa Brun, vol. 1, lib. II, cap. 13, no. 20, 245: "Pareciendo que no era justo, que ombres que son libres, y mandados tratar como tales, hiciesen oficios de bestias".

101 Solórzano, *Política indiana*, ed. Ochoa Brun, vol. 1, lib. II, cap. 13, no. 20, 245. Solórzano did

simply the boundary between humans and animals. His principal worry was that, because of their "continuous peregrinations", Indigenous carriers "could neither be well-instructed in the faith, nor were they left to live with their wives so that they were not there to procreate and raise their children, and underwent a great reduction and diminution".[102] In this sense, he sought to protect the reproduction of those who were destined to work under the yoke of the *mita*.

2 Colonial Law and Colonial Clamor

Around 1600, Potosí was one of the largest cities in the world. The population had more than doubled since the Toledan reforms and now numbered over 100,000.[103] In the burgeoning metropolis, roughly one in ten people were *mita* workers.[104] The harsh conditions in the depths of the Andean mines sparked public outcry in the Peruvian viceroyalty, especially among ecclesiastical men of letters. In 1596, the Jesuit Antonio de Ayanz wrote to the Spanish monarch that "in provinces between Potosí and close to Cusco, the Native population has declined to such an extent that the villages are empty and the *tambos* without people or service".[105] Three years later, university theologians of the Society of Jesus from Lima, Cusco, and Quito wrote a joint statement to the viceroy. They urged him to stop assigning more and more Indigenous tributaries for mining, in order to mitigate the increasingly alarming decline of their population.[106]

This situation was the result of several interrelated phenomena. Many Andeans perished in the mines, while others fled the *reducciones* to escape the *mita*. Still others chose to stay in Potosí after completing their draft term, working for mine owners in exchange for a better salary.[107] By 1600, more than half

---

not, however, make this claim with reference to his colleagues in Iberia; rather he pointed to Augustine's *The Lord's Sermon*, trans. Campbell and ed. Ramsey, lib. 1, cap. 19, no. 59, 57.

102 Solórzano, *Política indiana*, ed. Ochoa Brun, vol. 1, lib. II, cap. 13, no. 19, 244: "y que por traerles en estos tragines, y continuas peregrinaciones, ni podian ser bien instruídos en la Fé, ni aún les dexaban hacer vida con sus mugeres, con que faltaban á la procreacion, y crianza de sus hijos, é iban en gran menoscabo, y diminucion".

103 Elliott, *Empires of the Atlantic World*, 94; and Lane, *Potosí*, 37 and 95.

104 Lane, *Potosí*, 72.

105 Ayanz, "Breve relación de los agravios que reciben los indios", ed. Aldea Vaquero, 234.

106 "Parecer de los Padres de la Compañía de Jesús", ed. Aldea Vaquero.

107 Mumford, *Vertical Empire*, 152–153.

the Andeans at Potosí—as well as in Huancavelica—were skilled voluntary workers who bypassed the system in this way. The effect, however, was not the decline of forcible mining *tout court*. Juan de Solórzano would later claim that the cost of *indios voluntarios* exceeded the benefit they brought.[108] And indeed, those who ran the industry successfully lobbied for the centrality of coerced labor into the early 19th century.[109] Yet the fact that fewer Indigenous people could be drawn from the *reducciones* meant that the conditions for those who did remain under the yoke of the *mita* worsened. They were compelled to perform the most dangerous tasks, and many endured much longer turns than the system had originally envisaged.[110]

These developments prompted the intervention of the Council of the Indies. In 1601, it issued a landmark royal decree that became famous under the heading of *Servicio personal*, which sought to impose significant limits on the "personal service"—a synonym for *mita* labor—of Indigenous vassals. Presumably in response to local petitioners, the decree mandated that the existing system of coerced labor be abolished in favor of an alternative arrangement, where Natives offered their services voluntarily.[111] The practical purchase of this policy was limited, and it amounted to little more than a "mere declaration of intentions".[112] Under pressure from strong resistance overseas, another royal decree issued just eight years later re-legalized forced Indigenous labor as it had been previously practiced, and indeed, had continued all along.[113]

2.1 *Writing for the Viceroy*

For Spanish intellectuals, however, the 1601 decree *Servicio personal* marked a watershed moment in the debate over forced Indigenous labor. The first influ-

108 Solórzano, *Política indiana*, ed. Ochoa Brun, vol. 1, lib. II, cap. 6, no. 35, 177: "Indios voluntarios como se hallan en Potosí [...] se conducen á mucha costa, de manera que excede al provecho que rinden".

109 Lane, *Potosí*, 72; Robins, *Santa Bárbara's Legacy*, 91.

110 González Casanovas, *Las dudas de la corona*, 60–68; Robins, *Santa Bárbra's Legacy*, 77.

111 As Adrian Master has recently shown, "virtually all royal decrees" originated in petitions made by vassals of the Spanish empire and he calls the process of decree-making a "petition-and-response system". See Masters, *We, the King*, 6 and 21.

112 González Casanovas, *Las dudas de la corona*, 68: "La reforma no superó la condición de una mera declaración de intenciones".

113 The two decrees were sent separately to the viceroys of Peru and New Spain. See "Real instrucción sobre el trabajo de los indios: Valladolid, 24 de noviembre de 1601", ed. in Konetzke, *Colección de documentos*, vol. 2, 71–85; and as "Real cédula sobre los servicios personales y repartimientos de indios: Aranjuez, 26 de mayo de 1609", ed. in Konetzke, *Colección de documentos*, vol. 2, 154–168.

ential respondent to the royal edict was Miguel de Agia. Born in Valencia, he served as a professor of theology in the Franciscan convent of Guatemala from the 1560s. But like his fellow university theologians in the Old World, Agia had close ties to the governing elites.[114] He rose to fame when the Peruvian viceroy Luis de Velasco commissioned Agia to write a rhetorical rebuttal of the decree from Spain. The result was the *Tratado que contiene tres pareceres graves en derecho* (1604), which earned Agia the reputation as the most ardent defender of forced native mining.

Against the demands of the royal decree, he portrayed the *mita* as a corollary of "political or civil subjection".[115] Whereas Matienzo had made a similar point by comparing the duties of Castilian subjects on both sides of the Atlantic, Agia stayed true to his profession. He justified "personal services" with recourse to the scope of political power, pointing to the authoritative accounts of fellow university theologians like Vitoria, Soto, and Molina.[116] What is more, he followed in Acosta's footsteps and argued that "the *indios*, Spaniards, and other nations that reside in the Indies form one single body of a whole and perfect commonwealth, composed by true vassals of your Majesty that can and should justly be compelled and forced […] to serve and work in attendance of that body".[117]

At the heart of his argument was the defense of *mita* mining. Indigenous labor "in the Cerro of Potosí", he argued, was indispensable "for waging war against the enemies of the faith" as well as "to accumulate the riches, with which to support the public necessities of the entire kingdom, and all the other things of public and common utility".[118] For Agia, mining was the quintessen-

114 Chamberlain, "Review of Miguel de Agia," 301.

115 Agia, *Tratado*, segundo parecer, 56: "La subiection politica, o civil, en virtud de la qual son compelidos y forçados los indios a trabajar en servicio de la Republica".

116 Agia, *Tratado*, segundo parecer, 56: "Esta conclusion se prueva efficazmente porque la potestad politica o civil, que corresponde a la dicha subiection [i.e. of Indigenous peoples], es de ley natural como enseña Victoria […] Soto […] O alomenos tiene su origen y principio dela ley natural […] sigue Luys de Molina".

117 Agia, *Tratado*, segundo parecer, 59: "asi hazeindo los indios, y Españoles, y demas naciones que residen en las Indias un cuerpo solo de Republica entero, y perfecto compuesto de hombres verdaderos vasallos de su Magestad pueden y deven licitamente ser compelidos y forçados (siempre que convenga y sea necessario) a que sirvan y trabajen en servicio deste cuerpo". Agia did not, however, refer to Acosta and instead cited Cicero's speech in defense of Sextus Roscius to make this point.

118 Agia, *Tratado*, segundo parecer, 60 [incorrectly labeled as 68]: "Licitamente, et citra iniuriam puede su Mastad [sic] compeler los indios a que trabajen en la lavor de las Minas del cerro de Potosi […] para hazer guerra a los enemigos de la fe […] para hazer thesoros,

tial business that sustained the viceroyalty of Peru. Without it, he insisted, "the preservation of the commonwealth would fail".[119] And it was for this reason that the "*indios*" could be compelled to work in the mines without a violation of right.

Agia and his allies successfully argued their case. In 1609, the Council of the Indies abandoned its strict prohibition of *mita* mining, while maintaining its call for a transformation of the colonial economy.[120] The decree was received with enthusiasm in Peru, and plans for reform were quickly abandoned.

2.2 *Appealing to the King's Conscience*

Another Spaniard in the New World forcefully pushed back against such negligence. In a series of memorials in the 1610s, Juan de Silva—a former soldier turned Franciscan, who in his second career as *religioso* served as royal confessor and as a missionary in New Spain and Florida—petitioned the king for renewed intervention.[121] For Silva, the treatment of Indigenous vassals was "the most cruel end exorbitant tyranny that no nation in the world, as bad as they were, has imposed to this day".[122] The king's conscience, he insisted, would only be safe if he took steps to remedy the situation.[123]

In the Peruvian mines, Silva wrote, Andean tributaries were exposed to mortal danger and treated "as if they were fugitive slaves".[124] They were beaten to work, not properly paid, and neither given sufficient rest.[125] Most of the "thirteen thousand *indios*" inside the Cerro Rico never made it back home, Silva

---

y con ellos acudir a las necessidades publicas de todos sus reynos, y para las demas cosas de publica y comun utilidad".

119 Agia, *Tratado*, segundo parecer, 66: "la tierra del Piru para su conservacion no tiene otro comercio sino el de la plata, y oro, que se saca de las minas: el qual si faltasse faltaria la conservacion de la Republica".

120 "Real cédula sobre los servicios personales y repartimientos de indios: Aranjuez, 26 de mayo de 1609", ed. in Konetzke, *Colección de documentos*, vol. 2, 154–156.

121 Silva sent three memorials to Spain between 1613 and 1618, all of which were published together under the title *Advertencias importantes*. I will be citing from the edition by Paulino Castañeda Delgado. Biographical information on Silva is drawn from the opening section of Silva's third memorial (Silva, "Memorial tercero", in *Los Memoriales*, ed. Castañeda Delgado, 291–293); and from Kelly, "The Franciscan Missionary Plan", 280.

122 Silva, "Memorial tercero", in *Los Memoriales*, ed. Castañeda Delgado, 317: "Es también el dicho repartimiento y ley [...] la más cruel y exorbitante tiranía que hasta hoy con nación ninguna del mundo, por mala que fuese, se ha usado".

123 Silva, "Memorial tercero", in *Los Memoriales*, ed. Castañeda Delgado, 293.

124 Silva, "Memorial tercero", in *Los Memoriales*, ed. Castañeda Delgado, 322: "los tratan tan mal como si fueran esclavos fugitivos".

125 Silva, "Memorial tercero", in *Los Memoriales*, ed. Castañeda Delgado, 322–332.

maintained, "and the few who return are so mistreated, limping, with broken legs, and all of them so exhausted and ill that they pass from this life in very short time".[126] He painted an even gloomier picture of the Santa Bárbara mines at Huancavelica, to which "more than two thousand *indios* are assigned with the same force and harm".[127] Early moderns like Silva were well aware that the toxic mercury led to severe health issues like anemia, the loss of teeth, tremors—and death.[128] The relatives of those bound for Huancavelica, he wrote with a dramatic flourish, "farewelled them under much tears and regrets to never ever see them again, so that there is no tiger's heart that will not ache of such great misery".[129]

For Silva, the problem of mining was twofold. For one, it damaged Spain's reputation on an international level and was grist to the mill of those who portrayed the Spanish overseas ventures as cruel and inhumane. More importantly still, he argued, the destruction of the Native population effectively undermined the entire Spanish mission overseas.[130] "The empire of this New World" Silva wrote, was "a great grant of heaven, an *encomienda* of the eternal Father".[131] By casting the king as God's *encomendero*, he implied that the monarch was little different from his infamous representatives overseas, who had similarly neglected the divine mission and abused the Andeans in their strife for riches. Silva called on the king to clear his conscience and to save the souls of those under his authority.[132] To that end, he proposed a revival of the central dictum of the infamous royal decree *Servicio personal*: Indigenous labor should be voluntary rather than coerced.

126 Silva, "Memorial tercero", in *Los Memoriales*, ed. Castañeda Delgado, 321: "Primeramente para el cerro de Potosí se reparten trece mil indios, los cuales van de diversas partes del Perú [...] y estos pocos que vuelven, tan maltratados, cojos, perniquebrados y todos tan cansados y enfermos, que en muy breve tiempo pasan desta vida".

127 Silva, "Memorial tercero", in *Los Memoriales*, ed. Castañeda Delgado, 321: "A las minas de Guancabelica, que son las del azogue, también se reparten dos mil y tantos indios con la misma fuerza y agravios".

128 On what early moderns did and did not know about mercury poisoning, see Robins, *Mercury, Mining, and Empire*, 8.

129 Silva, "Memorial tercero", in *Los Memoriales*, ed. Castañeda Delgado, 321: "con qué lágrimas y con qué sentimiento se despiden para nunca jamas tornarlos a ver; de manera que no hay corazón de tigre que no se duela de tan gran miseria".

130 Silva, "Memorial tercero", in *Los Memoriales*, ed. Castañeda Delgado, 326–328.

131 Silva, "Memorial tercero", in *Los Memoriales*, ed. Castañeda Delgado, 355: "Vuestra Majestad goza del imperio deste nuevo mundo [...] por elección y donación divina; es una encomienda mayor del cielo, una encomienda del Padre eterno y inmenso Dios".

132 Silva, "Memorial tercero", in *Los Memoriales*, ed. Castañeda Delgado, 354: "no le va menos a Vuestra Majestad que asegurar su conciencia y la de sus consejeros y ministros con la de tantas almas que en este peligroso golfo se anegan".

A mining system "without force and violence", Silva explained, was already in place in New Spain.[133] The same approach, he argued, could equally be implemented "in all the mines of Peru, and in the great hill of Potosí".[134] Silva's point was that "the *indio* animated by good gain and by good treatment and liberty will work willingly, and with the greed of earning much for himself he shall also earn much for the miner, without any need for inflicting beating and lashes upon him".[135] If there were not enough voluntary workers, Silva added, "Your Majesty could mandate that the miners be given a quantity of Black slaves, whom the miners should pay out of their own pocket and by their estimation, little by little".[136] This latter point epitomizes the upshot of Silva's argument: being coerced to work in the mines was indeed a form of slavery. Even if a mining industry without the *mita* proved less economically fruitful, he stressed, "it is worth more to have little with a good conscience than to have a lot with a bad one".[137]

But in fact, the decree *Servicio personal* had not ruled out coercion altogether, and Silva knew this all too well. The royal edict had established that, due to great necessity, the "*indios*" could be obliged to offer their workforce voluntarily—also for mining.[138] While Silva remained firm on the matter of mining, he did concede that other forms of forced labor were subject to precisely that logic. This also included all the services of Indigenous vassals in the

133 Silva, "Memorial tercero", in *Los Memoriales*, ed. Castañeda Delgado, 345: "Esta manera de servicio de minas sin fuerza, ni violencia, se ha usado y usa tambien en todas las minas de Zacatecas, y en las mas de la Nueva Galicia, y Nueva Vizcaya, que es la gruesa de las minas de Nueva España". Mexican mining was indeed reliant on voluntary Native workers—alongside free and enslaved Africans as well as people of mixed descent—but was insignificant to the large-scale Peruvian industry of the time, and only really took off in the 18th century. See Lane, *Potosí*, 7; and Elliott, *Empires of the Atlantic World*, 99–101.

134 Silva, "Memorial tercero", in *Los Memoriales*, ed. Castañeda Delgado, 345: "podráse hacer acá lo mismo; y aún en todas las minas del Perú y del gran cerro de Potosí".

135 Silva, "Memorial tercero", in *Los Memoriales*, ed. Castañeda Delgado, 345.: "el indio convidado de la ganancia y del buen tratamiento y libertad trabaje de buena gana y con codicia de ganar mucho para sí, ganará también mucho para el minero, sin que sean menster palos ni azotes que ande sobre él".

136 Siva, "Memorial tercero", in *Los Memoriales*, ed. Castañeda Delgado, 346: "Mas para facilitar este inconveniente podría Vuestra Majestad mandar que se les diese a los mineros alguna cantidad de negros que por su cuenta y razón los vayan pagando poco a poco".

137 Silva, "Memorial tercero", in *Los Memoriales*, ed. Castañeda Delgado, 347; "*Melius est parum iustitia, quam multi fructus cum iniquitate*: que mas vale poco con buena conciencia, que mucho con mala. Y esto basta cuanto a las minas".

138 See the "Real instrucción sobre el trabajo de los indios: Valladolid, 24 de noviembre de 1601", ed. in Konetzke, *Colección de documentos*, vol. 2, 77–78.

households of Spanish settlers.[139] "Well, the thing is", Silva wrote, "Spaniards and *indios* already form one commonwealth, as Father Acosta says [...] and Christian charity demands that we help each other out and that we encourage each other in our necessities".[140] Silva shared the view that within the colonial body politic, Native vassals had the status of "natural slaves": they needed the guidance and governance of wiser men and were obliged to contribute to the commonwealth with their workforce.[141] In Silva's estimation, those in charge of the *reducciones* could therefore command all their Indigenous tributaries "with a certain Christian rigor and force [...] to rent themselves out voluntarily to the Spaniards who are present there" once a week—even for the individual benefit of *encomenderos*.[142]

Measured against the reality of forced labor at the time, Silva's proposal was indeed aimed at counteracting and moderating the abuses against Andeans. But by casting Indigenous subjects as "natural slaves", he tapped plainly into the argumentative logic of his intellectual predecessors. If historians today view Silva as a champion of the "liberty of the *indios*", they may be misled by his rhetorical redescription of what it meant "to participate freely and voluntarily in the viceregal economy".[143]

3 The Persistence of a Paradox

The decades that followed were tempestuous for Potosí. After a feud between Basque and Castilian miners had thrown the city into turmoil in the early 1620s,

139 Silva, "Memorial tercero", in *Los Memoriales*, ed. Castañeda Delgado, 347.

140 Silva, "Memorial tercero", in *Los Memoriales*, ed. Castañeda Delgado, 347.: "Y es que, pues indios y españoles hacen ya una República, como el Padre Acosta dice [...] y la caridad cristiana obliga que nos ayudemos y favorezcamos unos a otros en nuestras necesidades".

141 Silva, "Memorial tercero", in *Los Memoriales*, ed. Castañeda Delgado, 347–348.

142 Silva, "Memorial tercero", in *Los Memoriales*, ed. Castañeda Delgado, 347–348: "Para las demás granjerías de los españoles, servicio de casa y obrajes, y de personas particulares podrá ordenarse lo siguiente. [...] Lo cual se podrá hacer en esta forma: mandando los dichos caciques y governadores con algún rigor y fuerza cristiana, que todos los indios de servicio que en sus distritos hubiere [...] estén obligados a juntarse todos en el patio que está fuera del convento o iglesia, o en otra parte más acomodada, un día de la semana; y allí, delante de sus caciques y del sobredicho prelado, se alquilen voluntariamente a los españoles que allí estuvieren".

143 Zorrilla, "La doctrina misiológica", 311: "la idea que atraviesa la obra de Silva sobre cuestiones políticas y económicas es la libertad de los indios: libertad para abrazar la fe, para someterse políticamente a la corona española y para participar libre y voluntariamente en la economía virreinal".

a devastating flood in 1626 washed away many of Potosí's mills and refineries, leaving hundreds dead.[144] Around the same time, a new wave of Indigenous migration further intensified the mining industry's problems. Increasing numbers of tributaries managed to escape from their *reducciones* and joined other Indigenous settlements as "foreigners" (*forasteros*). Far away from their kinship group, they were required to pay taxes to the community's *caciques* but were no longer subject to tribute in the form of forced labor.[145]

The culmination of Potosí's mining crisis came in the mid-century. For years, those managing the Andean mints had tried to conceal the imbalance between rising demands for silver and declining supplies of ore by making coins lighter and by mixing the ostensibly pure silver with copper.[146] "The house of cards", as Kris Lane vividly puts it, "collapsed by the end of the year 1649", under the scrutiny of princes and merchants from around the world who had become aware of the fraudulent practices in Potosí.[147]

Even as the silver city's heyday was coming to an end, forced labor in the Cerro Rico remained an integral part of the Peruvian economy. Throughout the reign of Philp IV, "the *mita* continued to depopulate the Andes, reducing the number of Spain's subjects and burdening the royal conscience".[148] And it also remained at the forefront of debates among the viceroyalty's intellectuals.

3.1 *Mining by Prudent Reason of State*

One of them was Juan de Solórzano y Pereira. Educated at the University of Salamanca, Solórzano had been on track for an academic career before accepting a position as a judge in the Audiencia in Lima in 1609.[149] He had previously held a professorship in law at Salamanca and was later offered (but declined) the Prime Chair in that subject at the University of San Marcos in Lima. This background might explain why he first penned a major Latin treatise on the government and law of the Indies, the two-volume *De indiarum iure* (1629–1639).[150] When he later reworked it into a vernacular version under the title *Política indiana* (1648), Solórzano became one of the most widely read Spanish authors of his time.

---

144 See Lane, *Potosí*, 110–116 and 123–124.

145 González Casanovas, *Las dudas de la corona*, 74 and 102; Robins, *Santa Bárbara's Legacy*, 74–75.

146 Lane, *Potosí*, 127–133.

147 Lane, *Potosí*, 132.

148 Lane, *Potosí*, 145.

149 Biographical information on Solórzano is from García Hernán, *Consejero de ambos mundos*, 60–66 and 105–107.

150 Solórzano, *De indiarum iure*; Solórzano, *Tomum alterum de indiarum iure*.

By the time that Solórzano was writing, there was a growing awareness among Spanish settlers in Peru that the existing system of forced labor would be unsustainable in the long run. The dangers that it posed to the political fabric were not just metaphorical: the constant oppression of the Natives threatened to bring about their demise. The most contentious issue remained mining, as Solórzano was acutely aware. Public debates and the crown's conflicting legal policy had persisted well into the 17th century. A final resolution, he explained, was still pending and would ultimately "proceed from superior and more appropriate judgment"[151] than his own. Yet, despite this rhetorical recognition of monarchical authority, Solórzano did not leave it at that. Celebrations of *mita* mining were no longer tenable in his estimation. Even the royal decrees that permitted its practice, he noted, "admit the doubtfulness of the matter".[152] Much like Juan de Silva, he stressed that reforming the mining industry would free the Spaniards from moral scruples. And, in opposition to Acosta, he argued that "neither commerce with Spain, nor the propagation of the faith, nor the relief for wars would cease on account of this".[153] "True and prudent reason of state", Solórzano proclaimed, "is to lean and aspire only to what is licit, and no way that puts divine precepts and considerations behind human interests has ever proved beneficial".[154]

Solórzano did not call for the abolition of mining as such. Like all natural resources, he argued, the ores deep in the Andes were created by God "so that humans make use of them and help themselves, especially in times of such urgent necessities".[155] Prudent reason of state, in his understanding, was to

---

151 Solórzano, *Política indiana*, ed. Ochoa Brun, vol. 1, lib. II, cap. 17, no. 1, 290: "en la question de que vamos tratando del sercivio personal forzado de los indios para las minas [...] su última, y afinada resolucion pende, y procederá de juicio superior, y más acertado".

152 Solórzano, *Política indiana*, ed. Ochoa Brun, vol. 1, lib. II, cap. 17, no. 1, 290: "supuesto que algunas cédulas Reales han mandado, ó permitido que por aora se continúe, y eso es lo que se vá practicando, ellas mismas confiesan la duda del caso, y muestran desear el alivio de los Indios". On this point, See e.g., the "Real cédula sobre los servicios personales y repartimientos de indios: Aranjuez, 26 de mayo de 1609", ed. in Konetzke, *Colección de documentos*, vol. 2, 156.

153 Solórzano, *Política indiana*, ed. Ochoa Brun, vol. 1, lib. II, cap. 17, no. 3, 290: "no por eso cesarán los comercios con España, ni la propagación de la Fé, y socorros para las guerras, como lo advierte el Padre Josef de Acósta".

154 Solórzano, *Política indiana*, ed. Ochoa Brun, vol. 1, lib. II, cap. 17, no. 14, 291: "De qualquier manera que sea, la verdadera y prudente razon de estado es mirar, y aspirar á sólo aquello que es licito, y ninguna ha salido jamás provechosa que pospone los preceptos, y respectos divinos á los intereses humanos".

155 Solórzano, *Política indiana*, ed. Ochoa Brun, vol. 1, lib. II, cap. 17, no. 21, 292: "Pero no por

combine the merely advantageous with the morally right: the key to making mining legal was to go beyond the existing practice of forcing free vassals to do the work.[156]

One option was to switch to a system of "voluntary" mining, as envisioned by Juan de Silva. Solórzano noted that, to some extent, the major mines in the Peruvian viceroyalty relied on voluntary labor already.[157] But his attention was focused on different ways to reform the system.

An obvious alternative was the use of slaves. A century earlier, Juan de Matienzo had vehemently denied this option, as we know, and Solórzano was fully aware that harsh climatic conditions and high costs were contemporary arguments against the use of enslaved Black Africans instead of Andeans.[158] Yet as he stressed at various points in his *Política indiana*, mining was a quintessential form of slave labor. Abundant examples, from Roman times to the royal decree *Servicio personal*, proved this point.[159] "The right that we have over slaves", Solórzano argued,

> […] is much more extensive than the right we can claim over *indios*; and according to the law they are considered our very own property, and likened to the dead or to animals, and we may use them to our advantage and benefits with a little injustice, even if we expose them to some danger. There are even those who say that we can kill them, and that they are bound to obey to such an extent that they must put their own life and health behind that of their master.[160]

---

esto es mi intento decir, que dexen de buscarse, y labrarse las minas y sus metales que bien sé […] que los crió Dios, para que de ellos se valiesen, y ayudasen los hombres, y más en tiempo de tan urgentes necesidades".

156 I therefore do not agree that Solórzano simply sought to "Christianize" mining while advocating its continuation under the *mita* system, as argued in Bentancor, *The Matter of Empire*, 317 and 319.

157 Solórzano, *Política indiana*, ed. Ochoa Brun, vol. 1, lib. II, cap. 17, no. 25–26, 293–294.

158 See Solórzano, *Política indiana*, ed. Ochoa Brun, vol. 1, lib. II, cap. 6, no. 36, 177.

159 See especially Solórzano, *Política indiana*, ed. Ochoa Brun, vol. 1, lib. II, cap. 15, no. 21–28, 265–267.

160 Solórzano, *Política indiana*, ed. Ochoa Brun, vol. 1, lib. II, cap. 17, no. 23, 293: "Todavia es mucho más lleno el derecho que tenemos en los esclavos que el que podemos pretender en los Indios; y segun las disposiciones legales se juzgan por hacienda propria nuestra, y son comparados á los muertos, ó á los animales, y con menor injuria podemos servirnos de ellos para nuestros aprovechamientos, y comodidades, aunque se expongan á algun peligro; pues aún hay quien diga, que podemos matarlos, y que de tal suerte están necesitados á obedecer que deben posponer su salud y vida á la de sus amos".

In so arguing, Solórzano forcefully justified the call from Spain to employ enslaved persons in the Peruvian mines.[161] Yet the by-product of this juxtaposition of Indigenous vassals and slaves was an astonishing celebration of ancient chattel slavery—explosive even by the standards of his own time.[162]

Solórzano also proposed another way to reorganize the mining industry. If it was licit to send to the mines those who were "likened to the dead", mining could also be considered the equivalent of capital punishment, and therefore a form of civil punishment.[163] Solórzano highlighted the positive effects this would have: "it would act as a brake, so that fewer crimes would be committed here [...] and those who do commit them would pay for their sins in the mines, which is considered a clement punishment if they deserve the death penalty".[164] Solórzano supported this claim by pointing to several cities where this form of penal servitude had been used, from ancient Rome to Ming China.[165] He could have added that the same was true in his native Spain, where convicts worked alongside slaves in the mercury mines of Almadén.[166]

3.2 *The Feet of the Commonwealth*

For Solórzano, the problem with forced mining was not the coercion of Indigenous vassals per se, but the mounting death toll in the Andean mines that was undermining the very foundation of Spain's imperial economy. Indeed, he

161 See the "Real instrucción sobre el trabajo de los indios: Valladolid, 24 de noviembre de 1601", ed. in Konetzke, *Colección de documentos*, vol. 2, 78; and as "Real cédula sobre los servicios personales y repartimientos de indios: Aranjuez, 26 de mayo de 1609", ed. in Konetzke, *Colección de documentos*, vol. 2, 155–156.

162 Solórzano made the above-quoted argument drawing on a range of *loci* from Roman law, especially D.9.2.2 and D.50.17.32. He also referred to Mager von Schönberg, *De advocatia armata*, cap. 13, no. 69. In this passage, the Austrian court lawyer argued that slaves were bound to protect their masters, even at the cost of sacrificing their own lives, and did so in commentary on D.29.5.1.28. On the context of that treatise, which primarily called on the Holy Roman Emperor to protect the Catholic church in the context of the Thirty Years War, see Weber, "Von der normativen Herrschaftspflicht zum interessenpolitischen Instrument", 42–45.

163 This was a point that José de Acosta had already pondered in the preceding century, although without proposing a transformation of *mita* mining. See Acosta, *De procuranda*, ed. Pereña, vol. 1, lib. III, cap. 18, no. 1 and 4–5, 526 and 532–536.

164 Solórzano, *Política indiana*, ed. Ochoa Brun, vol. 1, lib. II, cap. 17, no. 32, 294: "Lo qual, si se introduxe en las Indias, serviria de freno, para que en ellas no se cometiesen tantos delitos, con reformacion general de costumbre, y los que los cometiesen pagarian allí su pecado, teniendo por clemente esta pena, si la merecieron de muerte".

165 Solórzano, *Política indiana*, ed. Ochoa Brun, vol. 1, lib. II, cap. 17, no. 33–37, 295.

166 See Pike, *Penal Servitude in Early Modern Spain*, ch. 2; and Martín Casares, "Maghrebian Slaves in Spain", 99.

insisted that the "*indios*" were urgently needed for a number of other tasks that were equally essential for the commonwealth. These included the construction of public buildings, bridges, and roads; agricultural work on fields and estates; work in textile workshops; or messenger services.[167] Unlike mining, these forms of forced labor remained unchallenged by Solórzano. They did not jeopardize the existence of the Indigenous population and ensured its "procreation and preservation".[168]

Solórzano justified the coercion of Andeans with reference to their position within the colonial society. He agreed with his intellectual predecessors that Spanish and Indigenous subjects "are now united and form one body in these provinces, both in spiritual and temporal terms".[169] Within this "one mixed commonwealth",[170] as he put it, some were naturally suited to work while others—"in whom there is more reason"[171]—should rule. The idea of natural slavery thus remained central to the ideology of forced labor in colonial Peru.

At the same time, Solórzano did not fully concur with the writings of his peers. The kingdom made of clay and iron from Nebuchadnezzar's dream, he noted, was an inappropriate metaphor for the social body, since—*pace* Acosta—that entire statue "collapsed and turned into dust".[172] Instead, Solórzano recovered another biblical image to illustrate his own vision of the colonial commonwealth: the idea of a corporate communion of Christians comprising "many members, yet but one body", as the apostle Paul had put it in his Epistle to the Corinthians.[173] Unlike Nebuchadnezzar's statue, this was an organic unity in which laborers, craftsmen, and pastors corresponded to the

---

167 For an extensive discussion of these forms of forced labor, see Solórzano, *Política indiana*, ed. Ochoa Brun, vol. 1, lib. II, cap. 8–14, 199–259.

168 Solórzano, *Política indiana*, ed. Ochoa Brun, vol. 1, lib. II, cap. 7, no. 30, 189: "importará este descanso, y el que se muden por veces en el trabajo para la procreacion, y conservacion de los mismos Indios".

169 Solórzano, *Política indiana*, ed. Ochoa Brun, vol. 1, lib. II, cap. 6, no. 1, 170: "las dos Repúblicas de los Españoles, é Indios, asi en lo espiritual, como en lo temporal, se hallan oy unidas, y hacen un cuerpo en estas Provincias".

170 Solórzano, *Política indiana*, ed. Ochoa Brun, vol. 1, lib. II, cap. 6, no. 15, 173: "los Españoles (que como se ha dicho, hacen yá una mezclada República con los indios)". *Pace* Levaggi, "Républica de indios", 425.

171 Solórzano, *Política indiana*, ed. Ochoa Brun, vol. 1, lib. II, cap. 6, no. 5, 171: "segun la disposicion de su estado, y naturaleza, unos sirvan, que son más aptos para el trabajo, y otros goviernen, y manden en quienes se halle más razon, y capacidad para ello".

172 Solórzano made this point in a different context: see his *Política indiana*, lib. II, cap. 16, no. 57: "todo vino abaxo, y se convirtió en polvo, como el mismo Daniél lo dice". Juan de Silva, too, had previously made this argument against Acosta. See Silva, "Memorial segundo", in *Los Memoriales*, ed. Castañeda Delgado, 43.

173 1 Corinthians 12:20.

feet, arms, and fingers of the political body. These individual members did not oppress but rather "help one another and carry each other's burden [...] for they are all inevitable and necessary, everyone in their office".[174]

And yet, harmony did not mean equality. Closer inspection reveals that Solórzano, too, perpetuated a fundamental duality between laboring Natives and governing settlers. This becomes more apparent in his account of agriculture, the type of *mita* labor that preserved the commonwealth by nourishing it. Solórzano argued that "forcing the *indios* to a task that appears so properly theirs, and that is so much in accordance with their nature, cannot be considered hard or unjust".[175] As laborers on the ground, he maintained, the "*indios*" were "the feet [...] that sustain the whole weight of the commonwealth".[176] Ultimately, Solórzano's organic social body was as oppressive as Acosta's composite commonwealth.

3.3 *The Treasure from the Indies*

This was duly noted by Diego de Avendaño, who had once embarked on the long journey to Peru with his compatriot Solórzano and then became professor of theology at the prestigious Jesuit College of San Pablo in Lima.[177] Almost unknown today, Avendaño is one of the most intriguing contributors to the debate on forced labor and—as we shall see in the final chapter of this book—he also intervened in the discussion about the legitimacy of the transatlantic trade in enslaved Africans. With his *Thesaurus indicus* of 1688, Avendaño brought together two different strands of contemporary literature: the tradition of commentary on theological questions originating with Aquinas, and the literature on the colonial administration of the New World. Avendaño himself

174 Solórzano, *Política indiana*, ed. Ochoa Brun, vol. 1, lib. II, cap. 6, no. 6, 171: "hace la Republica un cuerpo, compuesto de muchos hombres, como de muchos miembros, entre los quales, a los pastores, labradores, y otros oficiales mecánicos, unos llaman pies, y otros brazos, otros dedos de la República, siendo tódos en ella forzosos, y necesarios, cada uno en su ministerio, como grave, y santamente nos lo da á entender el Apóstol San Pablo".

175 Solórzano, *Política indiana*, ed. Ochoa Brun, vol. 1, lib. II, cap. 9, no. 5, 204: "Y no puede tenerse por duro, ni injusto, forzar á los Indios á ministerio, que parece tan proprio suyo, y se conforma tanto con su naturaleza".

176 Solórzano, *Política indiana*, ed. Ochoa Brun, vol. 1, lib. II, cap. 9, no. 11, 205: "y que los labradores son el higado ó los pies, como dijo Plutarcho, escribiendo à Trajano, que sustentan tódo el peso de la República". On this passage, see also Herrera Ángel, "Los pies de la república cristiana", 102–103.

177 Biographical information on Avendaño is from Muñoz García, "Introducción", 14–15; Fernández G., "Avendaño, Diego de", 303; and Losada, "El jesuita segoviano Diego de Avendaño", 424–427.

noted that this was "another genre of writing".[178] Quite immodestly, he claimed that his "Indian treasure" was the intellectual counterpart to the material treasures that the Spaniards were unearthing in the Indies.[179]

Drawing on debates that had originated in the Iberian lecture halls, Avendaño was above all concerned with the realities he encountered overseas. This brought him into a close dialogue with contemporary colonial intellectuals like Solórzano. To make sense of the politics of the Spanish empire in the Americas, as one historian has remarked, Avendaño relied on the *Política indiana* rather than Aristotle.[180] As it happens, the opening book of Avendaño's treatise bore the very same title that Solórzano had given to his Latin treatise on the law and government of the Indies.[181] Unlike the theological treatises penned in Iberia, then, the *Thesaurus* thus began with an intervention in a distinctly colonial discourse.

Avendaño justified forced Indigenous labor in the same terms as his intellectual predecessors. Pointing to Acosta, Silva, and Solórzano, he argued that "it is licit to force the *indios* to certain works for the commonwealth, especially those that are necessary, with Christian moderation".[182] Avendaño insisted, however, that those who had written before him had been troubled by the problem of forcing free vassals to toil in the deadly Andean mines. "It seems that nothing can trouble the conscience of kings more", he wrote, "for it seems that to be compelled to work in the mines is a kind of slavery, and surely a harsh one".[183]

178 Avendaño, *Thesaurus indicus*, Ingenuo lectori, without pagination: "Sacratoris theologiae partus iam pridem meditatus, ex quibus aliqui publicam iam lucem conspexerunt [...] aliud nunc scriptionis genus aggredior". Among Avendaño's other treatises were an extensive commentary on Psalm 44 entitled *Epithalamium Christi et sacrae sponsae*, as well as more straightforwardly moral theological works such as the *Problemata theologica* and the *Cursus consummatus*.

179 Avendaño, *Thesaurus indicus*, Ingenuo lectori, without pagination: "Tum etiam cum quod ex Indiis magnae in Europam transmittantur divitiae, quas Thesauri nomine usu frequentissimus indicat [...] divitiae sapientiae ex magnorum Auctorum scriptis [...] eductae, et in opus pro Indiis, et in Indiis elucubratum sollerter aptatae, indeque in Europam traiectae, ut ad plures etiam utilitas thesauri huius derivetur".

180 See Hofmeister Pich, "The Aristotelian Background of Diego de Avendaño's Moral and Legal Thought", 83.

181 See Avendaño, *Thesaurus indicus*, tit. I, I: "De indiarum iure, et Catholicorum Regum obligationibus circa illarum administrationem".

182 Avendaño, *Thesaurus indicus*, tit. I, cap. 14, §1, no. 128, 29: "Dico Primo. Licite possunt Indi ad labores aliquos reipublicae inprimis necessarios Christiana moderatione compelli, iuxta dicta superius. Sic Acosta [...] Solorzanus [...] Ioannes de Silva".

183 Avendaño, *Thesaurus indicus*, tit. I, cap. 12, no. 109, 24: "Reges Catholici [...] nihil videtur

The disastrous effects of mercury mining in Huancavelica had indeed troubled both critics and defenders of *mita* mining. Solórzano, who had personally witnessed the terrible effects of mercury on the health of the miners, explained that locals spoke of "*el mal de la mina*", the illness of the mine.[184] And even Miguel de Agia, the foremost advocate of forced Indigenous mining, acknowledged the inhumane conditions in the Santa Bárbara mines, which he had also visited. In the final pages of his *Tratado*, Agia stressed that the situation in Huancavelica was intolerable: there was "the malice and filth of the ores", the constant "danger of death", and most of all, "the many thousand *indios* that were killed and buried by the mines, without mentioning the many others that are about to die, and all the other damages that we could list on top of this".[185] Because of these mortal conditions, he advocated the closure of the Huancavelica mines.[186] In the face of Agia's overarching defense of forcible mining, this was a striking note on which to end his treatise.

Diego de Avendaño drew attention to this critical point. "Although the working conditions of the *indios* in that mountain cannot be said to be as terrible as they were when Father Agia inspected its depth", he said with an ironical tone, "the suffering continues with little difference".[187] In Avendaño's view, the Andeans under Spanish rule were in a situation comparable to that of the Hebrews under the yoke of Egypt: they were subjected to "intolerable labor" and thus "driven into the abyss of idolatry".[188] The Indigenous tributaries were

ita posse eorum solicitas conscientias agere, ut it, de quo quaestio et controversia praesens agitatur. Videtur enim haec ad mineras compulsio quoddam servitutis, et durae satis, genus".

184 Solórzano, *Política indiana*, ed. Ochoa Brun, vol. 1, lib. II, cap. 16, no. 21, 277. Solórzano visited the Santa Bárbara mines during his time as a short-term governor of Huancavelica from 1616–1619 (see García Hernán, *Consejero de ambos mundos*, 140–149).

185 Agia, *Tratado*, tercero parecer, 83–84: "la malicia y vascosidad de los metales [...] el peligro de despeñarse [...] y finalmente los muchos millares de indios que tienen muertos y sepultados sin otros muchos que estan para morir y todos los demas daños que a los dichos podria acumular".

186 Agia indeed proposed this on the very final page of his treatise. See Agia, *Tratado*, tercero parecer, 84.

187 Avendaño, *Thesaurus indicus*, tit. I, cap. 12, no. 115, 26: "Et licet modo Indorum labor in monte illo non ita dicatur esse terribilis, uti erat quando a praedicto Patre [i.e., Agia] profunditas est illa lustrata; semper tamen damna parvo discrimine perseverant".

188 Avendaño, *Thesaurus indicus*, tit. I, cap. 12, no. 117, 26: "Dum Hebraei in Aegypto intolerandis laboribus affliguntur, periclitatur fides, et in idolatriae barathrum eorum plurimi deturbantur". Bartolomé de Las Casas also compared the situation of Indigenous peoples to the Hebrews under Egyptian domination, although his aim was to criticize the Spanish domination of the New World more broadly, not just forced mining specifically. See Las

so frightened, he argued, that they resorted to "pagan" rites to protect themselves from the deadly consequences of the mines.[189]

Avendaño urged the Spanish monarch to act and "hasten to remove the oppression of this utterly harsh labor", warning that the advance of apostasy would put an end to the Spanish course of victories overseas.[190] In this way, he turned Miguel de Agia's argument against itself: rather than providing the necessities for the preservation of the commonwealth, the continued acceptance of forcible mining threatened to undermine the Spanish empire in the Americas.

3.4 Encomienda *Labor, Justice, and Conscience*

Another form of forced labor that remained controversial well into the 17th century was domestic *mita* service—the type of forced labor most closely resembling the formally abolished *encomienda* slavery.[191] According to Juan de Solórzano, it was permissible to employ Indigenous tributaries to build the homes of Spanish settlers because such work contributed to "human sustenance" and was analogous to how agricultural labor kept the commonwealth alive.[192] However, personal services of "*indios*" within these houses "were always forbidden and ordered to be abandoned".[193] Solórzano sidestepped Acosta's argument that forced labor in the homes of *encomenderos* could be justified by reference to settlers' public office. Instead, he argued that the *encomenderos* ignored all laws and abused Andean vassals with "haughtiness, cruelty, and greed".[194] Spanish nobles in possession of an *encomienda*—a select

---

Casas, "Memorial de Fray Bartolomé de Las Casas al Consejo de Indias (1565)", in *De regia potestate*, ed. by Pereña et al., 280. See also the discussion in Brading, *First America*, 71–72.

189 Avendaño, *Thesaurus indicus*, tit. 1, cap. 12, no. 116, 26.

190 Avendaño, *Thesaurus indicus*, tit. 1, cap. 12, no. 118, 27: "Ergo singularis protector fidei Rex Catholicus illam in suis indis radicandam accurret, durissimi laboris oppressione submota: sic victorias sibi de infestissimis poterit hostibus praeclaras et frequentes polliceri. Timeo enim ne idolatria in regionibus istis non penitus extirpata, cursum victoriarum impediat".

191 Puente Brunke, *Encomienda y encomenderos en el Perú*, 180–181 and 186–187.

192 Solórzano, *Política*, ed. Ochoa Brun, vol. 1, lib. II, cap. 8, no. 14, 202: "pues si se concede á la labranza, y crianza, y á otras cosas, que luego diremos, por decir que de ellas pende el sustento humano: tambien las casas, y habitaciones entran en esta cuenta".

193 Solórzano, *Política*, ed. Ochoa Brun, vol. 1, lib. II, cap. 3, no. 3, 148: "Todavia siempre se han prohibido, y mandando quitar [...] Y asi, fuera de las muchas Cédulas, que dexo citadas en los capitulos pasados, que tanto encargan, que los Indios sean tratados como vasallos libres". Solórzano cited a range of laws and decrees in support of this argument, including the decree *Servicio personal*.

194 Solórzano, *Política indiana*, ed. Ochoa Brun, vol. 1, lib. II, cap. 2, no. 22, 146: "considerando

few, including Solórzano himself[195]—should therefore only be entitled to demand tributary payments, not tributary labor, from Indigenous subjects.[196]

An even more assertive stance was proposed by his friend and follower Diego de Avendaño. He set out to redefine the very meaning of "personal service", which had thus far been understood as a synonym for labor coercion.[197] For Avendaño, however,

> Personal service (*servitium personale*) specifically speaking, in the way we treat it now, is a certain kind of coerced service, according to the will of those, who think that they are entitled to this right, either because they are *encomenderos* or because of other titles, by which they exercise a certain domination of the *indios*. And so they force them either to serve always against their will—having preserved the title of liberty—or on certain days, for a very meagre living allowance, so that on the other days they may work for their own benefit.[198]

The very definition of personal service Avendaño here provided already implied its injustice. In his understanding, it denoted the kind of labor that exclusively served the benefit of individuals and therefore—*pace* Acosta—lacked any grounding in the power structure of the commonwealth. "It is most certain", Avendaño insisted, "that this cannot be upheld without grave sin and

---

[...] la sobervia, dureza, y codicia de los Encomenderos, por muy justos, y moderados que sean los servicios, y obras, en que se los tasen, y adjudiquen, y las leyes, y formas, que para que no excedan de esto, se establecieren, las han de violentar, y traspasar tódas".

195 Solórzano obtained an *encomienda* in Guatemala in 1636, as a reward for his intellectual and administrative services for the crown. By that time, he was already back in Spain and it was a sign of unusual appreciation for the king to grant and encomineda to somebody who was not resident in the Indies. See García Hernán, *Consejero de ambos mundos*, 223–236.

196 Solórzano, *Política indiana*, ed. Ochoa Brun, vol. 1, lib. II, cap. 2, no. 22, 146.

197 See e.g., Solórzano, *Política indiana*, ed. Ochoa Brun, vol. 1, lib. II, cap. 2, no. 1, 141: "servicios, de los que en las Indias llaman personales. Debaxo de cuyo nombre (como lo advierte bien el Padre Josef de Acosta) se compreenden generalmente qualesquiera aprovechamientos, que pretendemos sacar del trabajo, obras, y servicio de ellos [...] públicos, o domésticos".

198 Avendaño, *Thesaurus indicus*, tit. I, cap. 13, no. 119, 27: "Servitium personale specialiter dictum, ut modo de illo disserimus, quoddam est serviendi genus coactum, ad voluntatem eorum, qui eam sibi licere existimant facultatem, sive quia Commendatarii, sive aliis titulis: ratione quorum aliquem erga Indos exercent dominatum. Itaque aut cogunt servire semper invitos, libertatis titulo conservato, aut certis diebus, tenuissimi victus stipendio, ut possint diebus aliis suo commodo laborare".

the burden of restitution".[199] He concluded that forcing the "*indios*" to work for the personal benefit of *encomenderos* was not a public service, but a form of slavery.[200]

Yet this was not the end of the story. If domestic labor coercion was unjust, Avendaño asked, what implications did this have for confessors conducting pastoral visitations in places "where this personal service perseveres" and "where people say that they cannot otherwise get hold of the things that are necessary for their sustenance, such as the fruits of the earth or the breeding of cattle?"[201] To answer that question, Avendaño distinguished between two scenarios. In the first, a penitent confessed to having compelled Indigenous people to perform domestic labor in bad faith, a situation, he argued, which required the intervention of confessors.[202] The same applied to anyone expressing doubts about the morality of their actions.[203] Following the judgment of his Iberian intellectual predecessors, Avendaño argued that absolution could not be granted to those who had violated justice and whose salvation was at risk.[204]

But there was also a second scenario that depended on another key idea of Catholic moral theology: invincible ignorance. If someone did not know about a law or doctrine and did not willfully or negligently ignore it, then the person was free of any guilt.[205] Avendaño explained that

> [...] if the penitent is in good faith, and the revelation [of the wrongdoing] makes it very likely that a grave sin is to be feared in the maintenance

199 Avendaño, *Thesaurus indicus*, tit. I, cap. 13, no. 120, 27: "Dico, uti, certissimum, sine gravi peccato, et restitutionis onere, id non posse constare".

200 Avendaño, *Thesaurus indicus*, tit. I, cap. 13, no. 120, 27: "Ratio est, quia hoc est genus quoddam servitutis, a quo Indi sunt prorsus eximii". See also Avendaño, *Thesaurus indicus*, tit. I, cap. 13, no. 121, 28: "Sufficiat ergo Indis quod semper cum metu vivant, hoc enim genus servitutis est".

201 Avendaño, *Thesaurus indicus*, tit. I, cap. 13, no. 122, 28: "Sed quid Confessarii facient ubi personale servitium perseverat, obnitentibus quibusdam urbibus aut etiam Provinciis, eo quod dicant non posse aliter ea, quae ad victum necessaria sunt, ex terrae fructibus, aut re pecuaria comparari?" On the notion that domestic forced labor was still in place despite the fact that it was prohibited, see also Avendaño, *Thesaurus indicus*, tit. I, cap. 14, § 3, no. 134–135, 31.

202 Avendaño, *Thesaurus indicus*, tit. I, cap. 13, no. 122, 28: "Respondeo tales, si in mala fide sint, nequaquam absolvendos, ut est copertum, cuius erit indicium, si de servitii talis coactione in Confessione se accusent".

203 Avendaño, *Thesaurus indicus*, tit. I, cap. 13, no. 123, 28.

204 Amongst others, Avendaño here referred to Sánchez, DSMS, vol. 1, lib. II, disp. 38, no. 8, 356.

205 See Toste, "Invincible Ignorance and the Americas", 284.

> of the [personal] service, the confessor may conceal it according to the widely received doctrine.[206]

Avendaño here followed the opinion of the Spanish Jesuit Fernando de Castropalao (1583–1633).[207] The latter had argued in his *Opus morale* that priests should admonish invincibly ignorant penitents only if it was for their own benefit. However, if the confessor's warning risked leading a person safe in conscience into damnation, this would betray the purpose of confession—for it would contravene the principle that the admonition should promote the penitent's well-being.[208] This had already been suggested by Francisco Suárez. Comparing the role of the confessor to that of the physician, Suárez argued that it was harmful to administer medicine when there was a risk that it might do more harm than good to the patient. In certain cases, therefore, confessors were obliged *not* to reveal what was just and lawful.[209]

Yet Avendaño's approach went far beyond the position of the Spanish Jesuits he cited. The issue in legitimizing forced labor, he argued, was not simply the penitent's good and conscience. The critical point was that it came at the expense of violating another person's right and liberty. For this reason, Avendaño ultimately needed a different authority to justify his position.

He found it in Éloi de la Bassée (1590/91–1670), a Capuchin theologian from the then Habsburg-controlled city of La Bassée near Lille. Bassée, a casuist who closely aligned himself with the laxist strand of Catholic theology, advocated "excessive leniency in moral theory".[210] That was precisely the kind of sup-

206 Avendaño, *Thesaurus indicus*, tit. I, cap. 13, no. 124, 28: "Si autem poenitens in bona fide sit, et ex manifestatione peccatum grave in retentione servitii verosimiliter timeatur, poterit dissimulare confessarius, juxta valde receptam doctrinam".

207 See Schmutz's brief entry on Hernando de Castropalao on *Scholasticon*.

208 Avendaño pointed to Castropalao, *Opus morale*, tr. XXIII, punctum 19, § 2, no. 7, 166: "Verum, si ignorantia praesumatur invincibilis […] potius times monitione facta in eodem statu poenitentem perseveraturum, nullo modo debes monere; sed absolutionem utpote recte dispositio impendere: quia, cum haec monitio in bonum poenitentis dirigatur, eo bono cessante, cessare debet".

209 Suárez, *Commentariorum ac disputationum*, vol. 4, disp. 32, sect. 4, no. 4, 446: "quando confessor non sperat fructum, vel quia probabiliter, et prudenter timet poenitentem non effecturum, vel certe non posse sine gravi incommodo id efficere, de quo admonendus est, potest et debet tacere, ac poenitentem in sua bona fide relinquere. […] Et explicatur, et confirmatur, quia medicus non debet adhibere medicinam, si timeat maius damnum allaturam, quam fructum".

210 This definition of laxism is from Fleming, *Defending Probabilism*, 6. On the importance of Bassée's thought and its relation to the work of contemporary theologians, see Schmutz, "Éloi de Bassée", 437–438.

port Avendaño had been seeking. Quoting from Bassée's *Flores totius theologiae practicae*, he underlined that a confessor was bound to remain quiet

> [...] even though the penitent's ignorance about his sin was to the detriment of his neighbor. The reason is that we must not set any traps for anyone. And in this case, to admonish would be nothing but to set a trap [...] since the penitent, in his state of good faith, would fall into a bad and dangerous state because of the confessor's warning.[211]

In so arguing, Avendaño provided a remarkable loophole for the continuation of *encomienda* slavery. Wherever personal service—as he defined the term—was "received" and contributed to the subsistence of Spanish settlers, confessors and preachers were required to "abstain from admonition".[212]

Despite his initial criticism of domestic *mita* service, Avendaño eventually offered an elaborate apology for the subjugation of Indigenous vassals by their *encomenderos*. To be sure, he was not the only one. But whereas Acosta had justified this form of forced labor by referring to the public offices held by Spanish settlers, Avendaño sanctioned an institution that, by his own standards, should have been illegal.[213] In this light, recent attempts to present Avendaño as "socially progressive" and as a champion of the "freedom" and "human rights" of Indigenous peoples seem misplaced.[214] Quite the contrary, the Jesuit theologian carved out a powerful justification for keeping *encomienda* slavery alive.

---

211 Avendaño, *Thesaurus indicus*, tit. 1, cap. 13, no. 124, 28: "sic loquitur Eligius Basseus [...] Quod scilicet cum nulla ex monitione speratur utilitas, et ignorantia invincibilis est [...] non tenetur confessarius docere, vel monere immo tenteur in hoc casu tacere propter inconvenientia, quae inde sequeruntur. Et hoc verum, quamvis per ignorantiam peccatum illud sit in detrimentum proximi. Ratio est, quia nulli laqueum debemus iniicere: sed admonere in hoc eventu nihil aliud esset quam laqueum [...] nam constitutus in statu bonae fidei, confessarii monitione in malo et periculoso versabitur". For the original passage, see Bassée, *Flores totius theologiae practicae*, verb. confessarius, sect. 4, no. 18, 67.

212 Avendaño, *Thesaurus indicus*, tit. 1, cap. 13, no. 124, 28: "Et quod de Confessario dictum est, de Praedicatore pariter afferendum. Si enim in aliquod veniat oppidum, in quo tale aliquid receptum usu perspiciat, et ex admonitione id timeat, quod diximus, debet ab admonitione temperare; cum praesertim monitiones huiusmodi gravia soleant incommoda suscitare".

213 Avendaño also employed this strategy in other contexts. For instance, with regard to a royal decree mandating that Spaniards who mistreated indios were to be punished more severely than indios who committed similar crimes against Spaniards. See Cuena Boy, "El castigo de las injurias causadas a los indios".

214 See Hernández Aparicio, "La doctrina de Avendaño sobre los repartimientos de indios", 419: "Avendaño se preocupó de los problemas laborales [...] y estableció unas normas

4 Subjection and Protection

The debates surrounding forced labor in colonial Peru reveal the fraught boundaries between freedom and slavery, as well as between legitimate political authority and illicit subjugation for personal gain. While no one claimed that Indigenous vassals were "matter" to be manipulated by the Spaniards—*pace* Bentancor—the political status of Native tributaries was contested.[215] At a time when there were no clearly demarcated boundaries of belonging in the sense that modern nation-states proclaim them, questions of inclusion and exclusion were always subject to debate, both on the level of the city and of empires.[216] To be sure, all the theologians, missionaries, and jurists discussed in this work emphasized that the "*indios*" were part of the newly formed colonial society. At the same time, contemporaries also insisted that the status of Indigenous subjects differed from that of Spanish settlers: Andeans alone were bound by the *mita*.

The idea of natural slavery provided a powerful justification for the fundamentally unequal configuration of the Spanish empire in the Americas. But in the original Aristotelian sense, "natural slaves" were placed outside the polity—they did not belong to the body of citizens. The early modern Iberian understanding of natural slavery seemed to echo this logic. Juan de Matienzo and Francisco de Vitoria, as we saw, likened that status of "*indios*" to that of Spanish peasants, who were seen as "brute animals".[217] This identification of peasants as "natural slaves" dates back to Thomas Aquinas's late-13th-century commentary on Aristotle's *Politics*. Despite the inherently political nature of human beings, and the Aristotelian dictum that only beast and gods could live outside society, Aquinas posited that some people did not live politically due to their "misfortune".[218] According to Aquinas, this was especially evident among peasants,

---

a tener en cuenta [...] Normas que, si tenemos en cuenta que el *Thesaurus* lo escribió entre 1622–1678, son sin duda, socialmente avanzadas". See also Losada, "El jesuita segoviano Diego de Avendaño", 428: "Es sin duda una de las primeras voces, equilibrada y libre de exageraciones, que se alza contra la esclavitud perpetua del indio y en defensa de su liberación física y moral". See also Yubero Galindo, "El 'Thesaurus indicus' de Diego de Avendaño", 399: "Realmente esta gran Obra del Avendaño es la Carta Magna de la defensa de los derechos del hombre, especialmente los 'marginados' para el Avendaño allí en América: los indios".

215 Bentancor, *The Matter of Empire*, 15.

216 This point is emphasized in Brett, *Changes of State*, 3 and *passim*; and in Benton and Clulow, "Introduction", 2.

217 Vitoria, *De indis*, in *Political Writings*, trans. Pagden and Lawrance, q. 1, a. 6, 250.

218 Aquinas, *Commentary on Aristotle's* Politics, ed. and trans. Regan, ad. 1.1, 20, 16.

"because poverty forces them to cultivate the fields or tend animals".[219] None of the Iberian thinkers, however, suggested that Indigenous tributaries in colonial Peru or peasants in Spain were outside the political community. In their view, natural slavery denoted the status of subjects who were governed but not governing themselves—and who were included in the polity on the premise that they contributed to the common good through their labor.

If Indigenous people were imagined as slavish by nature, they were also categorized as *personas miserables*, or "wretched persons". This colonial label, however, held the potential for Indigenous agency. As *personas miserables*, Indigenous vassals could claim special legal and judicial privileges derived from Roman and medieval canon law. What had originally been the prerogative of widows and orphans, as well as the poor and the sick, gradually emerged as a central category of imperial protection in Spanish America.[220] As *personas miserables*, Indigenous people had the right to appeal directly to the Audiencias, the highest courts, and were granted a variety of canonical privileges that ranged from baptism to marriage and beyond.[221] Recent scholarship shows that Andeans often successfully tapped into this language of guardianship so as to navigate the colonial juridical system to their advantage. Those who fashioned themselves as *personas miserables* were often far from socially or economically powerless agents.[222]

At first glance, the Spanish understanding of Indigenous vassals as "natural slaves" and *personas miserables* may appear contradictory, yet both ideas, in fact, had a common core. "Protection and legal privileges", as the historian Luigi Nuzzo writes, went hand in hand with "infinite tutelage".[223] Indeed, this was how contemporary intellectuals understood the matter. Consider Diego de Avendaño, who argued that the "*indios*" were "wretched persons" because of their "extremely downcast condition, their recent conversion, their poverty, their rural life, their poor discourse, like that of children".[224] And Juan de Solórzano similarly claimed that *personas miserables* were "all those who can-

219 Aquinas, *Commentary on Aristotle's* Politics, ed. and trans. Regan, ad. I.1, 20, 16. The other kind of people who fell into this category were those banned from the commonwealth.

220 See Duve, *Sonderrecht in der Frühen Neuzeit.* On the nexus of empire and protection more broadly, see Benton and Clulow, "Introduction"; and Haug, Weber, and Windler, "Einleitung".

221 See Duve, *Sonderrecht in der Frühen Neuzeit*, 167–180.

222 See especially Puente Luna, *Andean Cosmopolitans*, 148–154.

223 Nuzzo, "A Dark Side of the Western Legal Modernity", 207.

224 Avendaño, *Thesaurus indicus*, Additiones ad Tit. XI, §1, no. 141, 32: "Indos variis ex titulis miserabiles esse personas [...] abiectissima scilicet eorum conditio, novitas conversionis, paupertas, rusticatio, discursus inopia, puerorum adinstar". Note that this section appears

not govern themselves and need others who direct, rule, and assist them".[225] In this sense, the ideas of natural slavery and native wretchedness overlapped in crucial ways. Put more pointedly, the rationale underpinning native agency and protection also justified the subjection of Indigenous vassals to forced labor in the silver mines of Potosí.

at the very end of the volume, but with Avendaño's additions to his *Thesaurus* the pagination begins anew from 1.

225 Solórzano, *Política*, ed. Ochoa Brun, vol. 1, lib. II, cap. 28, no. 46, 427: "personas miserables [...] todas aquellas que no se pueden gobernar por sí y necesitan de que otros los dirijan, gobiernen y asistan".

CHAPTER 7

Revisiting Atlantic Slavery

As indicated in the opening vignette of this book, the moral issues surrounding the transatlantic trade in enslaved Africans reached the highest political circles of the Iberian empires. In 1685, King Charles II of Spain wrote to the Council of the Indies inquiring about the "benefits" that the presence of enslaved Black Africans brought to Spain's American empire, as well as the "harm" their absence might cause. He further asked "whether it is licit to buy them as slaves" and if there were "authors who have written about this issue".[1] In their response, the councilors highlighted the dramatic decline of the Indigenous population in the New World and the resulting shortage of tributaries for forced labor. They posited that prohibiting the slave trade would therefore amount to the loss of essential food supplies, so that "all of the kingdom, the estates that are principally based on the abundance of Black slaves, would be lost and America would be exposed to total ruin".[2] As for the justice of buying and owning enslaved Africans, the councilors pointed to the authority of Iberian theologians such as Luis de Molina or Tomás Sánchez, who not only elaborated a variety of legal justifications for enslavement but also reassured the conscience of those who had purchased slaves "in good faith and second-hand" from traders.[3]

Yet the Council of the Indies did not stop there. The letter to Charles II ultimately ended on a much more radical note:

---

1 Charles II of Spain, "Decreto de Carlos II a Vicente Gonzaga, Gobernador del Consejo de Indias, Madrid, 5 julio 1685", in Jaca, *Resolución sobre la libertad de los negros*, ed. Pena González, 339: "El Consejo de Indias me informará luego de qué conveniencia son los negros en la América y qué daños seguirían de no haberlos [...] a fin de reconocer si es lícito comprarlos por esclavos [...] si hay autores que hayan escrito sobre este particular, quiénes son".

2 Council of the Indies (Consejo de Indias), "Oficio del Consejo de Indias a Carlos II, Madrid, 21 agosto 1685", ed. Pena González, 350–351: "porque los indios han faltado [...] siguese necesariamente que si se prohibiese la continuación de conducirlos, cesaria el alimento preciso para todo: el común reino, las haciendas, que principalmente consisten en la caudal de los esclavos negros, se perderian exponiéndose la América a una total ruina".

3 Council of the Indies (Consejo de Indias), "Oficio del Consejo de Indias a Carlos II, Madrid, 21 agosto 1685", ed. Pena González, 352–353: "También hay quien hace distinción de los mercaderes que van a comprar, al tercero que compra después de conducidos con buena fe y de segunda mano, dando por licita la retención en este caso, como es el Tomás Sánchez, y el Molina".

 | DOI:10.1163/9789004760592_011

> [...] since this genus of people is born to serve, as many say, it is not necessary to consider the strict dispositions of the law of nations (*derecho de gentes*) as one does with respect to other people, so that any title that is not wholly improbable will suffice for buyers, since these slaves are so urgently needed to preserve this commonwealth, which cannot be maintained without them.[4]

This line of argument bears a striking resemblance to the claims about the necessity of forced Indigenous labor presented in the previous chapter. By the end of the 17th century, enslaved Africans had taken the place of Spain's Native vassals, at least in the colonial rhetoric emanating from Madrid. Yet again, this demonstrates how closely related contemporary agents of empire linked life under the yoke of the *mita* with slavery. The response Charles II received from his advisors illustrates the immediate political purchase of the Iberian imperial theorists' writings on slavery. Ultimately, however, the Council of the Indies was prepared to defend the business of African slavery even when it violated the prevailing standards of justice and morality.

What explains this sharp intervention? Part of the answer lies in Spain's waning hegemonic control over the transatlantic trade, for by the late 17th century, its Protestant rivals had become increasingly successful players.[5] Developments in Castile were equally bleak. "The prolonged struggles with the Dutch and the French, the revolts of the 1640s and Philip IV's increasingly desperate attempts to recover control over the newly independent kingdom of Portugal", as John Elliott writes, "placed enormous strains on a treasury perennially incapable of meeting the demands made upon it".[6] As the demand for wealth from the New World intensified, metropolitan elites fervently defended the significance of the slave trade.

However, this still does not explain why Charles II inquired whether the transatlantic slave trade was licit in the first place. After all, the practice of shipping enslaved humans to the Indies was hardly new. The problem, as the councilors explained in their letter to the king, was that "two Capuchins" in

---

4 Council of the Indies (Consejo de Indias), "Oficio del Consejo de Indias a Carlos II, Madrid, 21 agosto 1685", ed. Pena González, 353: "y siendo este género de gente nacida como lo dicen muchos para servir, no se ha de discurrir por las estrechas disposiciones del derecho de gentes que se discurre, respecto de otros gentíos, siendo para los compradores título bastante el que no fuere totalmente inverosímil, y siendo necesario con tanta precisión para conservarse aquella república, que sin ellos no se puede mantener".

5 Elliott, *Empires of the Atlantic World*, 226.

6 Elliott, *Empires of the Atlantic World*, 228.

the New World had recently "wished to persuade others that the enslavement of Black Africans is not licit", provoking such turmoil that colonial authorities overseas "feared an uprising".[7] One of these Capuchins was Epifanio de Moirans (1644–1689), a French theologian and missionary in the service of Rome. Traveling through the Caribbean and the province of New Andalusia (present-day Venezuela), he witnessed the violent realities of transatlantic slavery firsthand. This prompted Moirans to pen a treatise with the provocative title *Free Slaves, or the Just Defense of the Natural Liberty of Slaves* (1682).[8] This work was not only a polemic against the injustice of enslaving, trading, and possessing Black Africans. It also launched a blistering attack on the Iberian imperial theorists' accounts justifying Atlantic slavery.

∴

The manuscript of Moirans's *Servi liberi seu naturalis mancipiorum libertatis iusta defensio* lay buried in the Archive of the Indies in Seville for three full centuries. It was recovered only in 1982, when the Venezuelan historian José Tomás López García published a translation of Moirans's text, along with another treatise by Francisco José de Jaca—the second Capuchin mentioned by the Council of the Indies in its letter to Charles II—whom Moirans had met in Cuba.[9] Both men not only served as missionaries in the field but also intervened in pressing political and theological debates of their day, much like the Franciscan Juan de Silva we encountered in the previous chapter.[10] But while they were united in their critique of the African slave trade and effectively reached the same conclusions, Moirans's *Servi liberi* is "much more eloquent" and steeped in the language of natural law.[11] This makes his text particularly interesting. Although

7 Council of the Indies (Consejo de Indias), "Oficio del Consejo de Indias a Carlos II, Madrid, 21 agosto 1685", 351: "Y se arriesga tanto en discurrir este punto [...] por que dos Capuchinos predicaron en La Habana queriendo persuadir que no era licita la esclavitud de los negros, fue tanta la inquietud que causó a los naturales que se originó una conmoción tan grande que se temió una sublevación de aquel reino".

8 I will be citing from the only critical edition of Moirans's treatise that is currently available: Moirans, *Servi liberi*, ed. Pena González et al.

9 See López García's *Dos defensores de los esclavos negros*. We shall return to the relationship between Morians and Jaca, and their writings, below.

10 On this point, see also Lauren Benton and Lisa Ford's insitence that the making of imperial legal discourses was not limited to "the tomes of jurists" or "written charters and constitutions" (*Rage for Order*, 3).

11 Weller, "Humanitarianism before Humanitarianism?", 159. For a comparison between the two treatises by Moirans and Jaca, see Weller, "Humanitarianism before Humanitarian-

he probably never held an academic position, and little is known about his formation, Moirans's writing reveals his profound knowledge of moral theology and canon law. As one scholar put it, the *Servi liberi* "is perfectly in tune with the treatises *On Justice and Right* that were written over the sixteenth and seventeenth centuries".[12]

Ever since the rediscovery of Moirans's and Jaca's writings, scholars from diverse disciplinary and linguistic backgrounds have portrayed the two Capuchins as proto-abolitionists. López García suggested that their project paralleled Bartolomé de las Casas's defense of Indigenous freedom (without mentioning Las Casas's position on African slavery).[13] More recent commentators have gone further, claiming that Moirans and Jaca "created a truly antislavery project";[14] that "their aim was to theologically, morally, and juridically disapprove of any kind of slavery";[15] or that they "repudiated slavery and demonstrated why the institution goes against natural law, divine law, and the law of nations (*ius gentium*)".[16] Even otherwise cautious historians have spoken of a "'two-man-abolitionist-movement' *avant la lettre*".[17]

By contrast, this chapter argues that Moirans's advocacy of the natural liberty of Black Africans had very little to do with abolitionism. As Joseph Miller has urged, historians must decenter slavery in order to step out of the epistemic shadow of the antebellum American South—and the same is true for historical critiques of enslavement. The teleological fixation on modern abolitionist discourse that pervades studies of Moirans prevents us from understanding what the Capuchin himself actually wrote. In fact, Moirans did not reject the legitimacy of slavery *tout court*. The basis of his attack on Iberian theorists' apologies for the slave trade was the very discourse of natural law and the *ius gentium* on which the legality of slavery rested in the eyes of contemporaries. Rather than questioning the formal validity of the traditional titles of slavery, Moirans challenged how Iberian thinkers applied them to the concrete circumstances

---

ism?", 158–166. For a critical edition of Jaca's treatise, which was completed in 1681, see Jaca, *Resolución sobre la libertad de los negros*, ed. Pena González.

12 Pena González, "Estudio preliminar", xliii: "El *Servi liberi*, de Epifanio de Moirans, se encuentra en perfecta sintonía con los tratados de *Iustitia et iure* elaborados a lo largo de todo el siglo XVI y XVII".

13 López García, *Dos defensores de los esclavos negros*, 28. On Las Casas's shifting account of the African slave trade, see Clayton, "Bartolomé de las Casas and the African Slave Trade".

14 Montes D'Oca, "Two Capuchin Friars in Defense of African Slaves' Liberty", 93.

15 Noggler, "Die Kapuziner", 356: "Ihr Ziel [i.e., Moirans and Jaca's] ist es, mit ihren Schriften jegliche Sklaverei theologisch, moralisch und juristisch abzulehnen".

16 Obregón, "Spanish Colonial Critiques of Enslavement", 58.

17 Weller, "Humanitarianism before Humanitarianism?", 167.

of enslavement in the Atlantic world. He sought to beat the Portuguese and Spanish imperial theorists at their own game.

In what follows, I will argue that Moirans developed a distinctive world-historical understanding of slavery and salvation. The Capuchin missionary not only opposed Iberian theorists' defense of the trade in enslaved Black Africans in the language of natural law. He also rejected the claim that the Book of Genesis, especially its story of the curse of Ham, provided a legitimate basis for the enslavement of Black Africans. In Moirans's novel interpretation, the curse of Ham served a dual purpose: it underpinned Black African freedom, simultaneously justifying the enslavement of all Muslim "enemies of Christ" across the globe. A close reading of the *Servi liberi*, then, not only allows us to reconsider early modern Iberian apologies for the slave trade. It also brings us back to the nexus of slavery and religion, which was even more central to Moirans's thought than to that of the Iberian imperial theorists.

1 Revisiting the Foundations of the Slave Trade

Little is known about Moirans's early life and education.[18] He was born in a small village in the Province of Franche-Comté, near Geneva, in 1644. At the age of twenty-one, he entered the Capuchin order, which had grown out of a reform movement within the Franciscan order. Apart from doctrinal differences that are not relevant here, what distinguished the Capuchins from other religious orders discussed in this book was their placement under the aegis of the Sacred Congregation for the Propagation of the Faith, an institution of the Roman Curia. The missionaries of the so-called Propaganda Fide were thus subject to the Holy See rather than individual monarchs, irrespective of whether they were born in Italian, French, or Iberian territories. In fact, the very existence of the Propaganda Fide was due to the Curia's attempt to regain control over missionary affairs, which at the time were in the hands of European empires.[19]

Moirans crossed the Atlantic in 1678 and, after a brief stay on the Caribbean island of Martinique, moved on to the Spanish-dominated mainland.[20] His presence and missionary activities greatly displeased the local authorities.

18 Biographical information on Moirans is from Pena González, "Estudio preliminar", xvii–xxxi.

19 On the history and purpose of the Propaganda Fide, see Noggler, "Die Kapuziner", 351–354.

20 The next couple of paragraphs draw on Pena González, "Estudio preliminar", xix–xxxi. The episode is also recounted by Moirans himself, less comprehensively though, in the prologue of his *Servi liberi*, ed. Pena González et al., 1–16.

Under the pretext of lacking permission to enter Spanish territory, the governor of Cumaná had Moirans arrested and accused him of being a French spy. He was eventually released and managed to get to Cuba in the summer of 1681. In Havana, Moirans made the acquaintance of another Capuchin who shared his concern about the practice of enslaving Africans: the Aragonese Francisco José de Jaca (c. 1645–?). Both joined forces to preach on plantations and estates around the island's capital.

Moirans and Jaca soon became a thorn in the side of civil and ecclesiastical officials in Cuba. Rumor had it that they denied absolution to anyone who owned Black African slaves. Before long, they were excommunicated by the diocesan vicar of Havana and locked away in a convent. During their confinement, Moirans and Jaca began to document their arguments against African slavery in writing. The Capuchins also protested their imprisonment, arguing that as missionaries of the Propaganda Fide they were solely subject to the jurisdiction of the Curia or indeed the pope himself. After long negotiations, they were sent to Castile and eventually received permission to present themselves before the Propaganda Fide in 1684. The upshot of their hearing was, however, ambiguous. The Sacred Congregation neither endorsed nor criticized the process of excommunication to which the Capuchins had been subjected in Havana and ultimately "left the question open, closing the case without an exact conclusion".[21]

In the same year, the Propaganda Fide also received a petition from Lourenço da Silva de Mendonça, a self-styled descendant of the royal families of Kongo and Angola and leader of a Black lay confraternity in the Iberian empires. Mendonça called for the emancipation of all enslaved Africans who had been baptized.[22] In 1685, the Procurator General of the Capuchins submitted yet another memorandum to the Propaganda Fide, outlining eleven propositions on the transatlantic slave trade on behalf of the missionaries under his jurisdiction. Scholars widely agree that the document was strongly influenced

21 Pena González, "Estudio preliminar", xxix: "De esta manera, Propaganda no declara nulo el proceso llevado a cabo en La Habana contra los dos religiosos, aunque tampoco afirma que éste fuera correcto, dejando la cuestión en el aire y, zanjándola sin una conclusión precisa".

22 See Gray, "The Papacy and the Atlantic Slave Trade", 52–59; and Rowe, *Black Saints in Early Modern Global Catholicism*, 101–105. Against Gray, the historian José Ligna Nafafé recently argued that Mendonça went a decisive step further than that: "Mendonça's intention was to end the institution of slavery entirely—his was a demand for justice and an advocacy of human rights". Yet he does not offer documentary evidence to sustain this claim. See Lingna Nafafé, *Lourenço da Silva Mendonça*, 409. See also the discussion in Allemann, "Review of José Lingna Nafafé".

by Moirans and Jaca, since it denounced the trade in illegally enslaved Africans and demanded the liberation of all those who had been made slaves without a just title.[23] The matter was finally brought before the Holy Office, which "formally declared its complete agreement with every position".[24] And yet, the papal nuncios in Iberia were never actively encouraged to raise the issue with the Spanish and Portuguese crowns.[25] With the Council of the Indies' vigorous defense of the slave trade, the controversy was finally silenced and suppressed.

1.1 *A Principled Critique*

The intellectual foundations of Moirans's activism have been preserved in his treatise *Servi liberi*. At the outset, he listed five conclusions that summarized the main arguments of his pamphlet. First and foremost among them was the assertion that all the owners of Black African slaves had an obligation to free them and compensate them for the services they had rendered.[26] He also underlined the responsibility of enslaved people themselves, arguing that those who were forced to work on sugar plantations had the duty to flee to places where their spiritual salvation could be assured.[27] Finally, Moirans asserted that as a result of the injustice of the trade in human beings from West Africa to the Indies, Christian princes and clerics alike would lose their overseas possessions and eventually become "captives and slaves" themselves.[28] Divine punishment, as he argued elsewhere in his treatise, was already imminent: "By the just judgment of God", control of the transatlantic commerce with enslaved Africans had passed to the "English and Dutch heretics", who secured precious metals from the Indies—compared to the Spaniards, who traded all their wealth for slaves that "die instantly".[29] In this sense, the Spaniards were already "the slaves of other nations".[30]

---

23 A translation and discussion of the petition is available in Pena González, "Estudio preliminar", xxxiv–xxxvii. See also the discussions in Gray, "The Papacy and the Atlantic Slave Trade", 61–63; and Weller, "Humanitarianism before Humanitarianism?", 165–166.

24 Gray, "The Papacy and the Atlantic Slave Trade", 65.

25 Gray, "The Papacy and the Atlantic Slave Trade", 66.

26 Moirans, *Servi liberi*, ed. Pena González et al., argumentum libri, concl. 1–3, 4.

27 Moirans, *Servi liberi*, ed. Pena González et al., argumentum libri, concl. 4, 4.

28 Moirans, *Servi liberi*, ed. Pena González et al., argumentum libri, concl. 5, 4: "captivique et servi fient christiani".

29 Moirans, *Servi liberi*, ed. Pena González et al., cap. 11, no. 118, 178: "omne argentum et aurum deportant nationes asportantes nigros. Nigri statim moriuntur, ut plurimum, et pretium solutum, quod est magnum, est perditum. [...] dico quod hoc fit a Domino, iusto Dei iudicio, quo hodie Indiae cadunt in profectum aliarum nationum; sed, quod doleo, praesertim haereticorum anglorum et batavorum".

30 Moirans, *Servi liberi*, ed. Pena González et al., cap. 11, no. 118, 178: "Unde dico hodie quod hispani servi sunt aliarum nationum".

But Moirans's aim was precisely to prevent and counteract this unfolding scenario. As stated in his prologue, the treatise aimed to open the eyes of those whom avarice had blinded, "to undertake the just defense of the natural liberty of the slaves from Africa", and to suggest ways to remedy the wrongs so that "the destruction of Christian kingdoms" and "the captivity of the Catholics" might be avoided.[31]

The first step in this process, Moirans argued, was to recognize the root of the problem. Those involved in illicit practices of slaving "err in the beginning, in that they capture or buy slaves and carry them away to America, and they go wrong a hundred times in the end, by raising them like beasts and using them as if they were mules".[32] In his view, the entire transatlantic slave trade was based on the deduction of "a good conclusion from bad principles", whereby it was a syllogism gone wrong.[33] For Moirans, the only way to escape this philosophical and moral fallacy was to radically rethink everything from scratch. To that end, he called on his readers to join him in returning

> [...] from the end to the principle, from the end of the error to the principle of truth, from the end of the violation of right to the principle of natural law, and from the end of the land where slaves were captured to the principle of the homeland's soil, so that we may proceed according to the principles of natural law, divine positive law, the *ius gentium*, canon and civil law.[34]

1.2 *The Titles of Slavery Reappraised*

Moirans set out to assess the extent to which the traditional titles of slavery were applicable to contexts of slaving in West and Central Africa. He explained

31 Moirans, *Servi liberi*, ed. Pena González et al., prologue, 14: "Vae ergo europaeis, quia caeci sunt cupiditate. Ut ergo videant, aut saltem lumen habeant ad videndum, iustam libertatis naturalis mancipiorum ex Africa aggrediar defensionem [...] iniuriam remedium putans indicare, destructionem regnorum christianorum, captivitatemque catholicorum et ecclesiasticorum cupiens evitare".

32 Moirans, *Servi liberi*, ed. Pena González et al., cap. 1, no. 1, 18: "Catholici in omni iure et contra omnia iura committentes quantum ad mancipia, errant in principio, dum captivant eos aut emunt et asportant ad Americam, et centies aberrant in fine, dum educant eos ut bestias et utuntur veluti mulis".

33 Moirans, *Servi liberi*, ed. Pena González et al., cap. 1, no. 20, 34: "Bonam conclusionem faciebant in principiis malis et sollogysmo [sic] male concludente".

34 Moirans, *Servi liberi*, ed. Pena González et al., cap. 1, no. 24, 36: "Sed a fine principium, a fine errorum redeamus ad principium veritatis, a fine iniuriam ad principium iuris naturalis, et a fine terrae captivitatis mancipiorum ad principium patrii soli, ut procedamus secundum principia iuris naturalis, divini positivi, gentium, canonici et civilis".

that all those who had been condemned to servitude by public power were indeed just slaves, a status that extended to their children according to the Roman dictum *partus sequitur ventrem*.[35] However, Moirans argued that this title was inapplicable to regions such as Cape Verde and Guinea. In his estimation, the peoples who resided there "neither live politically nor do they have kings who rule them; rather everyone is of his own right, just like the *indios*, and they live without any public or political control".[36] This assessment strongly echoes the perspectives Tomás de Mercado and Miguel de Palacio put forth a century earlier—and Moirans was well aware of them.[37] However, none of these 16th-century thinkers actually questioned whether Sub-Saharan Africans were truly masters of their own affairs. Both Mercado and Palacio had expressly underlined that even if the "Aethiopeans" failed to live up to the standards of justice, they had the necessary features of political societies.[38] But Moirans claimed the exact opposite. The "Blacks" in Guinea and Cape Verde, he posited, "have no civil law or law of citizenship, neither kings nor judges, but […] all avenge themselves by private authority, and there is nobody who would administer justice".[39]

The picture of life in sub-Saharan Africa that Moirans painted was akin to a Hobbesian state of nature. "Whoever has more power and is stronger", he stressed, "seizes another and claims them as a slave".[40] Unlike Thomas Hobbes (1588–1679), however, Moirans argued that such practices of slaving were entirely at odds with the demands of the law of nature and in violation of man's natural liberty.[41] Whoever held enslaved Africans under the pretense of the title of public punishment was therefore obliged to set them free.[42]

35 Moirans, *Servi liberi*, ed. Pena González et al., cap. 2, no. 29, 42: "filii parentum qui peccatis suis iuste servi facti sunt potestate publica, nascuntur servi […] Unde dicitur: *Partus sequitur ventrem*".

36 Moirans, *Servi liberi*, ed. Pena González et al., cap. 2, no. 31, 44: "in Promontorio Viridi, in Guinea, nec vivunt politice nec reges habent dominantes eis, sed unusquisque sui iuris est, sicuti indi, et vivunt sine regimine publico aut politico".

37 Moirans referred to Mercado in the very context of this discussion: see Moirans, *Servi liberi*, ed. Pena González et al., cap. 2, no. 32, 44–46. For Moirans's explicit engagement with Palacio, see e.g., Moirans, *Servi liberi*, ed. Pena González et al., cap. 7, no. 81, 120–122.

38 See Mercado, *Suma*, ed. Sánchez-Albornoz, lib. II, cap. 21, § 4–5; and Palacio, *Praxis theologica*, lib. II, cap. 8, 153.

39 Moirans, *Servi liberi*, ed. Pena González et al., cap. 5, no. 58, 82: "in nigris Guineae, Promontorii Viridis […] nec habent ius civile aut quiritium, nec reges, nec iudices […] vindicant se omnes privata authoritas, et nemo est qui iustitiam administret".

40 Moirans, *Servi liberi*, ed. Pena González et al., cap. 2, no. 31, 44: "qui praevalet et fortior est rapit alium et sibi vendicat in servum".

41 Moirans, *Servi liberi*, ed. Pena González et al., cap. 2, no. 31, 4.

42 Moirans, *Servi liberi*, ed. Pena González et al., cap. 2, no. 35, 50.

As a corollary to his ethnographic account of West and Central Africa, Moirans rejected any claims that slavery could be justified by reference to "just wars". In regions where princely rule was absent, the more powerful entities simply preyed upon the weak, driven by the presence of European traders eager to buy such slaves without any moral hesitation.[43] Indeed, Moirans was as critical of the Portuguese ventures in Africa as he was of the deeds of local inhabitants. The only exception he allowed, for the time being, concerned captives taken in the Portuguese "just wars" against the kingdoms of Angola and Mutapa.[44] But apart from that, Moirans's verdict was devastating. "The Christians", he argued, "steal and seize Blacks whenever they can, for no other reason than the fact that they are Blacks and must be slaves, as if they were not truly human beings but sheep, or dogs and beasts".[45] Since God left nothing unpunished, Moirans argued, the Portuguese themselves, who were now routinely enslaved by the Muslims of North Africa, ended up in Ottoman hands. In this vicious circle, he concluded, Portuguese traders had become the "hens of the sea"—seized and passed on from one Muslim adversary to the next.[46]

The final two justifications for slavery addressed by Moirans centered on the right to sell oneself or one's children into slavery in cases of extreme necessity. Once again, acknowledging that these titles were valid in theory, he argued they were inapplicable to the slave trade. He was particularly adamant about repudiating Luis de Molina's famous claim that parents could enslave their offspring in grave, rather than extreme, necessity.[47] "We reject this doctrine from the fundaments", Moirans argued, because "only in extreme necessity will a father be allowed to sell himself or his children, to avoid natural death".[48] At first glance, it might appear that Moirans was simply reverting to the established Domini-

43 Moirans, *Servi liberi*, ed. Pena González et al., cap. 4, no. 52–53, 72–74: "Igitur inter illos non potest esse iustum bellum; sed qui fortior est illorum, et prevalet, capit sibi quos potest [...] et omnium malorum istorum in causa sunt negotiatores et mercatores, qui emunt nigros".

44 Moirans, *Servi liberi*, ed. Pena González et al., cap. 5, no. 61, 88. We shall return to this point in the next section.

45 Moirans, *Servi liberi*, ed. Pena González et al., cap. 5, no. 55, 78: "christiani [...] quando possunt furantur et rapiunt nigros, nullam aliam habentes nisi ipsos esse nigros et debere servos, quasi vero non essent homines, sed pecudes, ut canes et bestiae".

46 Moirans, *Servi liberi*, ed. Pena González et al., cap. 5, no. 57, 80: "Cum autem a Domino sit poena talionis et oculum pro oculo [...] iam videmus lusitanos fieri mancipia maurorum Africae, et in tantum ut communiter vocentur *gallinae maris* quas accipitres turcae sibi rapiunt, quot naves rapuerunt pyratae maurorum".

47 This is also noted in Montes D'Oca, "Two Capuchin Friars", 98–99.

48 Moirans, *Servi liberi*, ed. Pena González et al., cap. 6, no. 72, 106: "Sed a fundamentis doctrinam reiiciamus. Dico falsum esse in gravi necessitate posse patrem filium vendere, aut seipsum [...] in sola extrema necessitate ad evitandam mortem naturalem licebit".

can position on voluntary slavery from Domingo de Soto's *De iustitia et iure*. But, in fact, he advanced an entirely new argument with wide-ranging implications. According to Moirans, Christian merchants on the shores of Africa were morally obligated to provide aid and not permitted to profit from such cases of necessity: "The purchase of sons by Christians would thus have been unjust, because they would have been obliged to provide, freely and with charity, the necessities of life to those who were in extreme necessity".[49]

At the end of the day, Portuguese slave traders could not legitimately invoke this title, and by the same logic, they could not justly buy adult Africans who willingly offered themselves for sale. Iberian imperial theorists invoked the idea of Christian charity in order to protect fellow Christians from slavery while promoting the enslavement of "infidels". For Moirans, however, the religious affiliation of those in need was irrelevant. Charity, in his view, did not expand but rather defined and limited the rights of Christians vis-à-vis Black Africans.

2 Moirans against the Iberian Imperial Theorists

Moirans's reappraisal of the principles of African slavery centered less on the theory of enslavement itself than on its practical application. The same approach characterized his engagement with Iberian apologies of slave trade. Moirans was particularly critical of the Jesuits writers in the tradition of Luis de Molina, and this is hardly coincidental. His critique of the Iberian imperial theorists was deeply influenced by the work of yet another Jesuit, who had previously leveled sharp criticism against his intellectual predecessors: Diego de Avendaño.

The Lima-based university theologian was not only a recognized authority on questions of labor coercion but also intervened in the debate on the legitimacy of African slavery. A little over a decade before Moirans penned his *Servi libri*, Avendaño had dismantled the arguments in favor of the trade in enslaved Africans posited by luminaries as Luis de Molina, Tomás Sánchez, or Fernão Rebello in his *Thesaurus indicus*.[50] Avendaño explained this commerce was "illicit with regard to most slaves that are bought in these regions and comes

49 Moirans, *Servi liberi*, ed. Pena González et al., cap. 5, no. 59, 84: "non possent christiani emere filios, nam patri posito in extrema necessitate tenerentur sucurrere. [...] Iniusta ergo esset emptio filii a christianis, cum tenerentur gratis et charitate ministrare necessaria posito in extrema necessitate".

50 Avendaño, *Thesaurus indicus*, tit. IX, cap. 12, § 8, no. 180–199, 324–329.

with the burden of restitution".[51] He even declared it was unlawful to acquire *any* slaves transported from the shores of Africa to the Indies, since the suspicion of unjust enslavement was so strong.[52]

And yet, despite his forceful critique, Avendaño ultimately reached a radically different conclusion. After outlining the arguments against his intellectual predecessors' defense of African slavery, he proceeded to argue that "the aforementioned business in the Indies and Europe can in some way be justified".[53] It was precisely this abrupt reversal, as we shall see, that ultimately prompted Moirans to disagree with Avendaño. In the end, the Capuchin insisted that Avendaño was "contradicting himself" by abandoning his own principles—just like the Jesuits, who had previously written about the slave trade from Spain and Portugal.[54]

2.1 *The Portuguese War against Angola*

Among Iberian theorists, it was commonplace to stress that the Portuguese acquired enslaved Africans not just through trade but also through belligerent ventures. There was a general agreement with Luis de Molina that the war against the Kingdom of Angola constituted a legitimate cause for enslavement—and Moirans, at least initially, accepted this interpretation.

In Chapter 8 of his *Servi liberi*, however, Moirans turned to the opinion of Diego de Avendaño, who offered a re-reading of Luis de Molina's account of the Portuguese war in Angola, to claim that Molina himself had left room for doubting the justice of Portuguese intervention.[55] Indeed, Molina had admit-

51 Avendaño, *Thesaurus indicus*, tit. IX, cap. 12, § 8, no. 203, 329–330: "negotiatio dicta secundum maiorem parte mancipiorum, qui in illis partibus emuntur, est illicita, iniusta, et cum onere restitutionis".

52 Avendaño, *Thesaurus indicus*, tit. IX, cap. 12, § 8, no. 203, 330: "Mancipiorum copiam a mercatoribus, qui ea ex Africae regionibus asportant, non est licitum emere in Indiis, et Europa. [...] neque unum aut alterum mancipium licet emere ex eisdem stante suspicione, ob fundamenta dicta".

53 Avendaño, *Thesaurus indicus*, tit. IX, cap. 12, § 8, no. 204, 330: "Emptio dicta in Indiis, et Europa iustificari potest aliqualiter". This is also noted by Francisco Cuena Boy, who offers a compelling account of Avendaño's views on the legitimacy of the trade in enslaved Black Africans and his engagement with Iberian theorists who had previously addressed the issue. See Cuena Boy, *De servitue*, 209–237.

54 Moirans, *Servi liberi*, ed. Pena González et al., cap. 10, no. 110, 164: "Sibi ergo contradicit declinando, sicut et caeteri, quia omnes declinaverunt". See also Moirans, *Servi liberi*, ed. Pena González et al., cap. 11, no. 113, 170: "Cum autem dicat illos doctores favere hic iniustae negotiationi, siquidem probavit superius nullo modo favere, ergo sibi ipso contradicit. Sicut et caeteri".

55 Moirans, *Servi liberi*, ed. Pena González et al., cap. 8, no. 84, 126: "Sed certe, ut dubitari de

ted the possibility that the initial Portuguese military expedition, though formally about avenging a violation of right, might have been motivated "by the rumor [...] that there were many silver mines in this kingdom".[56] Molina suspected this was ultimately immaterial. Avendaño, however, emphasized that the uncertainty persisted as to whether the war had at least in part been motivated by the search for material riches.[57] His aim was not to invalidate the justice of the Angolan war *tout court*. Rather, he took issue with a curious remark made by Luis de Molina: the claim that slavery was permissible only "if its justice is clearer than light".[58]

This dictum, Avendaño recognized, was at odds with Molina's own advocacy of probabilistic reasoning. If taken seriously, he argued, "the Angolans captured in war could not be enslaved, because the justice of that war is not clearer than light".[59] The Peruvian professor thus sought to turn Molina's argument against himself. Although doubts surrounded the legitimacy of the said war, Avendaño underscored, a probable—not a crystal clear—title was sufficient to retain enslaved Angolans with a safe conscience.[60]

In the final stage of this multilayered and polyphonic exchange within the pages of the *Servi liberi*, Moirans staked his own ground in the debate. He followed Avendaño insofar as he, too, acknowledged the doubtful justice of the Portuguese war against Angola. And he concurred with Molina's assertion that

iustitia possit, dubitatio ipsius patris [i.e., Molina] facit". Moirans here cited verbatim from Avendaño, *Thesaurus indicus*, tit. IX, cap. 12, § 8, no. 190, 326.

56 Molina, *DIEI*, vol. 1, tr. II, disp. 34, no. 9, col. 171: "expeditionem a Rege Sebastiano ad iniuriam [...] vindicandam obtinuit. Neque parum ad eam comparandum ad contulit fama [...] esse in regno argenti fodinas non paucas". As Toby Green argues in his new economic history of early modern Africa, the myth of gold in Angola was a persistent and crucial motivation for Portuguese expeditions. See Green, *A Fistful of Shells*, 225.

57 Moirans, *Servi liberi*, ed. Pena González et al., cap. 8, no. 84, 126: "de avaritia esse satis fundata suspicio poterat, quando bellum illud non tantum ob vindicandas iniurias, sed propter argenti fodinas, quae in eo tractu esse fama vulgaverat, potius agebatur". Moirans here cited verbatim from Avendaño, *Thesaurus indicus*, tit. IX, cap. 12, § 8, no. 190, 326.

58 Molina, *DIEI*, vol. 1, tr. II, disp. 35, no. 19, col. 192: "neque aliter servitutis cuiusque illorum est permittenda, quam si luce clarius eam iustam esse constet".

59 Moirans, *Servi liberi*, ed. Pena González et al., cap. 8, no. 85, 128: "si titulus luce clarior ad servitutem permittendam requiritur, bello capti angolani non poterunt in servitutem redigi, quia iustitia illius belli non est luce clarior, ut numero praecedenti dicebamus". Moirans here cited verbatim from Avendaño, *Thesaurus indicus*, tit. IX, cap. 12, § 8, no. 191, 327.

60 Moirnans, *Servi liberi*, cap. 8, no. 85: "Tuta enim consciencia potest probabilis sententia teneri circa titulum huiusmodi, sicut circa alia et de bello est satis communis sententia inter recentiores". Moirans here cited verbatim from Avendaño, *Thesaurus indicus*, tit. IX, cap. 12, § 8, no. 191, 326 327.

titles of slavery needed to be "*luce clarior*".[61] Yet it was precisely through this selective agreement with the two Jesuits that Moirans ultimately rejected the opinions of each. "Because liberty is by natural law, and every single human being is in possession of their liberty", he maintained, "it is impossible to deprive them of their freedom unless there is a justified and verified title of slavery".[62] Therefore, Moirans concluded, "all Angolans are unjustly slaves [...] just like the rest of the Blacks".[63]

2.2 *Possession, Probability, and Human Freedom*

The claim that just titles of slavery left no scope for speculation was one of the central contentions of Moirans's treatise, and a direct attack on the probabilistic reasoning of Molina and all those writing in his vein. Throughout the *Servi liberi*, Moirans repeatedly underscored that "probability favors manumission rather than slavery", as Fernando Rodrigues Montes D'Oca has aptly put it.[64]

Where Iberian imperial theorists had focused, almost exclusively, on the validity of the master's right in the slave, Moirans introduced a novel perspective. He interpreted doubtful cases of enslavement as a conflict between two competing claims to the same thing: a human being's liberty. Unlike disputes between a possessor and a true owner of a mule, however, the contest between master and slave was framed by two different, hierarchically ordered systems of law. For Moirans, the two claims therefore differed in quality: "the possession that is by natural law prevails over the possession that someone has by the title of purchase, even if the doubt is equal, because the condition of the possessor by natural law is better than the title of purchase".[65] Human freedom was rooted in natural law, and in cases of doubt, Moirans insisted, the slave's right to freedom would always trump the master's claim to ownership, which rested on the law of nations.

---

61 Moirans, *Servi liberi*, ed. Pena González et al., cap. 8, no. 88, 134.

62 Moirans, *Servi liberi*, ed. Pena González et al., cap. 8, no. 88, 134: "Nam cum libertas sit de iure naturali, et quilibet homo sit in possessione suae libertatis, non potest privari illa nisi iustificato et verificato titulo iustae servitutis".

63 Moirans, *Servi liberi*, ed. Pena González et al., cap. 8, no. 88, 134: "Unde cum non constet de iustitia belli, omnes angolani iniuste servi sunt [...] sicuti et caeteris nigris".

64 Montes D'Oca, "Two Capuchin Friars", 107. On probabilism in early modern Catholic moral theology more generally, see Schüssler, *The Debate on Probale Opinions*.

65 Moirans, *Servi liberi*, ed. Pena González et al., cap. 7, no. 80, 120: "possessio quae est de iure naturali praevalet possessioni quam habuit titulo emptionis, etiam si dubium sit aequale, quia melior conditio possidentis de iure naturae quam titulo emptionis".

For Moirans, the idea that enslaved Africans could be justly owned in good faith was untenable for another reason. As he remarked, "it is astonishing what Molina says: although he seems persuaded that the majority of slaves from these places were unjustly subjected to slavery, he is not persuaded that this applies to all of them, and therefore he is not persuaded that it applies to any single slave at all".[66] In Moirans's estimation, Molina had thereby succeeded in "bringing together a contradiction that not even God could unite".[67]

This shift in focus from the rights of slaveholders to the rights of the enslaved also brought Moirans into disagreement with yet another theologian from the University of Évora; Molina's disciple Fernão Rebello. According to this Portuguese Jesuit, merchants could licitly acquire African slaves "*if they followed the royal ordinances on the examination of the titles of slavery*".[68] For Moirans, this was sheer hypocrisy. Since these captives had been purchased with the intention of shipping them across the Atlantic, he maintained, this trade was "worthy of damnation and illicit even if the royal ordinances have been kept".[69] Experience had shown that on the transatlantic slave ships Africans were exposed to "the most certain danger of death"—and because nobody had the right to impose such grave conditions on others, Moirans concluded, "this trade is illicit".[70] Emphasizing the principle that no one may endanger the physical and spiritual well-being of others, Moirans imported into the debate on the slave trade an argument that Iberian theologians had previously confined to the governance of slaves within the household. Once again, Moirans sought defeat the Iberian imperial theorists at their own game.

---

66 Moirans, *Servi liberi*, ed. Pena González et al., cap. 8, no. 91, 140: "Sed admirabile est quod dicit Molina: Licet persuadere videantur plurima mancipia ex illis locis iniuste servituti subiecta, non tamen persuadent omnia, ac proinde de nullo in singulari persuadent".

67 Moirans, *Servi liberi*, ed. Pena González et al., cap. 8, no. 91, 140: "Potens ergo Molina iungere contradictionem quam Deus non potest facere".

68 Moirans, *Servi liberi*, ed. Pena González et al., cap. 9, no. 92, 142, original emphasis: "*Cum aliis societatis nostrae magistris affirmat* [i.e., Rebello] *negotiationem esse licitam si mercatores ordinationes regias servent de examine circa titulum servitutis faciendo*". Moirans here cited verbatim from Avendaño, *Thesaurus Indicus*, tit. IX, cap. 12, § 8, no. 195, 328. For the original passage in Rebello, see his *Opus de obligationibus iustitiae*, pars 1, lib. I, q. 10, sect. 1, no. 4: "Non videtur regulariter illicitum emere Aethiopes [...] ubi forma examinandi titulum servitutis eorum a regibus Lusitanis tradita est, eaque observari praesumitur".

69 Moirans, *Servi liberi*, ed. Pena González et al., cap. 9, no. 97, 148: "Negotiatio autem principalis est ad asportanda mancipia ad alias regiones instituta, ergo damnabilis et illicita, etiam servatis regiis ordinationibus".

70 Moirans, *Servi liberi*, ed. Pena González et al., cap. 9, no. 97, 148: "miseros istos certissime mortis periculo in navigationibus exponi, ut quotidianis experimentis constat. Non licet autem exponere certissimo mortis periculo homines, ergo illicita negotiatio".

2.3 *Moirans* contra *Avendaño*

After his rebuttal of the Jesuits in Iberia, which he had developed through the lens of Diego de Avendaño's *Thesaurus indicus*, Moirans finally embarked on his critique of Avendaño himself. The Peruvian professor "fought for truth and justice, but not all the way to the end, and not legitimately", Moirans bemoaned, "and he swerved in the same way that other fathers of the Society [of Jesus] did".[71]

Among Avendaño's arguments in defense of the slave trade was the claim that "some doctors" justified African slavery even if it was "in a certain way illogical if measured against their own teaching".[72] He also maintained that Atlantic slavery was supported by the Castilian monarch and by ecclesiastical officials in the Indies.[73] Above all, however, the colonial intellectual fused an argument about the ostensible inferiority of Black Africans with a claim about their indispensability to the Spanish empire in the Americas: "these slaves are so necessary for the Indies that without them", Avendaño argued, "this commonwealth could not remain. Thus, because they are the vilest among humans, one can waive a certain requirement of the *ius gentium*".[74] Since these people "seem to be born to serve", he went on, all those who held Africans as slaves "should be content with a minor title".[75] This reasoning would later be echoed by the Council of the Indies in its letter to Charles II.[76]

In the same way that colonial thinkers had previously legitimated practices of Indigenous labor coercion, Avendaño invoked arguments of natural slavery and imperial expediency to justify the commerce in enslaved Africans. There was, however, a crucial difference between these two contexts. Unlike

71 Moirans, *Servi liberi*, ed. Pena González et al., cap. 10, no. 111, 166: "Pugnavit ergo pro veritate et iustitia, sed non usque ad finem, nec certavit legitime. Quapropter, sicut et alii Societatis Patres, declinavit".

72 Avendaño, *Thesaurus Indicus*, tit. IX, cap. 12, § 8, no. 204, 330: "doctores aliqui, licet eorum quidam inconsequenter ad suam ipsorum doctrinam, eam non esse aperte damnabilem affirmant, immo et illi favent, ut Molina, Rebellus [...] Fagundez".

73 Avendaño, *Thesaurus Indicus*, tit. IX, cap. 12, § 8, no. 204, 330. For Moirans's s critique, see his *Servi liberi*, cap. 12, no. 115–116.

74 Avendaño, *Thesaurus Indicus*, tit. IX, cap. 12, § 8, no. 204, 330: "quia pro Indiis adeo sunt necessarii, ut sine illis stare Respublica ista nequeat. Cum ergo vilissimi isti inter homines sint, dispensari cum aliquo requisito iuris gentium potest".

75 Avendaño, *Thesaurus Indicus*, tit. IX, cap. 12, § 8, no. 204, 330: "quia cum mancipia ista videantur ad serviendum nata, ut multi expendunt, non videtur circa illa eodem, quo circa alios, exactissimo iure agendum, sed minore titulo [...] emptores debere esse contentos".

76 Council of the Indies (Consejo de Indias), "Oficio del Consejo de Indias a Carlos II, Madrid, 21 agosto, 1685", 353.

the Indigenous peoples, enslaved Black Africans were forcibly dragged into the colonial body politic from outside. If the case for forced Native labor rested on the idea of an unequal, composite commonwealth, Avendaño's argument for the slave trade was grounded on the notion of a fundamentally unequal *world.* In Avendaño's vision of global power dynamics, the purportedly natural subservience of some licensed their quasi-lawless subjugation by agents from another commonwealth. This was precisely the kind of natural slavery *qua* chattel slavery that Francisco de Vitoria had vehemently repudiated in his *De indis*.

Epifanio de Moirans responded forcefully to these claims. Black Africans, he insisted, were human beings and therefore free by nature. Their servitude, far from being natural, resulted from the "greed and injustice of the Europeans".[77] Moirans acknowledged that many enslaved Africans were "dulled by intolerable labor", but he added that even more "surpassed their masters in wisdom and prudence".[78] In so arguing, he subverted Avendaño's appeal to the Aristotelian theory of natural slavery: the unjustly enslaved were, in fact, better suited to command the "crude" and "foolish" Spanish slaveholders.[79]

Moirans went even further, comparing Avendaño's justification of African slavery to the unjust subjugation of the Hebrews in biblical Egypt. He reminded his readers that the outcome for the Egyptians had been disastrous: instead of preserving their commonwealth, "they all died, and God struck them with terrible plagues."[80] Moirans warned that the Spanish oppressors of Black Africans faced a similar reckoning: "Let the Christians therefore fear the plagues of the Egyptians, for God is very angry!"[81]

---

77 Moirans, *Servi liberi*, ed. Pena González et al., cap. 12, no. 117, 176: "respondeo haec mancipia homines esse, ergo de iure naturae liberi […] Unde non sunt nati ad serviendum, sed factum hoc est cupiditate europaeorum et iniquitate".

78 Moirans, *Servi liberi*, ed. Pena González et al., cap. 12, no. 117, 176: "quantum ad ingenii vigorem, prae labore incomportabili hebetantur plurimi, sed quamplurimi praecellunt in sapientia et prudentia dominos".

79 Moirans, *Servi liberi*, ed. Pena González et al., cap. 12, no. 117, 176: "Et contra ius omne naturale et divinum et lumen ratinonis […] hos nigros servos esse talium rudium et stultorum dominorum, sicut dicitur […] ab Aristotele, ducto lumine rationis: Rudes et stulti naturaliter sunt servi sapientium".

80 Moirans, *Servi liberi*, ed. Pena González et al., cap. 12, no. 118, 178: "Immo hac de causa perierunt omnes et plagis horrendis percussit eos Dominus."

81 Moirans, *Servi liberi*, ed. Pena González et al., cap. 12, no. 118, 178: "Timeant ergo plagas aegipti christiani, quia iratus est Dominus valde!"

3 The Reinvention of Biblical Slavery

By the time Epifanio de Moirans was writing, Iberian justifications for the transatlantic slave trade were still largely based on the language of natural law and legal titles of enslavement. But an alternative legitimation of slavery that circulated in the 17th-century Iberian Atlantic rested on a story from the Bible. According to some, the skin color of sub-Saharan Africans was a sign of their eternal damnation by God and their predestined lives as slaves. This view of Blackness rested on the claim that Noah's curse of his son Ham in the Book of Genesis provided a divine foundation for the enslavement of Black Africans. Moirans, true to his polemical style, forcefully countered this reasoning. For him, the Book of Genesis testified to the divinely ordained *freedom* of Africans—and not to Black enslavement.

3.1 *The Curse of Ham—or Whom?*

The story commonly known as the "curse of Ham" (Genesis 9–10) is inextricably linked not only to the idea of slavery but also to broader discourses of human classification. It formed the starting point for "one of the most influential taxonomies of race" grounded in "the tripartite scheme derived from the story of Noah and his three sons".[82] In the most basic but historically influential reading, Shem was regarded as the ancestor of the Hebrews, Japhet of the Europeans, and Ham of the peoples dwelling in Africa.[83]

In Genesis 9, Ham enters Noah's tent and sees his drunken father naked. He then informs his brothers, who enter their father's tent, but avert their eyes to avoid witnessing Noah's nudity. When Noah learns of Ham's transgression, he curses Ham's son Canaan, and not Ham himself, condemning him to be a *servus servorum*, a "slave of slaves".[84] The genealogical account of Noah's descendants that follows in Genesis 10, however, does not offer a textual foundation linking Canaan to Blackness or slavery. In fact, it is Cush, another of Ham's sons, who is said to inhabit the African lands of Ethiopia.[85] Complicating matters further, Cush's son Nimrod is later situated in Assyria.[86] As Colin Kidd observes, the Bible itself is "colour-blind" and "tells us very little about the racial appearance of the figures and groups who feature within it".[87]

---

82 Kidd, *The Forging of Races*, 9.
83 Kidd, *The Forging of Races*, 36–37.
84 Gen 9:21–25.
85 Ezek. 29:10. The King James Bible here renders the Hebrew "Cush" as "Ethiopia".
86 Micah 5:6.
87 Kidd, *The Forging of Races*, 3.

Thus, the Bible neither explains how Noah's curse affected Ham's descendants, nor ties it to a specific geographic or racial lineage.[88] The so-called biblical justification for Black African slavery, therefore, was not rooted in the text itself but in the readers' interpretations. The centrality of descent in the Book of Genesis and its simultaneous "silence on matters of race" created a fertile ground for a plethora of interpretations of "racial meanings", stretching from antiquity to the modern era.[89]

A particularly salient theme is the long and complex history of (mis)identifying Ham as the subject of Noah's curse. The roots of this narrative can be traced to late antiquity and the medieval period.[90] Yet the rigid and fixed association of Ham with Africa, which later served as a justification for African slavery, has a significantly shorter history. As the historian Benjamin Braude notes, "much of what has been assumed to be medieval and well established turns out to be, in many respects, novel and modern."[91] By studying widely circulating texts like *Mandeville's Travels* or Hartmann Schedel's *Weltchronik*, also known as the *Nuremberg Chronicle*, Braude reveals the enormous variability—and vagueness—that characterized medieval understandings of Noah's offspring.[92] In part, this variability stemmed from the limited availability of biblical texts, mainly in fragments, and in a non-standardized form before the advent of print.[93] Ham was sometimes associated with Asia, and when portrayed as African, he was conventionally depicted as light-skinned.[94] The "medieval whiteness of Ham and most of his offspring" reflected the European imagination of Africa as a familiar Mediterranean space that was home to such Christian figures as Saint Augustine.[95]

According to Braude, the process of casting Ham as the forefather of Black Africans only began to take definitive shape with the Portuguese ventures in Western Africa. From the 15th century onward, European encounters with sub-Saharan Africans sparked polemical debates about their origin.[96] In some instances, scribes copying existing texts such as *Mandeville's Travels* altered the traditional allocation of the world's regions to Noah's sons in light of these emerging debates—transforming a formerly Asian Ham into an Africanized

88 Brion Davis, *Inhuman Bondage*, 66.
89 Kidd, *The Forging of Races*, 20.
90 See Goldenberg, *The Curse of Ham*, chs. 11–12.
91 Braude, "The Sons of Noah", 104.
92 Braude, "The Sons of Noah", 120 and *passim*.
93 Braude, "The Sons of Noah", 107.
94 Braude, "The Sons of Noah", 116–117.
95 Braude, "The Sons of Noah", 123.
96 Braude, "The Sons of Noah", 127.

figure.[97] In Gomes Eanes de Zurara's chronicles of the Portuguese ventures in Africa, we find an early manifestation of an express link between Noah's curse and the justification of Black slavery. Writing in the mid-15th century, Zurara claimed that the enslavement of sub-Saharan Africans was "in accordance with ancient custom, which I believe to have been because of the curse which, after the Deluge, Noah laid upon his son Cain [in fact: Cham], cursing him in this way".[98]

3.2 *Biblical Slavery in the Spanish Empire*

For Iberian imperial theorists, the idea of biblical slavery was inconceivable. They universally agreed that slavery originated from the *ius gentium*—the law of nations—rather than from any individual curse. Not surprisingly then, this was rejected by one Iberian theologian who had explicitly engaged with the story of Genesis 9. In his *Commentaries and Disputations on Justice*, Miguel Bartolomé Salón bluntly noted that only "heretics" claimed that slavery was introduced by divine law.[99]

By the 17th century, however, visions of biblical slavery had also begun to attract the attention of intellectuals in the Spanish empire. The most notable of these was the Jesuit theologian Alonso de Sandoval (1577–1652).[100] Born in Castile, Sandoval spent most of his life in the Americas. He studied at the College of San Pablo in Lima and later became the head of the Jesuit College in Cartagena, where he resided from 1624 until his death. Thousands of enslaved Africans passed through the port of Cartagena during this period, leaving a deep imprint on Sandoval's intellectual work. The Latin title of his vernacular treatise *De instauranda Aethiopum salute* (1627/47) was a tribute to the *De procuranda indorum salute* of his Jesuit predecessor Acosta.[101] Just as Acosta had been concerned with the salvation of the "*indios*", Sandoval was preoccu-

97 Braude, "The Sons of Noah", 118–119.

98 Zurara, *Chronicle*, vol. 1, cap. 16, 54. See the discussion in Goldenberg, *The Curse of Ham*, 175, which also touches on Zurara's mistaken mention of Cain rather then Ham.

99 Salón, *Commentariorum in disputationem de iustitia*, q. 3, a. 1, 112: "Praeter hos haereticos est opinio cuiusdam glossae in cap. 9 Gen. insinuantis servitutem essse iure divino introductae". This is also noted in Andrés-Gallego and García Añoveros, *La iglesia y la esclavitud de los negros*, 61.

100 Biographical information on Sandoval is from von Germeten, "Introduction".

101 While the title *De instauranda* is the title of the second edition of 1647, I follow the established scholarly convention of using this name for references to the earlier 1627 edition as well. In what follows, I will be drawing on the first edition: Sandoval, *Naturaleza*. The second edition was published as Sandoval, *Tomo primero De instauranda Aethiopum salute*. For an excellent overview of salient differences between the two editions, see Restrepo, "*De instauranda Aethiopum salute*".

pied with the salvation of the "Aethiopians". Since they had once been Christians, he referred to the *restoration* of their salvation. In this sense, Sandoval situated his project in the larger context of sacred history.[102]

Despite advocating for the re-Christianization of Africans, however, Sandoval advanced a remarkable interpretation of biblical slavery. Drawing on the church fathers, he argued that the true subject of Noah's curse was Ham, who, along with "all his offspring", was condemned to slavery.[103] Moreover, Sandoval explicitly associated Ham's lineage with sub-Saharan Africa. The blackness of the skin of the "*Etiopes*", he wrote, was both a consequence of "the curse that Noah placed upon his son Ham" and "an innate and intrinsic quality with which God created Ham [...] so that the sons he would engender appeared with this soot and as a marker of their descent from a man that had ridiculed his father, as a punishment for his insolence".[104] For Sandoval, therefore, the enslavement of Black Africans was ultimately sanctioned by divine will, even though he similarly acknowledged that slavery must proceed only under just titles, in the manner "eruditely" explained by "our doctor Molina in the first volume of *De iustitia et iure*".[105]

3.3 *The Foundation of African Liberty*

When Epifanio de Moirans revisited the question of biblical slavery, he did not explicitly mention Sandoval—or any other contemporary theologian. Yet his verdict was crystal clear: those who invoked the curse of Ham to justify Black African slavery were "mad with their own greed" because the one who had been cursed was not Ham "but his son".[106] It was Canaan and his progeny who

---

102 On this point, see von Germeten, "Introduction", xii.

103 Sandoval, *Naturaleza*, lib. 1, cap. 2, 14^v: "por aver maldecido Noe a su hijo Cham [...] y aun costandole quedar por esclavo el y toda su generacion, de los hermanos, que fue segun los santos Augustino, Chrisostomo, y Ambrosio, la primera servidumbre que se introduxo en el mundo". On Augustine, Ambrose, and Chrysostmo's accounts of Noah's curse, see Goldenberg, *The Curse of Ham*, 158–159.

104 Sandoval, *Naturaleza*, lib. 1, cap. 2, 14^r: "la tez negra en los Etiopes, no provino tan solamente de la maldicion que Noé echó a su hijo Cham (como veremos adelante) sino tambien de una calidad innata, e intrinseca, con que le crió Dios [...] para que los hijos que engendrasse, saliessen con esse tizne, y como marca, de que descendian de un hombre, qu se avia burlado de su padre, en pena de su atrevimiento".

105 Sandoval, *Naturaleza*, lib. 1, cap. 17, 65^r: "con todo me he determinado a tratarlo, dexando la determinacion de su justificacion a los Dotores, que tan doctamente han escrito cerca deste punto, principalmente a nuestro Dotor Molina en el tomo 1. de iustitia, & iure". On Sandoval's justification of Black slavery, see also Hofmeister Pich, "Alonso de Sandoval S.J. (1576/1577–1652) and the Ideology of Black Slavery"; and Ireton, "L'imaginaire éthiopien dans le premier monde hispanique".

106 Moirans, *Servi liberi*, ed. Pena González et al., cap. 3, no. 41, 58: "dico ipsos allucinatos esse

were enslaved, and, as Moirans argued, "there is nobody who would not see the difference between the peoples of Canaan and Black Africans", because "the Blacks were never slaves of the sons of Israel—those were rather the Canaanites and all the nations of Palestine—and they neither descend from the Canaanites".[107] He supported this claim by pointing to the geographic distinction between Canaanites and Africans: the former lived "in Palestine in Asia" whereas the latter "possess the West of Africa".[108] Moirans thus repudiated yet another contemporary justification for the transatlantic slave trade.

But he did not stop there. If Christians had assumed the place of the Hebrews and inherited from them the power over the sons of Canaan, as was commonly accepted, then this also included sub-Saharan Africans. For they too "belonged to the peoples who received the gospel", Moirans underscored with reference to the conversion of the "Aethiopeans" in the Book of Psalms.[109] Although he did not use the notion of "Aethiopean" as a synonym for all Black Africans, he situated the peoples of West Africa within the lineage of biblical Ethiopia. The consequences of this move were far-reaching, as Moirans went on to explain:

> [...] if anybody concludes with reason, he will conclude that the Blacks should hold the Canaanites as slaves, and they should all be free by divine positive law and be masters of the Canaanites. Therefore, those who deprive them of this right sin against divine positive law, and those who hold them as slaves sin against divine natural law.[110]

---

cupiditate sua, quia dato es ultra concesso quod nigri sint ex progenie Cham, quod tamen non fateor, dico quod non fuit maledictus et factus servus, sed Chanaan filius eius".

107 Moirans, *Servi liberi*, ed. Pena González et al., cap. 3, no. 41, 60: "Quid intersit autem inter populos chananeorum [sic] et nigros Africae nemo est qui non videat, cum nigri non fuerint unquam servi filiorum Israel, sed chananaei et cunctae nationes Palaestinae, nec sint de genere chananaeorum".

108 Moirans, *Servi liberi*, ed. Pena González et al., cap. 3, no. 41, 60: "Chananaei habitabant Palaestinam in Asia, et nigri occidentem tenent in Africa".

109 Moirans, *Servi liberi*, ed. Pena González et al., cap. 3, no. 41, 60: "Ad id quod dicitur christianos obtinuisse locum israelitarum dico, retroquendo argumentum: ergo nigri successerunt in hoc ius israelitarum, in filios Chanaan. Patet consequentia, quia nigri sunt ex gentibus, quae receperunt Evangelium, unde dicitur in psalmis: *Coram illo procident Aethiopes* (Ps 71) [...] psalmo 67, exponendo illud: *Aethiopia praeveniet manus eius Deo*". Moirans here referred to Ps 71:9 and 67:32 in the Vulgate.

110 Moirans, *Servi liberi*, ed. Pena González et al., cap. 3, no. 41, 60: "Igitur, si aliquid concluderet ratio, concluderet nigros debere habere chananaeos in servos, et liberos esse omnes iure positivo divino et dominos chananaeorum. Ergo contra ius divinum positivum peccant qui privant eos hoc iure et in naturale divinum committunt qui tenent eos in mancipia".

The inclusion of sub-Saharan Africans into the community of Christ thus protected them from slavery on multiple grounds. As Moirans argued, "Black Christians" were free by natural law "in their capacity as human beings", and they had an additional claim to freedom by divine law "in their capacity as Christians". Therefore, to enslave them constituted a "twofold violation of right".[111]

With this polemical re-reading of sacred history, Moirans laid the foundation not only for Black Africans' freedom but also for their God-given authority over others. Just as the enslavement of those who "sinned" against the Hebrews had been divinely ordained, he argued, so did Christians have the right "to take those as slaves who sin against the church and who are enemies of the church's sons, like the Turks and Moors, and all the Mohammedan enemies of the church".[112] But Moirans insisted "the Blacks" could not be counted among them, for "on the contrary, many are Christians".[113] In so arguing, Moirans echoed the arguments of enslaved Africans who fought for their freedom in Iberian courts in the 16th and 17th centuries, insisting that they had always been Christians and therefore illegally enslaved.[114] But Moirans went further, insisting that the peoples dwelling in West Africa were destined to be free, destined to be Christians, and ultimately destined to join the "holy wars" against the Muslims. Moirans's narrative of African liberty was part and parcel of a broader story of salvation that was inextricably linked to anti-Islamic sentiment and action.

The by-product of Moirans's vigorous intervention was thus a vindication of the kind of slavery whose ideological origins date back to the European Middle Ages. In the *Servi liberi*, the nexus between slavery and the faith was even stronger than in the writings of the Iberian imperial theorists. Although

---

111 Moirans, *Servi liberi*, ed. Pena González et al., cap. 3, no. 42, 60–62: "Itaque omnes nigri, christiani nigri non solum ius naturale habent in libertatem suam tanquam homines, sed divinum tanquam christiani. [...] nec possunt fieri servi, nisi duplici iniuria, ratione hominis et ratione christiani".

112 Moirans, *Servi liberi*, ed. Pena González et al., cap. 3, no. 43, 62: "Quia cum peccaverint [i.e., the Canaanites] in filios Israel, Dominus, completis iniquitatibus, subiecit eos filios Israel [...] Sic et christiani possunt habere in servos qui contra Ecclesiam peccant et hostes sunt filiorum Ecclesiae, sicuti turcae et mauri, omnesque mahumetani hostes Ecclesiae, non vero ex fratribus suis, nec ex gentibus que non sunt hostes eorum communes".

113 Moirans, *Servi liberi*, ed. Pena González et al., cap. 3, no. 43, 62: "Nigri autem nec sunt hostes christianorum, imo plurimi sunt christiani".

114 See Ireton, "Black Africans' Freedom Litigation Suits". As Karen Graubart has shown, enslaved Africans in late 17th-century Lima made a different argument for emancipation as well, claiming that as American-born subjects they should be considered Natives and therefore had the legal status of free Indigenous subjects. But in contrast to the court cases reconstructed by Ireton, Graubart's petitioners from Lima were not successful. See Graubart, "*Pesa más la libertad*".

Moirans condemned the treatment of enslaved Black Africans in the New World as animals rather than humans, his primary objection was not so much to the real inhumanity of slavery. Rather, he took issue with the fundamental incompatibility between life as a slave and life as a Christian.[115] Early in his treatise, Moirans lamented that female slaves in colonial households had been subjected to abuse by their masters, compelled to reproduce servile offspring, and coerced into sexual relations without the right of matrimony.[116] Plantation life was even harsher, prompting Moirans to urge enslaved Africans to escape from such places "where they were neither taught and instructed in the faith and customs nor were able to live in a Christian way".[117] Whereas the Iberian imperial theorists had previously prohibited the enslavement of fellow believers, Moirans considered this restriction insufficient. In his view, slavery and salvation were so fundamentally opposed that the ban of enslavement had to necessarily also extend to all Christians *in spe*. But at the same time, Moirans mounted a spirited defense of enslaving Ottomans, Maghrebians, and all other Muslim "enemies of the church".

---

115 See e.g., Moirans, *Servi liberi*, ed. Pena González et al., cap. 4, no. 56, 78: "Nec enim doctrinam fidei et morum accipiunt, sed accepto baptismo, sine doctrina relinquuntur, uti pecudes".

116 Moirans, *Servi liberi*, ed. Pena González et al., cap. 1, no. 8, 22: "quae remanent domi ancillae [...] procreare filios et educare, fructificareque domino, non copulatae coniugio, fructum quoque afferre in peccatis debent omnino".

117 Moirans, *Servi liberi*, ed. Pena González et al., cap. 1, no. 7, 22: "agriculturas, villas, domos campestres, habitationes quas galli vocant *sucreries* et hispani *ingenios*, in quibus nec docentur et instruuntur in fide et moribus, sed nec possunt vivere christiane". Apart from his initial conclusion that slaves on plantations were bound to escape, which we encountered above, this was Moirans's only other reference to plantation slavery in the *Servi liberi*.

CONCLUSION

Modes of Protection

The preceding chapters have explored a wide range of issues relating to slavery and empire in the writings of early modern Iberian theologians and jurists. This conclusion aims to synthesize select central findings of this study by highlighting a red thread that runs throughout the book: the political and legal logic of protection. Scholars have shown that the language of protection was at the heart of early modern political relations, both as a theoretical principle and a practical strategy. Its flexibility and ambiguity rendered it particularly effective for describing relationships within, between, and across polities. It could serve the interests of the weak and the powerful, and it left room for interpretation regarding who was protecting whom, under what terms, and for whose benefit.[1] The study of how protection arranged rights and power in the early modern period has been dubbed "a new way of characterizing the cultural politics of empires".[2] The final pages of this study seek to advance this endeavor by examining several modes of protection that were central to the ways in which Iberian imperial theorists conceptualized and addressed the problem of slavery in the 16th and 17th centuries.

Spanish and Portuguese theologians and jurists, who acted as protectors themselves, assumed the responsibility of offering practical guidance on how to align Catholic morality with realities that often appeared to conflict sharply with this ideal. As the correspondence between the Spanish monarch and the Council of the Indies reveals, the opinions of Iberian imperial theorists were used as guidelines for navigating the moral issues surrounding slavery and empire. Their writings focused on the limits of moral human agency, offering arguments aimed at protecting the souls of those who appeared to be in a state of mortal damnation. Consider Luis de Molina, who maintained that anyone who acquired enslaved Black Africans in good faith was safe in conscience, even if they later began to doubt the legitimacy of enslavement. Another strategy to protect the Christian conscience was to exploit the ambiguous status of slaves as both person and property. As Juan Azor argued, enslaved people abandoned by their careless masters lost their status as members of a domestic community and were treated as ownerless objects that could be seized by

1 See the contributions in Benton, Clulow, and Attwood (eds.), *Protection and Empire*; and in Haug, Weber, and Windler (eds.), *Protegierte und Protektoren*.

2 Benton and Clulow, "Introduction", 8.

anyone. Equally revealing is the case of Juan de Lugo, who argued that the marriage rights of enslaved "infidels" were ultimately irrelevant because the public authority of princes had overridden their individual rights through captivity in warfare.

Early modern Iberians viewed slavery itself as a mode of protection. In "just wars", enemies could be legitimately enslaved rather than killed. The same rationale applied to civil punishment, with slavery serving as an alternative to the death penalty. In cases of extreme necessity, enslaving oneself or one's children could effectively save human life, albeit at the expense of human freedom. University theologians, jurists, and missionaries agreed that in a world corrupted by original sin and plagued by wars and inequality, slavery offered protection to those who would otherwise face a legitimate or natural death.

Yet, from an early modern Catholic point of view, slavery remained morally problematic, and all the Iberian imperial theorists invoked charity to prohibit enslavement among Christians. Although the loss of human liberty was permissible in certain situations, it deprived humans of the very faculty that distinguished rational creatures from the rest of creation: the capacity to act according to one's own will and moral judgment. Accordingly, Spanish and Portuguese thinkers maintained that there could be no enslavement in "just wars" between Christian commonwealths. In their view, the *ius gentium*—which regulated and licensed slavery in warfare—had been partly abolished among Christians on the grounds of charity. Luis de Molina also made a similar argument regarding voluntary slavery. Charity, he argued, obliged Christians to aid fellow believers in necessity freely, or at least without enslaving them. But the very same virtue also justified the enslavement of non-Christians in need so that they might be converted in the process. In Molina's logic, charity protected Christians from losing their liberty while saving the souls of "infidels" through legal enslavement. This line of reasoning was later refuted by the French Capuchin missionary Epifanio de Moirans, the most outspoken contemporary critic of the Iberian imperial theorists. He asserted that charity extended not only to those who were already Christians, but also to those destined to convert, namely Black Africans. What united all these thinkers, however, was their shared insistence on the quasi-legal function of charity as a binding moral duty, which was layered on top of strictly juridical considerations and protected (would-be) Christians from slavery.

While the Iberian imperial theorists insisted that there was no enslavement within the Christian commonwealth, membership in that community, and thus protection from slavery, could be precarious. To be sure, enslaved "infidels" who were later Christianized remained in slavery according to Spanish and Portuguese thinkers. But those who joined a Catholic *civitas* as free subjects could, in their view, no longer be enslaved. This protection extended to such diverse groups as the inhabitants of the Christianized Kingdom of Kongo, Indigenous peoples in the New World—including enslaved Asians who were transported to colonial Mexico and considered free "*indios*"—and conquered former Muslims in Iberia. Nevertheless, the political status of neophytes in Iberian realms was unstable. As the debates about revolting Moriscos and rebelling Mapuche reveal, it was possible to legitimize the enslavement of vassals on both sides of the Atlantic by casting them as apostate or "infidel" enemies. Some Iberian theorists further complicated the matter by arguing that the baptized children of such rebels were protected from enslavement, since they remained innocent Christians within a hostile commonwealth. The boundary between those within and outside the political community was as tenuous—and consequential—as the line between those within and outside the spiritual community.

Spanish and Portuguese intellectuals also emphasized the rights of enslaved people, placing special importance on the natural right of self-preservation and, by extension, on the right to safeguard the human species through marriage. In their understanding, the natural right of marriage could not be eclipsed by enslavement, which was not a natural condition. Marriage served the basic purpose of procreation, but it also bore political implications, since the spouses were bound by mutual obligations that revolved around the joint administration of their household community. Enslaved people, who were servile subjects of one household, thus had an enforceable right to become heads of another household at the same time. However, if slaveholders came under the pressure of necessity, they too had a natural right of self-preservation: to secure their survival, they were permitted to sell enslaved people without restriction. Self-preservation was thus a double-edged sword. On the one hand, it was the foundation of enslaved people's rights and protected the integrity of their domestic communities. But on the other hand, self-preservation could also serve the interests of slaveholders by undermining the natural rights of slaves and reducing them to alienable property.

Within the household, enslaved people were also subject to a Janus-faced mode of protection revolving around care and punishment. The Iberian imperial theorists were keen to emphasize that slavery was more than a merely legal relationship. They underscored that, as heads of households, slaveholders had a duty to care for the physical and spiritual well-being of all their domestic subjects, including enslaved people. If masters contravened the good of the enslaved, they could be prosecuted by civil or ecclesiastical authorities. At the same time, however, early modern theologians and jurists defended the legitimacy of branding and imprisoning enslaved persons within Iberian households. In so arguing, they blurred the boundary between domestic discipline and public authority, advocating a vision of slave rule that combined care with coercive power.

A similar duality between protection and subjection is evident in Iberian thinkers' accounts of the political status of Indigenous vassals in the Americas. So-called "*indios*" were considered particularly vulnerable subjects and were therefore granted special legal and juridical privileges. But like enslaved people within the household community, Indigenous vassals were also placed at the very bottom of a deeply hierarchical and unequal colonial commonwealth. Iberian intellectuals writing from the New World drew on the Aristotelian idea of natural slavery to support this point: Indigenous vassals, they argued, were unable to lead a fully political life independently and required the guidance of others to govern them. Juan de Matienzo even went so far as to suggest that they were naturally equipped with strong bodies and weak intellects and therefore born to serve. The protection of Indigenous vassals could go hand in hand with a racialized understanding of "*indios*" as naturally inferior people who were simultaneously included in the community and excluded from the majority society.[3]

This portrayal of Indigenous subjects amounted to a justification of forced native labor as a necessary contribution to the preservation of the Spanish empire in the Americas. Iberian thinkers drew on the established idea that princes could compel their subjects to perform tasks indispensable to the maintenance of the commonwealth. At the most extreme, individual members could be justly sacrificed to keep the body politic alive, as evidenced by the classic example of subjects' obligation to fight in wars. Some Spanish voices in colonial Peru used this dictum to make an analogous argument about forced native labor. Juan de Matienzo and Miguel de Agia, among others, claimed that even deadly tasks such as mining could be imposed on Andeans because the economy sustaining the empire would otherwise collapse. However, others turned this argument on its head, asserting that the rising death toll among Indigenous workers in the silver mines of Potosí was what really undermined the colonial commonwealth. As the jurist Juan de Solórzano y Pereira contended, mining was so dangerous that it could only be imposed on enslaved people and criminals sentenced to death. Meanwhile, "*indios*" should be com-

---

3 I am here following Jean-Frédéric Schaub's understanding of race-making as a process whereby cultural and social characteristics are biologized and linked to arguments about descent, with the aim of identifying and suppressing a particular group within a given society. See Schaub, *Race Is About Politics*, 16–17 and 147. See also Schaub and Sebastiani, *Race et histoire*, ch. 3.

pelled to tasks that preserved both the empire and the Indigenous population. In this sense, the debate about forced native labor in colonial Peru not only reveals the intimate link between imperial protection and exploitation but also shows how contested the distinction between political subjugation and slavery was in the eyes of early modern Iberians.

Arguments centered on preserving Spain's colonial possessions in the New World ultimately also shaped debates about the legitimacy of the transatlantic slave trade. On one side of the spectrum, the theologian Diego de Avendaño argued that the Indies could not be upheld without enslaved labor. He insisted that Black Africans were born to serve, thereby invoking the very same natural slavery argument Matienzo had previously made in relation to Andeans. According to Avendaño, imperial expediency licensed the enslavement of Black Africans with an imperfect title, that is, even when it did not satisfy the demands of justice and morality. The Council of the Indies later adopted this line of reasoning and put forward a defense of Atlantic slavery that was steeped in the language of necessity and reason of state.[4] On the other side of the spectrum, the Capuchin missionary Epifanio de Moirans invoked a biblical comparison to state the exact opposite. Comparing the unlawful enslavement of Black Africans to the subjugation of the Hebrews in Egypt, he warned that continued injustice would lead to the demise of Spain's New World empire through divine punishment. For Moirans, safeguarding the colonial commonwealth required ending the slave trade and treating Black Africans as prospective Christians, whom charity shielded from slavery—lest the Catholics themselves become slaves to their Ottoman enemies, whom Moirans regarded as the ones truly destined for slavery.

4 On reason of state in the early modern Spanish empire, see Kattenberg, *The Power of Necessity*.

Bibliography

Printed Sources

Acosta, José de, *De procuranda indorum salute: Pacificación y colonización*, ed. and Spanish trans. Pereña, Luciano Vicente, Vidal Abril, Carlos Baciero, Antonio Garcia, Demetrio Ramos, José Barrientos, Francisco Maseda, 2 vols., Madrid 1984.

Africanus, Leo (Giovan Lioni Africano), "Della descrittione dell'Africa et delle cose notabili che ivi sono", in Ramusio, Giovanni Battista (ed.), *Primo volume delle navigationi et viaggi*, Venetia 1550: Lucantonio Giunta, 1^r–103^v.

Agia, Miguel de, *Tratado que contiene tres pareceres graves en derecho*, Lima 1604: Antonio Ricardo.

Aquinas, Thomas, *Scriptum super Sententiis*, ed. Alarcón, Enrique and Roberto Busa, Pamplona 2000 (http://www.corpusthomisticum.org).

Aquinas, Thomas, *Summa theologiae*, ed. Alarcón, Enrique and Roberto Busa, Pamplona 2000 (http://www.corpusthomisticum.org).

Aquinas, Thomas, *Commentary on Aristotle's* Politics, ed. and trans. Regan, Richard J., Indianapolis 2007.

Aristotle, *The Politics* and *The Constitution of Athens*, ed. Everson, Stephen and trans. Jowett, Benjamin, Cambridge 1996.

Aristotle, *Nicomachean Ethics*, ed. and trans. Crisp, Roger, Cambridge 2000.

Avendaño, Diego de, *Epithalamium Christi et sacrae sponsae*, Lugdunum 1643: Laurentius Anisson.

Avendaño, Diego de, *Thesaurus indicus seu generalis instructor pro regimine conscientiae, in iis quae ad Indias spectant*, Antverpiae 1668: Iacobus Meursius.

Avendaño, Diego de, *Problemata theologica*, Antverpiae 1668: Engelbert Gymnicus.

Avendaño, Diego de, *Cursus consummatus, sive recognitiones theologiae expositivae scholasticae*, Antverpiae 1686: Engelbert Gymnicus.

Avendaño, Diego de, *Thesaurus indicus*, ed. and Spanish trans. Muñoz García, Ángel, Pamplona 2001.

Ayanz, Antonio de, "Breve relación de los agravios que reciben los indios ... (1596)", in Aldea Vaquero, Quintín (ed.), *El indio peruano y la defensa de sus derechos (1596–1630)*, Madrid 1993, 234–331.

Azor, Juan, *Institutionum moralium*, 3 vols., Roma: 1600–1611: Aloysius Zannettus, Alfonsus Ciacconius, Aegidius Spada.

Azpilcueta, Martín de, *Manual de confessores y penitentes*, Salamanca 1556: Andrea de Portonariis.

Baldus de Ubaldis, *Commentaria in primam digesti veteris partem*, Venetia 1577: Iuntas.

Báñez, Domingo, *De fide, spe et charitate, Catholico Regi Philippo II: Scholastica commentaria in Secundam secundae Angelici doctoris partem*, Salamanca 1584: S. Stephanus.

Barros, João de, *Decada primeira da Asia, dos feitos que os portugueses fizeram no descobrimento e conquista dos mares e terras do Oriente*, Lisboa 1552: Germão Galharde.

Bartolus of Sassoferrato, *In II. partem Digesti novi commentaria*, Basilea 1588: Officina Episcopiana.

Bassée, Éloi de la, *Flores totius theologiae practicae, tum sacramentalis, tum moralis*, Duaci 1637: Ioannes Serrurier.

Bobadilla, Jerónimo Castillo de, *Política para corregidores y señores de vasallos*, Madrid 1597: Luis Sanchez.

Castropalao, Fernando de, *Opus morale, de virtutibus, et utiis contrariis ... pars quarta*, Lugdunum 1649: Ioannes Baptista Devenet.

Charles II of Spain, "Decreto de Carlos II a Vicente Gonzaga, Gobernador del Consejo de Indias, Madrid, 5 julio 1685", in Jaca, Francisco José de Jaca, *Resolución sobre la libertad de los negros y sus originarios, en estado de paganos y después ya cristianos: La primera condena de la esclavitud en el pensamiento hispano*, ed. Pena González, Miguel Anxo, Madrid 2002, 339.

Chavez, Tomás de, *Summa sacramentorum ecclesiae, ex doctrina fratris Francisci a Victoria*, Roma 1567: Iulius Accoltus.

Council of the Indies (Consejo de Indias), "Oficio del Consejo de Indias a Carlos II, Madrid, 6 agosto 1685", in Jaca, Francisco José de, *Resolución sobre la libertad de los negros y sus originarios, en estado de paganos y después ya cristianos: La primera condena de la esclavitud en el pensamiento hispano*, ed. Pena González, Miguel Anxo, Madrid 2002, 339–341.

Council of the Indies (Consejo de Indias), "Oficio del Consejo de Indias a Carlos II, Madrid, 21 agosto 1685", in Jaca, Francisco José de, *Resolución sobre la libertad de los negros y sus originarios, en estado de paganos y después ya cristianos: La primera condena de la esclavitud en el pensamiento hispano*, ed. Pena González, Miguel Anxo, Madrid 2002, 349–354.

Covarruvias y Leyva, Diego de, *In librum quartum Decretalium epitome*, Salamanca 1556: Ioannes de Canova.

Covarruvias y Leyva, Diego de, *Opera omnia*, 2 vols., Francofortum 1592: Sigismundus Feyerabend.

Diana, Antonino, *Resolutionum moralium pars septima*, Lugdunum 1645: Gabriel Boissat & Laurentius Anisson.

Durand de Saint-Pourçain, *In quatuor libros sententiarum quaestionum resolutiones*, Paris 1508: [Anon.].

Ercilla y Zúñiga, Alonso de, *Primera, segunda, y tercera partes de La Araucana*, Madrid 1590: Pedro Madrigal.

Fagundez, Estevão, *In quinque praecepta decalogi*, 2 vols., Lugdunum 1640: Laurentius Anisson & Gabriel Boissat.

Fagundez, Estevão, *De iustitia et contractibus et de acquisitione et translatione dominii*, Lugdunum 1641: Laurentius Anisson & Gabriel Boissat.

Filliucci, Vincenzo, *Moralium quaestionum de christianis officiis et casibus conscientiae*, 2 vols., Lugdunum 1622: Iacobus Cardon & Petrus Cavellat.

Gratianus, *Decretum magistri gratiani*, ed. Friedberg, Aemilius, Leipzig 1879 (https://geschichte.digitale-sammlungen.de/decretum-gratiani/online/angebot).

Gregory IX (Ugolino di Conti), *Liber extravagantium decretalium* (*Decretales Gregorii IX*), ed. Friedberg, Aemilius, Leipzig 1879 (http://www.columbia.edu/cu/lweb/digital/collections/cul/texts/ldpd_6029936_002/index.html).

Gregory XIII (Ugo Boncompagni), "Populis ac nationibus" (1585), in Metzler, Josef (ed.), *America Pontificia: Primi saeculi evangelizationis 1493–1592: Documenta pontifica ex registris et minutis praesertim in archivo secreto vaticano existentibus*, Vatican City 1991, vol. 2, 1228–1230.

Grotius, Hugo, *De iure belli ac pacis*, ed. Barbeyrac, Jean, Amsterdam 1720.

Hohberg, Wolf Helmhardt von, *Georgica Curiosa, das ist, Umständlicher Bericht und klarer Unterricht von dem Adelichen Land- und Feld-Leben*, Nürnberg 1682: Johann Friedrich Endter & Michael Endter.

Jaca, Francisco de, *Resolución sobre la libertad de los negros y sus originarios, en estado de paganos y después ya cristianos: La primera condena de la esclavitud en el pensamiento hispano*, ed. Pena González, Miguel Anxo, Madrid 2002.

Justinian I, *Corpus iuris civilis*, in Lassard, Yves and Alexandr Koptev (eds.), *The Roman Law Library* (https://droitromain.univ-grenoble-alpes.fr/).

Konetzke, Richard, *Colección de documentos para la historia de la formación social de Hispanoamérica, 1493–1810*, 3 vols., Madrid 1953–1962.

Las Casas, Bartolomé de, *De regia potestate o derecho de autodeterminación*, ed. Pereña, Luciano, José Manuel Pérez Prendes, Vidal Abril and Joaquin Azcarraga, Madrid 1969.

Las Siete Partidas del Sabio Rey Don Alonso el Nono, nuevamente glosadas por el licenciado Gregorio López, 4 vols., Salamanca 1555: Andrea de Portonariis.

Ledesma, Martín de, *Secunda quartae*, Coimbra 1560: Ioannes Alvarus.

Ledesma, Pedro de, *De magno matrimonii sacramento*, Salmantica 1592: Ioannes & Andera Renaut.

Leyes de Toro, Salamanca 1505: Pedro de Pascua (https://digibug.ugr.es/handle/10481/16415).

Lugo, Juan de, *De iustitia et iure*, Lugdunum 1642: Petrus Prost.

Machado de Chavez, Juan, *Perfecto confesor y cura de almas*, 2 vols., Madrid 1646: Francisco Martinez.

Mager von Schönberg, Martin, *De advocatia armata, sive clientelari patronorum iure et potestate*, Frankfurt 1625: Ludovicus König.

Mármol Carvajal, Luis del, *Historia del rebelión y castigo de los moriscos del reyno de Granada*, Malaga 1600: Iuan Rene.

Martyribus, Bartholomaeus de, *Theologica scripta*, ed. Almeida Rolo, Raul de, 6 vols., Braga 1973–1977.

Matienzo, Juan de, *Gobierno del Perú, 1567*, ed. Lohmann Villena, Guillermo, Paris 1967.

Mercado, Tomás de, *Suma de tratos y contratos*, ed. Sánchez-Albornoz, Nicolás, Madrid, 1977 (http://www.cervantesvirtual.com/nd/ark:/59851/bmc1c1t9).

Moirans, Epifanio de, *Servi liberi seu naturalis mancipiorum libertatis iusta defensio*, in Moirans, Epifanio de, *Siervos libres: Una propuesta antiesclavista a finales del siglo XVII*, ed. and Spanish trans. Pena González, Miguel Anxo, Carlos Baciero, José María Soto, Tarsicio de Azcona and J. Labiano, Madrid 2007, 1–221.

Molina, Luis de, *Concordia liberi arbitrii cum gratiae donis, divina praescientia, providentia, praedestinatione, et reprobatione, ad nonnullos primae partis D. Thomae articulos*, Olyssipone 1588: Antonius Riberius.

Molina, Luis de, *De iustitia et iure, Tomus primus* [= vol. 1], Moguntia 1614: Balthasar Lippius.

Molina, Luis de, *De iustitia et iure, Tomi tertii pars posterior* [= vol. 3.2], Colonia Agrippina 1614: Hermann Mylius.

Molina, Luis de, *De iustitia et iure, Tomus quartus* [= vol. 4], Colonia Agrippina 1614: Hermann Mylius.

Molina, Luis de, *De iustitia et iure: Über Gerechtigkeit und Recht*, ed. and trans. Kaufmann, Matthias, Alexander Loose and Danaë Simmermacher, 2 vols., Stuttgart-Bad Cannstatt 2019.

Molina, Luis de, *On Slavery and the Slave Trade*: De Iustitia et Iure, *Book I, Treatise 2, Disputations 32–40*, trans. Schwartz, Daniel and Jörg Tellkamp, Washington D.C. 2024.

Oliveira, Fernando, *Arte da guerra do mar*, Coimbra 1555: Iohão Aluerez.

Oliveira, Fernando, *Arte da guerra do mar* [The Art of War at Sea] (1555), trans. Igor Knezevic with the assistance of Rich Lizardo, in Cardim, Perdro and Nuno Gonçalo Monteiro (eds.), *Political Thought in Portugal and its Empire, c. 1500–1800*, (Cambridge: Cambridge University Press, 2021), 82–86.

Palacio, Miguel de, *Praxis theologica de contractibus et restitutionibus*, Salmantica 1585: Ioannes Ferdinandus.

Palacio, Miguel de, *Disputationes in quartum librum Sententiarum*, 2 vols., Salmantica 1577–1579: Ildefonsus à Neyla, Didacus à Benavides.

"Parecer de los Padres de la Compañía de Jesús … (1599)", in Aldea Vaquero, Quintín (ed.), *El indio peruano y la defensa de sus derechos (1596–1630)* (Madrid: CSIC, 1993), 335–344.

Peña, Juan de la, "An sit iustum bellum adversus insulanos (1560)", ed. in Pereña, Luciano Vicente, *Misión de España en América: 1540–1560*, Madrid 1956, 268–305.

Pérez, Fernando, "De acquisitione dominii in homines, sectio 1 [1587]", ed. and Portuguese trans. Tarrío, Ana Maria and Madalena Brito, in Calafate, Pedro and Ricardo Ventura (eds.), *A Escola Ibérica da Paz nas Universidades de Coimbra e Évora (século XVI): Volume III: Da restituição: Sobre a propriedade e a origem do poder civil*, Coimbra 2015, 324–381.

Pérez, Fernando, "Non nulla ante materiam de restitutione traditam a sapientissimo Doctore Patre Ferdinando Perez Anno Domini 1588", ed. and Portuguese trans. Tarrío, Ana Maria and Madalena Brito, in Calafate, Pedro and Ricardo Ventura (eds.), *A Escola Ibérica da Paz nas Universidades de Coimbra e Évora (século XVI): Volume III: Da restituição: Sobre a propriedade e a origem do poder civil*, Coimbra 2015, 382–495.

Rebello, Fernão, *Opus de obligationibus iustitiae, religionis et charitatis*, Lugdunum 1608: Hotarius Cardon.

Recopilacion de las Leyes destos Reynos, hecha por mandado de la Magestad Catholica del Rey don Philippe Segundo nuestro Senor, Alcalá de Henares 1569: Andres de Angulo.

Saliceto, Bartolomeo da, *Ad V., VI., VII., VIII. et IX. libros Codicis commentarii*, Lugduni 1560: Semanius.

Salón, Miguel Bartolomé, *Commentariorum in disputationem de iustitia … tomus primus*, Venetia 1592: Damianus Zenarius.

Sánchez, Tomás, *Disputationum de sancto matrimonii sacramento*, vol. 1, Genua 1602: Iosephus Pavone.

Sánchez, Tomás, *Disputationum de sancto matrimonii sacramento*, vol. 2, Madritus 1605: Ludovicus Sanchez.

Sánchez, Tomás, *Consilia, seu opuscula moralia duobus tomis contenta*, vol. 2, Lugdunum 1634: Iacobus Prost.

Sandoval, Alonso de, *Naturaleza, policia sagrada I profana, costumbres I ritos, disciplina I catechismo evangelico de todos etiopes*, Sevilla 1627: Francisco de Lira.

Sandoval, Alonso de, *Tomo primero De instauranda Aethiopum salute, historia de Aethiopia, naturaleça, policia sagrada y profana …*, Madrid 1647: Alonso de Paredes.

Seneca, *Epistles, Volume I: Epistles 1–65*, ed. and trans. Gummere, Richard M., Cambridge, MA 1917.

Seneca, *Moral Essays*, ed. and trans. Basore, John W., 3 vols., Cambridge, MA 1928–1935.

Silva, Juan de, *Advertencias importantes, acerca del buen govierno, y administracion de las Indias, asi en lo espiritual, como en lo temporal*, Madrid 1621: Viuda de Fernando Correa Montenegro.

Silva, Juan de, *Los Memoriales del padre Silva sobre predicación pacífica y repartimientos*, ed. Castañeda Delgado, Paulino, Madrid 1983.

Simões, Pedro, *Materia de restitutione explicata a doctissimo magistro patre Petro Simoes ex Societate Iesu Anno 1585*, ed. and Portuguese trans. Maurício, Sara and José Carlos de Miranda, in Calafate, Pedro and Ricardo Ventura (eds.), *A Escola Ibérica da Paz nas Universidades de Coimbra e Évora (século XVI): Volume III: Da restituição: Sobre a propriedade e a origem do poder civil*, Coimbra 2015, 224–323.

Solórzano y Pereira, Juan de, *Disputationem De indiarum iure, sive de iusta indiarum occidentalium inquisitione, acquisitione, et retentione*, Matritum 1629: Franciscus Martinez.

Solórzano y Pereira, Juan de, *Tomum alterum de indiarum iure, sive de iusta indiarum occidentalium gubernatione*, Matritum 1639: Franciscus Martinez.

Solórzano y Pereira, Juan de, *Política indiana*, ed. Ochoa Brun, Miguel Ángel, 5 vols. (Madrid: Ediciones Atlas, 1972).

Solórzano y Pereira, Juan de, *De indiarum iure* (*Liber III: De retentione indiarum*), ed. and Spanish trans. Baciero, Carlos, Francisco Cantelar, Antonio García, Jesús María García Añoveros, Francisco Maseda, Luciano Pereña and José Manuel Pérez-Prendes, Madrid 1994.

Soto, Domingo de, *In causa pauperum deliberatio*, Venetia 1547: [Anon.].

Soto, Domingo de, *In quartum sententiarum commentarii*, 2 vols., Salmantica 1569: Ioannes Baptista à Terranova.

Soto, Domingo de, *Relección "De Dominio"*, ed. and Spanish trans. Brufau Prats, Granada 1964.

Soto, Domingo de, *De iustitia et iure libri decem*, Salmantica 1556: Andreas à Portonariis.

Suárez, Francisco, *Commentariorum ac disputationum in tertiam partem Divi Thomae, Tomus tertius* [= vol. 3], Moguntia 1619: Balthasar Lippius.

Suárez, Francisco, *Commentariorum ac disputationum in tertiam partem Divi Thomae, Tomus quartus* [= vol. 4], Lugdunum 1613: Horatius Cardon.

Suárez, Francisco, *Defensio fidei catholicae*, Conimbrica 1613: Didacus Gomez de Loureyro.

Suárez, Francisco, *De legibus ac deo legislatore*, ed. and German trans. Bach, Oliver, Norbert Brieskorn and Gideon Stiening, 7 vols., Stuttgart-Bad Cannstatt 2013–2027.

The Holy Bible, King James Version, in King James Bible Online (www.kingjamesbibleonline.org).

Trigault, Nicolas, *De christiana expeditione apud Sinas*, Augusta Vindelicorum 1615: Christoph Mangius.

Trigault, Nicolas, *China in the Sixteenth Century: The Journals of Matthew Ricci 1583–1610*, trans. Gallagher, Louis J., New York 1953.

Vaca de Castro, Cristóbal, "Ordenanzas de tambos", in *Revista Histórica: Órgano del Instituto Histórico del Perú*, 3 (1908), 472–492.

Vázquez de Menchaca, Fernando, *Controversarium illustrium usuque frequentium libri tres*, Francofurtus ad Maenum 1572: Sigismundus Feierabend.

Vázquez, Gabriel, *Commentariorum ac disputationum in tertiam partem S. Thomae, tomus secundus*, Ingolstadium 1612: Martinus Nutius et Joannes Hertsroy.

Vitoria, Francisco de, *Relectiones theologicae XII*, 2 vols., Lugdunum 1557: Iacobus Boyerius.

Vitoria, Francisco de, *Comentarios a la Secunda secundae de Santo Tomás*, ed. Beltrán de Heredia, Vicente, 6 vols., Salamanca 1932–1952.

Vitoria, Francisco de, *Political Writings*, ed. and trans. Pagden, Anthony and Jeremy Lawrance, Cambridge 1991.

Vitoria, Francisco de, *Relecciones jurídicas y teológicas*, ed. and Spanish trans. Fernández-Largo, Antonio Osuna, Jesús Cordero Pando, Mauro Mantovani, Ramón Hernández Martín, Simona Langella and Ángel Martínez Casado, 2 vols., Salamanca 2017.

Zurara [Azurara], Gomes Eanes de, *The Chronicle of the Discovery and Conquest of Guinea*, ed. and trans. Beazley, Charles Raymond and Edgar Prestage, 2 vols. (London: Hakluyt Society, 1896–1869).

Literature

Abulafia, David, *The Discovery of Mankind: Atlantic Encounters in the Age of Columbus*, New Haven 2008.

Abulafia, David, *The Great Sea: A Human History of the Mediterranean*, Oxford 2011.

Adelman, Jeremy, "What is Global Histoy Now?" *Aeon*, 2 March 2017 (https://aeon.co/essays/is-global-history-still-possible-or-has-it-had-its-moment).

Adorno, Rolena, *Colonial Latin American Literature: A Very Short Introduction*, Oxford 2011.

Agamben, Giogrio, *Homo sacer: Il potere sovrano e la nuda vita*, Turin 2005.

Aichele, Alexander and Matthias Kaufmann, "Introduction", in Kaufmann, Matthias and Alexander Aichele (eds.), *A Companion to Luis de Molina*, Leiden 2014, xiii–xxxviii.

Allemann, Daniel, "Empire and the Right to Preach the Gospel in the School of Salamanca, 1535–1560", in *Historical Journal* 62:1 (2019), 35–55.

Allemann, Daniel, "Re-Reading Vitoria", in *Rechtsgeschichte—Legal History* 27 (2019), 338–340.

Allemann, Daniel, "After Vitoria: Natural Law and the Spanish Ideology of Empire", in Somo, Mark and Anne Peters (eds.), *The State of Nature: Histories of an Idea*, Leiden 2022, 82–113.

Allemann, Daniel, "Sklaverei, Heirat und 'Menschenrechte' in der iberischen Welt des 16. und 17. Jahrhunderts", in *Historische Zeitschrift* 317:2 (2023), 311–341.

Allemann, Daniel, "Review of José Lingna Nafafé, *Lourenço da Silva Mendonça and the Black Atlantic Abolitionist Movement in the Seventeenth Century*", in *Zeitschrift für Historische Forschung* 51:2 (2024), 381–382.

Alonso-Lasheras, Diego, *Luis de Molina's* De Iustitia et Iure: *Justice as Virtue in an Economic Context*, Leiden 2011.
Amorosa, Paolo, *Rewriting the History of the Law of Nations: How James Brown Scott Made Francisco de Vitoria the Founder of International Law*, Oxford 2019.
Andrés-Gallego, José and Jesús María García Añoveros, *La iglesia y la esclavitud de los negros*, Pamplona 2002.
Armenteros Martínez, Iván, *La esclavitud en Barcelona a fines de la Edad Media (1479–1516): El impacto de la primera trata atlántica en un mercado tradicional de esclavos* (Ph.D. Thesis), Barcelona 2012 (https://digital.csic.es/handle/10261/65489).
Armitage, David, "What's the Big Idea? Intellectual History and the *Longue Durée*", in *History of European Ideas* 38:4 (2012), 493–507.
Armitage, David, *Civil Wars: A History in* Ideas, New Haven 2017.
Aydin, Cemil, *The Idea of the Muslim World: A Global Intellectual History*, Cambridge, MA 2017.
Azevedo Alves, André and José Manuel Moreira, *The Salamanca School*, New York 2010.
Barrientos García, José, "El pensamiento económico en la perspectiva filosófico-teológica", in Gómez Camacho, Francisco and Ricardo Robledo (eds.), *El pensamiento económico en la Escuela de Salamanca*, Salamanca 1998, 93–121.
Barrientos García, José, *Repertorio de moral económica, 1526–1670: La Escuela de Salamanca y su proyección*, Pamplona 2011.
Becker, Anna, "Gender in the History of Early Modern Political Thought", in *The Historical Journal* 60:4 (2017), 843–863.
Becker, Anna, *Gendering the Renaissance Commonwealth*, Cambridge 2020.
Becker Lorca, Arnulf, *Mestizo International Law: A Global Intellectual History 1842–1933*, Cambridge 2014.
Beckert, Sven, *Empire of Cotton: A Global History*, New York 2014.
Belda Plans, Juan, *La Escuela de Salamanca y la renovación de la teología en el siglo XVI*, Madrid 2000.
Belmessous, Saliha, "Introduction: The Problem of Indigenous Claim Making in Colonial History", in Belmessous, Saliha (ed.), *Native Claims: Indigenous Law against Empire, 1500–1920*, Oxford 2012, 3–18.
Bennett, Herman L., *Africans in Colonial Mexico: Absolutism, Christianity, and Afro-Creole Consciousness, 1570–1640*, Bloomington 2003.
Bennett, Herman L., *African Kings and Black Slaves: Sovereignty and Dispossession in the Early Modern Atlantic*, Philadelphia 2019.
Bentancor, Orlando, *The Matter of Empire: Metaphysics and Mining in Colonial Peru*, Pittsburgh 2017.
Benton, Lauren, *A Search for Sovereignty: Law and Geography in European Empires, 1400–1900*, Cambridge 2010.
Benton, Lauren, "Afterward: The Space of Political Community and the Space of Au-

thority", in *Conceptions of Space in Intellectual History*, special issue of *Global Intellectual History* 3:2 (2018), 254–265.

Benton, Lauren, "The Legal Logic of Wars of Conquest: Truces and Betrayal in the Early Modern World", in *Duke Journal of Comparative & International Law* 28 (2018), 425–448.

Benton, Lauren, "Beyond Anachronism: Histories of International Law and Global Legal Politics", in *Journal of the History of International Law* 21:1 (2019), 7–40.

Benton, Lauren, *They Called It Peace: Worlds of Imperial Violence*, Princeton 2024.

Benton, Lauren and Adam Clulow, "Introduction: The Long, Strange History of Protection", in Benton, Lauren, Adam Clulow and Bain Attwood (eds.), *Protection and Empire: A Global History*, Cambridge 2018, 1–9.

Benton, Lauren and Adam Clulow, "Webs of Protection and Interpolity Zones in the Early Modern World", in Benton, Lauren, Adam Clulow and Bain Attwood (eds.), *Protection and Empire: A Global History*, Cambridge 2018, 49–71.

Benton, Lauren and Adam Clulow, "Interpolity Law and Jurisdictional Politics", in *Law and History Review* 42:2 (2024), 197–209.

Benton, Lauren and Lisa Ford, *Rage for Order: The British Empire and the Origins of International Law, 1800–1850*, Cambridge, MA 2016.

Benton, Lauren and Richard J. Ross, "Empires and Legal Pluralism: Jurisdiction, Sovereignty, and Political Imagination in the Early Modern World", in Benton, Lauren and Richard J. Ross, *Legal Pluralism and Empires, 1500–1850*, New York 2013, 1–17.

Benton, Lauren and Benjamin Straumann, "Acquiring Empire by Law: From Roman Doctrine to Early Modern European Practice", in *Law and History Review* 28:1 (2010), 1–38.

Birr, Christiane, "Rebellische Väter, versklavte Kinder: Der Aufstand der Morisken von Granada (1568–1570) in der juristisch-theologischen Diskussion der Schule von Salamanca", in De Benedictis, Angela and Karl Härter (eds.), *Revolten und politische Verbrechen zwischen dem 12. und 19. Jahrhundert: Rechtliche Reaktionen und juristisch-politische Diskurse = Revolts and Political Crime from the 12th to the 19th Century: Legal Responses and Juridical-Political Discourses*, Frankfurt 2013, 281–317.

Birr, Christiane, "Recht als Argument in Bartolomé de Las Casas" *Tratado sobre los indios que han sido hechos esclavos*, in Bunge, Kirstin, Stefan Schweighöfer, Anselm Spindler and Andreas Wagner (eds.), *Kontroversen um das Recht: Beiträge zur Rechtsbegründung von Vitoria bis Suárez = Contending for Law: Arguments about the Foundation of Law from Vitoria to Suárez*, Stuttgart-Bad Cannstatt 2013, 93–123.

Birr, Christiane, "Tradition and Innovation in Knowledge Production: Gregorio López' Commentary on the Siete Partidas (1555)", in *Rechtsgeschichte—Legal History*, 32 (2024), 81–106.

Blackburn, Robin, *The Making of New World Slavery: From the Baroque to the Modern, 1492–1800*, 2nd ed., London 2010.

Blackmore, Josiah, *Moorings: Portuguese Expansion and the Writing of Africa*, Minneapolis 2009.

Blumenthal, Debra, *Enemies and Familiars: Slavery and Mastery in Fifteenth-Century Valencia*, Ithaca 2009.

Bono, Salvatore, *Schiavi: Una storia mediterranea* (*XVI–XIX secolo*), Bologna 2016.

Bouza, Fernando, Pedro Cardim and Antonio Feros (eds.), *The Iberian World, 1450–1820* (London: Routledge 2019).

Bowser, Frederick P., *The African Slave in Colonial Peru 1524–1650*, Stanford 1974.

Brading, David A., *The First America: The Spanish Monarchy, Creole Patriots, and the Liberal State 1492–1867*, Cambridge 1991.

Bragagnolo, Manuela, "Managing Legal Knowledge in Early Modern Times: Martín de Azpilcueta's *Manual de Confesores* and the Phenomenon of Epitomisation", in Duve, Thomas and Otto Danwerth (eds.), *Knowledge of the Pragmatici: Legal and Moral Theological Literature and the Foundation of Early Modern Ibero-America*, Leiden 2020, 187–242.

Braude, Benjamin, "The Sons of Noah and the Construction of Ethnic and Geographical Identities in the Medieval and Early Modern Periods", in *The William and Mary Quarterly* 54:1 (1997), 103–142.

Braun, Harald E. and Edward Vallance, "Introduction", in Braun, Harald E. and Edward Vallance (eds.), *Contexts of Conscience in Early Modern Europe, 1500–1700*, Basingstoke 2004, x–xviii.

Brett, Annabel S., *Liberty, Right and Nature: Individual Rights in Later Scholastic Thought*, Cambridge 1997.

Brett, Annabel S., "The Good Man and the Good Citizen: Miguel de Palacios and an Aristotelian Question in the Spanish Second Scholastic", in Grunert, Frank and Kurt Seelmann (eds.), *Die Ordnung der Praxis: Neue Studien zur Spanischen Spätscholastik*, Tübingen 2001, 245–268.

Brett, Annabel S., "What is Intellectual History Now?", in Cannadine, David (ed.), *What is History Now?*, Basingstoke 2002, 113–131.

Brett, Annabel S., "Scholastic Political Thought and the Modern Concept of the State", in Brett, Annabel S. and James Tully with Holly Hamilton-Bleakley (eds.), *Rethinking the Foundations of Modern Political Thought*, Cambridge 2006, 130–148.

Brett, Annabel S., *Changes of State: Nature and the Limits of the City in Early Modern Natural Law*, Princeton 2011.

Brett, Annabel S., "Luis de Molina on Law and Power", in Kaufmann, Matthias and Alexander Aichele (eds.), *A Companion to Luis de Molina*, Leiden 2014, 155–181.

Brett, Annabel S., "Human Rights and the Thomist Tradition", in Slotte, Pamela and Miia Halme-Tuomisaari (eds.), *Revisiting the Origins of Human Rights*, Cambridge 2015, 82–101.

Brett, Annabel S., "Later Scholastic Philosophy of Law", in Miller, Fred D., Jr. and Carrie-

Ann Biondi (eds.), *A History of the Philosophy of Law from the Ancient Greeks to the Scholastics*, Dordrecht 2015, 335–375.

Brett, Annabel S., "Rights of and over Animals in the *Ius naturae et gentium* (Sixteenth and Seventeenth Centuries)", in *AJIL Unbound* 111 (2017), 257–261.

Brett, Annabel S., "Doing Without an Original: A Commentary on Martti Koskenniemi", in Etinson, Adam (ed.), *Human Rights: Moral or Political?*, Oxford 2018, 61–67.

Brion Davis, David, *Inhuman Bondage: The Rise and Fall of New World Slavery*, Oxford 2006.

Brieskorn, Norbert, "Die Sklaverei in der Beurteilung des P. Luis de Molina S.J.", in Meier, Johannes (ed.), *"… usque ad ultimum terrae": Die Jesuiten und die transkontinentale Ausbreitung des Christentums 1540–1733*, Göttingen 2000, 85–97.

Brufau Prats, Jaime, *La escuela de Salamanca ante el descubrimiento del nuevo mundo*, Salamanca 1989.

Brunner, Otto, "Das 'ganze Haus' und die alteuropäische Ökonomik", in *Neue Wege der Verfassungs- und Sozialgeschichte*, by Otto Brunner, 3rd ed. Göttingen 1980, 103–127.

Bunge, Kirstin, *Gleichheit und Gleichmass: Zur Rechtsphilosophie von Francisco de Vitoria*, Stuttgart-Bad Cannstatt 2018.

Burciaga Campos, José A., "Corona española, política económica e indígenas a través de la normatividad de las cédulas reales en la Audiencia de la Plata de los Charcas, siglo XVI", in Duve, Thomas (ed.), *Actas del XIX congreso del Instituto Internacional de Historia del Derecho Indiano*, Madrid 2017, vol. 2, 961–982.

Burgio, Santo, "Antonino Diana e la rivolta del Portogallo: Una testimonianza sulla crisi di metà seicento", in *Siculorum Gymnasium: Rassegna della Facoltà di Lettere e Filosofia dell'Università di Catania* 50:1–2 (1997), 89–104.

Burgio, Santo, *Teologia barocca: Il probabilismo in Sicilia nell'epoca di Filippo IV*, Catania 1998.

Burns, James H., "Scholasticism: Survival and Revival", in Burns, James H. and Mark Goldie (eds.), *The Cambridge History of Political Thought 1450–1700*, Cambridge 1991, 132–156.

Calafate, Pedro, "A antropologia portuguesa da época dos descobrimientos—os direitos dos povos descobertos", in Calafate, Pedro (ed.), *História do pensamento filosófico português*, Lisbon 2001, vol. 2, 35–49.

Calafate, Pedro and Álvaro Balsas, "Apresentação—Escola Ibérica da Paz: Direito Natural e Dignidade Humana", in *Revista Portuguesa de Filosofia* 75:2 (2019), 763–776.

Calafate, Pedro and Ramón Emilio Mandado Gutiérrez (eds.), *Escola Ibérica da Paz: A consciência crítica da conquista e colonização da América, 1511–1694 = Escuela Ibérica de la Paz: La consciencia crítica de la conquista y colonización de América, 1511–1694*, Santander 2014.

Calafate, Pedro and Ricardo Ventura, "The Iberian School of Peace: Natural Law and Human Dignity", in *Revista Portuguesa de Filosofia* 75:2 (2019), 793–836.

Cardim, Pedro, *Portugal y la monarquía hispánica (ca. 1550–ca. 1715)*, trans. Saúl Martínez Bermejo, Madrid 2017.

Cardim, Pedro and Nuno Gonçalo Monteiro, "Introduction", in Cardim, Pedro and Nuno Gonçalo Monteiro (eds.), *Political Thought in Portugal and its Empire, c. 1500–1800*, Cambridge 2012, 1–44.

Castelnau-L'Estoile, Charlotte, "Le mariage des infidèles au XVIe siècle: Doutes missionnaires et autorité pontificale", in *Mélange de l'École française de Rome* 121:1 (2009), 95–121.

Cavanaugh, Stephanie M., "Litigating for Liberty: Enslaved Morisco Children in Sixteenth-Century Valladolid", in *Renaissance Quarterly* 70 (2017), 1282–1320.

Chafuen, Alejandro Antonio, *Faith and Liberty: The Economic Thought of the Late Scholastics*, 2nd ed., Lanham, MD 2003.

Chamberlain, Robert S., "Review of Miguel de Agia, *Servidumbres personales de indios (1946)*", in *The Hispanic American Historical Review* 27:2 (1947), 300–304.

Chakraborty, Titas, "Slavery in the Indian Ocean World", in Pargas, Damian A. and Juliane Schiel (eds.), *The Palgrave Handbook of Global Slavery throughout History*, Cham 2023, 339–357.

Clayton, Lawrence, "Bartolomé de las Casas and the African Slave Trade", in *History Compass* 7:6 (2009), 1526–1541.

Cohen, Deborah and Peter Mandler, "*The History Manifesto*: A Critique", in *The American Historical Review* 120:2 (2015), 530–542.

Conrad, Sebastian, *What is Global History?*, Princeton 2016.

Cook, Karoline P., *Forbidden Passages: Muslims and Moriscos in Colonial Spanish America*, Philadelphia 2016.

Cooper, Frederick, "How Global Do We Want Our Intellectual History to Be?" in Moyn, Samuel and Andrew Sartori (eds.), *Global Intellectual History*, New York 2013, 283–294.

Costello, Frank Bartholomew, *The Political Philosophy of Luis de Molina, S.J. (1535–1600)*, Rome 1974.

Coxito, Amândio A., "Luis de Molina e a escravatura", in *Revista Filosófica de Coimbra* 15 (1999), 117–136.

Coxito, Amândio A. and Maria Luisa Couto Soares, "Pedro da Fonseca", in Calafate, Pedro (ed.), *História do pensamento filosófico português*, Lisbon 2001, vol. 2, 455–502.

Craveiro da Silva, Lúcio, "Luis de Molina", in Calafate, Pedro (ed.), *História do pensamento filosófico português*, Lisbon 2001, vol. 2, 547–557.

Cruz Cruz, Juan, "Predestination as Transcendent Theology: Molina and the First Molinism", in Kaufmann, Matthias and Alexander Aichele (eds.), *A Companion to Luis de Molina*, Leiden 2014, 89–121.

Cuena Boy, Francisco, "El castigo de las injurias causadas a los indios: Una página característica de Diego de Avendaño", in *Cuadernos de Historia del Derecho* 19 (2012), 9–25.

Cuena Boy, Francisco, *De servitute: Estudios jurídicos sobre la esclavitud en Roma, Castilla, Portugal y las Indias*, Granada 2024.

Danwerth, Otto, "*Política para Corregidores y Señores de Vasallos …*", in Dauchy, Serge, Georges Martyn, Anthony Musson, Heikki Pihlajamäki and Alain Wijffels (eds.), *The Formation and Transmission of Western Legal Culture: 150 Books that Made the Law in the Age of Printing*, Cham 2016, 144–148.

Davis, Robert C., *Christian Slaves, Muslim Masters: White Slavery in the Mediterranean, The Barbary Coast, and Italy, 1500–1800*, Basingstoke 2003.

D'Avray, David, "Slavery, Marriage and the Holy See: From the Ancient World to the New World", in *Rechtsgeschichte—Legal History* 20 (2012), 347–351.

Deardorff, Max, "¿Quién es morisco? Desde cristiano nuevo a cristiano viejo de moros: Categorías de diferenciación en el Reino de Granada (siglo XVI)", in *forum historiae iuris: Erste Europäische Internetzeitschrift für Rechtsgeschichte*, 26 March 2019 (https://forhistiur.de/2018-12-deardorff).

Deckers, Daniel, *Gerechtigkeit und Recht: Eine historisch-kritische Untersuchung der Gerechtigkeitslehre des Francisco de Vitoria* (1483–1546), Freiburg 1991.

Decock, Wim, *Theologians and Contract Law: The Moral Transformation of the* ius commune (*ca. 1500–1650*), Leiden 2013.

Decock, Wim, "Spanish Neo-Scholasticism", in Strawn, Brent A. (ed.), *The Oxford Encyclopedia of the Bible and Law*, Oxford 2015, vol. 2, 325–331.

Decock, Wim, "Collaborative Legal Pluralism: Confessors as Law Enforcers in Mercado's Advice on Economic Governance (1571)", in *Rechtsgeschichte—Legal History* 25 (2017), 103–114.

Decock, Wim, "Martín de Azpilcueta", in Domingo, Rafael and Javier Martínez-Torrón (eds.), *Great Christian Jurists in Spanish History*, Cambridge 2018, 116–133.

Díaz Ceballos, Jorge, *Poder compartido: Repúblicas urbanas, monarquía y conversación en Castilla del Oro, 1508–1573*, Madrid 2020.

Domingo, Rafael, "Tomás Sánchez", in Domingo, Rafael and Javier Martínez-Torrón (eds.), *Great Christian Jurists in Spanish History*, Cambridge 2018, 225–238.

Doyle, John P., *Collected studies on Francisco Suárez, S.J. (1548–1617)*, ed. Salas, Victor M., Leuven 2010.

Dunn, John, "Why We Need a Global History of Political Thought", in Kapossy, Béla, Isaac Nakhimovsky, Sophus A. Reinert and Richard Whatmore (eds.), *Markets, Morals, Politics: Jealousy of Trade and the History of Political Thought*, Cambridge, MA 2018, 285–309.

Dürr, Renate, "'German Home Towns' Reloaded oder wie weit kommt man mit einer postkolonialen Neuinterpretation des Alten Reiches?", in *Zeitschrift für Historische Forschung* 52:1 (2025), 47–67.

Duve, Thomas, "Der blinde Fleck der 'Oeconomia'? Wirtschaft und Soziales in der Frühen Neuzeit", in Kervégan, Jean-François and Heinz Mohnhaupt (eds.), *Wirtschaft und Wirtschaftstheorien in Rechtsgeschichte und Philosophie*, Frankfurt am Main 2004, 29–61.

Duve, Thomas, *Sonderrecht in der Frühen Neuzeit: Studien zum* ius singulare *und den* privilegia miserabilium personarum, senum *und* indorum *in Alter und Neuer Welt*, Frankfurt am Main 2008.

Duve, Thomas, "Kanonisches Recht und die Ausbildung allgemeiner Vertragslehren in der Spanischen Spätscholastik", in Condorelli, Orazio, Franck Roumy and Mathias Schmoeckel (eds.), *Der Einfluss der Kanonistik auf die europäische Rechtskultur*, Köln 2009, vol. 1, 389–408.

Duve, Thomas, "Salamanca in Amerika", in *Zeitschrift der Savigny-Stiftung für Rechtsgeschichte: Germanistische Abteilung* 132 (2015), 116–151.

Duve, Thomas, "The School of Salamanca: A Case of Global Knowledge Production", in Duve, Thomas, José Luis Egío and Christiane Birr (eds.), *The School of Salamanca: A Case of Global Knowledge Production*, ed. by Thomas Duve, Leiden 2021, 1–42.

Duve, Thomas, "Pragmatic Normative Literature and the Production of Normative Knowledge in the Early Modern Iberian Empires (16th–17th Centuries)", in Duve, Thomas and Otto Danwerth (eds.), *Knowledge of the Pragmatici: Legal and Moral Theological Literature and the Foundation of Early Modern Ibero-America*, Leiden 2020, 1–39.

Egío, José Luis, "La consolidación del estatuto teológico-político del pagano amerindio en los maestros 'salmantinos' y sus discípulos novohispanos (1512–1593)", in *The School of Salamanca Working Paper Series*, 1 (2015), 1–65.

Ehalt, Rômulo da Silva, "Jesuit Arguments for Voluntary Slavery in Japan and Brazil", in *Revista Brasileira da História* 39:80 (2019), 1–22.

Eisenberg, José, "Cultural Encounters, Theoretical Adventures: The Jesuit Missions to the New World and the Justification of Voluntary Slavery", in *History of Political Thought* 24:3 (2003), 375–396.

Elliott, John H., *Empires of the Atlantic World: Britain and Spain in America 1492–1830*, New Haven 2006.

Epstein, Steven A., *Speaking of Slavery: Color, Ethnicity, and Human Bondage in Italy*, Ithaca 2001.

Estenssoro Fuchs, Juan Carlos, *Del paganismo a la santidad: La incorporación de los indios del Perú al catolicismo, 1532–1750*, trans. Gabriela Ramos, Lima 2003.

Fastiggi, Robert, "Fransico Suárez as Dogmatic Theologian", in Salas, Victor M. Salas and Robert L. Fastiggi (eds.)., *A Companion to Francisco Suárez*, Leiden 2015, 148–163.

Ferguson, Niall, *The Ascent of Money: A Financial History of the World*, New York 2008.

Fernández G., Enrique, "Avendaño, Diego de", in O'Neill, Charles E. and Joaquín M.

Domínguez (eds.), *Diccionario histórico de la Compañía de Jesús*, Rome 2001, vol. 1, 303.

Finley, Moses I., *Ancient Slavery and Modern Ideology*, Princeton 1988.

Fitzmaurice, Andrew, *Sovereignty, Property and Empire, 1500–2000*, Cambridge 2014.

Fitzmaurice, Andrew, "Context and the History of International Law", in *Journal of the History of International Law* 20:1 (2018), 5–30.

Flaig, Egon, *Weltgeschichte der Sklaverei*, 2nd ed., Munich 2011.

Fleming, Julia A., *Defending Probabilism: The Moral Theology of Juan Caramuel*, Washington, D.C. 2006.

Flores, Jorge, "The Iberian Empires, 1400 to 1800", in Bentley, Jerry H., Sanjay Subrahmanyam and Merry E. Wiesner-Hanks (eds.), *The Cambridge World History, Volume 6: The Construction of a Global World, 1400–1800 CE—Part 1: Foundations*, Cambridge 2015, 271–296.

Foucault, Michel, *Sécurité, territoire, population: Cours au Collège de France (1977–1978)*, Paris 2004,

Freamon, Bernard K., *Possessed by the Right Hand: The Problem of Slavery in Islamic Law and Muslim Cultures*, Leiden 2019.

Freddoso, Alfred J., "Introduction", in *Luis de Molina: On Divine Foreknowledge: Part IV of the* Concordia, ed. and trans. Freddoso, Alfred J., Ithaca 1988, 1–81.

Garcés, María Antonia, *Cervantes in Algiers: A Captive's Tale*, Nashville 2002.

García Añoveros, Jesús María, *El pensamiento y los argumentos sobre la esclavitud en europa en el siglo XVI y su aplicación a los Indios americanos y a los negros africanos*, Madrid 2000.

García Añoveros, Jesús María, "Luis de Molina y la esclavitud de los negros africanos en el siglo XVI", in *Revista de India* 60:219 (2000), 307–329.

García Hernán, Enrique, *Consejero de ambos mundos: Vida y obra de Juan de Solórzano Pereira (1575–1655)*, Madrid 2007

Getino, Luis G. Alonso, *El maestro fray Francisco de Vitoria: Su vida, su doctrina e influencia*, Madrid 1930.

Gil Montero, Raquel, "Free and Unfree Labour in the Colonial Andes in the Sixteenth and Seventeenth Centuries", in *IRSH* 56 (2011), 297–318.

Glare, P.G.W. (ed.), *Oxford Latin Dictionary*, 2 vols., Oxford 1968.

Goldenberg, David M., *The Curse of Ham: Race and Slavery in Early Judaism, Christianity, and Islam*, Princeton 2003.

Gómez Camacho, Francisco, *Economía y filosofía moral: La formación del pensamiento económico europeo en la escolástica española*, Madrid 1998.

González Casanovas, Ignacio, *Las dudas de la corona: La política de repartimientos para la minería de Potosí (1680–1732)*, Madrid 2000.

Grafton, Anthony, "José de Acosta: Renaissance Historiography and New World Humanity", in Martin, John Jeffries (ed.), *The Renaissance World*, New York 2007, 166–190.

Grant, Daragh, "Francisco de Vitoria and Alberico Gentili on the Juridical Status of Native American Polities", in *Renaissance Quarterly* 72 (2019), 910–952.

Graubart, Karen B., "*Pesa más la libertad*: Slavery, Legal Claims, and the History of Afro-Latin American Ideas", in *The William and Mary Quarterly* 78:3 (2021), 427–458.

Gray, Richard, "The Papacy and the Atlantic Slave Trade: Lourenço da Silva, the Capuchins and the Decisions of the Holy Office", in *Past & Present* 115:1 (1987), 52–68.

Green, Toby, *The Rise of the Trans-Atlantic Slave Trade in Western Africa, 1300–1589*, Cambridge 2012.

Green, Toby, *A Fistful of Shells: West Africa from the Rise of the Slave Trade to the Age of Revolution*, London 2019.

Green-Mercado, Mayte, *Visions of Deliverance: Moriscos and the Politics of Prophecy in the Early Modern Mediterranean*, Ithaca 2019.

Grice-Hutchinson, Marjorie, *Early Economic Thought in Spain, 1170–1740*, London 1978.

Groebner, Valentin, *Das Mittelalter hört nicht auf: Über historisches Erzählen*, Munich 2004.

Groebner, Valentin, *Who Are You? Identification, Deception, and Surveillance in Early Modern Europe*, trans. Mark Kyburz and John Peck, New York 2007.

Groebner, Valentin, "The Carnal Knowing of a Coloured Body: Sleeping with Arabs and Blacks in the European Imaginagion, 1300–1550", in Eliav-Feldon, Miriam, Benjamin Isaac and Joseph Ziegler (eds.), *The Origins of Racism in the West*, Cambridge 2009, 217–231.

Groebner, Valentin, "Europas Grenzen? Über Seife, Apfelstrudel, Cafés, Zigaretten und historische Ressourcen", in Hohlmann, Michael and Pierre Monet (eds.), *Café Europa: Vorträge und Debatten zur Identität Europas*, Göttingen 2021, 111–123.

Gruzinski, Serge, *Les quatre parties du monde: Histoire d'une mondialisation*, Paris 2006.

Guimarães Pinto, António, "Pérez, Fernando", in Carvalho, Mário Santiago de and Simone Guidi (eds.), *Conimbricenses.org Encyclopedia*, 11 June 2021 (https://www.conimbricenses.org/encyclopedia/perez-fernando).

Guldi, Jo and David Armitage, *The History Manifesto*, Cambridge 2014.

Haar, Christoph Philipp, "Tomás Sánchez and Late Scholastic Thought on Marriage and Political Virtue", in Bunge, Kirstin, Marko J. Fuchs, Danaë Simmermacher and Anselm Spindler (eds.), *The Concept of Law* (lex) *in the Moral and Political Thought of the "School of Salamanca"*, Leiden 2016, 81–105.

Haar, Christoph Philipp, *Natural and Political Conceptions of Community: The Role of the Household Society in Early Modern Jesuit Thought, c. 1590–1650*, Leiden 2019.

Haar, Christoph Philipp and Danaë Simmermacher, "The Foundation of the Human Being Regarded as a Legal Entity in the 'School of Salamanca': *Dominium* and *Ius* in the Thought of Vitoria and Molina", in *Jahrbuch für Recht und Ethik* 22 (2014), 445–483.

Hall, Catherine, "Review of Colin Kidd, *The Forging of Races*", in *The American Historical Review* 113:2 (2008), 458–459.

Hanß, Stefan, "Sklaverei im vormodernen Mediterraneum: Tendenzen aktueller Forschungen", in *Zeitschrift für Historische Forschung* 40:4 (2013), 623–661.

Harris, Wendell V., "Child Exposure in the Roman Empire", in *The Journal of Roman Studies* 84 (1994), 1–22.

Haug, Tilman, Nadir Weber and Christian Windler, "Einleitung", in Haug, Tilman, Nadir Weber and Christian Windler (eds.), *Protegierte und Protektoren: Asymmetrische politische Beziehungen zwischen Partnerschaft und Dominanz (16. bis frühes 20. Jahrhundert)*, Köln 2016, 9–27.

Hayek, Friedrich von, "Lecture to the Memory of Alfred Nobel, December 11, 1974" (https://www.nobelprize.org/prizes/economic-sciences/1974/hayek/lecture/).

Helmholz, Richard H., "Diego de Covarrubias y Leyva", in Domingo, Rafael and Javier Martínez-Torrón (eds.), *Great Christian Jurists in Spanish History*, Cambridge 2018, 174–190.

Heng, Geraldine, *The Invention of Race in the European Middle Ages*, Cambridge 2018.

Heras Santos, José Luis de las, *La justicia penal de los Asturias en la corona de Castilla*, Salamanca 1991.

Hernández Aparicio, Pilar, "La doctrina de Avendaño sobre los repartimientos de indios", in Cuesta Domingo, Mariano (ed.), *Proyección y presencia de Segovia en América*, Segovia 1992, 411–419.

Herrera Ángel, Martha, "Los pies de la república cristiana: La posición del indígena americano en Solórzano Pereira", in Bonnett Vélez, Diana and Felipe Castañeda (eds.), *Juan de Solórzano Pereira: Pensar la colonia desde la colonia*, Bogotá 2006, 79–108.

Herzog, Tamar, *Defining Nations: Immigration and Citizens in Early Modern Spanish America*, New Haven 2003.

Herzog, Tamar, "Enslaved as Outsiders, Enslaved as Property: Understanding Slavery in a Global and Early Modern Context", in *Rechtsgeschichte—Legal History* 32 (2024), 42–56.

Hendrickson, Jocelyn, *Leaving Iberia: Islamic Law and Christian Conquest in North West Africa*, Cambridge, MA 2021.

Hespanha, António Manuel, "Luís de Molina e a escravização dos negros", in *Análise Social* 35:157 (2001), 937–960.

Hofmeister Pich, Roberto, "Alonso de Sandoval S.J. (1576/1577–1652) and the Ideology of Black Slavery: Some Theological and Philosophical Arguments", in *Patristica et Mediaevalia* 36 (2015), 51–74.

Hofmeister Pich, Roberto, "The Aristotelian Background of Diego de Avendaño's Moral and Legal Thought", in *Patristica et Mediaevalia* 38 (2017), 53–88.

Hofmeister Pich, Roberto and Alfredo Santiago Culleton, "Introduction: The Challenge of Investigating Latin American Colonial Scholasticism", in Hofmeister Pich, Roberto and Alfredo Santiago Culleton (eds.), Scholastica Colonialis: *Reception and*

Development of Baroque Scholasticism in Latin America, 16th–18th Centuries, Rome 2016, 1–34.

Höffner, Joseph, *Kolonialismus und Evangelium: Spanische Kolonialethik im Goldenen Zeitalter*, 3rd ed., Tier 1972.

Hont, István, *Jealousy of Trade: International Competition and the Nation-State in Historical Perspective*, Cambridge, MA 2005.

Höpfl, Harro, *Jesuit Political Thought: The Society of Jesus and the State, c. 1540–1630*, Cambridge 2004.

Huber, Vitus, *Beute und Conquista: Die politische Ökonomie der Eroberung Neuspaniens*, Frankfurt am Main 2018.

Idoya Zorroza, Maria, "Some Reflections on the Ethical Rationality in the Economic Theory of the School of Salamanca", in Alejandro Nestor García, Alejandro, Mario Šilar and José M. Torralba (eds.), *Natural Law: Historical, Systematic and Juridical Approaches*, Newcastle upon Tyne 2008, 85–107.

Idoya Zorroza, Maria, "Un discípulo salmantino en Coimbra: Martín de Ledesma", in *Humanística e Teologíoa* 37:2 (2016), 159–183.

Ireton, Chloe L., "Black Africans' Freedom Litigation Suits to Define Just War and Just Slavery in the Early Spanish Empire", in *Renaissance Quarterly* 73:4 (2020), 1277–1319.

Ireton, Chloe L., "L'imaginaire éthiopien dans le premier monde hispanique: Esclavage et baptême dans le Catéchisme évangelique de Sandoval", in *Revue d'histoire moderne & contemporaine* 68:2 (2021), 104–130.

Ireton, Chloe L., *Slavery and Freedom in Black Thought in the Early Spanish Atlantic*, Cambridge 2025.

Isaac, Benjamin, Joseph Ziegler and Miriam Eliav-Feldon, "Introduction", in Eliav-Feldon, Miriam, Benjamin Isaac and Joseph Ziegler (eds.), *The Origins of Racism in the West*, Cambridge 2009, 1–31.

Jansen, Nils, *Theologie, Philosophie und Jurisprudenz in der spätscholastischen Lehre von der Restitution: Ausservertragliche Ausgleichsansprüche im frühneuzeitlichen Naturrechtsidskurs*, Tübingen 2013.

Jarra, Álvaro, *Guerra y sociedad en Chile: La transformación de la guerra de Arauco y la esclavitud de los indios*, 2nd ed., Santiago de Chile 1972.

Joner, Henrique, "Impressions of Luis de Molina about the Trade of African Slaves", in *Patristica et Mediaevalia* 36 (2015), 39–50.

Kaiser, Wolfgang, "Sprechende Ware: Gefangenenfreikauf und Sklavenhandel im frühneuzeitlichen Mittelmeerraum", in *Zeitschrift für Ideengeschichte* 3:2 (2009), 29–39.

Kapila, Shruti, "Global Intellectual History and the Indian Political", in McMahon, Darrin M. and Samuel Moyn (eds.), *Rethinking Modern European Intellectual History*, Oxford 2014, 253–274.

Kapila, Shruti, "Armitage on Civil Wars", in *Global Intellectual History* 4:3 (2019), 318–321.

Kattenberg, Lisa, *The Power of Necessity: Reason of State in the Spanish Monarchy, c. 1590–1650*, Cambridge 2023.

Kaufmann, Matthias, "Subjektive Rechte als Grenzen der Rechtssetzung bei Luis de Molina", in Bunge, Kirstin, Stefan Schweighöfer, Anselm Spindler and Andreas Wagner (eds.), *Kontroversen um das Recht: Beiträge zur Rechtsbegründung von Vitoria bis Suárez = Contending for Law: Arguments about the Foundation of Law from Vitoria to Suárez*, Stuttgart-Bad Cannstatt 2013, 291–310.

Kaufmann, Matthias, "Slavery between Law, Morality, and Economy", in Kaufmann, Matthias and Alexander Aichele (eds.), *A Companion to Luis de Molina*, Leiden 2014, 183–225.

Kelly, Celsus, "The Franciscan Missionary Plan for the Conversion to Christianity of the Natives of the Austral Lands as Proposed in the Memorials of Fray Juan de Silva, O.F.M.", in *The Americas* 17:3 (1961), 277–288.

Kidd, Colin, *The Forging of Races: Race and Scripture in the Protestant Atlantic World, 1600–2000*, Cambridge 2006.

Kopytoff, Igor and Suzanne Miers, "Introduction: African 'Slavery' as an Institution of Marginality", in *Slavery in Africa: Historical and Anthropological Perspectives*, ed. by Suzanne Miers and Igor Kopytoff, Madison 1977, 3–81.

Korth, Eugene H., *Spanish Policy in Colonial Chile: The Struggle for Social Justice, 1535–1700*, Stanford 1968.

Koskenniemi, Martti, "Empire and International Law: The Real Spanish Contribution", in *University of Toronto Law Journal* 61 (2011), 1–36.

Koskenniemi, Martti, *To the Uttermost Parts of the Earth: Legal Imagination and International Power, 1300–1870*, Cambridge 2021.

Lagares Clavo, Manuel J., "Seis incógnitas y algunas respuestas sobre la vida de Fray Tomás de Mercado", in *Iberian Journal of the History of Economic Thought* 3:1 (2016), 68–77.

Lane, Kris E., *Potosí: The Silver City that Changed the World*, Oakland 2019.

Lanza, Lidia and Marco Toste, "The *Sentences* in Sixteenth-Century Iberian Scholasticism", in Rosemann, Philipp W. (ed.), *Medieval Commentaries on the* Sentences *of Peter Lombard*, Leiden 2015, vol. 3, 416–503.

Latasa, Pilar, "'If they remained as mere words': Trent, Marriage, and Freedom in the Viceroyalty of Peru, Sixteenth to Eighteenth Centuries", in *The Americas* 73:1 (2016), 13–38.

Laven, Mary, *Mission to China: Matteo Ricci and the Jesuit Encounter with the East*, London 2011.

Levaggi, Abelardo, "República de indios y república de españoles en los reinos de Indias", in *Revista de Estudios Histórico-Jurídicos* 23 (2001), 419–428.

Lingna Nafafé, José, *Lourenço da Silva Mendonça and the Black Atlantic Abolitionist Movement in the Seventeenth Century*, Cambridge 2022.

López García, José Tomás, *Dos defensores de los esclavos negros en el siglo XVII: Francisco José de Jaca y Epifanio de Moirans*, Caracas 1982.

Losada, Ángel, "El jesuita segoviano Diego de Avendaño, defensor de los negros en América", in Cuesta Domingo, Mariano (ed.), *Proyección y presencia de Segovia en América*, Segovia 1992, 423–444.

Lupher, David A., *Romans in a New World: Classical Models in Sixteenth-Century Spanish America*, Ann Arbor 2003.

MacGregor, Kirk R., *Luis de Molina: The Life and Theology of the Founder of Middle Knowledge*, Grand Rapids 2015.

Mahoney, James, *Colonialism and Postcolonial Development: Spanish America in Comparative Perspective*, Cambridge 2010.

Malcolm, Noel, *Agents of Empire: Knights, Corsairs, Jesuits and Spies in the Sixteenth-Century Mediterranean World*, London 2015.

Malcolm, Noel, *Useful Enemies: Islam and The Ottoman Empire in Western Political Thought, 1450–1750*, Oxford 2019.

Marcocci, Giuseppe, *A consciência de um império. Portugal e o seu mundo (sécs. XV–XVII)*, Coimbra 2012.

Marcocci, Giuseppe, "Conscience and Empire: Politics and Moral Theology in the Early Modern Portuguese World", in *Journal of Early Modern History* 18 (2014), 473–494.

Marcocci, Giuseppe, "Blackness and Heathenism: Color, Theology, and Race in the Portuguese World, c. 1450–1600", in *Anuario Colombiano de Historia Social y de la Cultura* 43:2 (2016), 33–57.

Marcocci, Giuseppe, "Iberian Theories of Empire in the Sixteenth and Seventeenth Centuries", in *Journal of the History of Ideas* 83:4 (2022), 671–683.

Mark, Peter and José da Silva Horta, "Being both Free and Unfree: The Case of Selected Luso-Africans in Sixteenth and Seventeenth-Century Western Africa: Sephardim in a Luso-African Context", in *Anais de História de Além-Mar* 14 (2013), 225–247.

Markus, Robert A., *Saeculum: History and Society in the Theology of St Augustine*, Cambridge 1970.

Martín Casares, Aurelia, *La esclavitud en la Granada del siglo XVI: Género, raza y religión*, Granada 2000.

Martín Casares, Aurelia, "Domestic Service in Spain: Legislation, Gender, and Social Practice", in ed. by Fauve-Chamoux, Antoinette (ed.), *Domestic Service and the Formation of European Identity: Understanding the Globalization of Domestic Work, 16th–21st Centuries*, Bern 2004, 189–209.

Martín Casares, Aurelia, "Maghrebian Slaves in Spain: Human Trafficking and Insecurity in the Early Modern Western Mediterranean", in Hanß, Stefan and Juliane Schiel with Claudia Schmid (eds.), *Mediterranean Slavery Revisited (500–1800) = Neue Perspektiven auf die mediterrane Sklaverei (500–1800)*, Zurich 2014, 97–113.

Martín Casares, Aurelia and Christine Delaigue, "The Evangelization of Freed and Slave

Black Africans in Renaissance Spain: Baptism, Marriage, and Ethnic Brotherhoods", in *History of Religions* 52:3 (2013), 214–235.

Martínez, María Elena, *Genealogical Fictions: Limpieza de Sangre, Religion, and Gender in Colonial Mexico*, Stanford 2008.

Matsumori, Natsuko, *The School of Salamanca in the Affair of the Indies: Barbarism and Political Order*, London 2019.

Masferrer, Aniceto, "Las *Siete Partidas* del sabio rey don Alonso el nono …", in Dauchy, Serge, Georges Martyn, Anthony Musson, Heikki Pihlajamäki and Alain Wijffels (eds.), *The Formation and Transmission of Western Legal Culture: 150 Books that Made the Law in the Age of Printing*, Cham 2016, 106–110.

Masters, Adrian, "The Two, the One, the Many, the None: Rethinking the Republic of Spaniards and Indians in the Sixteenth-Century Spanish Indies", in *The Americas* 78:1 (2021), 3–36.

Masters, Adrian, *We, the King: Creating Royal Legislation in the Sixteenth-Century Spanish New World*, Cambridge 2023.

McManus, Stuart M., "Partus Sequitur Ventrem in Theory and Practice: Slavery and Reproduction in Early Modern Portuguese Asia", in *Gender & History* 32:3 (2020), 542–561.

McManus, Stuart M. and Rômulo da Silva Ehalt (eds.), *Regimes of Bondage: The Encounter between Early Modern European and Asian Slaveries*, special issue of *Itinerario* 47:3 (2023).

McKee, Sally, "Inherited Status and Slavery in Late Medieval Italy and Venetian Crete", in *Past & Present* 182:1 (2004), 31–53.

McKinley, Michelle A., *Fractional Freedoms: Slavery, Intimacy, and Legal Mobilization in Colonial Lima, 1600–1700*, Cambridge 2016.

Metcalf, Alida C., *Go-Betweens and the Colonization of Brazil, 1500–1600*, Austin 2005.

Mikhail, Alan, *God's Shadow: The Ottoman Sultan Who Shaped the World*, London 2020.

Miller, Joseph C., *The Problem of Slavery as History: A Global Approach*, New Haven 2012.

Moreira, José Manuel and André Azevedo Alves, *De Salamanca a Coímbra y Évora: Caminos cruzados de una escuela singular*, Pozuelo de Alarcón 2018.

Morong Reyes, Germán, "Saberes hegemónicos y proyecto de dominio colonial: Los indios en la obra de Juan de Matienzo *Gobierno del Perú* (1567)", in *Fronteras de la Historia* 18:2 (2013), 77–103.

Mortimer, Sarah, *Reformation, Resistance, and Reason of State (1517–1625)*, Oxford 2021.

Moyn, Samuel, "On the Nonglobalization of Ideas", in Moyn, Samuel and Andrew Sartori (eds.), *Global Intellectual History*, New York 2013, 187–204.

Moyn, Samuel, *Christian Human Rights*, Philadelphia 2015.

Moyn, Samuel and Andrew Sartori, "Approaches to Global Intellectual History", in Moyn, Samuel and Andrew Sartori (eds.), *Global Intellectual History*, New York 2013, 3–30.

Muldoon, James, *Popes, Lawyers, and Infidels: The Church and the Non-Christian World, 1250–1550*, Philadelphia 1979.

Muldoon, James, *The Americas in the Spanish World Order: The Justification for Conquest in the Seventeenth Century*, Philadelphia 1994.

Mumford, Jeremy Ravi, *Veritcal Empire: The General Resettlement of Indians in the Colonial Andes*, Durham 2021.

Muñoz García, Ángel, "Introducción", in Avendaño, Diego de, *Thesaurus indicus*, ed. and Spanish trans. Ángel Muñoz García, Pamplona 2001, 13–169.

Noggler, Othmar, "Die Kapuziner: Ihr Verhältnis zur Sklaverei in Amerika", in *Zeitschrift für Missionswissenschaft und Religionswissenschaft* 92:3–4 (2008), 350–363.

Nuzzo, Luigi, "A Dark Side of the Western Legal Modernity: The Colonial Law and its Subjects", in *Zeitschrift für Neuere Rechtsgeschichte* 33:3–4 (2011), 205–222.

Obregón, Liliana, "Spanish Colonial Critiques of Enslavement", in *Beyond Law* 8:24 (2002), 41–66.

O'Callaghan, Joseph F., "Alfonso x", in Domingo, Rafael and Javier Martínez-Torrón (eds.), *Great Christian Jurists in Spanish History*, Cambridge 2018, 69–82.

Oschema, Klaus, *Bilder von Europa im Mittelalter*, Ostfildern 2013.

O'Toole, Rachel Sarah, *Bound Lives: Africans, Indians, and the Making of Race in Colonial Peru*, Pittsburgh 2012.

Owensby, Brian P. and Richard J. Ross, "Making Law Intelligible in Comparative Context", in Owensby, Brian P. and Richard J. Ross (eds.), *Justice in a New World: Negotiating Legal Intelligibility in British, Iberian, and Indigenous America*, New York 2018, 1–60.

Pagden, Anthony, *The Fall of Natural Man: The American Indian and the Origins of Comparative Ethnology*, 2nd ed., Cambridge 1986.

Pagden, Anthony, *Lords of all the World: Ideologies of Empire in Spain, Britain and France c. 1500–c. 1800*, New Haven 1995.

Pagden, Anthony, *The Burdens of Empire: 1539 to the Present* (Cambridge: Cambridge University Press, 2015).

Pagden, Anthony and Jeremy Lawrance, "Introduction", in Vitoria, Francisco de, *Political Writings*, ed. and trans. Pagden, Anthony and Jeremy Lawrance, Cambridge 1991, xiii–xxviii.

Pargas, Damian A. and Juliane Schiel (eds.), *The Palgrave Handbook of Global Slavery throughout History*, Cham 2023.

Patterson, Orlando, *Slavery and Social Death: A Comparative Study*, Cambridge, MA 1982.

Pena González, Miguel Anxo, "Estudio preliminar", in Moirans, Epifanio de, *Siervos libres: Una propuesta antiesclavista a finales del siglo XVII*, ed. and Spanish trans. Pena González, Miguel Anxo, Carlos Baciero, José María Soto, Tarsicio de Azcona and J. Labiano, Madrid 2007, xvii–lxxv.

Pena González, Miguel Anxo, *La Escuela de Salamanca: De la monarquía hispánica al orbe católico*, Madrid 2009.

Pennington, Kenneth, "Bartolomé de Las Casas", in Domingo, Rafael and Javier Martínez-Torrón (eds.), *Great Christian Jurists in Spanish History*, Cambridge 2018, 98–114.

Perdices de Blas, Luis and José Luis Ramos Gorostiza, "The Debate over the Enslavement of Indians and Africans in the Sixteenth- and Seventeenth-Century Spanish Empire", in Tellkamp, Jörg Alejandro (ed.), *A Companion to Early Modern Spanish Imperial Political and Social Thought*, Leiden 2020, 295–317.

Pereña, Luciano Vicente, *Misión de España en América: 1540–1560*, Madrid 1956.

Pétré-Grenouilleau, Olivier, *Les traites négrières: Essai d'histoire globale*, Paris 2004.

Phillips, William D., Jr., "Slavery in the Atlantic Islands and the Early Modern Spanish Atlantic World", in Eltis, David and Stanley L. Engerman (eds.), *The Cambridge World History of Slavery, Volume 3: AD 1420–AD 1804*, Cambridge 2011, 325–349.

Phillips, William D., Jr., *Slavery in Medieval and Early Modern Iberia*, Philadelphia 2014.

Pike, Ruth, *Penal Servitude in Early Modern Spain*, Madison 1983.

Piqueras, José Antonio, *Derecho antiguo y esclavitud moderna: Los esclavos, la ley y la justicia entre Europa y el Imperio español de América*, Madrid 2024.

Pocock, John G.A., "On the Unglobality of Contexts: Cambridge Methods and the History of Political Thought", in *Global Intellectual History* 4:1 (2019), 1–14.

Popescu, Oreste, *Studies in the History of Latin American Economic Thought*, London 1997.

Premo, Bianca and Yanna Yannakakis, "A Court of Sticks and Branches: Indian Jurisdiction in Colonial Mexico and Beyond", in *The American Historical Review* 124:1 (2019), 28–55.

Proctor, Frank T., III, *"Damned Notions of Liberty": Slavery, Culture, and Power in Colonial Mexico, 1640–1769*, Albuquerque 2010.

Puente Brunke, José de la, *Encomienda y encomenderos en el Perú: Estudio social y político de una institución colonial*, Seville 1992.

Puente Luna, José Carlos de la, *Andean Cosmopolitans: Seeking Justice and Reward at the Spanish Royal Court*, Austin 2018.

Pye, Tom, "Property, Space and Sacred History in John Locke's *Two Treatises of Government*", in *Modern Intellectual History* 15:2 (2018), 327–352.

Ramos, Gabriela, "Pastoral Visitations: Spaces of Negotiation in Andean Indigenous Parishes", in *The Americas* 73:1 (2016), 39–57.

Ramos Vázquez, Isabel, "Cárceles públicas y privadas en el derecho medieval y castellano: El delito de cárceles particulares", in *Revista de Estudios Histórico-Jurídicos* 28 (2006), 339–386.

Ramos Vázquez, Isabel, "Detenciones cautelares, coactivas o punitivas: La privación de la libertad en el derecho castellano como instrumento jurídico", in *Anuario de historia del derecho español* 77 (2007), 707–770.

Ramos Vázquez, Isabel, *Arrestos, cárceles y prisiones en los derechos históricos españoles*, Madrid 2008.

Rasilla del Moral, Ignacio de la, *In the Shadow of Vitoria: A History of International Law in Spain (1770–1953)*, Leiden 2018.

Reinhardt, Nicole, *Voices of Conscience: Royal Confessors and Political Counsel in Seventeenth-Century Spain and France*, Oxford 2016.

Reséndez, Andrés, *The Other Slavery: The Uncovered Story of Indian Enslavement in America*, Boston 2016.

Restrepo, Eduardo, "*De instauranda Aethiopum salute*: Sobre las ediciones y características de la obra de Alonso de Sandoval", in *Tabula Rasa* 3 (2005), 13–26.

Rexroth, Frank, *Fröhliche Scholastik: Die Wissenschaftsrevolution des Mittelalters*, 2nd ed., Munich 2019.

Robins, Nicholas A., *Mercury, Mining, and Empire: The Human and Ecological Cost of Colonial Silver Mining in the Andes*, Bloomington 2011.

Robins, Nicholas A., *Santa Bárbara's Legacy: An Environmental History of Huancavelica, Peru*, Leiden 2017.

Rodrigues Montes D'Oca, Fernando, "Two Capuchin Friars in Defense of African Slaves' Liberty: Francisco José de Jaca and Epifanio de Moirans", in *Patristica et Mediaevalia* 36 (2015), 91–108.

Rowe, Erin Kathleen, *Black Saints in Early Modern Global Catholicism*, Cambridge 2019.

Rubiés, Joan-Pau, *Travel and Ethnology in the Renaissance: South India Through European Eyes, 1250–1625*, Cambridge 2000.

Rugemer, Edward B., *Slave Law and the Politics of Resistance in the Early Atlantic World*, Cambridge 2018.

Ruhstorfer, Karlheinz, "Sola Gratia: Der Streit um die Gnade im 16. Jahrhundert, seine Auswirkungen für die Neuzeit und seine Virulenz in der Gegenwart", in *Zeitschrift für Katholische Theologie* 126:3 (2004), 257–268.

Scattola, Merio, "Sklaverei, Krieg und Recht: Die Vorlesung über die *Regula "Peccatum"* von Diego de Covarrubias y Leyva", in Kaufmann, Matthias and Robert Schnepf (eds.), *Politische Metaphysik: Die Entstehung moderner Rechtskonzeptionen in der Spanischen* Spätscholastik, Frankfurt am Main 2007, 303–355.

Scattola, Merio, "Die weiche Ordnung: Recht und Gesetz in der Naturrechtstheorie des Domingo de Soto", in Fidora, Alexander, Matthias Lutz-Bachmann and Andreas Wagner (eds.), *Lex und ius: Beiträge zur Begründung des Rechts in der Philosophie des Mittelalters und der Frühen Neuzeit = Lex and ius: Essays on the Foundation of Law in Medieval and Early Modern Philosophy*, Stuttgart-Bad Cannstatt 2010, 333–367.

Scattola, Merio, "Naturrecht und politische Theologie in der *Relectio regulae 'Peccatum'* von Diego de Covarrubias", in Bunge, Kirstin, Stefan Schweighöfer, Anselm Spindler and Andreas Wagner (eds.), *Kontroversen um das Recht: Beiträge zur Rechtsbegrün-*

dung von Vitoria bis Suárez = Contending for Law: Arguments about the Foundation of Law from Vitoria to Suárez, Stuttgart-Bad Cannstatt 2013, 261–289.

Schaub, Jean-Frédéric, *Race Is about Politics: Lessons from History*, trans. Lara Vergnaud, Princeton 2019.

Schaub, Jean-Frédéric and Silvia Sebastiani, *Race et histoire dans les sociétés occidentales (XVe–XVIIIe siècle)*, Paris 2021.

Schiel, Juliane, "Sklavennahme in der Seerepublik Venedig: Praktiken und Semantiken des Nehmens im spätmittelalterlichen Menschenhandel", in *Geschichte in Wissenschaft und Unterricht* 65:9–10 (2014), 586–599.

Schiel, Juliane, "Tatort Tana: Die Rolle Lateineuropas in der Sklavenökonomie des Schwarzmeerraums (ca. 1300–1500)", in *Historische Zeitschrift* 313:1 (2021), 32–60.

Schiel, Juliane, "Slavery in the Western Mediterranean", in Pargas, Damian A. and Juliane Schiel (eds.), *The Palgrave Handbook of Global Slavery throughout History*, Cham 2023, 179–193.

Schiel, Juliane and Stefan Hanß, "Semantics, Practices and Transcultural Perspectives on Mediterranean Slavery", in Hanß, Stefan and Juliane Schiel with Claudia Schmid (eds.), *Mediterranean Slavery Revisited (500–1800) = Neue Perspektiven auf die mediterrane Sklaverei (500–1800)*, Zurich 2014, 11–23.

Schirrmacher, Jonas, *Die Politik der Sklaverei: Praxis und Konflikt in Kastilien und Spanisch-Amerika im 16. Jahrhundert*, Paderborn 2018.

Schmidt-Voges, Inken, "Das Haus in der Vormoderne", in Eibach, Joachim and Inken Schmidt-Voges (eds.), *Das Haus in der Geschichte Europas: Ein Handbuch*, Berlin 2015, 1–18.

Schmutz, Jacob, "Éloi de Bassée (1590/91–1670)", in Foisneau, Luc (ed.), *Dictionary of Seventeenth Century French Philosophers*, vol. 1, 437–438.

Schmutz, Jacob (ed.), *Scholasticon* (Website discontinued; archived copy available at: https://web.archive.org/web/20230606112327/https://scholasticon.msh-lse.fr/index_fr.php).

Schnyder, Sibylle, *Tötung und Diebstahl: Delikt und Strafe in der gelehrten Strafrechtsliteratur des 16. Jahrhunderts*, Köln 2010.

Schumpeter, Joseph A., *History of Economic Analysis*, ed. Schumpeter, Elizabeth B., London 1954.

Schüssler, Rudolf, "Moral Self-Ownership and *ius possessionis* in Scholastics", in Mäkinen, Virpi and Petter Korkman (eds.), *Transformations in Medieval and Early Modern Rights Discourse*, Dordrecht 2006, 149–169.

Schüssler, Rudolf, *The Debate on Probale Opinions in the Scholastic Tradition*, Leiden 2019.

Schwartz, Daniel, *The Political Morality of the Late Scholastics: Civic Life, War and Conscience*, Cambridge 2019.

Scott, James Brown, *The Spanish Origins of International Law: Francisco de Vitoria and His Law of Nations*, Oxford 1934.

Seelmann, Kurt, "Selbstherrschaft, Herrschaft über die Dinge und individuelle Rechte in der spanischen Spätscholatik", in Kaufmann, Matthias and Robert Schnepf (eds.), *Politische Metaphysik: Die Entstehung moderner Rechtskonzeptionen in der Spanischen* Spätscholastik, Frankfurt am Main 2007, 43–57.

Seijas, Tatiana, *Asian Slaves in Colonial Mexico: From Chinos to Indians*, Cambridge 2014.

Seixas, Margarida, "Trabalho livre e trabalho escravo na obra da Francisco Suárez", in *Revista Portuguesa de Filosofia* 75:2 (2019), 1165–1194.

Senellart, Michel, *Les arts de gouverner: Du* regimen *médieval au concept de gouvernement*, Paris 1995.

Silva Horta, José de, "Perspectivas para o estudo da evolução das representações dos Africanos nas escritas portuguesas de viagem: o caso da 'Guiné do Cabo Verde' (Sécs. XV–XVII)", in Rodrigues, Joé Damião and Casimiro Rodrigues (eds.), *Representações de África e dos Africanos na historia e cultura: Séculos XV a XXI*, Ponta Delgada 2011, 409–425.

Simmermacher, Danaë, " 'Non qua servus est, sed qua homo': Der rechtliche Status von Sklaven bei Luis de Molina", in *The Salamanca Working Paper Series* 2 (2014), 1–41.

Simmermacher, Danaë, *Eigentum als ein subjektives Recht bei Luis de Molina (1535–1600): Dominium und Sklaverei in* De iustitia et iure, Berlin 2018.

Sinha, Manisha, *The Slave's Cause: A History of Abolition*, New Haven 2016.

Skinner, Quentin, "Meaning and Understanding in the History of Ideas", in *History and Theory* 8:1 (1969), 3–53.

Skinner, Quentin, *The Foundations of Modern Political Thought*, 2 vols., Cambridge 1978.

Skinner, Quentin, "A Genealogy of the Modern State", in *Proceedings of the British Academy* 162 (2008), 325–370.

Sousa, Lúcio de, *The Portuguese Slave Trade in Early Modern Japan: Merchants, Jesuits and Japanese, Chinese, and Korean Slaves*, Leiden 2019.

Sperling, Jutta, "Marriage at the Time of the Council of Trent (1560–1570): Clandestine Marriages, Kinship Prohibitions, and Dowry Exchange in European Comparison", in *Journal of Early Modern History* 8:1–2 (2004), 67–108.

Spierenburg, Pieter, "Prison and Convict Labour in Early Modern Europe", in de Vito, Giuseppe and Alex Lichtenstein (eds.), *Global Convict Labour*, Leiden 2015, 108–125.

Stegmüller, Friedrich, "Zur Literaturgeschichte der Philosophie und Theologie an den Universitäten Evora und Coimbra im XVI. Jahrhundert", in *Spanische Forschungen der Görresgesellschaft, Erste Reihe* 3 (1931), 385–438.

Stegmüller, Friedrich, *Geschichte des Molinismus*, Münster 1935.

Stella, Alessandro, *Histoires d'esclaves dans la péninsule ibérique*, Paris 2000.

Strathern, Alan, "Catholic Missions and Local Rulers in Sub-Saharan Africa", in Po-Chia Hsia, Ronnie (ed.), *A Companion to Early Modern Catholic Global Missions*, Leiden 2018, 151–178.

Subrahmanyam, Sanjay, *Empires Between Islam and Christianity, 1500–1800*, Albany 2019.

Tarruell, Cecilia, "Prisoners of War, Captives or Slaves? The Christian Prisoners of Tunis and La Goleta in 1574," in De Vito, Christian G. and Anne Gerritsen (eds.), *Micro-Spatial Histories of Global Labour*, Cham 2018, 95–122.

Tau Anzoátegui, Víctor, "Provincial and Local Law of the Indies: A research Program", in Duve, Thomas and Heikki Pihlajamäki (eds.), *New Horizons in Spanish Colonial Law*, Frankfurt am Main 2015, 235–255.

Tau Anzoátegui, Víctor, *El jurista en el Nuevo Mundo: Pensamiento. Doctrina. Mentalidad*, Frankfurt am Main 2016.

Tellkamp, Jörg Alejandro, "Über den Zusammenhang von Freiheit und Sklaverei bei Vitoria und Soto", in Kaufmann, Matthias and Robert Schnepf (eds.), *Politische Metaphysik: Die Entstehung moderner Rechtskonzeptionen in der Spanischen* Spätscholastik, Frankfurt am Main 2007, 155–175.

Tellkamp, Jörg Alejandro, "Francisco de Vitoria and Luis de Molina on the Origin of Political Power", in Culleton, Alfredo Santiago and Roberto Hofmeister Pich (eds.), *Right and Nature in the First and Second Scholasticism—Derecho y naturaleza en la primera y segunda escoláscita*, Turnhout 2014, 231–247.

Tellkamp, Jörg Alejandro, "Rights and *Dominium*", in Kaufmann, Matthias and Alexander Aichele (eds.), *A Companion to Luis de Molina*, Leiden 2014, 125–153.

Tellkamp, Jörg Alejandro, "Introduction", in Tellkamp, Jörg Alejandro (ed.), *A Companion to Early Modern Spanish Imperial Political and Social Thought*, Leiden 2020, 1–13.

Thornton, John, "The Slave Trade and the African Diaspora", in Bentley, Jerry H., Sanjay Subrahmanyam and Merry E. Wiesner-Hanks (eds.), *The Cambridge World History, Volume 4: The Construction of a Global World, 1400–1800* CE*—Part 2: Patterns of Change*, Cambridge 2015, 135–159.

Thornton, John, *Africa and Africans in the Making of the Atlantic World, 1400–1680*, Cambridge 1992.

Thornton, John, *A Cultural History of the Atlantic World, 1250–1820*, Cambridge 2012.

Tierney, Brian, "Aristotle and the American Indians—again: Two critical discussions", in *Cristianesimo nella storia* 12 (1991), 295–322.

Tierney, Brian, *The Idea of Natural Rights: Studies on Natural Rights, Natural Law, and Church Law, 1150–1625*, Atlanta 1997.

Tierney, Brian, *Liberty and Law: The Idea of Permissive Natural Law, 1100–1800*, Washington, D.C. 2014.

Toste, Marco, "Invincible Ignorance and the Americas: Why and How the Salamancan Theologians Made Use of a Medieval Notion", in *Rechtsgeschichte—Legal History* 26 (2018), 284–297.

Trivellato, Francesca, "The Moral Economies of Early Modern Europe", in *Humanity* 11:2 (2020), 193–201.

Tuck, Richard, *Natural Rights Theories: Their Origin and Development*, Cambridge 1979.

Tuck, Richard, *The Rights of War and Peace: Political Thought and the International Order from Grotius to Kant*, Oxford 1999.

Van Deusen, Nancy E., *Global Indios: The Indigenous Struggle for Justice in Sixteenth-Century Spain*, Durham 2015.

Von Germeten, Nicole, "Introduction", in Sandoval, Alonso de, *Treatise on Slavery: Selections from* De instauranda Aethiopum salute, ed. and trans. von Germeten, Nicole, Indianapolis 2008, xi–xxx.

Vargas, José María, *Historia de la cultura Ecuatoriana*, Quito 1965 (http://www.cervantesvirtual.com/nd/ark:/59851/bmcht301).

Velázquez Gutiérrez, María Elisa, *Mujeres de origen africano en la capital novohispana, siglos XVII y XVIII*, Mexico City 2006.

Von Weber, Wilhelm, *Wirtschaftsethik am Vorabend des Liberalismus: Höhepunkt und Abschluss der scholastischen Wirtschaftsbetrachtung durch Ludwig Molina S.J. (1535–1600)*, Münster 1959.

Weber, Wolfgang E.J., "Von der normativen Herrschaftspflicht zum interessenpolitischen Instrument: Zum Konzept der Protektion in der Frühen Neuzeit", in Haug, Tilman, Nadir Weber and Christian Windler (eds.), *Protegierte und Protektoren: Asymmetrische politische Beziehungen zwischen Partnerschaft und Dominanz (16. bis frühes 20. Jahrhundert)*, Köln 2016, 31–48.

Weller, Thomas, "Humanitarianism before Humanitarianism? Spanish Discourses on Slavery from the Sixteenth to the Nineteenth Century", in Klose, Fabian and Mirjam Thulin (eds.), *Humanity: A History of European Concepts in Practice from the Sixteenth Century to the Present*, Göttingen 2016, 51–168.

Winius, George D., "Bibliographical Essay: A Treasury of Printed Source Materials Pertaining to the 15th and 16th Centuries", in Winius, George D. (ed.), *Portugal, the Pathfinder: Journey from the Medieval toward the Modern World, 1300–ca. 1600*, Madison 1995, 373–401.

Wisnoski, Alexander L., III, "'It is Unjust for the Law of Marriage to be Broken by the Law of Slavery': Married Slaves and their Masters in Early Colonial Lima", in *Slavery & Abolition* 35:2 (2014), 234–252.

Yubero Galindo, Dionisio, "El 'Thesaurus indicus' de Diego de Avendaño", in Cuesta Domingo, Mariano (ed.), *Proyección y presencia de Segovia en América*, Segovia 1992, 399–410.

Zamora, Romina, *Casa poblada y buen gobierno*: Oeconomia *católica y servicio personal en San Miguel de Tucamán, siglo XVIII*, Buenos Aires 2017.

Zamon Davis, Natalie, *Trickster Travels: A Sixteenth-Century Muslim between Worlds*, New York 2006.

Zeron, Carlos Albeto de Moura Ribeiro, "Pombeiros e tangomaus, intermediários do tráfico de escravos na África", in Loureiro, Rui Manuel and Serge Gruzinski (eds.),

Passar as fronteiras: Actas do II Colóquio Internacional sobre Mediadores Culturais: Séculos XV a XVIII, Lagos 1999, 15–38.
Zeron, Carlos Albeto de Moura Ribeiro, *Ligne de foi: La Compagnie de Jésus et l'esclavage dans le processus de formation de la société coloniale en Amérique portugaise (XVIe–XVIIe siècles)*, Paris 2009.
Zeuske, Michael, *Sklavenhändler, Negreros, Atlantikkreolen: Eine Weltgeschichte des Sklavenhandels im atlantischen Raum*, Berlin 2015.
Zeuske, Michael, *Sklaverei: Eine Menschheitsgeschichte von der Steinzeit bis heute*, Stuttgart 2018.
Zorrilla, Víctor, "La doctrina misiológica, política y económica en tres memoriales de Fray Juan de Silva", in *Cauriensia* 11 (2016), 299–314.

Index

www.ingramcontent.com/pod-product-compliance
Ingram Content Group UK Ltd.
Pitfield, Milton Keynes, MK11 3LW, UK
UKHW020822290926
15470UKWH00003B/1314

9 789004 760585